PRINCIPLES
OF REAL ESTATE
MANAGEMENT

Contributing Editor:
Nicholas Dunlap, CPM®

Editorial Review Team:
Christopher Mellen, CPM®, ARM®
Kimberly Mitchell, PhD
Patricia Nooney, CPM®, ARM®
Fred Prassas, CPM®

Nadia Geagea Pupa
Managing Editor, Publications

Ronald Gjerde
Senior Director, Publishing & Content Services

Nancye J. Kirk
Chief Strategy Officer/Education, Advocacy, Outreach

PRINCIPLES
OF REAL ESTATE
MANAGEMENT

Seventeenth Edition

IREM Institute of Real Estate Management

The Institute of Real Estate Management, Chicago 60611.

© 2011, 2018 by the Institute of Real Estate Management
of the NATIONAL ASSOCIATION OF REALTORS®

All rights reserved. Sixteenth edition 2011
Seventeenth edition 2018

SKU: 971-17
ISBN: 978-1-57203-259-0

Cover © iStock/naqiewei

Text and Cover Composition:
Nadia Geagea Pupa
Managing Editor, Publications

IREM® logo, IREM®, CERTIFIED PROPERTY MANAGER®, CPM®, the CPM key logo, ACCREDITED RESIDENTIAL MANAGER®, ARM®, the ARM torch logo, ACCREDITED MANAGEMENT ORGANIZATION®, AMO®, the AMO circle logo, Income/Expense Analysis®, Expense Analysis®, *JPM*® and MPSA® are registered marks of the Institute of Real Estate Management.

IREM practices diversity. We are an inclusive organization that embraces and values differences and welcomes individuals of all races, genders, creeds, ages, sexual orientations, gender identities, and national origins and individuals with disabilities, providing an equal opportunity environment among its members, vendors, and staff.

IREM is dedicated to supporting real estate management strategies that advance an environmentally sustainable and economically prosperous future.

Library of Congress Cataloging-in-Publication Data

Names: Dunlap, Nicholas, 1982- editor. | Institute of Real Estate Management, issuing body.
Title: Principles of real estate management / developmental editor, Nicholas Dunlap, CPM.
Description: Seventeenth edition. | Chicago, IL : Institute of Real Estate Management, [2017] | Includes index.
Identifiers: LCCN 2017028590| ISBN 9781572032590 (hardcover : alk. paper) | ISBN 1572032596 (hardcover)
Subjects: LCSH: Real estate management.
Classification: LCC HD1394 .P74 2017 | DDC 333.5068--dc23 LC record available at https://lccn.loc.gov/2017028590

Table of Contents

CHAPTER 7:
STAFF MANAGEMENT

CHAPTER 8:
MARKETING AND TENANT RETENTION 217

CHAPTER 9:
UNDERSTANDING THE LEASE 249

CHAPTER 13:

Preface

Simply put, real estate as an industry has evolved. Gone are the days where a career in real estate just meant selling homes or brokering mortgages. Today, the industry is global and accounts for trillions of dollars of economic activity and encompasses trades like brokerage, construction, development, finance, investment, management, and valuation. With the emergence of new and specialized segments of the industry, skillsets are dynamic, specialized, and refined. Whether managing properties on Main Street or Wall Street, there are many new players and new faces in the game; however, the basics are the same. Real estate management has become its own career path, one where there are hundreds of roles, titles, responsibilities, and endless opportunities to become successful.

Although the industry has gone through some changes, many of the skills and traits of a successful real estate manager have stayed the same. The need for good people skills, analytical skills, and strong written and oral communication have only been bolstered or enhanced by technological advancements. However, this being an aging business and one where 60 percent of the workforce will be at retirement age within the next five years, the need to attract, train, and retain new talent is amplified. Old stereotypes die hard and real estate management, historically characterized as the less exciting and even lower-paying cousin of the brokerage or investment sectors, has undergone a reinvention of sorts.

During the economic downturn and the Great Recession, real estate managers were called upon en masse to play the role of receiver and help financial institutions account for, stabilize, and manage their holdings, ranging from single-family residences to strip shopping centers, office buildings, and mixed-use developments. Real estate managers helped to remove an element of stress from a highly-distressed real estate market and played a critical behind-the-scenes role in helping the economy recover. This is not the first time that real estate managers were called upon to help restore normalcy to the markets. In the late 1980s and early 1990s, the same was done for a government-owned asset management company known at the Resolution Trust Corporation (RTC).

Real estate management was mostly associated with the physical upkeep and guidance of an asset. While fiscal management was also a component, it occupied less of the real estate manager's time and focus than, say, caring for curb appeal. Today, real estate managers are relationship masters and market experts, who help investors understand the marketplace and the community as it relates to their investment. The relationship between owner and operator (or investor and real estate manager) is one driven by value-add. Real estate managers are no longer just physical custodians, but financial architects who create value. The real estate manager plays an integral role in the investment process, while also helping to ensure a quality experience for customers and maximizing returns for their clients.

Just as the ownership landscape has changed, so too has the management business. Today's management professional is more sophisticated, plugged-in, and informed than ever. The *Principles of Real Estate Management* is in its seventeenth edition and has been revisited, revised, and remastered to include the best practices of yesterday and the best tips for today. Whether you are a seasoned professional looking for additional insight or a beginner just starting out, there is something in this textbook for you. Use it as a roadmap to your future success, or as a support tool when you need help along the way.

New and exciting information included in this seventeenth edition includes a transformed marketing chapter with an emphasis on branding and social media marketing, along with new visual diagrams and exhibits, creating a more stimulating read. There are both useful and practical suggestions that will help to inspire and empower you to make changes to your personal and professional approach. There is also additional information about the owner-ship landscape that is changing, what it means for your business, and how you can benefit from it.

It is an exciting time to be a part of the real estate industry especially as the property management business is thriving like never before.

On behalf of the Institute of Real Estate Management (IREM®)
Nicholas Dunlap, CPM®

Acknowledgments

First and foremost, the Institute of Real Estate Management (IREM®) gratefully acknowledges James C. Downs (1905–1980), one of the IREM founders in 1933, who wrote the first edition of *Principles of Real Estate Management* in 1947. He revised this book through its twelfth edition in 1980. Downs was the first property manager to receive the CERTIFIED PROPERTY MANAGER® (CPM®) designation and firmly believed that the best means of developing qualified real estate managers is through education, certification, professionalism, and ethical practices.

IREM is grateful for the contribution of the editorial reviewers of this seventeenth edition of *Principles of Real Estate Management*: Christopher Mellen, CPM®, ARM®, Vice President of the Simon Companies and 2016 IREM Past President; Kimberly Mitchell, PhD, previous Director of Property Management and Associate Teaching Professor at Drexel University; Patricia Nooney, CPM®, ARM®, Senior Managing Director at CBRE and 2003 IREM Past President; and Frederick Prassas, CPM®, Program Director at the University of Wisconsin-Stout, founder of PMC Management Group, and 2006 IREM Past President. These real estate management professionals provided a peer review of the manuscript for accuracy of information, timeliness of content, and ease of reading.

IREM also gratefully acknowledges Nicholas Dunlap, CPM®, for greatly contributing to the revision of this seventeenth edition of *Principles of Real Estate Management*. With his subject matter expertise and oversight, IREM was successful in revising the book's content and creating an updated, clear, and concise guide for both seasoned professionals and those new to the real estate management industry.

Dunlap is currently the Director of Property Management for Avanath Capital Management. He oversees the firm's day-to-day property management operations, capital projects, and due diligence. Prior to joining Avanath, Dunlap was the Vice President of Dunlap Property Group, a full-service real estate investment firm specializing in the syndication and management of multifamily and commercial complexes in the southern California area.

He is an internationally published author, featured columnist, and speaker. He has served as President and also on the Board of Directors of the Apartment Association of Orange County (AAOC), the Orange County Commission on Housing and Community Development (OCCHCD), the Board of Directors of the Fair Housing Council of Orange County (FHCOC), and on the Editorial Advisory Board of the *Journal of Property Management*® (*JPM*®). In 2011, he published his first book, *The Four Benefits: Commercial Real Estate Investing & You*. In 2014, he published his second book, *Brick and Mortar Piggy Banks: Your Guide to Creating Life Changing Wealth Through Real Estate Investment*.

Dunlap is a graduate of the University of California, Los Angeles, and is a licensed real estate broker in California and Texas.

Ronald Gjerde
Senior Director, Publishing & Content Services

1 An Overview of Real Estate Management

Real estate professionals work in a dynamic, ever-changing environment. Understanding the demands of clients and being able to analyze their needs are essential skills for the real estate manager. Having a critical eye, paying close attention to detail, and being able to effectively communicate with a variety of people—along with having a tech-savvy edge—are important elements for success. Succeeding as a real estate manager will require many skills, but having a positive approach and working with people are truly essential and will help to reap great rewards.

THE PROFESSION OF REAL ESTATE MANAGEMENT

Professional real estate management is a thriving and satisfying career that many people *choose* as their occupation. In order to better understand the growth and development of the profession to date, it is important to understand the history and to reflect back to 1907 to the founding of the *National Association of Building Owners and Managers.* This association focused specifically on office buildings, but it wasn't until 16 years later that this organization created a division that specialized in managing rental apartments and other types of commercial properties. However, only local real estate boards were members of the Property Management Division.

As a result of dire circumstances, businesses that survived the stock market crash in 1929 were in an uncertain position. They had already suffered substantial losses, and the poor management of their real estate holdings would result in additional losses. A strong need to establish standard management practices and methods of accrediting real estate managers became evident. The National

Association of Building Owners and Managers subsequently reorganized the Property Management Division into a different type of body.

In 1933, one hundred real estate management firms joined together to form the *Institute of Real Estate Management* (IREM®) as an affiliate of the National Association of Real Estate Boards, today known as the National Association of Realtors® (NAR®). Five years later, the founders of IREM agreed that accrediting individual real estate managers was more fundamental and beneficial than recognizing the integrity of management firms. IREM inaugurated the Certified Property Manager® (CPM®) designation to acknowledge the individual professional achievement of real estate managers who successfully complete a series of real estate management courses after working a certain number of years in the profession and managing a portfolio of a required size—other factors involving the individual's professional experience are also considered.

As IREM has grown, it has responded to and accommodated changes in the real estate management profession by developing additional credentials—the Accredited Management Organization® (AMO®) in 1945, the Accredited Residential Manager® (ARM®) in 1974, and in 2006, the Accredited Commercial Manager (ACoM) certification.

Since education is one of the most vital qualifications of a professional real estate manager, the *Principles of Real Estate Management* presents the information managers need to learn to become professionals. Being able to identify areas of economic, social, and political change, and to understand the ways they affect certain properties, is truly essential for this profession. This book assists in creating programs to respond to such changes, which are a major component in laying the foundation of success.

What Is Real Estate?

Before diving into the nuances of different property types, it's important to first examine *real estate*, which is solely the land and all of its parts—landscapes, timber, waterways, roads, fences, structures, utilities, and all other permanently attached improvements and structures. While farms, golf courses, and even deserts are real estate as well, the definition of real estate is often limited to nonagricultural property that houses individuals or families or accommodates commerce, industry, professions, or other activities. Any changes or new trends related to these properties directly affect real estate and the way it is managed. Depending on the ways our society expands and changes, real estate managers need to respond to the effects of population shifts—either to capitalize on them or to minimize their effects on the real estate that is in their care.

As a homeowner, one is considered an *investor* in real estate. However, owning an apartment building is considered an investment in *income-producing* real estate—property that is rented or leased to others who pay rent. Investment in real estate can range from a small shopping center in a neighborhood to a high-rise apartment community. No matter what type of use or service occurs on the land, the success or failure of the investment relies on many factors that include but are not limited to the following:

- Governmental regulations and taxes
- Accessibility to and from the property
- Financing limitations
- Topography or the features of the land surface
- Economic conditions (local and global)

Real estate has typically been a steady and *appreciating* investment vehicle over time. When purchasing a home became more affordable in the 1940s and 1950s, the dream of homeownership became a reality for many. Investments from that period have perhaps doubled, tripled, or even quadrupled in value. Similarly, the same result is expected if one invests in the stock market, a 401(k), or another investment medium—but those investments are intangible. Real estate, however, is a tangible investment that has the ability to change and adapt to future trends. For this reason, investing in real estate usually carries with it a feeling of pride and satisfaction. However, while the goal of an owner is to create and increase value, real estate assets can decline. If a property is not well cared for, that is easily detectable. Owners who are unable to stay up to date with changing demands hire *real estate managers* to oversee their properties and to maintain all operations and the physical condition of the property to the highest standards.

The Role of Real Estate Managers

A *real estate manager* is responsible for conducting the operations, marketing, leasing, and financial reporting of the property to meet the objectives of the owner. Planning for the future of the property by proposing physical and fiscal strategies that will enhance the value of the real estate asset is another major component of the job.

Since larger buildings cost more to build and maintain, and fewer individuals can afford them, financing by outside sources became prevalent, and that created a new type of ownership. Ownership by groups, or pooled capital, emerged due to the demand and need, but such ownership required different handling. For instance, larger properties required more full-time attention and higher financing costs. These larger assets also required greater scrutiny of *cash flow,* or monies remaining after all expenses have been paid. The interests of multiple owners required intermediary or third-party managers, and that entailed increased duties for managing the financial aspect of the asset, rather than simply overseeing the maintenance and collection of rent. As the role of real estate managers evolved, two major property types became specialties: (1) residential and (2) commercial.

When land prices in cities rose because of the heightened demand for space, that prompted the construction of large, higher-density projects and, over time, the upgrading of residential conditions and equipment. Central heating, air conditioning, additional bathrooms, and other improvements became standard features in apartment buildings. Maintenance requirements grew with each additional feature, increasing the need for specially trained,

Real estate management as a profession is the result of four major occurrences:

1. Development of a legal system that granted individuals the right to own real property
2. Increased complexity and size of buildings and their components
3. Changing economic conditions that required professional management and advice to achieve sound fiscal operation of income-producing property
4. Satisfying the needs and desires of those people who live, work, and shop in these properties

professional management of residential property. Commercial properties, which include industrial, office, and retail spaces, have seen major changes throughout history. With advances in structural engineering, high-rise buildings emerged; they housed some of the earliest office buildings. With every additional floor, the number of tenants increased; the increased numbers required the special skills of a full-time staff—real estate managers, leasing agents, and a large maintenance staff—to serve the tenants and their customers.

To meet the needs of growing markets, shopping centers developed and evolved from smaller strips of independent stores to large enclosed malls with unified themes. They, too, required real estate managers. Over time, these trends in residential and commercial development sparked an increasing demand for management and ultimately led to further specialization into the three most common specialties today: (1) residential, (2) office, and (3) retail. However, the transition from some owners allowing real estate managers to deal with such large investments to the general acknowledgment of the profession didn't happen overnight. The next section describes the cycles of real estate management throughout history, how management came to be what it is today, and what that will mean for our future.

THE CYCLES OF REAL ESTATE MANAGEMENT

Historically, major events in the world and the economy have had an impact on the real estate industry. It's important to understand how these occurrences changed the way real estate managers function today, how the profession was perceived throughout history, and how property ownership evolved into such a widely recognized and valued commodity to investors in the United States and all over the world.

From 1920 to the Stock Market Crash of 1929

Due to rapid business expansion and a consequent demand for rental space, many owners became quite wealthy and chose to travel for long periods or even to move to warmer climates altogether. Since these investors settled far from their properties, they hired real estate managers to collect rents, manage the maintenance staff, and oversee general utilities. After paying the basic expenses, the real estate manager forwarded the remainder of the income from the rents to the owners. However, an owner's specific authorization was usually necessary for any other expenditure. Owners also negotiated leases personally, so the extent of real estate management during the 1920s was still limited.

Before the U.S. economy collapsed in the stock market crash of 1929, there was unparalleled urban prosperity and building construction was at a high. Many building projects were financed through private loan services, other building associations, and insurance companies. Coast-to-coast networks of chain stores emerged; that development held great promise for real estate managers.

After the crash, the country's income-producing real estate was left in the hands of mortgage holders. Banks were unwilling or unable to renew loans; many borrowers had only one option—to default on the loans and let the banks foreclose. For the first time, a large amount of property was gathered under one ownership, one policy, and one common perspective. While it was something of a luxury for an owner to hire a real estate manager before the crash, banks absolutely needed real estate managers in large numbers to assist them with this onslaught of property.

Recovery Period After the Great Depression, 1934 to 1939

Following the Great Depression, real estate management experienced years of trial and error, while the operators of lender-owned real estate adopted other views. They needed professional, knowledgeable experts who could provide sophisticated analysis, market research, and an organized approach to property administration.

After the recovery years, ownership was redistributed to new owners. Real estate promised once again to be a profitable opportunity for investors. Individuals and partnerships (sometimes called *syndicates*) purchased property from lenders who were reducing their real estate portfolios as they prepared to resume their other activities. In many cases, to ensure the highest and best use of the properties, the new owners retained the real estate managers who were previously hired by the banks. The upsurge in occupancy, rental rates, and property values characterized the recovery period (1934 to 1939).

At the end of 1941, when the United States entered into World War II, the demand for rental space was so high that owners easily rented their own properties, so the need for professional real estate management in the residential area diminished. However, the Society of Industrial Realtors (SIR)—later to be called the Society of Industrial and Office Realtors (SIOR)—was formed in response to World War II. The U.S. Department of War greatly needed space in and availability of vacant industrial buildings, which led to a need for professional property managers.

Post–World War II, 1940 to 1950

Phenomenal construction from 1946 until 1956 satisfied the demands for housing after World War II and after the Korean War. The number of residential units built exceeded the demand for new space. Much of this construction occurred in newly developed suburbs, which had increased due to more people owning cars. This period also marked the beginning of the baby boom. For many, the suburbs became the place of choice to live—especially because many business executives decided to move farther from the city. As a result, their companies and businesses essentially moved with them, which created more jobs and opportunities away from the city in the suburbs.

As this tendency grew, many mid- and high-rise apartment buildings became popular in metropolitan areas beginning in the late 1950s; such buildings could house hundreds or thousands of people in the area of a city block. This concentration of population intensified service requirements and consequently increased the need for knowledgeable and professional real estate management.

From 1960 to 1970

Condominiums emerged in the 1960s and 1970s and offered real estate managers even more opportunities because of the ownership structure involved. For commercial properties, an enormous demand for office space characterized this period. As companies prospered, they outgrew their existing quarters. Office operations became more complex and companies needed more space for newer equipment. Retail space also developed, as did the number and size of shopping centers, especially in the suburbs.

A steady increase in the supply of mortgage money during the 1960s and 1970s affected the real estate management industry because it made way for the development of large, income-producing properties. *Real estate investment trusts* (REITs) and pension funds were among the sources of mortgage money. A REIT is an entity that sells shares of beneficial interest to investors and uses the funds to invest in real estate or mortgages. This form of investment permits those with limited capital to participate in large real estate investments. REIT units can be traded privately, and some of the larger ones are traded on public stock exchanges, thus, providing significant flexibility. However, REITs are inherently subject to fluctuations in the real estate market and the stock market, the integrity of the administration of the trust, and changes in governmental policy.

After the passage of the Employment Retirement Income Security Act (ERISA) in 1974, pension funds and insurance companies began to take an interest in real estate as a means of diversifying their portfolios and capitalizing on the rapid appreciation of real property developments, and that led into the role of pension funds in the 1980s.

From 1980 to 1990

The decade started with a booming real estate industry and ended with a crash. Between 1980 and 1982, the United States suffered the next recession since the Great Depression. During that period of double-digit inflation, investors viewed real estate as a way to preserve capital. The recession finally gave way to a period of prosperity, and construction boomed. One reason for the nation's rebound from recession in 1983 was the availability of credit, which resulted from changes in federal regulations related to banks and savings and loan associations (S&Ls). Previously, the federal government prohibited S&Ls (also called *thrifts*) from lending money for commercial real estate development and from investing directly in real estate, but it removed those restrictions in the early 1980s.

These changes, combined with the Tax Reform Act of 1980 (1980 Act), offered numerous incentives for real estate investment and fueled unprecedented development. Large syndicates and partnerships organized to take advantage of the credit and tax opportunities. Pension funds also played an increasingly important role in real estate investment, and REITs rebounded from their disfavor and again became important sources of investment. This record growth eventually faltered because of the following two significant and almost concurrent events:

1. As a result of overbuilding, the market saw an overabundance of available rentable space. Many developers lost their properties because high vacancy rates reduced their cash flow and prevented them from making their loan payments. Massive foreclosures ensued.

2. The federal government enacted the *Tax Reform Act of 1986 (1986 Act)*, which repealed most of the income tax incentives granted through the 1980 Act. In particular, the new law defined rental income from real property as *passive activity income*—income in which the investor does not materially participate in earning the funds. Similarly, losses from such passive activities, which had been deductible from *active income* (i.e., salary) under the 1980 Act, could no longer be deducted under the 1986 Act. The changes significantly reduced the attraction of real estate for most long-term investors.

The oversupply of vacant property, coupled with hundreds of poorly conceived developments and numerous failing syndicates and partnerships, lowered the value of the properties that the banks and S&Ls had seized. As a result, many of the financial institutions that held the properties went bankrupt and were taken over by federal regulators.

In the late 1980s, many more REITs were created as a result of companies not being able to sustain themselves. They reemerged as publicly traded companies and consequently incurred more restrictions. By early 1989, a significant portion of the savings and loan industry had collapsed. Thrift failures were so widespread that the U.S. government dissolved the Federal Savings and Loan Insurance Corporation (FSLIC)—the agency that insured deposits in participating S&Ls.

The federal government needed an organization to efficiently manage and dispose of the assets from the thrifts that were in receivership, so it created several new governmental agencies. The *Resolution Trust Corporation (RTC)* was among them. Upon its creation, the RTC became the largest landowner in the United States. At the end of 1995, the RTC had taken over 747 thrifts with total real estate assets of all types valued at nearly $402.6 billion. Among other strategies, the RTC contracted with real estate management firms to manage and market many of those assets for disposition. The RTC had no way to finance the sales of the properties they were trying to liquidate, which led ultimately to the creation of the Commercial Mortgage-Backed Security (CMBS).

From 1990 to 2000

In many markets, office vacancy rates remained high throughout most of the decade. In addition to the consequences of earlier overbuilding, numerous corporate mergers and restructurings (workforce downsizing) reduced companies' space needs. Technological advances allowed people to work at home while being linked electronically to their places of employment.

Technology also affected retailing. Encryption software enabled online credit card purchases, and so-called e-commerce thrived as new businesses started online while established retailers rushed to online advertising as an additional marketing and sales tool. *Power shopping centers*—centers dominated by large space users that sold goods at discount prices—made major inroads (power shopping centers are explained in more detail in Chapter 13).

In 1994, the North American Free Trade Alliance (NAFTA) was passed; it eliminated all non-tariff barriers to agricultural trade between the United States and Mexico. Increasingly, manufacturers produced goods outside of the United States at lower cost, which meant fewer manufacturing jobs and less space used for production. While heavy industry declined, the development of low-rise, flexible structures (*flex space*) that could be configured as offices or used for light manufacturing grew. Apartments built in the 1990s often included amenities more typical of single-family homes, such as *great rooms*—combined living/dining room and kitchen—with larger bathrooms and walk-in closets. Those changes added to the appeal of renting versus home ownership and helped keep average rents high.

With the increased global reliance on technology and the failure of established programming to anticipate dates overlapping with the previous century, the world expected the crashing of computers around the world to herald the dawn of the twenty-first century. While that issue did not materialize on any scale, other problems loomed on the horizon. The economic growth of the 1990s slowed after 2000. Even though the economy slowed, productivity increased, and that kept job growth low and affected the office and industrial real estate markets because the demand for additional office space was low. However, the discipline of lenders slowed new development and prevented the recession in real estate from being as deep as it had been in the 1990s.

The United States continued to maintain a *negative balance of trade*—importing more goods than were exported—which resulted in the loss of even more manufacturing jobs. At the same time, many corporations increasingly outsourced professional jobs, many in technology fields, to developing countries where educated populations would work for low wages. The year 2000 saw another wave of bankruptcies as online service providers and retailers found they were unable to generate sufficient revenue or obtain needed capital to sustain their operations.

Effects of 9/11 on Real Estate Management

The terrorist attack on the United States on September 11, 2001, was a defining moment in U.S. history. The repercussions of that event continue to resonate, and the American way of life has changed forever—including the real estate management industry. The economy continued to slow in 2001 along with the pace of hiring. In most industries, wage increases were small or nonexistent, and employees in some industries had to accept pay reductions. The travel and tourism industries were hit the hardest. Increased security checks after 9/11 made travel an aggravation, and major airlines went through bankruptcy proceedings.

The effects of 9/11 had a lingering impact on real estate management in the form of increases in management time and property operating costs. Other challenges included higher costs in finding and obtaining adequate property insurance coverage that contained provisions related to terrorism, requiring more intensive screening of prospective residential and commercial tenants—for security issues as well as financial concerns—and developing more comprehensive emergency procedures that emphasized preparation against acts of terrorism.

The U.S.A. PATRIOT Act—the acronym stands for "providing appropriate tools required to intercept and obstruct terrorism"—addressed security issues from 9/11. Residential properties intensified their screening of rental applicants, in particular the verification of each prospect's identity and citizenship or immigration status. Commercial properties increased security measures and paid more attention to the activities of their tenants, visitors, and guests. *Executive Order 13224,* issued September 23, 2001, required those leasing commercial space to check the names of officers of prospective tenant companies against the *Specially Designated Nationals and Blocked Persons list,* which identifies individuals suspected of terrorism or related activities.

The Enron Scandal

October 2001 saw the bankruptcy of the Enron Corporation, a Texas-based energy company. Many executives at Enron were indicted for a variety of charges and were later sentenced to prison. In addition to being the largest bankruptcy reorganization, Enron was attributed as the biggest audit failure—their $63.4 billion in assets made it the largest corporate bankruptcy in U.S. history until WorldCom's bankruptcy the following year. As a consequence of the scandal, new regulations and legislation were enacted to expand the accuracy of financial reporting for public companies. One piece of legislation, the *Sarbanes-Oxley Act (SOX),* expanded repercussions for destroying, altering, or fabricating records in federal investigations or for attempting to defraud shareholders.

After the SOX legislation, property management companies were required to recognize the SOX compliance and to continually manage compliance as information and technologies change. Since new SOX compliance brought more challenges, management companies had to set their policies and controls carefully by contracting consulting experts, regardless of whether they decided to pursue automated or manual controls.

Were it enough to simply *list* the ethical standards a company expects from its employees, Enron's implosion and the Wall Street collapses might not have come to pass. To state ethical intentions when company leaders act in direct contrast to those intentions clearly sends a contradictory message to the entire organization.

From 2003 to 2010

The array of high-tech equipment used for businesses demanded office buildings that could support state-of-the-art technology. Developers designed new office buildings to meet those requirements. If retrofitting older office buildings for tenants' technology needs was costly or otherwise impractical, owners and developers converted the old buildings to other uses, including hotels, condominiums, and apartments.

Trends toward urban living as well as neighborhood and downtown retailing increased. In addition, the *green movement* began. Efforts to minimize urban sprawl and achieve reductions in our "carbon footprint" had a great influence on developers. By encouraging downtown residential development—both as new construction and by conversion of commercial buildings—major cities became desirable places to live, work, and play. Suburban areas saw increasing numbers of *common interest developments* (CIDs) such as townhouse communities and low- and mid-rise condominiums.

Single-family homes were increasingly built in gated (common interest) communities as well.

Beginning in 2004, the Chairman of the Federal Reserve Bank began to raise the federal funds rate and the discount rate in small increments (25 basis points—one-fourth of one percent—at a time) to control inflation as the economy continued to recover. Home buyers and home owners benefited from the low interest rates as they financed and refinanced home purchases.

The Great Recession of 2008 was very similar to the recession of the 1980s in that it was deep, lasting, and affected those individuals and corporations that many would have thought were untouchable. One of the top two owners of shopping malls in the United States, whose revenues were in excess of $3.3 billion and whose assets were valued at $29.6 billion in December of 2008, filed bankruptcy just four months later—citing an inability to refinance its maturing debt. Although General Growth Properties, Inc. (GGP) would survive this, when the market realized that the real estate was worth more than the stock, a company with a huge, profitable portfolio and much less debt than the property value still could not find long-term financing because the lending community was unable to assess risk in that environment. Similarly, other owners who took out short-term, interim financing were faced with an inability to refinance. Fueling the fire, lenders became reluctant to loan funds at all, let alone at the loan-to-value ratios common when the economy was more stable. Compounding that problem was declining revenue caused by reductions in overall market rental rates and an increase in concessions needed to retain tenants in the owners' centers and buildings.

Tenants who relied upon lines of credits to maintain their monthly cash flow positions saw those credit lines shrink or be eliminated altogether—virtually closing them down overnight. This reduction in revenue reduced property value even further, which left little or no option for sources of financing. As a result, lenders heightened their scrutiny of their real estate portfolios, and real estate managers were literally forced into the mix between lenders and owners. This required examining the fine print of loan documents that were virtually ignored in the past, and it added another layer of skills that real estate managers needed to master.

According to the U.S. Bureau of Labor Statistics, in January 2008, the average unemployment rate was 5.4 percent. By December of that year, it was 7.1 percent. As the economy soured, unemployment reached its peak of 10.4 percent in January of 2010. The real estate meltdown produced some moderately good developments; however, they included:

- The *Housing and Economic Recovery Act of 2008* established a tax credit for first-time home buyers
- The *American Recovery and Reinvestment Act of 2009* expanded the first-time home buyer credit by increasing the credit amount for purchases made in 2009 before December 1, and the *Worker, Homeownership and Business Assistance Act of 2009* extended that deadline even further
- The IRS provided economic stimulus monies
- Taxpayers who bought new vehicles qualified for sales tax and other tax and fee reimbursements
- Some unemployment benefits were made tax free

These numerous incentives and rebates were designed to put additional monies in consumers' pockets that, if spent, would stimulate the economy into a period of recovery. Unfortunately, that plan faltered, and most Americans held onto their funds as the market's uncertainty unfolded. Consumer confidence remained at an all-time low. At that same time, public employers were forced to lay off many of their employees, while private employers reduced wages and other benefits and cut out all unnecessary expenses to weather the storm.

Not only did the economy change, so too did the residential rental sector. With millions of Americans forced out of their homes during the foreclosure crisis that occurred during the Great Recession, many of these homes were acquired by Wall Street-based investment banks. Historically, this is a first for big investment banks who tend to prefer the multifamily sector, but this would lead to additional opportunity for real estate managers and increased competition for residential rentals.

In 2010, while the federal government issued statements that the economic crisis was over, unemployment remained higher than ever. Real estate investors were still struggling to hang onto their investments and qualify for refinancing in order to avoid bankruptcy. Although wages were creeping up slightly to their pre-recession levels and spending increased somewhat, the "valley" that the economy was in at that time remained level—longer than recession valleys of the past. The agonizing climb to the top of the peak took even longer than previous recovery periods.

From 2010 to 2017: Short Sales and the New Shareconomy

The Great Recession had a lasting impact not just on the economy, but on our way of life. The GDP shrank more than five percent, while the economy lost approximately 8.7 million jobs. And with rapid changes in the online, information technology, and application space, it has made measuring the recovery all the more challenging. Today, however, has shown job growth and a recovery. Unemployment is down from 8.9 percent to 4.5 percent, and GDP is up 80 basis points. While there is growth occurring, it is minimal—and there is a reason for that. There is currently a new and different GDP, one that fails to account for what is projected to be a $335 billion dollar *Shareconomy.* It's increasingly common for people to shrug off the employee title for the freedoms of self-employment by becoming independent contractors and people renting out or selling items directly to consumers—bypassing more traditional methods of trade.

Real estate markets also changed as the effects of the foreclosure crisis loomed heavily on the economy. With the creation of a shadow rental market in the single-family residence and condominium space, markets across the country found competition in these newly available rental units. A new generation of buyers, the millennials, would also enter the market, but have the impact of the foreclosure crisis fresh in their minds. As such, the term "lifestyle renter" became widely utilized to describe those who could purchase but instead choose to rent.

Even with somewhat lower prices and historically low interest rates, financial regulation known as the *Dodd Frank Act* had a significant impact on the for-sale and for-rent sectors of the residential market. While these regulations were aimed at preventing another financial fiasco, the ultimate effect would stifle buyers and drive occupancy in the rental space. With more people renting and population trends on the rise, only additional supply of rental housing stock could solve the problem. But through the downturn, housing starts dropped off from a peak of 2.2 million units in 2006 to just more than 600,000. The result of this shortage would lead to several consecutive years of strong, double-digit rent growth in many markets across the United States—in some cases surpassing the previous high watermark reached before the downturn.

Time will prove critical as there are a number of real-estate focused items on the table, including the affordability crisis, tax reform, environmental regulations, and, of course, Dodd Frank.

The Economic Future for Real Estate Management

The fluctuations of the real estate market are generally considered a casualty of other worldwide events that are out of the control of real estate managers and investors. Regulation by all levels of government will continue to grow, and new technologies will affect the way buildings are built and used. The ebb and flow of our economy and the state of affairs, regionally and globally, will continue to challenge real estate managers of all types of properties as they strive to keep vacancies to a minimum, operate efficiently and effectively, and achieve the owner's objectives for the property.

During a recession, real estate managers must take responsibility for deciding what specific projects to address for their specific properties. They must make decisions to hold off on less visible projects and to undertake others that more directly benefit the bottom line. Tenants and residents will readily see the benefits, and owners are more likely to support such undertakings, especially if they will improve the overall return on investment (ROI). By and large, real estate managers have endured this evolution with great dignity and perseverance by learning new skills and adapting in ways appropriate to survive an economic recession, and they will continue to do so in this ever-changing world of real estate management and investment.

TYPES OF REAL ESTATE ASSETS

Almost every type of real estate investment—from boat marinas to vacation resorts—needs professional management. The base principles outlined in this book apply to all of them. An owner of a single-family home rental is essentially "managing" a real estate asset. Whatever the property type, management not only ensures that the properties are well maintained, it ensures that owners and tenants perceive that they are receiving the highest value possible for their respective investment and rental dollar. The following sections explore in more detail the main types of properties that need professional management.

Residential

Unlike commercial property, rental housing is in use 24 hours a day and must meet all of the housing needs of the residents' daily lives. This continuous occupancy tends to increase the demand for highly skilled professional management, maintenance, and repair. Managers of residential property must have superior customer service skills in addition to proficiency in the administrative functions of the profession.

Government-Assisted Housing. Any residential rental property in which the property owner receives part of the rent payment from a governmental body is considered government-assisted housing. *Public housing,* on the other hand, is generally owned and managed through a local or state governmental agency. As a rule, governmental housing subsidies are either resident based or property based.

Resident-Based Rental Assistance. The individual or family who receives a housing voucher is responsible for finding a suitable housing unit in properties that accept such vouchers. The Public Housing Agency (PHA) then pays the subsidy directly to the property owner on behalf of the participating renter. The voucher program also has provisions that outline resident and owner responsibilities. In addition to the traditional resident screening by property owners, the U.S. Department of Housing and Urban Development (HUD) permits PHAs to screen applicants for assistance.

Project-Based Rental Assistance. Section 8 *Project-Based Rental Assistance* is also available directly from HUD. Under this program, HUD makes up the difference between the rent that a low- or very low-income household can afford and the approved rent for an adequate housing unit in a multifamily project. Eligible renters pay rent based on their income. HUD originally provided such project-based assistance in connection with new construction or substantial rehabilitation of existing structures. However, the government repealed those programs in 1983. While funding is no longer available for new commitments, units previously approved under long-term contracts (20 to 40 years) may continue to receive subsidies.

Subsidized Housing. The need for effective management of subsidized and public housing creates a demand for real estate managers skilled in balancing the interests of all the parties involved—owners, governmental agencies, residents who receive subsidies, residents who do not, citizens' action groups, and resident (tenant) associations. In addition to understanding the principles of real estate management, managers of subsidized housing must thoroughly understand all applicable regulations. For example, to continue to receive housing benefits, residents of subsidized housing must periodically be recertified by the manager. These real estate managers must understand the role and structure of the governmental agencies involved, and they must work within budgets that are limited because of lower rental income. Under most federal, state, and local housing programs, the real estate manager must submit an extensive series of forms and reports. In subsidized housing, the lines of communication must be established to overcome a multitude of barriers—ethnic, economic, social, and linguistic. In addition to maintaining peaceful coexistence at the property, the improved relations that result from the manager's efforts help the community and society at large.

Condominium Associations

Although residential in use, the operation of a condominium complex or association is a bit more like a commercial property. Condominium owners are typically members of an association, and the association is managed by a professional firm whose job it is to oversee the structure, upkeep, and appearance of the property while hosting periodic meetings and generating financial statements and reports for members of the association on a consistent basis. Association managers will administer the Codes, Covenants and Restrictions (CCRs) that were put in place by the developer or the association to ensure quality controls are in effect.

Commercial Properties

Commercial properties consist of office buildings; specialty office projects such as medical facilities and research facilities; malls and shopping centers; industrial properties; warehouses; and storage or self-storage facilities. While managing commercial property is similar in many ways to managing residential property, a number of important differences exist. The general involvement with commercial tenants over the period of their tenancy can sometimes be much greater than it is with residential tenants.

Regular Offices. Office buildings are a unique type of commercial property that has special management requirements. Tenant selection, rent determination, and lease negotiations require special consideration. With an office tenant, the initial lease term can range from 3 to 10 years. Throughout their tenancy and at lease renewals, office tenants can expand their leased premises, relocate to a more favorable location within the building, or downsize as their needs require. This accommodation is usually not present at a residential site unless the numbers of occupants change.

Office Condominiums. Spaces that offer ownership of the office space as an alternative to leasing are prevalent in office condominiums. They appeal to medical and dental practitioners, real estate firms, financial planners, entrepreneurs, and small companies that need 1,000 to 10,000 square feet of space. Not only do owners acquire equity in the property, but they are also better able to project and control their costs of occupancy. However, office condominiums do not offer much flexibility to expand or contract as business needs change. Like residential condominiums, office condominiums offer new challenges for professional real estate managers that will be discussed later in this book.

Medical Office Buildings (MOBs). Buildings whose space is leased primarily to medical and dental professionals must be modified to meet those tenants' needs for additional (sometimes specialized) plumbing and electrical wiring. The nature of their clients and the services they provide mandate special care in cleaning and waste disposal—e.g., bloodborne pathogens and other hazards. The lease must address those issues. Entrances and other common areas—including parking—must accommodate disabled and ailing individuals; and possibly include larger doorways for stretchers and/or unique entrances for specialized transportation vehicles. In addition to doctors and dentists, other possible tenants for a medical building include pharmacies, biomedical laboratories, physical therapists, optical services, pain management clinics, and health maintenance organizations.

Shopping Centers. A shopping center differs from a retail district in a city center or a residential area in that it is usually a single project in a suburban area and it typically has on-site parking. However, shopping centers are not exclusively located in the suburbs; major cities also foster their development downtown, both as new buildings and as adaptive uses of old ones. A shopping center has a unified image, and the property is planned, developed, owned, and managed on the basis of its location, size, and types of shops as they relate to the trade area the center serves. There are two classes of shopping centers: (1) enclosed malls and (2) open-air centers—each is further classified into many subcategories (explained in more detail in Chapter 13).

Industrial Properties. Industrial properties include large single-user buildings, incubator space for small business start-ups, multi-tenant business parks, self-storage facilities, and business continuity services (records maintenance). They often have a mix of uses that combines office, retail, distribution, and storage at a single site. Technology has affected industrial users' space needs as it has those of office and retail uses. Manufacturers can often maintain minimum stocks of raw materials, parts, and packaging because computer inventory systems coupled with overnight shipping services allow just-in-time delivery that keeps pace with their production levels.

Warehouses. The spaces used in warehouses are leased for storage of inventory, records, excess raw materials, and the like. Warehouse management services may include shipping and receiving, with charges based on gross weight of materials handled or the number of packages shipped and received. In the storage environment, control of temperature and humidity are critical for many materials; federal and other laws mandate labeling to identify specific hazards of materials transported in interstate commerce. These requirements may affect management procedures.

SUMMARY

The real estate manager's role is to oversee the operation and maintenance of real property in a manner that aligns with the objectives of the owner. The overall development of real estate management resulted from a number of factors. The major demand for management expertise arose in the 1930s after lenders foreclosed on thousands of mortgages and discovered that the management of those properties required specialized skills. Since that time, the need for professional management has intensified because of absentee ownership of real estate, ownership by groups of investors through syndicates and partnerships, increased urbanization, and recognition that professional management is often necessary to maximize income and value.

Recognizing the need to establish professional standards of management, a group of real estate managers gathered during the Great Depression and founded IREM. The Institute grants four credentials—the Certified Property Manager® (CPM®) designation for individuals, the Accredited Management Organization® (AMO®) accreditation for management firms, the Accredited Commercial Manager (ACoM) for managers of commercial buildings, and the Accredited Residential Manager® (ARM®) certification for residential managers. Recipients must meet personal education and experience requirements, and all must pledge to adhere to ethical business practices.

Through the many educational programs available, there will always be continual improvements in the abilities to expand and refine the services that real estate managers offer to their clients. It's also important to note that learning does not always occur in the classroom. Each day, real estate managers are exposed to contractors who work on equipment and have innovative ideas on repairs and maintenance. Learning opportunities are everywhere. Most important is having the enthusiasm for higher learning that will motivate tradesmen, colleagues, and staff to actively pursue education as a means to gaining personal and financial rewards.

Types of Real Estate Managers and Their Responsibilities

There are many professions within the field of real estate management. This chapter explores the many positions available to new and seasoned real estate managers alike. Real estate management is not the typical nine-to-five job and can at times be quite stressful. For this reason, it's important to choose an area of expertise within the field that best suits the personality type and work ethic—one that invokes a strong passion and that will carry a career for many years.

TYPES OF REAL ESTATE MANAGERS

Although residential and commercial property types are very different, they do have much in common. Staffing, specifically at the site level, is perhaps the most important position in either sector. On-site representatives are the property owner's first line of communication and interaction with their customers. As such, it is important to attract and retain top-notch personnel at the smallest apartment community or biggest high-rise alike. Whatever the specific titles, professional management of a property and its primary goals are similar to managing a *business.*

Site Management

Site managers are responsible for the overall prosperity of the property and the general satisfaction of its residents. They manage all of the day-to-day dealings with residents, leasing, rent collection, and overall supervision of property maintenance. The title typically applies to managers of apartment buildings or other residential properties. Site managers are also commonly called *community managers, business managers, resident managers,* or *property managers.* On-site residential managers often maintain basic accounting records related to rent collection, unit occupancy, and tenant files, while property managers retain control of the management agreement, insurance policies, and complete accounting records. For example, the site manager of an office building may be called the *building manager* or *general manager,* and the site manager for a shopping center may be called the *mall manager* or *general manager.*

Real estate site managers regularly inspect the interior and exterior of the properties they manage, using appropriate inspection checklists to detail their findings. Although maintenance staff might regularly examine particular sections or components of the property—if the property is large enough to support such additional personnel—the site manager should be available to consult with the staff, supervisor, or owner on any problems they might find. The site manager is also responsible for identifying, analyzing, recommending, and implementing major maintenance or remodeling projects. Since managers are ultimately responsible for such activities and are not necessarily experts on every aspect that warrants attention, they usually rely on the advice of knowledgeable staff, skilled professionals, or trustworthy contractors.

The term "site management" often implies maintaining the physical structure of the property, but updating documents and records is also a principle aspect of this role. Aside from accounting records, site managers must maintain numerous other forms and documents (such as insurance policies, tenant files, the management agreement, and other property-related documents and information) in a logical and chronological order. All insurance records should be kept where they can immediately be accessed when needed, and the site manager should be able to retrieve tenant files quickly. A cross-referencing system is necessary to keep specific time-sensitive documents available well in advance of their expiration. Since many residential leases renew annually, being well organized ensures adequate time for marketing and resident retention. Keeping records current also ensures continuity in the operation of a property and gives the manager more time to invest in other responsibilities. For example, in government-financed, low-income housing, accurate, up-to-date records are required to maintain low-income status and receive government funds.

The owner has primary responsibility for compliance with governmental regulations with respect to the property, but the site manager must be knowledgeable in this area to avoid (or at least minimize) liability for noncompliance and to advise the owner regarding applicable regulations. Changes in income tax laws, fair housing, anti-discrimination laws, environmental regulations, zoning ordinances, or property taxation rules are just some ways in which government at all levels can affect the operation of income-producing property. The role of a real estate manager includes advising the owner when to seek legal counsel. Such advice requires knowledge about certain legal and tax ramifications.

Although the responsibilities of real estate management are broadly applicable, the skills required to carry out these responsibilities may be refined or tailored to a specific type of property. The duties and requisite skills for operating a skyscraper office building can differ substantially from the requirements for managing a 20-unit multiple dwelling in the suburbs. Perhaps the most challenging property to manage is the *mixed-use development,* which may combine office, retail, entertainment, and residential uses in a single property.

Property Manager

A *property manager* may be responsible for operating a single large property or a portfolio of several properties, while also supervising the site managers. This position is also referred to as the *property supervisor.* In most cases, the property manager has the responsibility of communicating with the owner of the property. They are sometimes responsible for creating management plans and annual or long-range budgets, and for carrying out the directives of each. Property managers provide accounting records and management reports to the client on a monthly basis, noting any variances or extenuating circumstances needing attention. In addition, this position may recommend major repairs or improvements to the property and identify sources of funding needed to carry them out. In general, the property manager has the ultimate responsibility for the financial and physical well-being of the property, which also includes the satisfaction and contentment of the residents, tenants, and any on-site personnel.

Regional Manager

The *regional manager* supervises on-site residential or commercial property managers and sometimes the property managers within the management firm. This position is also referred to as the *regional property manager, portfolio supervisor,* or sometimes *senior property manager.* Regional property managers sometimes obtain their titles due to the geographical area of the assets they manage. Whatever their titles, their roles are similar to the property manager role in that the overall health and well-being of the property and its residents or tenants—along with the satisfaction of the owner—are their ultimate responsibility.

Asset Manager

The focus of a real estate *asset manager* is on the property—residential or commercial—as a financial asset, and the general decisions this person makes can directly impact a property's financial performance. In many cases, the asset manager is the representative of the owner and is responsible for selecting a third-party management company and monitoring the performance of that company. In all cases, the emphasis of asset management is on activities that will add value to each property under management. Operational functions, performance goals, and caretaker roles are left to the property and site managers.

The definition of asset management continues to evolve, and the responsibilities of an asset manager vary greatly from one professional setting to the next. Regardless, as a rule, the asset manager should always have an eye toward long-term appreciation of the property as well as short-term cash flow. Overall, when performing asset management functions, the manager progresses through the property's life cycle and is involved from acquisition through operational oversight throughout the holding period and eventually the sale of the property. To perform competently, the asset manager must have the following four skills:

1. Must be in tune with the changing market opportunities and economic factors affecting tenancy
2. Must be knowledgeable on leasing rates and other incentives to offer tenants to stimulate leasing
3. Must generally be aware of financial developments that can lead to alterations in the physical or financial structure of the project itself
4. Must be knowledgeable of capital markets and financing opportunities

An asset manager views a property from the perspective of its present and potential value to the owner—its ability to meet the owner's goals, whether for income-producing or for owner-occupied property. Even though an owner may consider the property solely from an investment standpoint, effective asset management requires a working knowledge of property management duties and valuation procedures. A thorough evaluation to determine highest and best use can lead an asset manager to identify and analyze alternative uses of a property. If an alternate use such as converting an aging office building into residential units seems feasible, the manager must be able to encourage the owner to implement a plan to change the property's use—if it's financially feasible. Yet, another aspect of asset management is analyzing properties to identify and recommend what to buy, sell, refinance, or reposition in the market—possibly through a change of use—which requires knowledge of capital markets as well as local conditions.

Defining the Corporate Supervisory Team

Titles and positions are not typically interchangeable, but when it comes to some of the corporate supervisory roles held by managers, the portfolio manager and/or executive portfolio manager are often held by senior company executives, who may actually hold titles such as president, senior vice president, or president. While these titles or positions vary depending on the firm's organizational structure, the roles will remain similar and be somewhat compatible.

Portfolio Manager

Portfolio managers are typically responsible for assembling real estate assets to achieve specific investment plans and goals—similar to the management of a mutual fund or other pooled investment. Portfolio managers can also attain this title by managing many properties at once in a local area—either for one owner or many owners. In this role, a portfolio manager might regard their portfolio as one large entity, or they might manage each particular property as a single entity.

Executive Property Manager

The *executive property manager* is responsible for overseeing management, ensuring profitability, and acquiring new business, and is usually reserved for one or more of the officers of a management firm or its owner. The executive property manager may oversee an entire department of property managers, regional managers, or maintenance staff, and often is an intermediary between the owner of the property and the property managers assigned to that client. The executive property manager may report directly to the management firm's owner or CEO.

PRIMARY RESPONSIBILITIES OF A REAL ESTATE MANAGER

Whatever role a manager has towards a property, there are primary responsibilities associated with managing a real estate asset.

These responsibilities will be fully explored in later chapters, but it's important to review them while discussing the various professions and related professions in real estate management.

The training, education, and duties of the real estate manager can be categorized under four responsibilities:

1. Management of the physical site
2. Management of on-site and off-site personnel
3. Management of funds and accounts
4. Management of leasing activities and tenant services

These responsibilities are components of the overall responsibility as the *agent* of the owner. The agent is seen as the owner's fiduciary and is entrusted to act in the owner's best interests. Real estate management often involves fiduciary responsibility for millions of dollars in assets and cash flow. For this reason, property owners choose real estate managers who have strong ethical backgrounds.

The following is a brief listing of the principle responsibilities of the real estate manager:

- **Meet the owner's goals.** Having the owner's goals in mind helps develop the path for which the real estate manager is held accountable.
- **Develop a management plan to operate the properties.** The property management plan serves as a guidebook throughout the property's management cycle.
- **Develop and implement marketing plans.** There are specific tools needed to conduct a regional, neighborhood, market, and property analysis, which are used to determine the rental rates and target audience for marketing purposes.
- **Develop and administer a maintenance program.** This can be developed by the real estate manager or with the expertise and advice of maintenance professionals, the facility's personnel, or outside service providers. Setting up standards for replacements will make maintenance tasks less daunting if planned beforehand.

- **Anticipate and respond to residents' and tenants' needs.** Knowing what to expect and how to meet those expectations of residents and tenants is always a top priority. It's important to remember that it takes less effort and expense to retain a current tenant or resident than to procure a new one.

- **Administer the collection and deposit of rents.** Security measures, accounting for deposits, and managing the collections of funds are important, required skills that will be explored later in more detail.

- **Monitor and pay expenses.** Managing expenses and spending is just as important as the collection of property rents.

- **Prepare comprehensive budgets and cash flow projections.** Similar to the management plan, a budget, long-range budget, and cash flow projections are a guidebook to the property. While budgets are generally just estimates, the owner will expect the real estate manager to adhere to their projections for expenses and income. Knowing how to compensate for emergencies and inevitable variances will become a key skill.

- **Negotiate terms and leases.** Real estate managers play a key role in the occupancy of the building. Knowing how to negotiate properly for the benefit of both the owner and the resident or tenant is a skill that is learned over time and through experience.

- **Communicate with property owners and investors.** At each step in the management process, real estate managers must properly and effectively communicate their actions and outcomes to the owner or investors. This communication is critical in the overall development of the working relationship. In this business, there's no holding back—even if the news isn't good. It's the real estate manger's job to report the truth and to find and recommend solutions for any existing problems.

- **Administer human resources activities for the property and professional management company.** Each person who works on the management team for a property is just as important as the next. As previously mentioned, the successful management of a real estate asset requires numerous people with a common goal. Managing personnel and resources is a critical skill in the overall real estate management experience.

- **Assess, minimize, and mitigate risk.** Not only do real estate managers repair and maintain properties, they also anticipate future liabilities. This can include everything from ensuring that the property is adequately insured to conducting daily or weekly risk assessments to identify safety issues and to proactively correct them.
- **Develop an emergency procedures plan.** Emergencies can come in all forms—from earthquakes, to fires, to power outages. Regardless of the situation, the real estate manager is responsible for ensuring the safety of the residents and tenants on the property. Planning in advance of how these emergencies will be handled will ensure the best success possible.
- **Increase the property's value.** Increasing value can come quite naturally with the proper application of skills and tools. Increasing wealth is one of the primary reasons an owner invests in real estate. Real estate managers who conduct their management plan with that goal in mind will be well on their way to rewarding and successful careers.

OTHER REAL ESTATE MANAGEMENT PROFESSIONS

Real estate management most often requires the efforts of many people working as a team. Many other vital career opportunities in the real estate management arena are just as rewarding as managing real estate assets. The following list includes some major examples, but is not all-inclusive:

Leasing Agent

Professional *leasing agents*—sometimes referred to as *leasing brokers*—provide the skills and knowledge necessary to secure tenants for their buildings, and they have many opportunities to thrive. These individuals can be employees of a management or brokerage firm that specializes in leasing, or they can be freelance or contracted workers. They may be licensed in the state in which they lease space. They typically earn a base salary plus commission, but oftentimes they are paid commission only. Professional leasing agents may lease apartments in communities, office suites, or other commercial properties, such as shopping centers, industrial sites, or warehouse space.

The duties of leasing agents require interaction with prospective residents or tenants from start to finish. They develop and implement the marketing program or plan, serve as the initial contact for those seeking rental space, provide tours of the properties, close the sale, complete the required screening and lease documents, and provide the new resident or tenant with move-in instructions, lease, and rules and regulations.

It's essential that these professionals have extensive customer service skills. Maintaining a high level of enthusiasm and motivation helps lessen the stress level for those seeking space. In fact, leasing agents do not maintain the typical nine-to-five job schedule. They often perform their duties on weekends and evenings when their prospective tenants are not working. Leasing agents take pride in a job well done, which is evidenced by their *closing ratios*—the number of prospects who actually became residents or tenants due to their efforts.

Marketing Director

Marketing directors or *marketing managers* play a significant role in the overall success of the real estate asset. Typically, marketing directors provide their services to large, enclosed shopping malls, but they can be found in large apartment communities or office buildings as well.

For apartment communities, marketing directors are in charge of the entire marketing campaign from lease-up of a new property to managing the leasing activities of the property. Marketing directors ensure that the property is targeting the appropriate tenant and that the advertising campaign and leasing activities follow suit. Marketing directors might also be responsible for maintaining model units, overseeing the seasonal decorations, overall signage, or creation of advertisements and brochures.

For office buildings, marketing directors typically provide the same services as provided in residential communities. However, they are geared toward a different audience—the business client.

Marketing directors who work at a large shopping mall generally have a wider range of duties. For example, the *Mall of America* in Minnesota is 96.4 acres—the size of seven baseball stadiums. This megamall has a mini-amusement park, conference and meeting centers, a hotel, and baby-sitting services. It also holds many events throughout the year and numerous other activities designed to attract shoppers and tenants. In the past, shopping mall marketing directors were in charge of special events and dealt with specific issues such as arranging photos with Santa during the holidays. However, these events entail so much more. Other events might be arranging political or celebrity appearances or local performances. This is obviously an extreme example of a marketing director's potential duties; however, the example shows there is no end to the activities that a marketing director may perform.

Accounting and Financial Services

As previously mentioned, real estate managers have a fiduciary responsibility to their clients. They must collect rent and fees, pay expenses, and manage the overall cash flow of the property. To do this properly and efficiently, real estate managers must rely on accounting personnel to accomplish those tasks.

Accounting services can range from accounts payable to accounts receivable to corporate accounting for the management firm, as well as payroll services. Some property accountants perform these functions and are assigned to one or a few properties as full-charge accountants. Entrusting these services to qualified personnel is a much better solution than relying on someone who might not have the required experience or knowledge base. Some accountants who work for property management firms have also earned their CPA degrees with an emphasis on real estate.

Building Engineers, Mall Managers, and Construction Managers

Building engineers and facilities and construction managers typically work for a real estate management firm or a construction company. Some are freelance operators or consultants.

Building engineers are usually assigned to one or more office properties. They care for the mechanical systems that are present, such as HVAC, boilers, elevators, communications, electrical systems, and even green-building technologies. Building engineers must have a wide range of knowledge and expertise in all building systems. They may not physically repair or maintain the systems, but they must have enough knowledge to ensure that the systems function properly. Because such systems can be extremely expensive, the building engineer's expertise is critical to the overall *useful life* of the systems and to the value of the building.

Mall managers are well-rounded, experienced individuals who manage the physical aspect of malls and retail shopping centers. They provide or arrange the proper care of vital parts of the property, such as asphalt in parking lots, common area lighting, HVAC equipment, roofing, structural elements, and security systems. They usually work for a management firm and assist real estate managers as part of the management team. They may work closely with tenants as well, arranging for maintenance or repair issues. They may provide their expertise to one or many assets, and their knowledge is highly in demand.

Construction managers usually provide expertise when an owner or tenant makes improvements to the property. Improvements can entail *vanilla shell work*, which is provided by an owner prior to a tenant's move-in, or they can be changes made by the tenant in preparing the space for their particular use. These managers ensure that the contractors performing the work are properly licensed and insured, and that the proposed methods of installing the improvements are sound and not detrimental to the building. Construction managers add value to the work by recommending efficient ways to cut costs. They finalize jobs by verifying that the work performed was as planned, passes applicable codes, and all lien releases have been received. They sign off on the project as a whole.

Construction managers' services are invaluable to a real estate manager because they typically have a construction or engineering background, which most real estate managers do not. Poor workmanship can cost owners thousands of dollars and reduce a property's value. Construction managers ensure that any improvements made to the facility are just that—improvements that add value to the asset.

Facility Management

Properties owned by public (government and military), nonprofit (colleges and universities), and private entities (for-profit corporations) are often managed by *facility managers.* In general, a facility manager coordinates the needs of people, equipment, and operational activities within the physical workplace; the role is somewhat different from that of a real estate manager. Facility managers who work for corporations have responsibilities similar to those of on-site or property managers.

The Real Estate Executive

In addition to the corporate roles and/or titles included earlier in this chapter, there are other roles a *real estate executive* can hold; these include, but are not limited to, the following:

- Senior Portfolio Manager
- Director of Real Estate Services
- Director of Client Services

Typically, these individuals fill a supervisory role; they manage multiple real estate managers, numerous personnel within the entire firm, or even several apartment communities that have regional real estate managers that supervise on-site personnel. These executives usually have a college degree, along with a higher level of related experience in other aspects of real estate management. They may also play a key role within the management firm or even be a partial owner.

Brokerage Services

Real estate brokers are either employed by a brokerage firm or a management firm, or they are freelance workers. *Brokers* are licensed individuals that provide owners with the knowledge and expertise needed to buy and sell real estate assets as an investment—acquisition and disposition. Brokers must have extensive knowledge in a variety of areas including finance, value

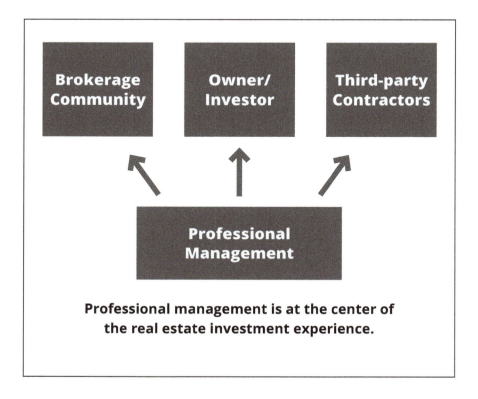

Professional management is at the center of the real estate investment experience.

determination, listing and marketing, sales ability, and many more. Brokers generally have an extensive clientele and many business associates or acquaintances with whom they build relationships that benefit both parties. For example, Broker A may know an investor looking for property in the northwest, while Broker B may have a listing for property in the same area. Those brokers, working together, help fulfill their respective clients' goals, and in turn, each reaps financial rewards related to the transaction.

Brokers usually work on some form of commission structure in which the brokerage house pays a minimal salary plus commission; they sometimes work on commission only, and the brokerage house receives a portion of the broker's commission. Buying and selling real estate is a fast-paced career that is not for everyone. Brokers must go after their work because the work does not fall into their laps.

Administrative Personnel

Throughout the entire real estate management industry, reliance on support personnel is essential. *Administrative personnel* include receptionists, office managers, filing clerks, and assistant property managers. They normally work onsite and provide supportive administrative duties that are essential to the success of the firm, the real estate management team, and, ultimately, the client.

Assistant real estate managers frequently become the next real estate managers in the firm. That is a natural progression, because if they are trained properly, they understand the product, the management cycle, and the appropriate delivery of management services.

SUMMARY

Roles, titles, and job descriptions can vary widely depending on the organization's size and structure. From site manager to asset manager, each position provides a distinct and unique service to the property and the client for whom they manage. One must never underestimate the impact of site-level employees on the financial performance of the asset. They are on the frontline dealing with the public, prospective tenants, current tenants, or occupants while advising others firsthand about technical aspects of the property and needed corrective action.

As with many professions, there are various career specialties that revolve around real estate management. On occasion, site managers and property managers work alongside other professionals and they may be called upon to hire outside leasing agents, marketing directors, accountants, engineers, construction and facility managers, and a multitude of other experienced professionals. Few industries or professions are more team oriented or team driven than real estate management. Since the world of real estate management can be complex, varied, and specialized, and it can involve many people, it's important to remember that each person adds value to the client or investor and provides unique talents and skills necessary to succeed.

Regardless of the title one holds or the type/size of the property that one manages, the responsibilities of the real estate manager are very similar. While each asset is unique, the basic need for knowledgeable and professional services remains constant. The real estate manager must take care of the physical and financial asset, preserving or enhancing its value, while managing the people necessary to provide these services and accounting for funds and overseeing a certain amount of financial management that includes analysis, planning, and budgeting. Other responsibilities for all property types include marketing and leasing, resident and tenant retention, human resources, risk management and emergency preparedness, and many more—all of which help to preserve and enhance the value of a real estate asset.

3 | Real Estate and Economics

Simply put, the core focus of the real estate manager is to increase and preserve the value of the managed property. As commercial or investment real estate is valued based on the income stream associated with a particular asset, it is imperative to ensure that rents are at or near market and expenses are managed. A property's performance will depend on the market as driven by the economy and economic trends, in particular, have a significant impact on a property's operations. In order to understand the impact of economic trends on real estate, it's important to first understand the fundamental principles of economics.

BASIC ECONOMICS

Economics is the study of the range of activities necessary for the satisfaction of human needs. These activities include the production, distribution, and consumption of manufactured goods and agricultural products as well as the various services provided to individuals and businesses. Fundamental to all of these activities is the use of land and the construction of buildings to house these activities—real estate is an important component of economics in general. In fact, ownership of land was once the principal measure of wealth in one's lifetime.

Today, money is the measure of wealth. The material substance of wealth—an automobile, a home, furnishings, stocks, bonds, and other investments—is expressed as the money value of those items. The interrelationship between money and the goods and services it can purchase goes beyond money's role as a *medium of exchange.* Money allows comparison and measurement of the values of goods and services that are otherwise not readily comparable or measurable—it serves as a *standard of value.* Money itself has value based on its purchasing power—it serves as a *store of value* during the time between specific transactions. The value of money fluctuates over time because of changing factors in the marketplace, such as interest rates, inflation, money supply, and world events.

The Marketplace

In any study of economics, an important element is the *market*— the place in which the exchange of goods and services between willing sellers and buyers actually takes place. The town square market, a retail store, and a real estate office are all markets. In these markets, purchases and sales take place between people who are face to face. In other markets—such as the New York Stock Exchange, Chicago commodity markets, and online—the seller rarely sees the buyer. The marketplace continues to be complex and multifaceted. Many elements are part of or have an effect on the market for a particular item. Price, supply, and demand have direct effects on rental space and employment levels. These phenomena are themselves affected by changes in technology and in the value of money. These elements of the market are of particular interest to real estate managers.

Price. In a complex economy where money is the medium of exchange used to measure the value of goods and services, the *price* of an item is the amount of money required in exchange for a unit of the item. Market factors determine the price of any item, and the price must be acceptable to both the buyer and the seller. If the price the seller wants is higher than the amount a buyer is willing to pay, no transaction will take place.

Supply and Demand. Prices in the marketplace are subject to the quantity of available goods and services and the relative value of money. The availability of goods and services is called *supply.* Availability of goods and services for sale is related to price, and more goods or services are offered as prices rise. When the amount of merchandise available for sale exceeds the amount that people are willing to buy, the excess volume reduces the value of the individual units and therefore lowers the price.

Price is not the only factor that limits supply. The price of one item can affect the supply of another related item. The supply of corn drops if the price of soybeans rises because farmers choose to grow the more profitable crop. Supply of a finished product depends on the price and availability of its components. An increase in the number of sellers of a specific product increases the supply of that product. Reduction of import restrictions permits foreign-made goods to compete with comparable domestic products and increases the overall supply. Sellers' expectations are another consideration. For example, oil production may temporarily fall (i.e., be delayed) if prices are expected to rise in the future.

Another market factor that affects price is *demand*—the amount of goods or services for which purchasers are available. Conversely, price affects demand. Generally, the amount purchased increases as prices drop. Factors other than the price of an item also affect demand. The price of related goods is one example. A simple illustration of this is how the demand for tea increases when the price of its substitute, coffee, rises. On the other hand, demand for sugar, a complement to coffee, drops when coffee prices rise. Because the price of coffee with sugar rises as the price of coffee rises, reduced coffee consumption will lower the demand for sugar. Another example is income. People spend more as their income rises, increasing demand. People also spend less when confidence in the economy is low. People's preferences also are a factor in demand, and advertising may alter preferences. An increase in the number of buyers will increase the demand for goods or services.

Over time, prices tend to be stable when supply meets or is equal to demand. When supply is less than demand, prices tend to rise; when supply exceeds demand, prices tend to fall. Taken together, these statements are the *laws of supply and demand*.

The Laws of Supply and Demand Relative to Price

 When demand exceeds supply, prices rise.

 If supply exceeds demand, prices drop.

= When supply equals demand, prices are stable.

Rental Space. These same supply-and-demand phenomena occur in the real estate market. Successful companies change their operations when demand for products or services drops. For real estate managers, this focuses on the need to:

1. Anticipate trends and market shifts
2. Collect and accurately assess and analyze data
3. Stay on the cutting edge (create demand)

For example, when demand for rental space is strong, rents should go up. A growing or shrinking work force signals a need to evaluate office space needs. Rising income encourages consumer spending, and that creates a demand for retail businesses and, potentially, store space. An increase in manufacturing, warehouse and distribution, and research and development triggers a strong demand for industrial space.

Rising rents stimulate investment in existing income-producing properties (apartments, office buildings, shopping centers, industrial parks) as well as construction of new ones. As rental rates increase, the value of the asset increases. New development eventually increases the supply of apartments, offices, industrial, and store spaces beyond the demand for them, and rents stabilize or decrease. However, the value of the real estate assets inevitably decreases as its rental income diminishes.

Employment Levels. The labor market, too, is subject to the laws of supply and demand. The workforce consists of both employed and unemployed individuals. Full employment is an unachievable ideal. As new jobs are created, other jobs are removed from the market. Unemployment can result from corporate downsizing and outsourcing of jobs, long-term decline of a specific industry, or a general downturn of the economy. Full employment (in economic terms) can only result when everyone who wants to work can find a job.

Significant unemployment affects the real estate industry in several ways, most notably as a reduction of the income stream of a property. People who are not working do not have income from which to pay rent for housing. Rather than struggle to meet expenses on their own, renters may double up to share expenses, or young adults may return to their parents' homes. Inability to pay rent may

Employment, Unemployment, Underemployment, and Rent

The Bureau of the Census measures employment by surveying 58,000 households every month to gather information on their labor-market activities during the preceding week. From the data, the Bureau of Labor Statistics estimates the number of people employed and unemployed during that month. It classifies everyone over age 16 as employed, unemployed, or not in the labor force based on a specific definition of employment. The unemployment rate is the number of unemployed divided by the number in the labor force (the number of employed plus the number of unemployed). For real estate managers, levels of employment and unemployment, particularly as they change within a localized area, reflect people's—and businesses'—ability to pay rent. The employment levels also indicate whether the need for housing or commercial space will increase or decrease.

force residents to vacate apartments or face eviction. This cycle has been seen during the Great Recession.

Reduction of the work force means businesses have fewer employees. For most businesses, fewer employees mean reduced work space requirements. Unemployed people are generally not consumers, so retail businesses may have to cut back on inventory and the amount of space used to display merchandise. They may opt to relocate to smaller stores. In factories, the initial reaction may be the reduction of the length or number of work shifts, but eventually manufacturers may eliminate redundant equipment and then seek smaller sites. As the slowdown of business reduces the demand for space, it also reduces the demand for new construction. The market cannot absorb additional rental space, and the market for a specific type of space becomes overbuilt and rents drop.

The office building market is particularly affected by changes in the level of employment. High employment means that companies typically need more space to house their operations and personnel. However, high unemployment means companies need less space—they will also be less inclined to move because of the expenses involved. If they stay and renew a lease, they may seek to reduce the amount of space rented. If they do move, it will be because they have found a smaller space that meets their needs. The ultimate effect of major unemployment on office space is higher vacancy levels and slow absorption of new space. Some resort to sub-leasing space from companies that would like to downsize but can't afford to move, or are hoping for a speedy recovery of their business. These prospective tenants have now found space outside of the pool of vacancies, thereby diminishing potential occupancy.

Technological Change. One of the most far-reaching causes of change in the marketplace is the increasing speed of new technologies for both consumers and businesses. With greater efficiency in production, improved modes of transportation, innovations in communication, and development of totally new products, technology has reshaped the way people live and work. New technology can affect production, distribution, supply, and demand, and the jobs created by technological change have a direct impact on the labor market.

Technology also has an impact on rental space. For example, development and widespread use of computers contributed to a growing demand for new office buildings because retrofitting of older buildings for the high-tech equipment used in many businesses can be very costly. On the other hand, the use of computers and their adjuncts may increase productivity in the workplace and have a negative impact on demand.

More specifically, home computing which began in the '90s affected both the demand for office space and the way it is used. Computers, smartphones, and other new technologies made it possible for workers to perform job tasks at home or at locations other than their employers' offices. These workers could telecommute or establish a home office, where they could conduct their business with the tools they need. In such situations, the employer might need less space overall. A company might not maintain office space for a particular employee, but instead set aside a cluster of spaces for those staff members who only needed to work in the office periodically—a practice called *hoteling*.

Computers also altered inventories. Increased supplies of crops and manufactured goods generally increase demand for warehouse space. However, the ability to maintain accurate counts of items in stock, coupled with manufacturers' desire not to invest large amounts of capital in inventory and their ability and willingness to ship small quantities on short notice (just-in-time delivery), reduced the need for storage space among distributors and retailers. And, the longer a product is held, there is more chance of damage, misplacement, and reduced value. The direct effect of this phenomenon was increased demand for *smaller* store and warehouse spaces.

By-products of technology provide other examples of technology's impact on rental space. Prior to the 1980s, video stores did not exist. However, by the early 1980s, video rentals could be profitable in just about any size store, and those operations consequently leased space in every type and size of shopping center and provided additional profits to supermarkets, drug stores, bookstores, and other businesses until the mid 2000s. By 2010, video stores became nearly extinct as new devices and online video streaming (e.g. Netflix, Amazon Video, Hulu, Sling TV) made movies and TV shows directly available to rent and/or purchase.

The 1990s brought the ability to transact sales securely online without specific need for a brick-and-mortar site. The full impact of this change on the demand for rental retail space has yet to be fully realized; however, warehouse and distribution facilities have already experienced a noticeable impact. For example, portable devices for downloading and storing individual songs online significantly impacted retailers who sold music. Today, nearly all music is sold online. In addition, with the introduction of e-reading devices like Kindles and iPads, book retailers have also been greatly impacted, with Borders Book Stores declaring bankruptcy in early 2011.

Just as the co-working phenomenon is booming with companies like WeWork, who allow business owners and employees alike the freedom of being able to travel the country, pop in to a location, and set up shop with a rented desk or work station, so too is the hospitality space doing battle not only with each other but also with app-driven sites such as Airbnb and VRBO. These companies are just a part of the billion-dollar "Shareconomy" that is disrupting the traditional economy by offering a peer-to-peer as opposed to business-to-customer platform.

The Role of Government

The U.S. government has an impact on the economy in numerous ways. The government is also a purchaser of goods and services from private industry, and that stimulates production and fosters competition. On the other hand, specific legislation and regulatory programs add to consumer prices and skew the costs of doing business (e.g., requiring governmental agency approval of drugs, pesticides, and other products before marketing; setting minimum wage rates; taxing specific products such as tobacco, alcoholic beverages, and gasoline). *Price controls* (supported prices for agricultural products) and regulation of competition in U.S. markets (limitations on imports, subsidies for domestic products) are other examples.

In addition to its participation in the economy, the federal government also measures economic activity. It collects information on wholesale and consumer prices, interest rates, money supply, levels of production and consumption of goods, construction starts and permits issued, sales of new and existing homes, population and more. Trends and changes in these *indicators* are used to chart economic growth, inflation, and the place of the U.S. economy in the world at large.

Other indicators are also relevant to real estate and its management. Fluctuations in interest rates are a measure of the availability of funds for borrowing—for investment, construction, and operating capital. The U.S. Federal Reserve System may lower the discount rate at which it lends money to its member banks as a way to stimulate economic growth. The *Producer Price Index (PPI)* and the *Consumer Price Index (CPI)* are measures of inflation at the wholesale and retail levels, respectively. (In leases written before the 1990s, real estate managers often used the CPI for rent increases based on increased operating costs. The CPI is discussed in detail later in this chapter.) The number of building permits issued, the number and value of construction starts, and the absorption rates for newly constructed space chart the health of the U.S. real estate market. Real estate professionals in general and real estate managers in particular follow many of these economic indicators as a matter of course, which may help guide their decision-making processes.

Measures of Productivity

For decades, the productivity of the U.S. economy was measured as *gross national product (GNP)*. The GNP is the market value of all final goods (tangible objects such as canned food and automobiles) and services (intangible objects such as entertainment activities and transportation) produced by an economy in one year's time. It measures output attributable to U.S. residents *regardless of their geographic location*. Because foreign trade provides some of the goods and services Americans purchase, its effects are also included in the measurement of GNP. It accounts for the volume of goods and services exported to and imported from other countries. When imports exceed exports, the net value of the GNP is negative (as it was during the late 1980s in particular).

Beginning in 1991, however, U.S. productivity has been reported as *gross domestic product (GDP)*, which measures the same factors for economic activity located *only within the United States*. (Nearly all other countries measure productivity as GDP, so use of GDP facilitates comparisons of U.S. economic activity with that of other countries.)

The U.S. GDP is currently measured in billions of dollars. The amount is calculated by adding together the value of personal consumer purchases (durable and nondurable goods and services) and government purchases of goods and services at the federal, state, and local levels, plus the investment of private capital in new plants and equipment, commercial buildings, and residential structures (fixed investment), and new stocks of business inventory. The investment amount is adjusted for depreciation (using up) of the existing capital stock during the process of production. A rapidly rising GDP may signal rising interest rates or the beginning of a period of increasing inflation. A declining GDP may forecast falling interest rates or impending recession. (Some economists consider two consecutive quarters of declining GDP as an indicator of recession.)

Real estate is a significant portion of GDP (10 percent in 2010). It comprises construction, professional services, and real estate finance and accounts for designing, building, brokering, financing, and managing real properties (residential, office, retail, industrial) built or traded for investment. It excludes building materials and construction of public facilities. Real estate's contribution to the GDP exceeds those of durable and nondurable goods manufacturing, wholesale and retail trade, and the cost of government as individual sectors.

Of all the functions of government; however, taxation on income, regulation of banking, and control of interest rates are among those of greatest interest to the real estate manager. (The specific role of the various levels of government in the real estate market is discussed later in this chapter.)

Taxation. The functions of government, including the services it provides, have inherent costs. In order to pay those costs, the government must have income. Government derives its income from various sources, the most significant of which is taxes. In the United States, the federal government taxes the income of individuals and businesses. State and local governments impose taxes primarily on property, although some tax income and sales of goods and products as well.

The federal income tax, as its name implies, is a tax on personal and business income. Changes in the law have from time to time specifically encouraged or discouraged investment in income-producing property. In the early 1980s, the law provided for higher tax rates on higher incomes, but it also created a variety of tax shelters. An individual or entity could invest in property that generated little or no income and still make a profit on paper. The level of continuing inflation essentially guaranteed a selling price higher than the property's purchase price. In addition, investors could use losses from real estate investments to offset income from wages and other sources. That reduced the property owner's taxable income and, in some cases, lowered the tax bracket. However, the *Tax Reform Act of 1986* changed that, and investment in real estate became less attractive because the act greatly reduced tax incentives. Property owners could no longer use losses that resulted from real estate operation to offset other income. The tax reform blocked them from sheltering that income from taxation. Owners who previously bought property for tax breaks found themselves in the position of having to use income from other sources to support their real estate investments that were operating in the red. Those who did not have extensive resources had few options, and they elected sale, foreclosure (default), and sometimes bankruptcy. Inflation slowed and property values no longer appreciated quickly—especially in overbuilt markets. As a result, the number of distressed properties on the market increased.

Changes in the federal income tax laws affect the amount of capital people are willing to invest in real estate and other assets. The *Economic Growth and Tax Relief Act of 2001* lowered individual tax rates, and the *Jobs and Growth Tax Relief Act of 2003* made further adjustments, including the reduction of the long-term capital gains tax rate from 20 to 15 percent. (Those capital gains rate cuts were to be effective for the tax years ending on or after May 6, 2003, and signed into law on May 28, 2003, but nearly all of the cuts—individual rates, capital gains, dividends, estate tax have expired after 2010.) Favorable capital gains tax rates encourage the sale of appreciated property. On the other hand, changes in the rules regarding depreciation—the method by which taxpayers are allowed to recover the cost of their investment—can encourage or discourage investment. The current long cost-recovery periods for real estate investment (27.5 years for residential property and 39 years for commercial property) diminish the rate of return on the owner's investment.

Financial Regulation. A significant role of government relates to money. It produces the nation's money and regulates the amount in circulation. When governments mint and print additional currency, they create inflation. When they reduce the amount of currency in circulation, they cause deflation. Printed money and coinage were traditionally backed by some type of convertible commodity. Each country fixed a value of the commodity for its particular currency so that international exchange could take place. Previously, gold was the accepted standard. However, the present standard involves a mixture of floating- and fixed-exchange rates. The value of the U.S. dollar floats with respect to the major currencies of the world.

The U.S. government also regulates banking. Deregulation of the thrifts in the 1980s gave rise to several phenomena. Branch banking (and branch S&Ls) became widespread, and the government allowed S&Ls to offer negotiable order of withdrawal (NOW) checking accounts and to lend money for commercial investment. A large number of banks and S&Ls entered the real estate market directly, often lending money in a manner that allowed them to participate in the property ownership. Many of those institutions had no prior experience in real estate investment, and they frequently made loans for the development of marginal properties. In addition, they allowed assets held in reserve to reimburse depositors to fall below required levels—sometimes as a result of real estate assets having lost value. When the borrowers defaulted on the loans, the financial institutions foreclosed on the properties. By the end of the 1980s, the market was glutted with troubled properties. Failures of S&Ls became widespread, and the *Federal Savings and Loan Insurance Corporation (FSLIC),* which guaranteed the deposits in the institutions, was required to pay back the insured deposits. The *Financial Institutions Reform, Recovery, and Enforcement Act (FIRREA),* which the U.S. Congress enacted in 1989, transferred the responsibilities of the FSLIC to the *Federal Deposit Insurance Corporation (FDIC),* which is the insuring body for deposits in banks and in the few remaining S&Ls. As a consequence of the savings and loan crisis of the 1980s, the Resolution Trust Corporation (RTC)—a United States government-owned asset management company—was charged with liquidating assets (primarily real estate-related assets, including mortgage loans) that had been assets of S&Ls declared insolvent by the Office of Thrift Supervision. Although the RTC was first established in 1989, it was overhauled in 1991.

Beginning in the late 1990s, the government began allowing banks to acquire or merge with banks in other states. It modified the Bank Holding Company Act to authorize banks to underwrite and sell insurance and securities, conduct both commercial and merchant banking, and invest in and develop real estate, among other activities. However, the act limits the kinds of nonfinancial activities in which those new entities can engage. (Banks are not allowed to act as agents in real estate transactions.) National banks are allowed

Money and the International Arena

International trade requires the exchange of the U.S. dollar for other nations' currencies. In free markets, currency values generally *appreciate* in countries where inflation rates are lower than those in the rest of the world. Foreign demand for those countries' goods drives up the value of the currency. Likewise, in countries with lower-than-average economic activity (specifically, low imports), exchange rates (currency values) rise. Countries where interest rates are high attract investment capital from all over the world. The reverse is also true: Currencies *depreciate* in value in countries with high inflation rates, high levels of economic activity, or low interest rates. The U.S. dollar has a floating exchange rate against foreign currencies, most notably the British pound, the euro, and the Japanese yen.

In the United States, the Federal Reserve System regulates the money supply by changing the required *reserve ratio* (the amount of reserves a bank must have on hand in relation to the deposits on its books), by changing its policy on lending to banks (raising or lowering the *discount rate*), or through open market purchase and sale of government securities. To increase the money supply, the Federal Reserve purchases U.S. government bonds (treasury bills or T-bills) that pay a fixed number of dollars of interest annually for various terms (one-year T-bills, 10-year notes, 20-year bonds). Increasing the money supply results in higher bond prices and lower interest rates. Conversely, when the Federal Reserve sells bonds, the money supply decreases, and lower bond prices and higher interest rates result. For example, consider a bond that pays $90 a year. It will yield a return of nine percent when the bond price is $1,000. However, if the bond price falls to $900, the bondholders will receive a 10 percent return.

Real estate investors and managers use the interest rate on treasury bonds as a benchmark—a *risk-free rate of return.* They use it to determine how much additional interest a real estate investment must return to compensate for its illiquidity and other risk factors. For example, if the risk-free rate of return on treasury bonds is six percent, a real estate investor may require an eight percent or larger return. Internationally, the London Inter-Bank Offering Rate (LIBOR) provides a similar benchmark. The LIBOR rate quoted in *The Wall Street Journal* is an average of the rates at which five major banks would be willing to deposit U.S. currency for a set period. It compares most closely with the U.S. rate on one-year T-bills.

to underwrite municipal bonds. As a result, things became dramatically tighter due to the Dodd-Frank Act that was signed on July 21, 2010. It was enacted to promote financial stability by improving accountability in the financial system, to protect taxpayers by ending bailouts, and to protect consumers from abusive financial service practices. The Dodd-Frank Act changed the existing regulatory structure by creating a multitude of new agencies to streamline the regulatory process, increase oversight of specific institutions, and amend the Federal Reserve Act by promoting transparency and other changes.

Interest Rates. As part of its regulation of banking, the U.S. government controls the money supply by adjusting interest rates, and that has widespread effects. When the Federal Reserve System lowers the discount rate charged to its member banks (to stimulate economic growth), the banks, in turn, may lower the commercial *prime interest rate* they charge their most credit-worthy customers for short-term loans. This can lead to a reduction in the interest rate paid on deposits as well. Conversely, the Federal Reserve System may raise the discount rate to reduce the money supply or to discourage banks from excessive leniency in their lending and investment policies.

Interest is a major inducement for people to save. When an individual's income exceeds the amount required to take care of basic needs, the surplus income can be spent immediately for personal enjoyment (to acquire possessions, for recreation, etc.) or set aside for future use.

Savings deposited in banks and related financial institutions do more than earn interest for the saver. That money works to produce more money. Banks use savings deposits to finance various types of lending. Consumers borrow money to purchase homes, automobiles, major appliances, recreational equipment, vehicles, etc. Businesses borrow money for operating capital, which they use to purchase raw materials for processing into finished products or to provide inventory of products for sale. Both individuals and businesses borrow money to invest in income-producing real estate. They pay the borrowed money back to the lenders with added interest. In fact, the amount borrowed often depends on the rate of interest charged.

When money is plentiful, interest rates tend to be low, and banks readily lend money to willing borrowers. Throughout the 1990s and into the 2000s, interest rates were kept low to fight inflation, despite a recovering economy. The low interest rates encouraged a boom in single-family home purchases and in refinancing, and the country enjoyed a strong economy in the latter part of the 1990s.

The exuberant purchasing and refinancing began to wane in 2004 when the Federal Reserve Bank began to raise the federal funds rate and the federal discount rate, which in turn influenced the prime rate quoted by financial institutions. When money is tight, however, interest rates tend to rise, and individuals and businesses tend to borrow less. High interest rates encourage saving and discourage borrowing. Changes in interest rates are among the factors that contribute to inflation and deflation, and periods of inflation and deflation affect the sale and purchase of goods and services, usually in a cyclical manner. Controlling interest rates is one way the government attempts to control inflation and the amount of money available for borrowing. However, the recession of the late 2000s made credit tight and interest rates remained at a historically low level. As a result, consumers and businesses could not obtain credit as easily as they did before the collapse, but the steadily decreasing interest rates created easy credit conditions for a number of years prior to the Great Recession.

The Business Cycle

Periods of economic expansion or contraction may be short-lived (a few months), or they may go on for many years. Sometimes one region of the United States or the world is affected more than another region. Occasionally a single industry or a single market is the focus of economic change, but that is rare. Businesses and industries today are interrelated in such complex ways that whatever affects one significantly affects most, if not all, of them. Poor sales of consumer merchandise slow a retailer's business, the retailer orders less from wholesalers and distributors, and they in turn take less of a manufacturer's production. A raw material shortage curtails a manufacturer's production, less merchandise is available for wholesalers and distributors to move to retailers, and consumers cannot purchase products they desire. Changes in technology, development of new materials, and discovery of new uses for existing materials are some factors that contribute to massive economic changes. They may make current materials and technologies obsolete, or they may create entirely new industries.

When business is good, selling goods or services is simple. Demand exceeds supply, prices are high, and making a profit is easy. When business is poor, supply exceeds demand, prices are low, and losses often replace profits. These various periods of inflation and deflation of an economy are known as the *business cycle.* The business cycle generally has four successive stages: recession, depression, recovery, and prosperity (Exhibit 3.1). By convention, professional economists look at the downside first, perhaps because its causes and effects are more readily apparent.

Recession. During periods of prosperity, all sectors of the economy expand. The increased demand for goods and services tends to raise prices. Prosperity also results in higher wages. When personal income increases, people have a tendency to spend that income—buying a more luxurious car, paying more in rent for a larger apartment, etc.—but only up to a point. Once their needs and wants are satisfied, many people will store their surplus income in the form of savings or investments.

When people actively save money, a corresponding reduction in consumer spending generally occurs. However, savings invested in banks or in stocks and bonds provide the capital for commercial investment. Spending by business firms temporarily offsets the absence of spending by consumers. The lessening of consumer

EXHIBIT 3.1

The Business Cycle

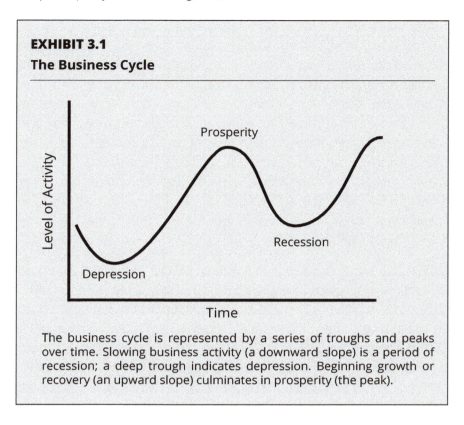

The business cycle is represented by a series of troughs and peaks over time. Slowing business activity (a downward slope) is a period of recession; a deep trough indicates depression. Beginning growth or recovery (an upward slope) culminates in prosperity (the peak).

spending affects businesses in two ways. Because merchants can no longer rely on the same level of sales, their income decreases, and they cannot afford to maintain the same inventory levels. Manufacturers still have to pay for raw materials, wages, and other costs of production.

Providers of services are also affected. Businesses may postpone or defer equipment maintenance and repairs. To control costs, they may have in-house staff provide services that they previously outsourced. Conversely, they may opt to reduce staff and outsource services that they can contract for less. To increase profit margins, manufacturers of consumer goods may deal directly with retailers, eliminating the wholesale distributor. Some may even choose to deal directly with consumers via factory outlet stores, direct mail (catalogs), or online. Competition increases as businesses try to

Economic Indicators

A number of economic factors measured by the U.S. government on a regular basis move upward and downward in the same pattern as the business cycle. Some of these indicators lead the cycle, some run concurrent with it, and others follow it. Of particular interest are the indexes of business activity—building permits, total output, employment, business formation, and new orders. A period of recession often follows sustained downturns in one or more of these indicators.

Indicators that relate directly to real estate include the total value of new construction put in place (all property types), nonresidential investment as a percentage of gross domestic product (GDP), total manufacturing and wholesale trade inventories, and retail sales. Other indicators of interest to real estate professionals reflect the general economy. These include consumer and producer prices, net exports, employment, and interest rates (especially the prime rate).

Indicators that tend to rise or fall in advance of a general rise or fall in business activity are called *leading indicators*. They are the most important because they give advance warning of future economic events. Normally they turn down before a recession and up before an expansion of the economy. The U.S. Department of Commerce publishes a composite *index of leading indicators* that is a weighted average of twelve of their leading indicators. Four components of this index are new building permits, net change in inventories, stock prices, and the money supply. The index of leading indicators is one of the most widely used indicators in the U.S. economy; however, its accuracy in forecasting recessions is not absolute because components of this composite index do not move together in exactly the same rhythm.

maintain or increase their share of a dwindling consumer or industrial market. In order to maintain inventories and meet payroll expenses, businesses turn to bankers. Meanwhile, the bankers become cautious; their willingness to lend money to business for expansion may not extend to providing operating capital. Tightening credit also reduces the funds available for new construction. Prices cannot continue to rise in this environment. Not enough buyers are available—demand has reduced. This slowdown in business activity signals the beginning of a period of economic *recession.*

Soon, manufacturing costs catch up with selling prices. Banks raise their interest rates and may even refuse to make loans; businesses cannot borrow additional capital. The inability to obtain funds from banks leads to the failure of some businesses, and that can have a domino effect. One business may depend on payment from a second business to meet its obligations on a loan. When that payment does not come, the first business fails. Business failures mean banks and other lenders cannot collect their outstanding loans, and eventually the financial institutions themselves fail, which happened with the subprime mortgage lending crisis in 2008 and 2009. The term *subprime* refers to the credit quality of particular borrowers, who have weakened credit histories and a greater risk of loan default than *prime* borrowers. The banks' faulty practices are a large part of what led to the Great Recession. Lending practices became so much tighter that even people with good credit experienced difficulty in obtaining loans, which further stifled the recovery and caused more businesses to fail.

Depression. A widespread reduction in business activity ultimately results. Employment drops, wages fall, and consumer demand declines. Surviving businesses try to sell all they can and buy as little as possible so they can meet contractual obligations, pay their debts, and avoid failure. As demand continues to decline, so do prices. The most serious outcome of all of these negative factors is a period of *depression.* Stocks of goods diminish as businesses sell and do not replenish their inventories. The rate of production is slow and prices are low. Interest is down and so are wages. Unemployment is widespread. Depression eliminates the weakest businesses and banks, and less competition exists in the marketplace.

Recovery. During a depression, however, business costs also decline because rents, wages, and prices for raw materials decline.

Businesses will eventually have to replace machinery and equipment they did not maintain or replace during the depression. The need for new machinery creates a demand for capital equipment, and increased demand stimulates other businesses and leads to higher prices. These are early signs of *recovery.* After most recessions in the United States, once recovery gets started, employment and wages increase; however, the Great Recession did not follow typical recovery and was referred to as a "jobless recovery." Eventually, recovery with jobs should occur. Additional income will increase the demand for consumer goods and services and tends to raise prices. Production costs will not rise as quickly as prices because rents, interest rates, and wages—which react more slowly to change—will remain low for some time.

Prosperity. When prices rise faster than the costs of production, business income increases in the form of higher profits. The reviving economy heads for prosperity once again. *Prosperity* is a period of good business. Businesses foresee opportunities for profits, so they borrow capital, increase their production, and try to enlarge their share of the market. Banks are willing to lend money for business expansion because such loans are easy to repay. Lending expands the banks' business. The expansion of one business creates a demand for the products and services of other businesses, and that tends to raise prices. High prices in the marketplace attract other businesses to it, resulting in competition.

Population growth also fuels economic growth. In the United States, immigration has significantly affected the population. Foreign-born individuals represented 7.9 percent in 1990, 11.1 percent in 2000, and 13.5 percent in 2015. Changes in the size of the population affect the size of the work force. A growing work force means larger numbers of consumers as well. The Baby Boom generation dramatically increased the size of the work force beginning in the 1970s. However, they produced fewer offspring than their parents. As the Baby Boomers passed into middle age (in the 1990s and beyond), their children entered the work force—but in much smaller numbers. Only a few years ago, many Baby Boomers were likely to have retired as they reached age 65; however, with the financial turmoil from the Great Recession, which has sharply reduced the home values and financial investments of millions of boomers just as they approach retirement, this is no longer the case. For the first time, at least three generations of individuals will be in the work force together. The Bureau of Labor Statistics provide numbers of employed persons by detailed occupation and age, including median age—specifically in the real estate industry (Exhibit 3.2).

Prosperity tends to feed on its own momentum. Employment levels rise as businesses expand. Business expansion leads to new construction of office, industrial, and retail properties. High wages permit workers to purchase luxury items and invest in home ownership. During these times, housing starts to increase, especially single-family homes. Investment, savings, and purchases on credit are on the rise. Meanwhile, rents and interest rates begin to escalate as leases and contracts expire. The economy starts to slow down, checked by rising prices, wages, rents, and interest rates—all of which make money tighter—and the cycle repeats itself.

EXHIBIT 3.2

LABOR FORCE STATISTICS FROM THE 2016 POPULATION SURVEY:
Employed persons by detailed industry and age*

Ages	20–24	25–34	35–44	45–54	55–64	65+	Median age
Real estate	119	434	545	655	606	381	49
Rental and leasing services	30	114	79	74	59	29	40.6
Commercial, industrial, and other rental assets	4	30	25	22	18	3	41.9

*Numbers are in thousands (i.e., 119 represents 119,000).

NOTE: Median age represents the midpoint in the age distribution such that half of workers are younger and half are older.

Throughout the business cycle, rents, interest, and wages do not change as quickly as other prices. Rents and interest rates usually remain fixed for a time; leases and other contracts run for months or years. Wages and salaries also remain fixed for extended periods, sometimes by contract. As general prices for goods increase, rents, interest, and wages are slow to catch up. The disparity in these costs of production in relation to the prices commanded for goods is part of the fuel behind prosperity. Rents, interest, and wages eventually catch up with prices, however, and that has the effect of reducing profits and creating losses—ultimately fueling a recession. The numbers of potential buyers diminishes, depressing real estate prices. Unavailability of capital precludes investment in improvements, and the real estate market becomes glutted with distressed properties. In the end, the credit crunch that results promotes recovery by limiting new building.

A period of depression does not always follow a recession, and recovery is not always a separate stage in the business cycle. Sometimes periods of prosperity follow periods of mild recession; economic expansion and contraction are apparent but not pronounced. Often a scientific breakthrough or development of a promising new technology can be a significant contributor to economic recovery. The real estate industry is part of the general economy, and it reacts to the same economic pressures, but its reactions are slower and stronger. (The nature of the real estate cycle is discussed later in this chapter.)

REAL ESTATE ECONOMICS

The amount of land available for use is strictly limited. Land also has unique characteristics based on its location and its inherent qualities. These factors give value to land and affect its desirability. Value is also created when land is made *usable*—i.e., prepared for development by grading, draining, and installation of curbs, sidewalks, sewers, and streetlights. Ultimately, the use or potential use of land determines its market value. Fertile farmland that yields more grain per acre is more valuable than less productive acreage. However, neither will be as valuable if the grain cannot be transported to the marketplace. A location that includes access to transportation is a key factor in the value of farmland. Land in urban areas is often considered more valuable than suburban land because of its intensive use. For instance, population density is very high for residential uses—a 100-unit apartment building may occupy the same amount of land as two or three single-family homes.

In some urban areas, residents accept high rents as a trade-off against long, expensive commutes to work. They expect ready access to public transportation and the cultural and entertainment features of the city as well as the amenities of the building to compensate them for that rent. Businesses willingly pay high rents for office space in urban areas because they have access to a large labor pool and to all the services available in a city. (Exceptions do exist. Some cities have lower rents per square foot than their surrounding suburbs.) Retailers will pay high rents to have store space in an area where wealthy people shop or to have access to large numbers of potential customers.

The Real Estate Market

Markets for specific products and services exist wherever willing buyers and sellers of those products and services exist. The products themselves and the people who provide the services can move from one location to another. While land is fixed in location, owners of real estate may not be local. Large commercial properties, in particular, are typically traded at the national level and in international markets. However, the ultimate users are local.

The value of land in the local market depends on its use and any improvements to it. Because buildings and other improvements on land have a long physical life, the commitment to a specific use is not readily subject to change. Land use is affected by many factors, among them industry, population, highways—and supply and demand.

Credit Card Debt

Yet another contributor to the down side of an economy is credit card debt. With easy availability of credit, consumers are as likely—or more likely—to make purchases with credit cards than with cash. When the credit card bills come in, some may have a tendency to pay only the minimum amount due, carrying forward a growing balance at a high rate of interest. Competition among credit card issuers encourages consumers to pay off an existing credit card balance using a new card at a lower interest rate. Those who continue to use credit cards without paying down the balance may become overwhelmed. And, with a flat salary or fluctuations in employment, bankruptcy can be an appealing option. Their creditors—merchants, property owners, and others—may be able to collect only a small portion of the debt owed—or nothing at all.

The Bankruptcy Abuse Prevention and Consumer Protection Act of 2005 (BAPCPA) made it more difficult for consumers to file for bankruptcy. The Act requires that incurred debts are discharged only after the debtor has repaid some portion of their debts instead of forgiving the entire debt. The legislative changes affected consumers and business bankruptcies. The Act requires the debtor's income to be compared to the median income of the debtor's state. If the income is above the median income, they are subject to being found "abusive" or in violation of filing for bankruptcy.

Industry. Changes in industry and the economy also affect land value. Inflation, wide fluctuations in the availability and cost of mortgage money, and the cost and availability of foreign crude oil are factors that affect the real estate market at the regional, national, and international levels. At the local level, empty factories and warehouses on the edge of a city may no longer be as useful as industrial properties. Creative developers and architects can usually find a way to convert them to other uses. Vacant warehouses that could not be sold or were no longer usable for their original purpose have been renovated and converted to housing.

Factories, post offices, railroad stations, and historic buildings have been made over as shopping centers. Such changes, intended to increase the income from the property and therefore increase its value, also preserve landmarks and conserve raw materials.

Changes in a region affect land use. The growth that occurred in the *Sunbelt* (the Southwest) in the 1980s had nationwide impact. Many industries relocated there from the northeastern United States. The areas they left behind became known as the *Rust Belt*—also known as the Manufacturing Belt or Factory Belt in the Northeastern section of the United States running west of the Megalopolis (Washington D.C, Baltimore, Philadelphia, New York City, and Boston) through Pennsylvania, Indiana, Ohio, Michigan, and to the western shore of Lake Michigan. High technology and petroleum were the booming Sunbelt businesses. They brought jobs that created demand for new office space. However, dependence on them to the exclusion of other types of industries eventually had severe effects locally. Increased importation of petroleum reduced domestic exploration and production. Higher prices for domestic oil increased the production costs of products derived from it. When the oil and high-technology industries faltered, many cities—especially Dallas and Houston in Texas—suddenly had phenomenal amounts of vacant new office space and interrupted construction. Property values declined drastically.

Population. Changes in population size have a direct impact on land values. When the population in an area grows, land value increases. The increase in demand for the fixed amount of land leads to higher prices. Population growth is a direct result of the formation of new industries that provide jobs. New manufacturing industries attract support businesses (suppliers of raw materials or parts and distributors of finished goods), which also increase the number of available jobs. When the local population declines—particularly if significant numbers of people move away and others do not move in to replace them—demand for land decreases, land values decline, and prices fall. Population decline results when industries close down because they have become obsolete or lost their share of the market. Those satellite businesses that depended on the major industry may close down earlier because the components they supply are no longer needed or later because there are no finished products for them to distribute. These shifts in industrial activity that affect population size also affect the local economy by increasing and decreasing the amount of income available for discretionary spending.

Ample discretionary income and ready availability of credit encourage shopping, and that creates a demand for shopping centers. In order to meet the demand and create unique shopping environments, major malls include food courts, movie theaters, and other forms of entertainment, which also serves to lengthen the shoppers' stay.

The U.S. population is aging rapidly, and more people are living longer than ever before. An aging population increases the demand for senior communities and retirement housing (which may be comparatively smaller and are likely to be more expensive and include recreational amenities). Such housing provides opportunities for specialty management. The aging population also increases the need for senior housing, nursing homes, and health care facilities.

Supply and Demand. In the real estate market, the laws of supply and demand are also at work. Usually the value of real estate in a given market is based on the present worth of projected future benefits to be derived from the investment. Stable values result when a balance exists between the supply of a given land use and the economic demand for that use. Supply may be limited and is not quickly increased. Supply declines because of deterioration, demolition, and destruction by hazards (e.g., fire). Change of use reduces the supply of one use while adding to the supply of another. Existing properties are part of the total supply even if they are not used. Demand changes, however, and many factors influence it. Population, income, credit, personal tastes and preferences, as well as governmental actions, taxes, and cost savings have an impact on demand. The imbalance between supply and demand means real estate investment can be riskier than other types of investments whose markets are more predictable.

When a particular use (e.g., office space, shopping centers) is in oversupply, the value of that type of property declines. An overbuilt market is a renter's market. More space is available than renters who desire such space, so prospective tenants can negotiate lower rents and other favorable terms—some or all of which can have negative long-term effects on property value. An under-built market is more appealing to investors because it favors the property owner. When demand exceeds supply, the available space commands high rents because less competing space exists.

Government and Real Estate

Governments at all levels affect real estate transactions in numerous ways. Local governments tax real property based on its value *(ad valorem tax)*. The tax burden affects the value of a particular parcel of land and is therefore an important consideration in the investment in real estate. Local *zoning* ordinances impose limits on land uses, and compliance with them—or efforts to change zoning—can be costly. Appropriate zoning is particularly important in real estate development.

Federal regulations that affect financial transactions also have an impact on the real estate market. Acceptable interest rates and the availability of funds for mortgage loans determine how much buyers can borrow. As stated, high interest rates discourage borrowing. The amount of *debt service* (mortgage principal and interest payments) affects the return that an investor can derive from the purchase of a rental property. To meet debt service requirements, the property must generally produce more income. The amount of income needed to pay debt service reduces the amount of income the owner can keep.

Government ownership of land in national and state parks, highways and rights of way, public buildings, and military bases makes the government a major participant in the real estate market. The presence of various government-owned properties can increase or decrease real estate values, depending on what and where they are. A military base, for example, may be desirable because it brings jobs to an area. Conversely, if it attracts undesirable businesses to the area (e.g., bars or adult entertainment), a military base does not enhance surrounding property values.

Numerous governmental subsidy programs have an influence on property values and real estate investment decisions. Some housing programs subsidize rents for lower-income groups and may limit rental rates for private properties that participate in the program. Other programs encourage home ownership by offering more favorable terms for mortgage loans than are available in the private sector, in effect, competing with it. (Chapter 11 provides more information on government-subsidized housing.)

Federal programs are often the key to land development or rede-velopment. One such program is *urban renewal,* which opens land in cities to new uses. Urban renewal has both short-term and long-term effects. The short-term effects are often negative because urban renewal displaces the original users to land elsewhere and results in a loss of property value in the sale. When urban renewal eliminates housing, the residents move elsewhere, often to the suburbs. It also encourages the movement of businesses and industries to the suburbs.

The displaced owners may have to accept less than market value for their properties because that is all they can get. (The sale price of a property may reflect low values of adjacent, blighted properties.) In the long term, however, urban renewal has many positive aspects, especially as it revitalizes the area. Development of a parcel of land for one use usually attracts development of adjacent land, often for a different use. Industrial development may attract research facili-ties and offices. Residential development tends to attract retailing and entertainment enterprises. Occasionally, the reverse is true.

Different levels of government occasionally impose *rent controls,* usually with the intent of setting upper limits on rental rates to maintain a pool of affordable housing. In general, rent controls interfere with the operation of the laws of supply and demand in the marketplace. In the absence of rent controls, more rents would tend toward the average rate rather than the extreme high (uncontrolled) and low (controlled) rates. Rent controls create an artificial lack of movement in rents at the lower end of the rate range. People tend to not vacate rent-controlled apartments.

The stagnation at low and middle rental rates forces those who are moving to go to areas where rents are higher. When controlled rents are substantially lower than market rents, the demand for those units is often disproportionately high, and the demand for units at market rates is consequently low. The reduction in rental income that results when controls are in place means less money is available for maintenance and repairs, so property owners defer maintenance. The lower income and the deferred maintenance contribute to lowering the property's value. In order to sell a property after rent controls have been in place, the owner may have to take a loss. A loss may result anyway through deterioration, which can remove the property from the overall supply and curtail rental income altogether.

Some regulations affect real estate both directly and indirectly. Laws enacted to protect the environment offer a useful example. Concerns about the presence of asbestos in buildings led to demands for containment or removal of the material from certain classes of existing buildings and the use of other materials for fireproofing new buildings. The direct effect was tremendous costs to building owners for containment or removal of asbestos. These demands also had an effect on property value because the presence of asbestos made a building less desirable to prospective buyers. The potential for long-term liability if asbestos was discovered after the sale of the building added to the problem. Although the demand for removal or containment of this potential hazard changed as more research emerged, the effect on the real estate market did not go away. All levels of government can enact environmental regulations, and owners must comply with the most stringent requirements that apply in a given situation. Because of this, the environmental aspects of a property will continue to be a major concern for real estate owners and managers as well as potential investors.

Laws regarding fair housing are of particular interest to real estate managers. All levels of government make *fair housing laws,* and they specifically regulate how houses are sold and how apartments are rented (see Chapter 11). Federal income tax laws (discussed earlier in this chapter) specifically how it affects investment in real estate.

Real Estate Cycles

Just as other businesses have a cyclical nature, so does the real estate market. Statistics regarding real estate sales, new housing (single-family and multiple dwellings), mortgage lending, new construction, and absorption rates for rental space show periods of high and low levels of activity. Historically, the total of real estate transactions or sales recorded in real estate markets throughout the United States has operated on a long cycle that averages more than 18 years. However, some cycles have been longer and others have been much shorter. Discrepancies in duration often relate to important historical events (depressions, wars, or major technological changes). A short cycle that lasts up to five years also exists. It relates to the availability of mortgage funds, shifts in money markets, and governmental housing programs.

Like the business cycles previously mentioned, the real estate cycle has four components (Exhibit 3.3). They generally follow their business counterparts. As a result of *overbuilding,* demand begins to decline, absorption slows, and rents weaken further just as construction peaks. Overbuilding is a consequence of prosperity (or sometimes perceived prosperity), which cannot last forever. It precedes and then coincides with recession. The real estate market then undergoes an *adjustment*—demand continues to decline,

EXHIBIT 3.3

The Business Cycle and the Real Estate Cycle

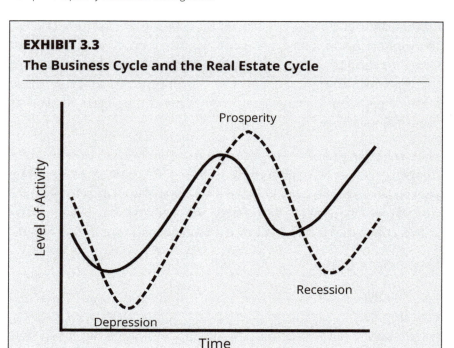

The solid line indicates the business cycle; the broken line shows the real estate cycle, which follows it. Slowing business activity (a downward slope) is characteristic of a period of recession. In the real estate cycle, new construction declines because of overbuilding (a peak) and leads to a period of adjustment during which occupancy declines and rent concessions are widespread. A deep trough indicates depression; occupancy and rents reduce severely. An upward slope signals beginning growth or recovery. In the real estate cycle, this reflects accelerated demand for rental space and increased new construction. The business cycle culminates in prosperity (the peak) which leads to new levels of overbuilding.

occupancy diminishes further, and rent concessions become widespread. New building slows decidedly during periods of recession and depression. This is followed by *stabilization,* a period in which demand begins to increase despite declining construction starts, making inroads into the excess supply. This coincides with the depths of recession or depression and is the real estate equivalent of recovery. The last stage is *development.* As prosperity returns to the rest of the economy, occupancy is high, rents are rising, and absorption levels are high. Demand accelerates and the market needs new construction to meet the increased demand.

Activity in other sectors of the economy drives real estate demand, which consequently tends to lag behind the upward movements in the general economy. However, real estate demand tends to exceed the heights of the peaks and the depths of the troughs of the general economic cycle. Recovery and prosperity are reflected in high occupancy levels, high rental rates, strong real estate sales, large amounts of money available to lend at acceptable interest rates, and large volumes of new construction. Conversely, during periods of economic recession and depression, vacancies increase, delinquencies in mortgage and rent payments rise, and real estate sales decline in numbers of sales and prices. New construction slows and the numbers of mortgage loans and their dollar values decline.

Many of the factors that influence real estate cycles are inherent in the real estate market itself. Real estate is not always a mirror of the general economy. By its very nature, it is local, which has a greater impact on the local real estate market. However, conditions outside the immediate market area frequently generate real estate booms and busts. Globalization and institutionalization of investment capital had key roles in the U.S. real estate market in the late 1980s and early 1990s. The impact on the real estate cycle of the prolonged period of low levels of inflation and high unemployment in the mid to late 1990s and early 2000s are significant. If unemployment stays high and inflation stays low, both inflationary expectations and the price/wage spiral start to slow. In particular, the extended period of low interest rates may have ameliorated the effect of higher unemployment to some extent.

The consequences on today's market have also been affected by the housing prices that peaked in early 2006, and then started to decline in 2006 and 2007—referred to as a "housing bubble," which can occur in both the local or global real estate markets. It was reported in December of 2008 to be the largest price drop in its history. In October of 2007, the U.S. Secretary of the Treasury called the bursting housing bubble "the most significant risk to our economy" because it had a direct impact on the value of home and also on the nation's mortgage markets, real estate, and home supply and retail outlets. The rapidly growing housing prices forced many residents to flee the expensive centers of many metropolitan areas to more suburban areas, which further explain how other factors can affect the real estate cycles.

Occupancy levels reflect the relationship between supply and demand at current rent levels. Changes in occupancy levels are of particular concern to real estate managers. However, the public sets the tone of the market. Occupancy levels that are extremely high indicate a probable space shortage and may justify higher rents. High vacancy, on the other hand, suggests a weak market in which renters are likely to resist rent increases.

The rental price level reflects the strength of the current real estate situation. It moves up and down in response to changes in supply and demand. When demand exceeds supply, higher rental rates can be charged, and rent increases as renewal of leases or as automatic adjustments under escalation clauses (in commercial leases) are more readily accepted. Real estate managers must know the prevailing trends in rental rates in their area.

Mortgage lending reflects the lenders' confidence in the safety and desirability of real estate as an investment. Lenders must believe the property is sound, that it will retain its value or increase in value over time, and—most important from their perspective—that it will generate sufficient income to ensure repayment of the loan. Real estate managers should keep abreast of current interest rates in their area because rising interest rates adversely affect mortgage lending.

Building activity is a measure of the economic potential of vacant land. Large-scale construction can increase the supply of a specific use and depress the market for that type of space. When a surplus

Consumer Price Index and Rent

The *Consumer Price Index (CPI)* is the most commonly used measure of inflation. The U.S. Department of Labor calculates the current year's cost of a particular array of goods and services consumed by a typical family and reports it as a percentage of the cost of those same goods and services in a *base year* (also set by the Department of Labor). Among the goods and services "consumed" are food and beverages, housing, apparel, transportation, medical care, and entertainment.

The CPI is computed and published monthly or bimonthly for most of the *metropolitan statistical areas (MSAs)* in the United States. As a measure of inflation, the CPI provides the basis for raising wages and for adjusting Social Security benefits, pension benefits, and income tax schedules. Real estate managers may use it as a guideline for rental rate increases, but this practice has lost favor, especially in commercial real estate where it was once common.

Because existing long-term leases may still include references to the CPI, the following additional information is included here. Upward movement of the CPI favors the real estate manager whose leases include specific provisions for rent increases based on the CPI. The CPI provides a rationale (measure of inflation) and a rate (the percentage change) for the scheduled rent increases based on a reputable, nonbiased statistic provided by the government.

Because the CPI measures inflation over time, annual rent increases based on the change in the CPI are usually realistic. (A rent escalation clause based on the CPI enables the property owner to retain the current value of rent dollars.) However, downward movement of the CPI for any length of time can reduce or cancel the benefit expected. Many leases that contain CPI language usually have a floor and ceiling (minimum/maximum) so as to moderate times of extreme swings in the CPI.

of space exists, construction slows, and that has wide-reaching effects beyond the real estate market itself. Unemployed construction workers may not be able to pay rent. They certainly will not have income to spend for consumer goods, and that will affect other segments of the economy.

Mortgage foreclosures reflect the inability of owners of real property to generate enough income from their properties to pay the debt on them. In general, foreclosures of income-producing real estate are an effect of economic recession or depression. Real estate loses earning power because of reductions in occupancy levels and rental rates. However, the absence of foreclosures does not necessarily signify prosperity. Real estate managers must understand the conditions that lead to foreclosures and be aware of foreclosure activity in the local market.

SUMMARY

Since the real estate manager's goal is to preserve and increase the value of a property through good management, it can best be done by trying to achieve the highest and best economic use for the property. An evaluation and understanding of economic trends is necessary to the accomplishment of this goal.

Economics covers the activities of production, distribution, and consumption of manufactured goods and agricultural products. Real estate is a part of the economic picture because land is fundamental to economic activity.

Value is attributed to the products of economic activity by agreement to exchange one kind of goods for another. The use of money facilitates exchange because it functions as a standard of value. It allows the measurement and comparison of the value of goods and services that otherwise cannot be readily measured or compared. Money is also a store of value through its purchasing power.

The marketplace is subject to the laws of supply and demand. When supply is less than demand, prices tend to rise; when supply exceeds demand, prices tend to decline. Changes in the supply of money in relation to the volume of goods available for purchase affect the overall economy. More money than goods signals inflation; the opposite signals deflation. Because the federal government can control the supply of money, its actions can lead to inflation and deflation.

In general, business activity is cyclical in nature. Prosperity is a period of economic growth, but economic growth cannot continue forever. Workers who have met their needs and wants tend to save their excess wages. When workers are saving and not spending their income, banks and other financial institutions have capital to lend to businesses for expansion. However, reduced consumer spending reduces business income, and financial institutions that lend freely for expansion become disinclined to lend money for operating capital. When the economy slows, prosperity is followed by a period of recession; supply exceeds demand, prices drop, and production decreases; profits fall off and businesses have less income to pay for operating expenses; wages decrease and unemployment increases; and borrowing slows and businesses fail.

At its lowest point, the economy may enter a period of depression. However, the surviving businesses take stock of their situations. Their inventories are low, and they have to replace equipment. Orders for new merchandise and machinery create demand, which leads to increasing prices, and the economy begins to recover. Recovery soon becomes prosperity, which is a period of high demand in comparison to supply. This is apparent in high profits, high levels of borrowing, and increased production. Unemployment is low, wages are high, and prices for consumer products are high.

Real estate is part of the overall economic picture primarily because of the relationship between land and economic activity. However, the real estate market is itself subject to the laws of supply and demand, and factors in the general economy of the nation and the world can have an impact on it. The real estate market is also affected by governmental actions, both those related specifically to real estate and those that affect the economy at large.

The real estate business is cyclical, and it follows a pattern similar to that of the business cycle. Changes in occupancy levels, rental rates, and mortgage financing are among the specific components of real estate cycles. Often, the cycles of real estate are reflections of the state of the general economy, although they tend to follow other trends and to be more extreme.

CHAPTER 4

The Logistics of Real Estate Ownership

While there are four primary benefits to owning real estate, there are many reasons to invest. These reasons will vary widely from one owner to the next, and ownership itself can take many forms depending on the individual or the entity involved. It's important for real estate managers to thoroughly understand the goals and objectives of the client. To do so, it's important to first know the process and reasons behind owning property, how the property was financed/acquired, what the owner hopes to accomplish, and the entity that will take ownership. The answers to these items will definitely affect how the income-producing real estate is managed.

MEANS AND REASONS FOR INVESTING IN REAL ESTATE

Most people aspire to invest in real estate at some point in their lives—people usually buy a home or condominium, but they might not consider it an investment. A new homeowner usually says, "I bought a house," instead of, "I invested in real property." But purchasing real property is always an investment—regardless of how the owner uses the property.

Means of Investing

Investors purchase property in one of two ways: (1) they buy it outright as an all-cash purchase, or (2) they finance part of the purchase price through a loan. Both purchases have specific advantages and disadvantages for the investor.

All-Cash Purchase. An all-cash buyer is able to keep all of the NOI from a property and yields greater cash return. When a property is financed, the NOI is divided between the owner and the lender in the form of mortgage payments (*debt service*). Most investors, even if they have substantial amounts of cash available, do not generally pay cash for their real estate investments. This is because the benefits of *leverage (use of borrowed funds)* can produce a higher return with a smaller cash investment.

On the other hand, real property is considered an *illiquid asset.* The owner can only convert real estate into cash in two ways: (1) sell or (2) refinance the property. Neither is quick, and both require agreement on the property's value. For example, selling property can sometimes take years, depending on the type of property and strength of the market. For a six-year period starting in 2008, the real estate market became especially challenging—nearly all forms of real estate assets suffered a huge loss in value, which made both selling and refinancing nearly impossible.

Financing. Borrowing funds to purchase an income-producing property is often necessary or desirable. When a financial institution approves a loan, it drafts numerous instruments often referred to collectively as *loan documents.* The most significant of such documents are the *mortgage* and the *promissory note*. Among other things, the mortgage places a *lien* on the property in favor of the lender. The borrower pledges the property as *collateral* to secure the mortgage loan. The lender has the right to foreclose the mortgage, sell the property, and apply the proceeds to the outstanding debt—in the event the borrower defaults on the loan.

The *promissory note* is the legally binding document that stipulates the loan conditions, including repayment terms, but borrowers and lenders alike commonly use the words *mortgage* and *loan* interchangeably. In place of a mortgage, some states use a *deed of trust*, which pledges the property as collateral—the buyer holds title to the property as a *warranty deed,* and the financial institution and the buyer execute a note as evidence of the debt.

Mortgage Conditions. Mortgages for all real property loans contain three major conditions: (1) They require the repayment of the *principal,* or the amount borrowed, (2) they require the payment of interest on the principal, and (3) they require a specific schedule of payments. The *debt service,* or process of repayment, addresses all three of these conditions. Borrowers usually pay debt service monthly, and the amount of the payment depends on the interest rate for the loan, the duration of the loan, and whether part of the payment is to pay back principal.

When the debtors' payments gradually reduce the principal with each succeeding payment over the term of the loan to a final payment in which the balance is completely paid off, the loan is a *fully amortized* loan. When the loan is fully amortized, allocation of the payments between principal and interest are determined by a mathematical formula. In the early years of the loan term, the lender allocates most of the borrower's monthly debt service payment to interest and applies only a small portion to pay down the principal. However, if the payment amount and interest rate remain the same, the portion the lender allocates to interest gradually decreases as the borrower pays the principal down over time, and the portion the lender allocates to principal slowly increases. The type of loan determines whether the lender uses the debt service payment to amortize the principal, and if so, how much it uses for that purpose. In real estate investment, the best loan is usually the one that has the lowest annual debt service because paying less debt service increases the property's *before tax cash flow*.

In addition to monthly payments, most mortgages have start-up costs such as points and application fees. A *point* is one percent of the total loan amount. If the borrower must pay two points to secure a $100,000 loan, the lender will receive $2,000 at the closing of the purchase, or the beginning of the loan. Because the acquisition of real estate involves more than the purchase price of the property, some owners consider these additional costs as part of their *initial investment base*. Investors will add additional funds to the investment base if there are initial improvements required to make the newly purchased property operational or to enhance its ability to generate income, such as installation of new appliances to upgrade apartments for achieving higher rental rates.

Mortgage Types. Lenders offer many types of mortgages. Some of the more common types are (1) fixed-rate, (2) variable-rate, (3) adjustable-rate, and (4) balloon-payment mortgages. The type of loan a borrower will use will be a function of the owner's goals and of the market availability for mortgage funds. While a basic description of each type of loan follows, the actual loan put in place by a borrower must be analyzed for its ability to help the owner achieve its goals.

Fully Amortized Loan

A *fully amortized* loan is characterized by periodic payments that include a portion applied to interest and a portion applied to principal. In the early years of the mortgage, a greater portion of the payment is applied to the interest. As the loan matures, a greater portion of the payment is applied to the principal, and the entire debt obligation is extinguished at the end of the loan term.

Over the course of a fully amortized loan, the borrower builds equity in the property, and the lender gains additional cushioning against loss in the case of default of payment. There are two types of fully amortized loans: (1) fixed-rate and (2) adjustable-rate.

An *amortization schedule* shows the periodic interest and principal components of each individual payment and the amount of the outstanding loan balance after each scheduled payment. An amortization schedule can be generated for monthly, annual, or any other schedule of periodic payments.

Year	Principal	Interest	Balance
1 (1–12)	$43,630.46	$117,029.38	$1,276,369.54
2 (13–24)	47,723.31	112,936.53	1,228,646.23
3 (25–36)	52,200.05	108,459.79	1,176,446.18
4 (37–48)	57,096.81	103,563.03	1,119,349.37
5 (49–60)	62,452.88	98,206.96	1,056,896.48
Annual Debt Service Payment = $160,659.84 each year			

*Source: IREM Educational Course, Investment Real Estate: Financial Tools (FIN 402)

1. **Fixed-Rate Mortgage.** In a *fixed-rate mortgage,* the interest rate is constant throughout the term of the loan. This type of loan was once the industry standard. The individual monthly payments on a loan with a long amortization period, such as 30 years, are generally lower than payments on the same loan with a shorter amortization, such as 15 years. Lower payments can be beneficial, especially when the income from the property is low. However, a longer amortization period usually has a much higher cumulative cost because the portion of each debt service payment the lender applies to the principal is smaller, the borrower makes more payments over time, and the total amount of interest paid for the same financed amount increases.

2. **Variable-Rate Mortgage.** On the other hand, a *variable-rate mortgage* permits the lending institution to raise or lower the interest rate of the loan based on changes in a prescribed index, such as the average Treasury bill yield or the prime rate. Interest on most variable-rate mortgages is a few percentage points above the *prime rate,* which is the lowest interest rate available from banks for short-term loans to their most credit-worthy customers. The rates are generally lower in the initial years of the loan term than they are for fixed-rate mortgages of comparable dollar amounts. While having a lower rate during the initial term, investors need to be prepared to see the increase in the rate in time and be able to pay the higher amounts due—that became a major issue with the housing crisis from 2008 onward.

3. **Adjustable-Rate Mortgage.** An *adjustable-rate mortgage* (ARM) is a type of variable-rate mortgage in which the interest rate is adjusted at fixed intervals—semiannually or annually—based on changes in the appropriate index. Variable-rate mortgages may have an upper limit, or *cap,* on the amount of change allowed in a year and over the term of the loan. It's important to note that without such a cap, investors are subject to wide swings in their monthly payments, based on how the market

is faring at the particular time the loan is adjusted. If indexes are on the upswing, an ARM might be a great loan to secure. However, a downswing could occur and greatly limit cash flow.

4. **Balloon Mortgage.** Lenders sometimes permit repayment of a loan based on an amortization period that is longer than the term of the loan. For example, the fixed debt service payment may be based on a 25-year amortization, but the loan is actually due in 10 years. The monthly payments allocate a small amount to the reduction of principal—the bulk of the payment goes to interest—and the borrower pays a very large *balloon payment* at the end of the term of the loan, that is, in 10 years. The balloon amount pays off the remaining principal balance due. The benefit of this loan structure is that the monthly payment is smaller than the 10-year fully amortized loan at the same interest rate. The requirement of a balloon payment compounds the risk inherent in borrowing. If funds are not available for the balloon payment, the borrower must refinance—typically only possible if the property has appreciated in value—and the interest rate and monthly payments for the refinancing may be higher. If the borrower is unable to refinance, they must sell the property to cover the debt or risk foreclosure.

While financing has many advantages, purchasers must understand that their equity in the property will be some amount less than 100 percent of the asset's value until the principal of the mortgage is fully amortized. To calculate one's equity, simply find the current market value and subtract from it the current outstanding amount of the loan.

Reasons for Investment

Prior to investing in real estate, one must understand whether liquid or illiquid assets are best suited for their investment needs. Generally, the earnings of liquid investments derive from just a few sources. Growth in the value of precious metals is based on demand

and, therefore, investors often buy metals to preserve capital. The value of stock can appreciate from both demand for the stock and increasing value (profitability) of the company. Stocks often pay a periodic dividend as well, while the only earnings from a savings account are periodic interest payments. Bonds purchased at less than face value have a fixed maturity date and accrue interest over the period they are held. While some bonds, such as municipal bonds, are tax free, the income from others may be taxable when the bond matures, when the investor converts it to cash, or throughout the holding period as the interest accrues. Unlike real estate, investors have little to no control over their investment in these liquid assets.

Even though real estate is an illiquid investment, the allure of owning property and the financial rewards of ownership make real estate one of the largest storehouses of wealth. What's more, real estate provides comfort through physicality in that the assets are typically large and built out—serving greater functional purpose in a space than just an investment vehicle. As previously noted, there are four benefits to owning real estate, including: (1) capital preservation, (2) capital appreciation, (3) periodic return or regular income, and (4) income tax advantage. While a major consideration in real estate investment is financial return, it has nonfinancial considerations as well—it can also be a means of diversifying an extensive investment portfolio.

Capital Preservation. Many people believe that investment in real property is a way to preserve capital. Property values tend to rise with the inflation rate if the property is in a good location and the economic environment of the area is healthy. Land and real property are similar to precious metals because they have an *intrinsic value*—they are inherently useful. The intrinsic value of a property should increase at least at the same rate as inflation. Investors interested primarily in the safety of their capital look for property with extremely low risk. The following lists the qualities that indicate low risk:

- Prime location
- Durable construction
- Architectural style that will not become outdated
- Excellent potential to increase in value over time
- Established tenancy
- Long-term leases containing *pass-through clauses*—provisions that allow property owners to pass to tenants increases in certain operating expenses and rent escalations
- Sufficient income from property to pay expenses and debt service (if financed)
- Intrinsic property value nearly equal to purchase price
- Absence of encumbrances, such as mechanics' liens or zoning restrictions

Capital Appreciation. *Appreciation* is the increase in the value of an asset over time. In real estate investment, capital appreciation is realized when an owner sells a property for more than its original purchase price. Since it does not materialize until the owner sells or refinances the property, capital appreciation can be the ultimate goal of a long-term investment, although appreciation is also possible for a short-term holding. The equity generated by appreciation can also be used to diversify an investor's real estate holdings. If there is sufficient equity, it can be drawn through a refinance of the property, thereby making cash available for other investments. It's important to note that *depreciation* can also occur, cutting cash flow, and increasing debt for the short or long term.

Real estate managers play an important role in the capital appreciation of the investment by positioning the property to meet its highest and best use, producing as much income as possible, controlling operating costs as much as possible, and maintaining, preserving, and improving the structure itself. This has become even more challenging in recent years because more investors have lost properties to foreclosure or bankruptcy. In turn, new owners or banks have sought out real estate managers with specific skills in turning around troubled properties to bring them back to the market.

With regard to distressed assets or troubled properties, there are seven major factors that contribute to the decline of property value:

1. Neighborhood decline
2. Impact of unfavorable transportation
3. Controls and regulations
4. Wear and tear
5. Supply and demand
6. Lack of proper maintenance
7. Pressure to sell

The community surrounding the income property can change in many ways that can dramatically affect a property. Increased vacancy leads to reduced rents, which in turn means reduced maintenance, causing building deterioration, which then causes the surrounding area to slip into decline—initiating a domino effect that amplifies the general decline in value. The nearby construction of facilities such as prisons, sewage treatment plants, and airports also contributes to an adverse effect on the location and value of the property. Comparably, the construction of a major highway or intersection includes additional noise and inconveniences that drive tenants away. Basically, if the property is not maintained, the value of the investment in real estate is reduced; this is referred to as *economic obsolescence,* which is the failure to generate enough income to offset operating expenses because of the physical condition of the property.

With regard to market conditions, there are two main factors that can cause values to go down: (1) overbuilt properties and (2) stringent funds. With the multifamily sector, *overbuilt* implies that more apartment units are available to rent than there are tenants to rent the units. Simple economic principles of supply and demand tell us that a surplus of supply will not promote rent growth. On the contrary, under-built markets will see demand and pricing increase. Having stringent funds applies to the unavailability of long-term financing options from lenders, which means there will be fewer qualified buyers for rental property.

Despite particular challenges in a down economy, value can still increase for several reasons. If income increases and exceeds any increase in expenses, the property will be more desirable and can sell for a higher price. An improvement in the economy of the area, greater demand for property in the area, rehabilitation of the property, or a change in its use can drive value up as well.

Periodic Return. The relationship between purchase price and cash flow is a consideration for investors who seek regular, periodic income from their property. *Before tax cash flow* refers to the amount remaining after subtracting operating expenses and debt service from gross receipts. In the same manner that the capital appreciation of the property is enhanced, the amount of periodic income derived from property operations can also be influenced. However, the amount of income a property can generate is subject to prevailing conditions in the market. The investor's income is usually expressed in dollars, i.e., cash flow, or as a percentage rate of return.

Income Tax Advantage. Federal and state governments in the United States and elsewhere commonly grant tax incentives for real estate investment. Incentives for property ownership help drive the U.S. economy. To increase the amount of housing stock available, federal and state governments allow income tax deductions for mortgage interest, operating expenses, and depreciation of income-producing residential property. Owners of income-producing commercial properties can take the same kinds of deductions—the deductibility of mortgage interest encourages borrowing, which keeps money in circulation. The demand for loans encourages lending institutions to seek savings and investments, which in turn generates additional tax dollars. The deductibility of operating expenses provides an incentive for the owner to reinvest in the property and keep it well maintained.

Depreciation. *Depreciation,* also called *cost recovery* for income tax purposes, is particularly enticing because it is a noncash expense that the property owner can take as a deduction from income. The

Basis of Investment Value—Appreciation and Depreciation

The value of an owner's investment in real estate is *equity*. An all-cash purchase gives the owner 100 percent equity. If a real estate purchase is financed, the investor's initial equity is the amount of the cash down payment. When an owner has an amortizing loan and holds a property over time, the owner's equity increases as the principal of the loan decreases. If the owner then sells the property for more than the original purchase price, the increase in the market price is the result of an *appreciation* in value, and the amount of appreciation becomes part of the owner's equity. For example, if an owner pays $10,000 down on a $100,000 real estate purchase and finances the remaining $90,000, the owner's initial equity is $10,000. If the property sells for $120,000 five years later, the seller's equity at that time will be *at least* $30,000 ($10,000 initial equity plus $20,000 in appreciation *plus* whatever equity—if any—has accumulated through amortization).

Investment, on the other hand, typically extends for a longer holding period and offers investors fundamental opportunities. For example, an owner/investor may purchase real estate to obtain a steady source of income over a specific time period. The cash flow will provide a rate of return that can be compared to other investments and is enhanced by the tax shelter effects of the real estate, such as *depreciation*. The strength of a rent roll or market will greatly impact the quality of the cash flow that the owner will receive.

Consider a residential building and a commercial building (placed in service in 1995) that were each bought for $1.3 million. The land is worth $300,000, which gives a recoverable basis of $1 million. For the residential building, straight-line cost recovery over 27.5 years means subtracting 1/27.5 of the recoverable basis each year. For the commercial building, straight-line cost recovery over 39 years means subtracting 1/39 of the recoverable basis each year. The following calculates the adjusted basis of both buildings at the end of the sixth year of ownership.

	Residential Building	Commercial Building
Original basis land	$1,300,000	$1,300,000
	300,000	300,000
= Depreciable basis	**= $1,000,000**	**= $1,000,000**
Depreciation 1st year	$36,364	$25,641
	(1/27.5 x $1 million)	(1/39 x $1 million)
Depreciation 2nd year	36,364	25,641
Depreciation 3rd year	36,364	25,641
Depreciation 4th year	36,364	25,641
Depreciation 5th year	36,364	25,641
Depreciation 6th year	36,364	25,641
= Total depreciation	**= $218,182**	**= $153,846**
= Adjusted basis	**= $1,081,818**	**=$1,146,154**
	(book value)	**(book value)**

U.S. income tax laws permit an owner to assume that a building has a specific *useful life* in which it will produce income and to recover the cost of the building over a period of years. The depreciation period (or useful life) varies for different types of properties. In theory, if the depreciation period is 39 years, the property owner can deduct 1/39th of the purchase price of the property, excluding the land, each year for 39 years. However, the calculation of income tax deductions for depreciation is more complicated. The tax law sets the periods of useful life for various classes of property. For real estate investments, the depreciation period depends on the type of property, such as residential or commercial.

Capital Improvements. The depreciation deduction also applies to *capital improvements*—investments in equipment or alterations that last for more than one year and increase the value, productivity, or useful life of the property. The number of years the government allows for depreciation of capital improvements varies, and the deduction may be larger during the early years of the depreciation period—*accelerated cost recovery*. The IRS also distinguishes between a capital improvement and a *repair* that preserves the investment in a property but does not lengthen its useful life. For example, adding granite countertops to existing apartments is a capital improvement or added value—fixing a hot water heater is a repair. The cost of a repair is tax deductible as an operating expense for the year in which it is made.

Tax advantages of ownership vary with changes in federal income tax laws. At times, the amount of interest, real estate tax, and depreciation claimed in a given year may result in a taxable loss, which is subject to passive loss limitations and other factors in an individual's investment portfolio.

Pride of Ownership. In addition to the financial reasons to own income-producing property, investors sometimes own real property because of an inherent pride of possession. Real estate is more tangible than stock certificates or other assets. Property ownership can be a symbol of financial security, wealth, or power. Certain aspects of a property make the owner a contributor to the community—that alone can give an owner satisfaction. In addition, owners sometimes live on the premises, have an office there, or even operate a retail business in the income-producing property they own—an owner's relationship to the property can have more dimensions than just being a source of income. Sometimes the simple pride that owners exhibit in their properties is likely to increase net income. Especially when the owner gives more attention to maintenance and repairs, the property has more potential to attract tenants and higher rents. Deductibility of maintenance and improvement costs offers tax incentives, and dedicated care makes capital preservation and capital appreciation more likely outcomes.

PRINCIPAL FORMS OF INCOME-PROPERTY OWNERSHIP

Investors can own an interest in property in many ways and each form of ownership provides the investor with different capabilities and limitations in making a profit from the property (Exhibit 4.1). No particular form is necessarily ideal—each has certain advantages and disadvantages. Depending on the property and the goals of the investors, one form can be more beneficial than others. Income-property ownership takes five common forms: (1) sole proprietorships, (2) partnerships, (3) corporations, (4) real estate investment trusts (REITs), and (5) joint ventures.

Exhibit 4.1

Characteristics of Ownership Forms

Ownership Form	Taxation Status	Investor Liability	Management
Sole Proprietorship	Single	Unlimited	Personal
General Partnership	Single	Unlimited	All partners
Limited Partnership	Single	Limited	General partner(s)
Limited Liability Company	Single	Limited	Manager member
C Corporation	Double	Limited	No restrictions
S Corporation	Single	Limited	No restrictions
REIT	Modified Single*	Limited	Trustees

*Tax losses cannot exceed cash distributions.

Sole Proprietorship

The mainstay among ownership forms is a *sole proprietorship,* which has total control and unlimited liability. Sole proprietors benefit directly from the profits that the property produces. They are also directly liable for all financial losses and may be able to take deductions for such losses on their personal income tax. However, deductibility rules vary—passive loss limitations apply. Due to this variability, the property manager, along with the owner, should scrutinize tax provisions and seek the guidance of legal or tax advisors regarding the deductibility of losses.

Partnerships

A very common association of individual investors is a *partnership,* which is an arrangement that allows each partner to participate in the profits and losses of their mutual investment. A partnership distributes all profits and losses to the partners based on the amount of their investments or as stated in their partnership agreement. Although it must report annual information on income, gains, and losses, the partnership itself pays no income tax. The income (or loss) of the partnership affects the tax reporting of the individual partners based on their shares in the investment.

A partnership or other form of multiple ownership may be certified as a legitimate business entity. Depending on state law, a partnership may sue or be sued in the names of the partners or in the firm name. The ownership form does not insulate individual investors from liability. If a partnership is sued and found liable, the general partners would be liable individually and collectively for damages— *joint and several liability*.

Partnerships usually take one of two forms: (1) general partnership or (2) limited partnership. The following sections also discuss two special types of partnerships: (1) syndicates and (2) limited liability companies.

General Partnership. A *general partnership* involves two or more investors who agree to be associated for business purposes. Title to property is held in the name of the partnership. All partners share in the rights, duties, obligations, and financial rewards to the extent of their own participation—or in accordance with the partnership agreement. However, the partners' personal liability for the debts of the partnership is unlimited. Any general partner can commit the other partners to a financial obligation without their consent or knowledge—provided the partner makes the contract for the service or material on behalf of the partnership and not on behalf of the individual. A small number of investors who know each other well and are reasonably certain they can work together coopera-tively sometimes enter into a general partnership. Because general partners are personally and fully liable for the property, they can lose personal assets along with their investment in the partnership if the property faces bankruptcy or a lawsuit.

As the name implies, *limited liability general partnerships* (LLGPs) actually do limit the liability of the general partners. Depending on state laws and the partnership agreement, a general partnership may dissolve if one partner chooses to remove their interest. Even if dissolution is not mandatory, it may be unavoidable because selling a partial interest in an established partnership is difficult.

Successfully managing a property for a general partnership can be difficult if all the partners do not agree on an issue, and if they do not have a general partnership agreement that defines a decision process. Even among the most cooperative partners, occasional differences of opinion are inevitable. Although the partners may agree that they must take a vote on certain actions and that those who own the majority of the investment must agree to enact a change, one dissenting general partner among five may have equal authority over the property.

The real estate manager is usually in a good position to reconcile any differing points of view, but that consumes time that could be spent more productively. If the real estate manager reports to more than one person, then multiple reports need to be distributed, which also uses more time and resources. To avoid financial harm to the property because of, or during a dispute, the partners can name one of their members as a managing partner with whom the real estate manager will work exclusively. Such action centralizes the management control and places the obligation for settling differences where it belongs—among the partners.

Limited Partnership. A more popular form of partnership is the *limited partnership* (LP), which consists of one or more general partners who supervise the investment, plus a number of limited partners who participate in the arrangement—only to the extent of their financial investment. As in a general partnership, the liability of the general partners is unlimited. The limited partners assume no liability beyond their capital investment. It's important to note that a partnership can organize as a *limited liability limited partnership* (LLLP), which limits the liability of the general partners.

Two forms of limited partnerships exist: (1) private limited partnerships and (2) public limited partnerships. *Private limited partnerships* have 35 or fewer investors and usually do not have to register with the Securities and Exchange Commission (SEC)—although they may have to file a certificate with state authorities. *Public limited partnerships* have an unlimited number of participants and must register with the SEC when the number of partners and the value of their assets reach certain levels.

Individual investment in a limited partnership does not necessarily require a large amount of capital, so this type of partnership is attractive to an investor with limited resources who wants to participate in a large venture. As in a general partnership, the tax benefits and obligations pass through to the individual partners based on the provisions in the partnership agreement.

Limited partners have no say in management policies, and they may consider that a disadvantage. The decisions made by the general partners in a limited partnership affect more than their personal investments—the potential exists for all of the partners to lose their investments. If the property requires additional funds because of adverse economic conditions, the general partners are obligated to invest additional capital, but the limited partners are not. Limited partners may make additional contributions to protect their original investment—but they typically do not do so.

The challenges to management of a limited partnership are about the same as those of a general partnership. However, if some limited partners become frustrated with the general partners' decisions, they may try to appeal directly to the real estate manager. If a limited partner is permitted to have direct influence on the management of the property, the Internal Revenue Service (IRS) can reclassify the partnership as an association that is taxable as a corporation. The IRS could also reclassify the limited partner as a general partner, and that person would lose the liability protection extended to limited partners.

The real estate manager might be obligated to report to *all* investors in a limited partnership, but such reporting is potentially expensive. To avoid this reporting requirement, include in the management agreement a clause that clearly explains the form, frequency, and recipients of reports. To minimize or discourage conferences between the real estate manager and anyone other than the general partners, the agreement should also state an hourly fee for discussion with limited partners, their attorneys, accountants, heirs, executors, or anyone else. In turn, the partnership agreement should provide that the individual who requires special services must pay the charges for them. (Chapter 5 provides more details about the management agreement.)

Syndicate. A real estate *syndicate* is a special type of partnership formed by any combination of owners who purchase an interest in a property together. The investor may be an individual, a general or limited partnership, a joint venture, an unincorporated association, a corporation, or a group of corporations. Syndication is a way to pool both capital and experience for a property's success. Another advantage of syndication is that people of differing backgrounds can make a formal agreement to accomplish one specific goal. The flexibility of investment is another advantage—the purpose of a syndicate can be to purchase a particular property or to rely on the experience of a *syndicator* to acquire property that appears promising. If more funds are necessary, the syndicate can sell additional partnership interests.

Limited Liability Company. A *limited liability company* (LLC) is another form of ownership that allows multiple owners to invest in real estate. Its owners are called *members,* and the managing entity may be a participating investor (*manager member*) or a nonparticipant appointed by the members. An LLC is created by state statute, and most states have adopted such laws—although the rules and fiduciary responsibilities vary. For federal income tax purposes, the IRS classifies an LLC as a partnership. Unlike the general partners in a partnership, however, *all* LLC members enjoy limited liability—no one member may be held liable for debts or other obligations of the company. In addition, LLCs have lesser tax reporting requirements than do C or S corporations described below.

Corporations

The difference between a *corporation* and any other association of investors in the United States is its recognition by federal and state governments. A corporation is chartered by a state, and it is considered to have a legal life of its own. It is an independent legal entity—it can sue and be sued. If a corporation goes bankrupt or loses a lawsuit, the liability of the corporate owners, or the stockholders, is limited to the amount of their investment. As an independent legal body, a corporation must pay local, state, and federal income taxes—it cannot transfer its tax deductions to its shareholders. Depending on the structure of the corporation, corporate profits may be subject to *double taxation*—at the corporate level and again at the individual shareholder level when dividend distributions are made. Income tax law in the United States recognizes two types of corporations for tax purposes: (1) C corporations and (2) S corporations.

C Corporations. The government legally defines most corporations as *C corporations.* These entities pay income tax and have no restrictions on the number of shareholders they have or the types of stock they issue. The obligation of a C corporation to pay income tax is the main limitation on its ownership of real estate as a primary business endeavor. Even so, the attraction of limited liability for all participants (directors as well as shareholders) is a positive feature for some real estate investors.

S Corporations. Unlike a C corporation, an *S corporation* combines the ownership features of a corporation with those of a partnership. It does not pay federal income tax, so it does not incur double taxation—profits (and losses) pass directly to the shareholders. Because the investors are shareholders and not partners, their individual liability is limited to the value of the stock they own. Stock ownership inherently provides the election of a board of directors, a factor that ensures centralized management. In addition, ownership of the investment is more easily transferred through stock shares than it is in a limited or general partnership.

The eligibility requirements for classification as an S corporation are strict. To be eligible, the corporation must have no more than 75 shareholders, and it can offer only one class of stock. All shareholders must be individuals or estates; other corporations or business ventures cannot hold stock in an S corporation. Classification as an S corporation is by choice—otherwise, a corporation is classified as a C corporation. Some states may not recognize S corporation status and may impose state corporate taxes in spite of the designation.

Working for a corporation may involve more administrative procedures than working for a sole proprietor or a partnership because the corporation must report to the government, its directors, and its shareholders. The board of directors may be the authority for management decisions, although the contact may be someone other than a board member whose primary responsibility is unrelated to real estate. Decisions involving the property may require

Corporations as Real Estate Owners

While a group of investors may form a corporation specifically to purchase and operate one or more income-producing properties, corporations created for purposes other than real estate investment also become real estate owners.

Such a corporation may own the building in which it conducts its business and derive additional income from the property by leasing any excess space. For example, one of the major department stores that holds a shopping mall may own all or part of the mall. A manufacturing company may develop land around its factory into an industrial park. A bank, advertising firm, or other service company may build or purchase a premier office building for its business operations and rent out the space it does not use.

This type of rental income is generally secondary to the income generated by the main business operation of the corporation, such as retail sales and manufacturing. A real estate manager for corporate-owned real estate will have broad responsibilities that include acquisition and disposition in addition to real estate management specifics, such as property maintenance, record keeping, and reporting.

formal documentation and board approval. Budgets and financial statements for the property may have to conform to the accounting standards of the corporation—even though such standards may not be suited to real estate management. The corporation may require one budget for the calendar year and another for the fiscal year if the two are different, and it may require both cash- and accrual-basis accounting. Duties may include annual audits and filings with the SEC. Because working with a corporation can create the potential for uncomfortable compromises between confidentiality and mandatory public disclosure, all information must be maintained in the strictest confidence—only the corporation should release its information.

Real Estate Investment Trusts

Another vehicle that permits small investors to engage in large real estate ventures is a *real estate investment trust* (REIT), which is a specialized trust fund that invests exclusively in real estate. Dealing with a REIT can take one of three paths: (1) direct investment, (2) investment through mortgage lending, or (3) both. A REIT issues *shares of beneficial interest* that can be traded publicly, and its passive losses cannot exceed the cash distributions to the trust beneficiaries. For a REIT to avoid double taxation, it must distribute at least 95 percent of its taxable income to the shareholders—if a REIT has any retained income, corporate taxation rules may apply—and it must meet several requirements to ensure that most of its income is derived from real estate. Investors in a REIT are liable only to the extent of their investment.

Because REITs operate through shares, they offer greater security than limited partnerships because they diversify their assets among properties in several locations—provided the trust is astutely managed and the REIT is significantly large. If shares of the REIT are publicly traded, the beneficiaries have two distinct advantages: (1) they profit from real estate investment and (2) their funds remain liquid. However, REITs must distribute most of their earnings, and adequate reserves may not be available for capital improvements to or additional investments in a property owned by a REIT. Likewise, a REIT has few options for preserving its capital. If the real estate market becomes unfavorable, most owners of real property can liquidate their assets, possibly taking a one-time loss, and invest the remaining capital in something else. A REIT, by definition, must keep its money in real estate.

Joint Venture

Investors can use any combination of ownership forms to establish a *joint venture*—the purpose is to share the risks and the rewards jointly by contributing the appropriate knowledge, skill, or asset. The advantages, disadvantages, and tax obligations depend on the type of business entity selected for the joint venture. Some of the most common joint venture relationships are between a developer and an institutional investor—or a lender who undertakes a new project. The lender invests capital, land, or both, and the developer contributes knowledge to make the project succeed. Foreign capital is often invested in real property in the United States via joint ventures. In that case, a domestic entity nurtures the development and the foreign investor provides the capital.

The challenges of managing real estate owned by a joint venture depend on the type of business entity the joint venture chooses.

SUMMARY

Investors can purchase real estate with cash or a combination of cash and financing. Mortgage loans commonly have a fixed maturity and interest rate, but some mortgages have flexible terms that take advantage of market fluctuations. The terms of the loan can have a profound impact on the property's success based on changes in the property's income, the overall economy, and the owner's expectations from the investment. The reasons for owning real estate include capital preservation, capital appreciation, periodic return (cash flow), income tax advantages, and pride of ownership. Any of these reasons alone may be sufficient for an investor to purchase a property. However, the investor usually considers a combination of these factors before making a purchase.

A comparison of investment options reveals that real estate is highly illiquid when compared to stocks, bonds, and other investment vehicles that an investor can convert to cash relatively quickly and easily. However, the various forms of real estate ownership and the many advantages of that ownership sustain real estate's popularity as an investment.

The principal forms of property ownership are sole proprietorships, partnerships (including limited liability companies), corporations, real estate investment trusts (REITs), and joint ventures. Each ownership form has advantages and disadvantages, and no single form is necessarily ideal. Each has different effects on income from the property, payment to the investor, tax obligations, and the relationship between the owner and the manager. Understanding the subtleties of the owner's reasons for investing in a property and knowing the form of ownership gives the real estate manager the basis for determining how to manage the property and how to improve its productivity.

5 | The Management Agreement and Plan

Regardless of the property type, and whether working with a private owner or public agency, there are no two documents more important than the management agreement and the management plan. Together, these two documents help establish a strong foundation for the investment relationship and help protect the real estate manager by outlining the owner's goals and overall strategy. Essentially, the property owner's goals become the same goals for the real estate manager. These goals, which must be shared and be achievable, are the basis of the *management agreement* and the *management plan*.

THE MANAGEMENT AGREEMENT

In most cases, owners hire real estate managers because they need professionals who possess the knowledge, skills, and patience to do the job. Oftentimes, tenants do not know who owns the property and sometimes confuse the real estate manager for the owner. This is a common conclusion—from the legal aspect, real estate managers establish the leases, set rents, and safeguard the property. While operating the property on the owner's behalf, the real estate manager is representing not only the owner to residents and others who have business with the property, but also the real estate management company associated with the property. When representing a company, there are expectations that should be consistent with the company's brand identity. To respect and formalize the relationship between the owner and real estate manager, there must be a variety of agreed-upon terms and responsibilities.

A management agreement is a formal and binding document that establishes the real estate manager's legal authority over the operation of the property. The real estate manager is technically an agent of the owner and serves as the owner's fiduciary or trustee of the funds and assets associated with the property.[1]

The management agreement is a legal contract that should be prepared in consultation with a lawyer. The agreement establishes the relationship between the real estate manager and property owner for a fixed period, along with addressing the financial obligations of the owner. It also defines the real estate manager's authority and compensation for services provided by specifying what those limits are. The following lists the specific contents of a management agreement:

• Full name and identification (alongside the owner's)
• Description of the owner's property
• Term (duration) of the agreement
• The real estate manager's overall responsibilities
• Financial management
• Reports to ownership
• Owner's obligations to the real estate manager and the property
• Insurance
• Compensation for property management services
• Operating and reserve funds
• Liability

A solid management agreement also includes provisions for termination of the arrangement under specific conditions, as well as numerous clauses related to general legalities.

---

1. Agency relationships and independent contractor are not mutually exclusive. Most companies are independent contractors and legal agents for the property owner.

Establishing the Management Direction

Two major real estate management documents are prepared before a property is managed:

1. **Management Agreement.** A formal contract that defines and explains the duties and responsibilities of the owner and the real estate manager and establishes the business relationship, along with the real estate manager's compensation.

2. **Management Plan.** A logical, deductive, intensive analysis of all factors related to the property, such as its location, physical condition, financial status, competitive position, and highest and best use.

Basic Components of an Agreement

Fundamental to every contract are (1) the names of those entering into it, (2) the purpose of the agreement, and (3) the duration of the agreement. In a management agreement, these elements are (1) the parties, (2) management of the property, and (3) the term (or duration). The parties to a management agreement—the property owner and the management company or an independent real estate manager—must establish their authority to negotiate and sign this agreement. In particular, individuals who represent a partnership or a corporation must have specific authorization to sign contracts. Although the street address may uniquely identify the property, including the legal description of the property according to its title documentation may be appropriate. If the property has a special name, the agreement usually lists that name as well. The term of the agreement refers to the duration—usually stated as a specific number of years that include the beginning and ending dates. Provisions for automatic renewal on an annual basis when the initial term expires are also included—provided it is not otherwise officially terminated. The duration of the agreement and its renewability are negotiable, as are all of the other terms and conditions.

Working as the Owner's Agent

As a real estate manager (*agent*) acting on behalf of the owner (*principal*), the words and actions are binding on the owner. In the role of agent, a standard of care must be exercised in managing money and the property for the owner (*fiduciary capacity*). Being a fiduciary creates certain legal obligations, such as being loyal to the interests of the client by not engaging in activities contrary to that loyalty. This means paying scrupulous attention to handling the owner's funds and not accepting any fee, commission, discount, gift, or other benefit that has not been disclosed to and approved by the owner-client.

When achieving the Certified Property Manager® (CPM®) designation, the real estate manager is subscribing to a specific code of ethics. In addition to the fiduciary obligation noted here, the *IREM Code of Professional Ethics* requires real estate managers to hold proprietary information in confidence, to maintain accurate financial and business records for the managed property, and to protect the owner's funds. This code of ethics also outlines the duties to the manager's employer, to former clients and employers, and to tenants and others. It sets forth requirements for contracting management and managing the client's property and addresses relationships with other members of the profession and compliance with laws and regulations. Ethical practices are an important part of professionalism in real estate management and are usually a licensing requirement in most states.

Responsibilities of the Real Estate Manager

Financial management, reporting, and general property management activities are among the normal duties of a typical real estate manager. Much of this work is interrelated—reporting and record keeping are natural functions of both financial management and general property management. The management agreement formalizes the job, often providing specific software requirements, procedures to follow, and sometimes stating intervals of time (daily, monthly, or annually) for the performance of various duties.

Financial Management. Within the management agreement are specific details regarding the financial arrangements between the property owner and real estate manager. The following lists the details of these financial agreements and the components managed by the real estate manager:

- Treatment of bank accounts
- Owner's and real estate manager's funds
- Security deposits
- Income
- Expenses
- Lending
- Audits

Establishment of Bank Accounts. The establishment of an *operating account* is an important provision of the management agreement.[2] The management company usually chooses the financial institution and establishes the account—although the owner may participate in the decision. Receipts and expenditures flow through the client's operating account. It's important to remember that the management agreement should require a minimum balance to remain in the operating account at all times. Apart from the necessity of having adequate funds to pay the operating expenses of the property, the bank or the management agreement may require a minimum balance that remains in the account at the end of every month or accounting period.

The agreement to maintain more than one bank account is also discussed when creating the management agreement. Security deposits and reserve funds are often separate from operating funds for residential properties, but not normally for commercial properties. In fact, security deposits for commercial properties are recorded on the tenant's ledger, but they are disbursed to the client as *owner proceeds* upon receipt. The security deposits are represented on the books as a liability and the management reports

---

2. Operating accounts are accounts from which property invoices and deposit rents are paid. These can be trust accounts or a regular account over which the real estate manager has signature authority.

state that "any security deposits received within the month are included in the owner proceeds distribution." State requirements for the handling of resident security deposits vary widely, from the requirement to pay interest on said funds to the handling of the deposit once received by the manager. It's important to consult with the state's real estate department or bureau in order to avoid running afoul of any licensing laws. However, most state laws require that security deposit funds be held in a separate account.

Regardless of the number of accounts necessary to maintain the property's funds, the management agreement usually mandates that deposits be in federally insured accounts. Real estate managers are obligated to inform the owner if the balance in any account for the property exceeds the federally insured amount.

Separation of Funds. The management agreement should clearly state that the owner's and real estate manager's funds should not be mixed or *commingled*—this is not just a legal requirement, it's actually a matter of professional ethics, good business practice, and a requirement in the IREM Code of Professional Ethics. All funds earned by the property—directly or indirectly—belong to the owner. Real estate managers are entitled to compensation from the property's income and have the authority to pay themselves, but must fully disclose all financial transactions to the property owner(s).

Collection of Income. The management agreement authorizes the real estate manager to collect rent and any other income for the property—along with late fees and fees for bounced checks, credit checks, document preparation, and other administrative work. Some real estate managers retain fees collected from residents for these services as compensation for these exceptions to regular practices. Others receive separate management compensation on the fees collected, while some may not benefit at all. Unless state law prohibits it, the management agreement should specifically state the compensation for such collections and the arrangement—which is negotiated between the manager and the owner.

Payment of Expenses. Payment of expenses is another portion of the real estate manager's duties. Expenses include debt service in addition to normal operating expenses. The remainder after all income has been collected and expenses have been paid—i.e., cash flow—is sent to the owner on a schedule established in the management agreement. If the property has more than one owner, the management agreement should state the proportionate distribution of the funds.

Provision for Audits. The owner usually has the right to audit the accounts of the property at any time—although a routine schedule is agreed upon for this procedure and clearly stated in the contract. Audits are also at the owner's expense unless discrepancies in excess of a predetermined percentage are found. The real estate manager might be financially responsible for the audit if a discrepancy greater than the limit has resulted. The management agreement should state that all ledgers, receipts, and other records pertaining to the property belong to the owner even though they are usually in the possession of the manager.[3] When the agreement ends, the real estate manager must send the records to the owner, while maintaining copies (or the originals) as required by state law.

Reports to the Owner. Real estate managers send the owner(s) a monthly management report that often consists of the following parts:

- Statement of operations
- Record of income
- Record of disbursements
- Narrative report of operations

The *narrative of operations*, which reveals budget variances and

---

3. This is an evolving issue with the predominance of property management software, which allows the owner to have access to all records at any time. The real estate manager should include in the agreement that, if the owner pulls information from the property records during any accounting period, the owner understands that he or she is viewing unadjusted records that may need to be changed prior to the issuing of financials.

their causes is one of the best ways to effectively communicate with the owner. The real estate manager typically prepares the annual budget for operating the property—the agreement usually states how and when that is to be done.

The number of written reports and their formats are definitely negotiable items. Institutional owners usually require the reports to conform to the institution's forms, or they may require the use of specific software, which can involve additional time and expense. Since this can sometimes become an issue, the management fee and requirements for preparing the reports should be discussed and negotiated in the agreement.

General Property Management. Real estate managers provide a service and are either (1) self-employed or (2) an employee of a management company. That means they are not an employee of the owner—the management agreement should clearly state this fact. The following lists the general activities that should be described in the management agreement that details the manager's authority in managing the property:

- Promoting and advertising the property
- Executing leases
- Hiring and supervising staff
- Administering the payroll
- Overseeing maintenance

Advertising the Property. Since all advertising is at the owner's expense, these objectives should be established and stated in the management agreement. Although advertising available space for lease in a small office building, strip shopping center, and residential property are all very similar, advertising is more prominent when dealing with commercial tenants because it's an integral part of the leasing activity.

Executing Leases. Regardless of a particular leasing role, it's important to understand the particulars of each lease because the real estate manager will ultimately administer its terms, collect the rents, and provide services to the resident or the commercial tenant. Because of their depth of experience, most real estate managers usually advise the property owners if certain lease clauses work to their disadvantage; they can offer suggestions regarding the language or clauses to protect the owners' interest and property. (More information about leases can be found in Chapter 9.)

For residential properties, executing leases usually includes authorization to select residents, set rents, and enforce lease terms—in which case the owner and real estate manager should agree in advance on the lease form. In addition, state law may require the real estate broker, or principal broker, to sign or review rental agreements within a short time after execution. Multi-family leases have nearly all provisions in common. While they will specify the unit address, amount of rent, names of occupants, term, and whether pets are agreed upon, nearly all other provisions are the same.

Commercial leases, on the other hand, can vary widely within a single building. When dealing with commercial properties, lease renewals or new leases are normally negotiated, but the real estate manager will not typically execute them. For larger commercial properties, the manager might serve as the leasing agent and receive compensation for the leasing specified in the management agreement. However, a separate leasing agent may also be hired through a *listing agreement* to handle most of the leasing.

Keep in mind that the complexity of the leases, rents for commercial space, and number of vacancies or renewals may dictate the manager's role. *Leasing agents* may be employees of a property, but because of their specialized role, they often have separate contracts and receive commissions based on the value of the negotiated leases. For a new property, the real estate manager may supervise the initial lease-up and then be directly responsible for renewing leases as they expire.

Hiring Staff and Administering Payroll. Although the owner is the employer of the property's staff, it's the responsibility of the real estate manager to hire and supervise them, along with administering payroll. However, multiple properties are managed for separate owners, the staff would be employees of the management company. Since many owners cannot afford to pay benefits (and depending on the management agreement), the management company sometimes pays benefits, charges them to the owner through a pro-ration or cost per person, or charges an additional management fee to cover the cost of benefits. The property staff usually includes maintenance personnel, site managers, and anyone else who works full- or part-time on the property. If the owner pays the expenses of employment, including salaries, benefits, employment taxes (Social Security, Medicare, and unemployment), and workers' compensation insurance premiums, these expenses are paid out of the property's operating funds.

Managing Maintenance. The real estate manager has the authority to perform all necessary and ordinary repairs and replacements to preserve the property by making alterations required to comply with lease agreements, governmental regulations, and insurance requirements. Apart from specific budgeted expenditures, the management agreement usually states a maximum dollar amount that can be spent on individual items of maintenance without obtaining prior approval from the owner, except in the event of an emergency. The management agreement may include a provision that requires the real estate manager be bonded or especially insured, which usually states the amount of liability involved.

The Owner's Obligations

Essentially, the owner is usually responsible for insuring the property, and the agreement should require that the real estate manager is identified on all policies as an additional named insured party. If the owner is the employer of record, the manager's name or the management company should be listed as an alternate employer on the owner's workers' compensation insurance policy. Premiums and deductibles are the owner's expenses, even though these might be paid out of the operating funds. The types of insurance required depends on the specific property, local practice, or state law. Consult with insurance agents to determine the best coverage for the property.

An important issue to negotiate for the management agreement is whether to establish and maintain a *reserve fund*. For residential properties, the reserve fund is usually a percentage of the property's gross receipts or *net operating income (NOI)* to be set aside on a regular basis. For commercial properties, a specific amount per square foot of building area is sometimes set aside.

The agreement should state the owner's responsibility for the property's compliance with applicable governmental regulations, such as environmental laws and building codes, or any associated insurance requirements. It should also indemnify the agent, or real estate manager, against liability for noncompliance. If the owner does not cure any discovered noncompliance, the manager could become liable since he or she is working as the owner's agent. However, the agreement should require the manager to advise the owner of any known noncompliance, the owner must then decide to implement changes or corrections and authorize the manager to do so.

Compensation for Management Services

Typically, the usual compensation, or *management fee,* for real estate management services can be a fixed fee, but it is usually the greater of a minimum fixed fee or a percentage of the gross receipts *(effective gross income)* of the managed property. The specific percentage is always negotiated or could be a minimum monthly fee. This should be finalized and stated in the agreement to ensure the manager of compensation in case of a shortfall in collections. In setting a fee, the real estate manager should be certain of adequate compensation for the full range of services provided.

Negotiating separate fees or commissions may be appropriate for services not generally part of the regular management duties, such as executing commercial or residential lease renewals, and overseeing construction, rehabilitation, or remodeling. With commercial properties, the gross receipts should be clarified in advance since they provide the total cash income from all sources.

THE MANAGEMENT PLAN

After finalizing the management agreement with the owner, the next step is to outline all of the details and include them in the management plan. The *management plan* should include an analysis of the current physical, fiscal, competitive, and operational conditions of the property in relation to the owner's goals. If the conditions are not suitable for attaining the owner's goals, the management plan should be used to recommend and support physical, financial, or operational changes. The management plan also evaluates the feasibility or practicality of plans the owner has for the property. Completing a management plan is an essential start to any new management account since it strengthens the knowledge base of the property being managed.

There is no definitive or standard structure for the management plan because every property is unique in its own way. For some properties, an operating budget and a list of the real estate manager's observations might suffice. For others, a full and detailed document (that can be hundreds of pages) might be necessary to give a complete perspective on the current condition of the property and the programs required to make its operation effective—or to justify a loan from a financial institution to support the necessary work. Regardless of the size of the plan, the appearance and presentation is always important. Logical assertions and conclusions and clear statements of the facts exemplify the real estate manager's skills and ability to communicate effectively.

The usual starting point for a management plan is a definition of the owner's goals for investment in the property. (See Chapter

4 for more details.) The owner's goals help narrow the scope of the research and recommendations in the management plan. If the owner expects rapid capital appreciation from a property, the management plan may center on improvements that offer a short period for return. Ways to increase NOI are another important inclusion because a higher return from a property increases its value. For owners who want a consistent return from their investment, a schedule should be created that outlines gradual improvements and/or cost saving measures that will ensure a high occupancy rate and create the potential for steadily increasing cash flow. (NOI and cash flow are described in detail in Chapter 6.)

The goal, as exhibited throughout the management plan and the actual management of the property, should agree with and complement the owner's goal. That goal is usually for the property to reach its *highest potential in its current use,* meaning that it generates the highest NOI possible and attains the best possible use based on its location, size, and design. When developing a specific management plan, the following evaluations are usually performed:

- National analysis
- Regional analysis
- Neighborhood analysis
- Property analysis
- Market analysis
- Analysis of alternatives
  - o Operational changes
  - o Structural changes
  - o Changes in use
- Cost-benefit analysis
- Conclusion and recommendations

National Analysis

Location, location, location—it's the most important aspect of a property's value. To gain a clear understanding of the effects that supply, demand, and location have on a property, its surroundings must be defined and thoroughly described. Two identical buildings, one located on Wall Street in Manhattan and the other in a small rural town, obviously will have different dollar values even though their designs and structures might be the same. A building's physical attributes and location are obviously not easy to change. The demand for space in any income-producing property impacts its value as well. The amount of income it can produce depends on the number and quality of the rental spaces of that type, availability of those same rental spaces locally, and proximity to the subject property.

Since value is mostly dependent on location, it's important to understand the economic, legal, demographic, environmental, and physical conditions that affect a property. After logically outlining the major national concerns, the next phase of the evaluation is with the region.

Regional Analysis

The *regional analysis* outlines the general geographic area in which changes in the economic and demographic conditions, as well as geographic features of the area surrounding the property, will impact a piece of real estate. The geographic features relate to environmental situations such as soil contamination and airports or highway access that affects noise issues in specific areas. Those conditions affect occupancy and the demand for space in a particular property. However, when there is an over-supply of any product or service, success is achieved through adapting the product or service to meet existing needs in other ways. Therefore, the recognition and adaptation of poorly utilized real estate is an invaluable skill to possess.

Demand ultimately gives value to real estate. Since people and their economic means create the general demand, investigating this demand will provide pertinent information about the region, especially through collection of historical data and growth projections.

The collected data includes the following general *demographic profile:*

- Business and industry
- Tourism and recreation
- Public improvements and facilities
- Transportation and traffic conditions
- Educational system
- Local economy

When evaluating these data, seek trends that signal: (1) future growth and opportunity, (2) little or no change from the current conditions, or (3) eventual decline. The government and social climate of a region also greatly affect the value of its real estate, so carefully investigate and analyze these regional components as well.

The Federal Government. The following lists the primary resources from the federal government that provide data for a regional analysis that are helpful when formulating statistical compilations:

- U.S. Department of Commerce, *commerce.gov*
- U.S. Bureau of Economic Analysis, *bea.gov*
- U.S. Census Bureau, *census.gov*
- Department of Labor, *dol.gov*
- U.S. Bureau of Labor Statistics, *bls.gov*
- U.S. Department of Housing and Urban Development (HUD), *hud.gov*

The U.S. Department of Commerce and the U.S. Census Bureau produce many statistical profiles in conjunction with federal departments and agencies. *The Census Catalog and Guide* lists the reports available and their publication dates. A few publications that are especially valuable are the *American Housing Survey,* conducted every other year in odd-numbered years, and the *Economic Census,* conducted at five-year intervals in years ending in two and seven.

The annual *Statistical Abstract of the United States* is a compilation of more recent information added to the census data. A fair amount of local data can be found through regional planning authorities.

Commercial Real Estate Brokerage Firms. Numerous real estate brokerage firms compile and publish demographic data in both print and electronic formats. Many of these firms are subsidiaries of companies, such as insurance companies and savings associations that already maintain vast databases. They sometimes combine their data with census results or compare their results with correlative census figures to verify accuracy. The following lists a few major real estate brokerage firms:

- Marcus and Millichap *(marcusmillichap.com)*
- Grubb and Ellis Company *(grubb-ellis.com)*
- Ramsey-Shilling Company *(ramsey-shilling.com)*

Most brokerage firms sort data on the basis of census tracts, city blocks, zip codes, area codes, phone prefixes, or any other specific boundaries identified. Such reports are economical in consideration of the time necessary for compilation—some firms promise delivery of the reports within a few days.

Professional Associations. Professional associations publish property-specific reports for regional, national, and market comparisons. However, the most valuable information within the region itself is available through state and local governmental agencies, utilities, local industries, financial institutions, chambers of commerce, and local economic development agencies. The following lists major professional associations and the specific types of publications they publish:

- Institute of Real Estate Management (IREM®), *irem.org*
  - *Income and Expense Analyses® Reports* for specific property types, including office buildings, shopping centers, federally assisted apartments, conventional apartments, and condominiums

- Urban Land Institute (ULI), *uli.org*
  - *Real Estate Market Analysis* explains how to get started, where to get information, and how to apply the basic techniques to a variety of development types
- Building Owners and Managers Association International (BOMA), *boma.org*
  - *Market Analysis for Real Estate: Concepts and Applications in Valuation and Highest and Best Use* has information on market and marketability analysis along with data collection and analysis
- International Council of Shopping Centers (ICSC), *icsc.org*
  - *Dollars and Cents of Shopping Centers*® provides the income and expenses for convenience, neighborhood, community, regional, and super-regional shopping centers; reports by region, center type, and age; and data on sales for centers in urban, suburban, and rural locations
- National Apartment Association (NAA), *naahq.org*
  - *Income and Expense Surveys* supply information on operating income and expenses, specifically in rental apartments, based on data supplied by NAA members

Neighborhood Analysis

The next area of research for the management plan is an in-depth study of the immediate neighborhood, or localized area, in which properties compete for prospects. Similar to the regional study in content but more narrowly focused, the *neighborhood analysis* is an evaluation of data related to nearby sites and the competition—centering on the immediate surroundings of the subject property. Without a thorough national and regional analysis, however, the neighborhood analysis can either be too optimistic or too pessimistic. Just as changes in the neighborhood affect a property, changes in the nation and region affect the neighborhood as well.

Many factors contribute to prospects choosing a specific neighborhood. For instance, mapping sites like Google Maps (maps.google.com) provides basic information about a neighborhood in terms of its geographic and physical features (bridges, walkways, bike paths, traffic information, and any areas with open land) and allow capabilities to virtually walk a neighborhood. Review and recommend websites like Yelp (yelp.com) contain feedback written by consumers about neighborhood businesses; such sites are another possible sources of information about competitive properties or about the specific property being managed.

Other Online Resources

The following lists other online resources that might provide more general demographic information:

- *demographicsnow.com*
- *melissadata.com*
- *fedstats.com*
- *statelocalgov.net*

Boundary Definition. Analyzing a neighborhood first requires a definition of boundaries. The neighborhood of a particular property may consist of a few adjacent buildings or it may comprise an area of many square blocks. Neighborhood boundaries are often natural or constructed barriers—such as rivers, lakes, ravines, railroad tracks, parks, and streets—that separate discrete areas that have common characteristics in population or land use. Sometimes neighborhood boundaries are not visually discernible; information can be complied from sources such as the U.S. Census Bureau, municipal and county governments, local government offices, local utility companies, newspaper reports, the local library, the school board, and social agencies to map a neighborhood precisely. Post office as zip codes help define the boundaries as well.

The objective of analyzing the neighborhood is to characterize the population, economic elements, and property types that are dominant. Considerations such as age, education, ethnic groups, income levels, and institutions (colleges, hospitals, etc.) are part of the characterization of a residential neighborhood. The types of businesses (complementary and competitive) and their clientele and employees differentiate the neighborhood of a commercial property; however, many newer, urban developments such as mixed-use properties are built to sustain both housing and commercial business elements.

Physical Inspection. A physical inspection of the neighborhood is also essential. The general *curb appeal* and overall cleanliness of the area should be inspected to determine whether or not the neighborhood is well maintained. In reporting the analysis, particular features in the neighborhood might be singled out that favor the subject property. In the neighborhood analysis for an apartment building, the location and quality of schools, accessibility to stores, and the level of public transportation service are good items to mention. Important components of the neighborhood analysis for an office building would be transportation, restaurants, and types of business services.

An overall physical inspection should identify comparable properties to study trends in their surrounding area. For office buildings, the *micro-market* (neighborhood) may encompass just a few blocks or a few buildings. Merchandise categories and price lines of retail operations and the numbers of similar businesses—or their absence—along with a demographic profile of shoppers define the *trade area* (neighborhood) of a shopping center.

Property Analysis

The analytical methods used for the regional and neighborhood analysis are also applied to the *property analysis,* which includes a careful inspection of the building and a description of its rental space and common areas. Other factors related to analyzing the property are the basic architectural design and the overall physical condition. The following are some of the questions to answer when conducting a property analysis:

- **Building size.** How many units or leasable square feet does the building contain? What size are the spaces—the number of rooms and square feet in each apartment or the configuration and method of measuring commercial space?

- **Condition.** What is the physical condition of the building structurally in regard to maintenance—roof, masonry, elevators, HVAC, other mechanical equipment, cable and wiring, windows and trim, asphalt, doors, other hardware? Is *functional obsolescence*—the loss or change of value brought about by a change in design, technology, taste, or demand—correctable? For example, what would happen to a playground in a residential community that was recently converted to individuals 55 and older? How can functional inadequacies be corrected? Will a structural engineer or other professional need to be consulted about the condition of any elements of the building? Should a useful-life study be conducted on major expensive systems such as HVAC units, roofs, or asphalt? What major improvements or repairs will be needed in the first year, after three years, after five years? And will those repairs extend the useful life of that system?

- **Common areas.** What is the condition of the most heavily used elements—floors, floor coverings, lobbies, entrance halls, elevator cabs, escalators, hallways, stairways, storage areas, and amenities such as fitness centers? (Concrete sidewalks, ADA requirements, lighting, landscapes, and trees can have a significant impact on safety, compliance, and visibility, to name a few.) Does the building meet all fire codes, and have all fire prevention systems been properly tested and maintained over the years? Does the property have a history of environmental issues? Was the property a prior fueling station? Was there ever asbestos? Is there evidence of mold? Are the light fixtures and elements properly maintained or corrected?

- **Residents'/tenants' individual spaces.** How attractive is the rentable space—layout, exposure, view, features, and décor? Are there pest issues due to the tenant's lack of cleanliness? Are appliances or other fixtures such as toilets, tubs, and sinks outdated in terms of colors (pink, avocado green, etc.)? Are kitchen appliances stainless steel or white? Are counters granite or Formica? (Numerous factors can have unwanted financial and legal consequences as well—therefore, it is important to look to the future and the predictable shifts such consequences may entail.)

- **Occupancy.** What has been the trend in occupancy? What is the current occupancy level? What is the composition and character of tenancy—for example, two adult roommates with no children and two dogs in apartment 101, a law office with 100 employees in suite 1800, or a convenience store in unit 3? Do outside factors such as being located next to a college or university affect occupancy? Swings in occupancy can mean excessive costs of turnover, advertising, payroll, and a myriad other financial impacts. (Frequent turnover can also provide opportunities to raise rents and other charges.)

- **Curb appeal.** How desirable is the property—visual impression, age, architectural style, grounds, layout, approaches, public space, and signage? Having a clean, inviting property and office with all amenities in excellent shape can result in the subject property being selected first over the competition.

- **Building-to-land ratio or floor area ratio (FAR).** What is the relationship between the building and the land on which it is located, for example, the current zoning and parking? Can the owner use the building or the land more efficiently? Have there been changes in the zoning code that would impact the building-to-land ratio if the owner wants to expand? Differences in FAR can be good or bad depending on the circumstances. It's essential to understand that ratio is not the only element to analyze. High density in any area can mean higher maintenance costs with higher use, but more people in smaller spaces means more rent per square foot. Is there ample parking—far more than is required per leases or per code? The owner may consider building outparcels if allowed by zoning, or obtaining a variance to maximize potential income and increase value. Simply knowing and being aware of the area's possibilities makes the land more valuable to a potential purchaser.

- **Compliance status.** Are violations of health, safety, or environmental standards evident? Is the building compliant with the Americans with Disabilities Act (ADA)? For residential properties, have they had an excessive number of police calls? Compliance issues or having violations will prevent anyone from getting financing for the building, which establishes the importance of maintaining the market value.

- **Current management.** What are the current standards of building management? What policies and procedures are in effect for selecting residents, hiring and training staff, maintaining the building and grounds, collecting rents, controlling purchases, and administering the policies and procedures? Are they documented in an operations manual? If management is lax, other areas such as maintenance, accounting, billing, and customer service may be lacking as well. In general, all deficiencies can affect the property's value by increasing vacancy, deferred maintenance, and disgruntled tenants.

- **Staff.** How is the property staffed? What are the staff attitudes, capabilities, training, and goals? Properly trained staff can add significant value through increased customer service and better attention to service. Staff has the power to increase or decrease a building's value and to establish or damage its reputation. A property's staff can cause it to lead or trail the market.

- **Financial integrity.** What is the status of the property with respect to NOI? What is its level of debt? Are expenses high or low compared to competing properties?

One of the most important aspects of the property analysis concerns tenant leases. It's important to review the status and language of existing leases, which are the basis of the property's revenue stream. For commercial properties, lease negotiations in progress may be a consideration. Additionally, if leases are not properly abstracted, money can remain uncollected. *Abstracting* is the process of extracting and condensing the most important terms and financial clauses of the lease into a form that is more easily accessible and understandable. As the leases and their abstracts are reviewed, the lease language might allow for certain common costs to be passed through to the tenant. If those costs have not been passed through, the property's revenue will be increased by collecting those costs.

In the examination of the property and analysis of the information obtained, keep in mind that the owner's ultimate goal is usually to achieve the greatest return on his or her investment by putting the property to its highest and best use. At this point, the information gathered in the regional, neighborhood, and property analyses have been described, but the next and most essential component of the management plan is the market analysis.

Market Analysis

The term *real estate market* has different meanings in such diverse aspects of real estate as mortgage interest rates, development, property cost, property value, rental rates, and even property amenities. All of these, except mortgage interest rates, relate in some way to the level of competition and the demand for rental space in a particular property. A *market analysis* evaluates the supply and demand conditions for rental space in a specific building in comparison to the demand for space in other competitive buildings—along with details like rental and vacancy rates. The market analysis gathers information about specific comparable properties and compares their features to the subject property.

Once the features are described, the advantages and disadvantages can be evaluated accordingly. The market analysis should only focus on competing buildings within the neighborhood and the region based on the information derived from the regional, neighborhood, and property analyses. After comparing the property to its competitors and analyzing the region and neighborhood, conclusions can be made to identify factors that affect, or could affect, the performance of the subject property. This study is conducted based on the current condition of the property.

The four principles of conducting the market analysis are essentially the same for all types of property: (1) find which properties are competitors, (2) complete a comparison grid analysis to compare the subject property to the competition, (3) set the correct rental rates based on the comparison, and (4) write a narrative report.

Define the Competition. Buildings in direct competition with the subject property obviously define the competition. To find which buildings are legitimate competitors, examine the subject property at the *submarket* level, which is a segment of the overall geographical area limited by a particular market factor—office, retail, industrial, apartment, or single-family home markets. This property categorization reduces the focus and number of potential residents and, thus, potential competitors. In some cases, ask prospects which other buildings they are considering. If a prospect is lost to a competitor, figure out why.

Other factors narrow the field even further. Prospective residents usually locate in one portion of the region by limiting their search to the part of town they prefer. They also commonly search for a particular type of rental space—households of three or more are obviously not interested in studio apartments, convenience store owners do not seek supermarket-sized spaces, and couples often make decisions based on a shorter commute if a suitable accommodation cannot be found at a midpoint.

Because prospects narrow their focus, narrow the focus of the market analysis to determine the true competition. The subject property is compared to similar properties in the neighborhood or general vicinity—not compared to property across town or in another region. However, even if a property across town is not in direct competition with the subject property, its standing in the market will have an influence because it is a part of the market as a whole—the narrative description of the market accounts for this influence.

Since the facts learned in the regional and neighborhood analyses basically indicate which buildings are in direct competition with the subject property, compare their features and amenities and rate them appropriately. The same concept applies to the property type—different information is needed for residential properties compared to commercial properties. The sections below describe the specific information that should be gathered for each type.

Residential Markets. Prospective residents are looking for the perfect new home and their expectation is that it will contain one or more specific qualities or characteristics. Each of these elements can be allocated to a dollar value. The prospect will pay a certain amount to have a feature a competitor does not, or the prospect will do without it if the price is appropriately adjusted. For this reason, when comparing the subject property to the competition, list those influential features and amenities that might persuade a prospective resident to sign a lease. The following considerations pertain to most residential markets:

- Number and types of apartment units available within the area
- Average age and character of the building
- Features that are similar in most units within the market—size, layout, equipment, and amenities that define a typical unit
- Quality of staff and the services they offer, such as concierge, food delivery, dry cleaning pickup, and even credit card acceptance for rental payments
- Current rent for an average unit on a monthly and square-foot basis
- Cost of utilities—gas, electricity, water, sewer, and even parking—and if they are paid by the resident or owner
- Availability of public transportation or access to major highways or arterial streets
- Rental rates and occupancy levels in recent years

Commercial Markets. The following lists the types of property characteristics to compile for commercial spaces when learning about the market:

- Square footage of the space—office, retail, and industrial
- Average age, character, and condition of the building
- Types of commercial tenants, major space users, or professionals in private practice—doctors, lawyers, direct retail sales, or manufacturers of finished goods and suppliers of component parts
- General mix of commercial tenants in a building
- Accessibility via public transportation
- Availability and cost of parking—especially in a central business district
- Presence of amenities that serve commercial tenants' employees, such as restaurants or banks
- Current base rate per square foot and how it is quoted—monthly or annually
- Whether and how the common area is included in the rent—add-on factor
- Types of concessions negotiated in leasing space of the type—free rent, moving allowance, or tenant improvement dollars
- Typical lease terms, or numbers of years, and provisions for rent escalations—flat rate, consumer price index (CPI), or other index or calculation
- Types and cost of operating expenses—common area maintenance (CAMs) or operating expenses—passed through to commercial tenants via their pro-rata share or some other generally acceptable method
- Whether retailers pay percentage rents (percentage of their sales)
- Occupancy level of the type of space—office, retail, or industrial—in the market that is superior, average, and inferior
- Trends in rental rates and occupancy levels in recent years

When conducting the market analysis, many questions should be asked. How do the rent and occupancy trends compare with real estate market trends in general? How do vacant apartments or commercial spaces in the area compare to those in the subject property with regard to size, age, condition, amenities, and rents? Based on the results of the neighborhood analysis, is the number of prospective tenants for the subject property increasing or decreasing? Is the *absorption rate*—the amount of space leased compared to the amount of space available—positive or negative?

Complete a Comparison Grid. To make an effective comparison, categorize the features of the competitive properties with respect to the subject property using a *comparison grid* (Exhibits 5.1 and 5.2). Specific features are listed at the left, and the comparable properties are indicated as column headings. Most of the categories are straightforward, but some might require additional explanation. A "pets allowed" category may be listed as a straight "yes or no" for most residential properties, but some apartments may have very specific provisions—separate pet agreement, additional rent, or fees. For commercial properties, rental rates account for additions to base rent—operating expenses and percentage rent— and a comparison of major and minor space users should also be included.

When completing the comparison grid, consistency in rating or ranking is most important. In preparation of the comparison grid, use the same rules of assessment for each category of analysis for all properties. Describing and rating "location" on the comparison grid can be difficult, yet the location of a property within the neighborhood is its prime marketable feature. Keep in mind there is no standard for a good location. For instance, being a block from a supermarket or a mass transit stop would ordinarily be a promotable feature for a residential property, but being next door to the bus depot or to the parking lot of the supermarket would not. On the other hand, being next door may be more attractive than being three miles away from those amenities. Location next door to a hospital is a selling point for offices designed for physicians

EXHIBIT 5.1

Sample Comparison Grid (Residential Property)

	Subject	Comp #1		Comp #2		Comp #3	
Name/Address							
Type of Unit							
Square Feet in Unit							
Rental Rate							
Rate/Square Foot							
Categories	**Descrip.**	**Descrip.**	**Adj.**	**Descrip.**	**Adj.**	**Descrip.**	**Adj.**
Location							
Age							
BUILDING CONDITION							
Exterior							
Grounds							
Common Areas							
PARKING							
Condition							
Open/Covered/Garage							
Ratio							
Other							
APARTMENT INTERIOR							
Floor/Carpet							
Drapes/Blinds							
Stove/Refrigerator							
Dishwasher							
Washer/Dryer							
Closets/Storage							
Air Conditioning							
Other							
AMENITIES							
Laundry Room(s)							
Swimming Pool(s)							
Other							
Owner-Paid Utilities							
Pets Allowed							
Other							
Total Rent Adjustments							
Adjusted Rent /Unit							
Adjusted Rent /Sq. Ft.							

If the feature in the subject property is better than that in a comparable property, the rent for the comparable is adjusted upward; if the subject property's feature is not as good as the comparable's, the rent for the comparable is adjusted downward. The adjustments for each comparable property are totaled, and the rental rate is changed—increased or decreased—based on the net adjustments.

EXHIBIT 5.2

Sample Comparison Grid (Commercial Property)

	Subject	Comp #1		Comp #2		Comp #3	
Property Name							
Base Rental Rate							
– Concessions							
+ Expense Pass-Throughs							
+ Tenant Improvements							
+ Tenant Effective Rent							
Categories	**Descrip.**	**Descrip.**	**Adj.**	**Descrip.**	**Adj.**	**Descrip.**	**Adj.**
Location /Accessibility							
BUILDING CONDITION							
Age							
Exterior							
Grounds							
Common Areas							
Commercial Space							
Other							
BUILDING SYSTEMS							
Elevators							
HVAC Efficiency							
After-Hours Charges							
Life Safety							
Other							
AVAILABLE SPACE							
Location							
Floor Plate							
Storage							
Telecommunications							
Other							
PARKING							
Open/Covered/Garage							
Visitor Spaces							
Parking Ratio							
Cost to Tenant							
Other							
AMENITIES/FEATURES							
Vacancy Rate							
Total Rent Adjustments							
Rentable Square Foot							
× R /U Ratio							
Usable Square Foot							

This form is typical of those used to evaluate office buildings. Concessions and tenant-paid improvements are prorated based on the R /U (rentable area /usable area) ratio (see Chapter 12). Comparison data for a shopping center would emphasize anchor draw, tenant mix synergy, visibility from the street, signage, and the amount of drive-by traffic. Information about deal-making rents, percentage rates, and specific pass-throughs might also be included.

and allied health professionals, but it is a detriment for industrial space with heavy incoming and outgoing truck traffic. Being near a courthouse is a desirable feature for space usable as law offices, but that location is not a selling point for stores seeking high-end retail tenants.

Because most factors involving location are relative and complex, a separate location analysis can help evaluate how the property's location affects demand—Exhibit 5.3 lists some of the factors that influence prospective tenants' perceptions of location quality.

Comparison grid analysis determines how the rental space in the subject property compares to similar space in the market on a feature-by-feature basis. The purpose is to show whether a particular feature at a comparable property is better than or not as good as the same feature in the subject property and how the total of these features affects quoted rents. By attributing a dollar value to each feature, a market-level rent can be determined for the subject property based on the comparison. If the feature in the subject property is better than in a comparable property, the rent for the comparable is adjusted *upward.* If the feature in the subject property is not as good, the rent for the comparable is adjusted *downward.* The adjustment amount, whether it's negative or positive, is based on what a resident would pay for the feature or would not pay because of its absence. For each property, the adjustments and changes to the rental rate are totaled to reflect the net adjustments. Finally, the rents for the comparable properties are analyzed to determine a market rent on a per-unit or a per-square-foot basis. Typically, a comparison grid analysis is completed for each type of apartment unit in a residential property.

Set Rents. Evaluating the quoted rents and occupancy levels of the competing rental apartments or commercial spaces helps to determine the rent that the owner should charge for the subject property—based on quality, services, amenities, and other attractions. The comparison grid also indicates whether the rent for the type of space in the subject property is below, at, or above market

EXHIBIT 5.3

Factors That Influence Location Quality

RESIDENTIAL PROPERTIES
- Convenience of local facilities
- Central business district (CBD)
- Convenience store or center
- Neighborhood shopping center/supermarket
- Regional mall or larger shopping center
- Major employment locations (if different from CBD)
- Schools and colleges
- Parks, sports, and fitness centers, and other recreational facilities
- Cultural/entertainment centers
- Social services (government and human services centers)

OFFICE BUILDINGS
Availability of Business Services
- Adequate to cutting-edge communications facilities, services, and support
- Printing and related services
- Delivery/shipping services and messengers
- Office, computer, and photocopying supplies and support
- Industry-specific support services and suppliers
- Temporary staffing agencies
- Professional consultation (accounting, legal)

Availability of Services for Employees
- Restaurants and other food outlets
- Daycare facilities
- Fitness facilities
- Dry cleaning, shoe repairs, valet services
- Drug/sundry stores

RETAIL PROPERTIES
- Amount of traffic passing the property (vehicular and/or pedestrian)
- Visibility from the street
- Signage possibilities
- No one-way streets or limitations on turns
- Nearby streets, highways, and thoroughfares
- Amount and configuration of parking
- Adequate access to receive merchandise deliveries
- Age and condition of suite amenities such as heating, ventilation, and air-conditioning (HVAC) units for which they may become responsible
- ADA compliance

rates. Based on this information, the current *rental schedule* of the subject property can be evaluated and compared it to the rental schedules of other properties on the comparison grid.

To determine whether to adjust the current rental schedule of the subject property, there must be a search for an optimum balance between vacancy and maximum income. While the ideal is maximum rent and maximum occupancy, reality dictates that vacancies will be present. In fact, an increase in rent may initially increase vacancies. With this in mind, a realistic maximum rent should be chosen that will minimize the impact on the occupancy rate. Rents and vacancies are important considerations in estimating changes in gross receipts and NOI that will result from an increase in rents. The prices are then applied to each unit or space according to its location, view, and amenities.

Write a Narrative Report. The market analysis generally includes a narrative overview of market trends and observations, such as the evaluation of the absorption rate and regional and neighborhood trends, including population changes.

Absorption Rate. The absorption rate in the neighborhood or region usually warrants discussion. The *absorption rate* of a property type is the amount of space leased compared to the amount of space available for lease over a given period—usually a year. The rate relates to both construction of new space and demolition or removal from the market of old space. Different property types within the same region have different absorption rates.

If demand exceeds supply, the absorption rate is favorable because overall vacancy decreases. If supply exceeds demand, the absorption rate is unfavorable, and lenders tend to curtail their financing of the development of similar properties, which eventually causes a slowdown of growth. A negative absorption rate can also result from other changes in a market. If a major industry closes and not enough jobs are available, people will move away from the area, and the lack of jobs will discourage others from moving in. The amount of residential space available for lease will quickly exceed demand—irrespective of any new construction. The commercial sector may also slow down based on this major change. However, the effect of reduced demand is not always immediately apparent. Construction might continue because the financing is in place. If the developer obtained financing when the level of demand was high, market trends may be unfavorable when construction starts, and stopping construction may cost more than completing the project. As the new space fills over time, demand will again exceed supply and the absorption rate will again be favorable—encouraging new construction and causing the cycle to repeat.

Trends. The narrative portion of the market analysis includes trends observed in the regional and neighborhood analyses that can affect the subject property. For a residential property, a shift in the demographic profile of the neighborhood (for example, from families to empty nesters) would be noted here—along with conclusions regarding the favorable or unfavorable effects that shift may have on the demand for rental apartments. If the regional analysis showed that a nearby company, such as Boeing or Microsoft, would be expanding its operations and hiring more people, it could be presumed that demand for rental space will increase. And with further reasoning—based on the comparison grid—the competing buildings in the neighborhood are better suited to profit from the anticipated population growth.

Population changes also affect the leasing of commercial space. Education levels and technical skills determine the caliber of potential office workers. Household income levels indicate the price levels of merchandise that will sell in a particular area—Bloomingdale's and Nordstrom obviously offer different price lines than do Target and Walmart. These considerations should guide the development of a marketing program for the property that will capitalize on any positive trends and insulate the property from the impact of negative trends. (Chapter 8 provides more information on marketing.)

Many management plans conclude with the market analysis. The research to this point can substantiate a need for a new rental schedule and indicate the increase that the property can attain without compromising its competitive strength. In other words, if implementation of a new rental schedule alone will place the property in a condition of highest and best use—enough said. However, many properties, particularly commercial properties, demand a more comprehensive examination of their future prospects.

Data Evaluation

Data evaluation essentially determines three major factors about the property: (1) what management direction to take, (2) what conclusions are justified, and (3) what recommendations will ultimately be made to the owner. A neighborhood is not a static environment—it changes continually and its changes can affect the property in numerous ways. Always examine the changing neighborhood conditions, include definitions of those trends in the neighborhood analysis, and explain why they are occurring. The changing numbers of individuals in different age and income groups and changes in household sizes indicate population shifts. Fluctuating real estate sales prices and rental rates, along with the amount of vacant space, which are readily ascertained in a physical inspection, reflect economic shifts. Differences in types of property development (new vs. renovated), changes in land value and use, rental rates, and vacancy rates are other indicators of specific trends.

If results of the neighborhood analysis seem incomplete or uncertain, always investigate further. A complete and fair perspective is essential to an accurate market analysis. Population growth often indicates prosperity for a neighborhood such as leading to higher occupancy, but it can also signal the reverse. For example, an excess of vacant commercial space may be the result of new development in response to increased demand or a sign of challenging economic times. In established properties, vacancies can signal an inability to support retail and other businesses—leading to even more vacancy. With the numerous sources available for data, it would be unwise to predict a change in land value from a single statistic. Evaluation of its cause in the context of other specific statistics is essential to understanding a particular trend and its impact on value or even use.

It's important to continually monitor current trends to know whether conditions are improving, staying the same, or declining. These trends can signal the need to modify the way the property is managed, while continuing to meet the specific goals and needs of the owner—improving conditions may lead to increased market rents. Staying the same—perhaps adding new amenities for tenants—might help retain or improve occupancy. If conditions are declining, perhaps improvements to the physical aspects of the building may lead to other property owners in the area improving their buildings—thereby reversing that trend. Further, current trends may signal the need to project future trends, which lead to a variety of new conclusions and recommendations that can prepare the property owner for the coming changes.

Analysis of Alternatives

Some properties require changes in operations or some form of physical change to justify a rent increase. Examples are elevating the occupancy level, controlling expenses, and subsequently bringing such properties to their highest and best use. In the effort to improve the performance of a property, investigate the range of possible changes and evaluate their anticipated effects—in other words, conduct an *analysis of alternatives.* The intent of the changes proposed in this section of a management plan is to increase NOI, which is the tangible and measurable benefit of the investment in the property, and thereby to increase the property's value. Each proposed change carries with it a cost, so the analysis will compare the costs and the benefits of each proposal or combination of proposals made in the analysis of alternatives.

In some instances, improvements to real property may preserve value rather than increase income—upgrading an HVAC system and replacing a roof are examples. Ignoring the needed improvement could result in decreased rents, lower occupancy, increased operating expenses, and a lower property value. Preserving value and the capital invested in the real estate are important to every investor. Such investments in capital improvements also warrant a cost-benefit analysis because their costs may be factored into the residents' rents or result in reductions of operating expense increases—and the owners will need to know how long the *payback period* will be until they recoup their investment. Some capital improvement projects are the financial responsibility of the owner, while others can be passed through to the tenants—raising operational expenses that the tenants pay.

In analyzing alternatives, consider potential operational and physical changes. Operational changes are procedural, whereas physical changes can range from rehabilitation or modernization of the current building to outright change in the use of the building or the site.

Operational Changes. These changes affect procedural methods or efficiency but not the physical makeup of the property. The net effect is to increase income or reduce operating expenses and thereby increase NOI. Operational changes range from adopting a new rental schedule based on the market analysis to using low-wattage bulbs in common-area lighting. Strategies to reduce outside service expenses include renegotiating contract terms with certain service providers, such as elevator maintenance, or calling for bids on recurring services that are not under contract—landscaping or parking lot sweeping. Along with reducing expenses, it's important to keep in mind the numerous enhancements and improvements of operations as well. Many residents and tenants actually place a value on the efforts made to sustainable changes to the property. It attracts attention and has the potential to gain more residents. It's important to keep in mind that investors will want to see a return for the risk they take in greening their assets, for improving sustainability, and in achieving particular levels of accreditation on the environmental performance of their buildings.

Although the intent of operational changes is to reduce operating expenses, the property's quality is what always needs to be maintained. After completing the market analysis, it's important to be acutely aware of the services provided at competing properties. Any recommendation that sacrifices any similar services may be more costly than the savings achieved. However, examination of the competition may lead to the discovery of new methods that will reduce operating costs yet preserve or enhance service standards.

Structural Changes. Rehabilitation and modernization can lengthen the economic life of a property. *Rehabilitation* is the process of renewing the equipment and materials in the building—it entails correcting deferred maintenance. *Modernization,* the correction of functional obsolescence, is inherent in the rehabilitation process. To make the property competitive, similar equipment of more modern design will replace the original equipment. New carpeting, wood floors, upgraded electrical service, Wi-Fi, equipment that is more energy efficient, or any other physical improvement that does not affect the use of the property can be rehabilitative. The list of possibilities in this arena is virtually endless. When physical changes are proposed, the management plan must include an expense budget and/or a capital budget showing the allocation of funds for the changes and the anticipated return on investment, impact on NOI, cash flow, and property value. The owner may also require an analysis of debt service—if the funds are borrowed—and cash flow.

Changes in Use. A recommendation to change the use of a property must be well founded since changing the property is complex, expensive, and therefore, not typical. However, the rewards of a successful change in use are often substantial. Once a change of use is implemented, reverting to the original condition is clearly difficult. The property owner should carefully weigh the anticipated improvement in performance expected from a change in use against the risks of that change. The most common changes include adaptive use, condominium conversion, and demolition for new development.

Adaptive Use. *Adaptive use* (or recycling) of existing structures is usually more economical than building new structures. Capitalizing on an existing shell and foundation eliminates the cost of demolition and part of the cost of new materials. Old factories, warehouses, train stations, and post offices have gained new life as offices, shopping centers, apartments, and entertainment complexes—some office buildings have become hotels and condominiums.

Adaptive use is a way to reduce development costs to meet new market demands, preserve historical architecture, or revive a location that is not achieving its highest and best use. A recycled building may not achieve the same rent per square foot as a new one, but the initial costs are lower and the debt service requirements are usually less. Adaptive use projects make sense when cash flow per square foot will be greater than the cash flow from the original use. Old buildings, whole city blocks, and even sections of towns have been preserved and made profitable through adaptive use.

Condominium Conversion. The primary advantage of *condominium conversion* is the potential to achieve a high profit in a short time. The appeal is even greater when cyclical changes or market conditions cause increases in financing costs, which always reduces cash flow. Converting a rental property to condominium ownership allows the original owner to recapture their investment, pay off the mortgage, and keep any excess funds as profit. If rent control restricts a property owner's ability to increase rents to market levels, condominium conversion may circumvent the potential loss of income, although current renters may have the right to remain despite the conversion. Review of state and local laws regarding condominium formation and conversion is essential to determine the feasibility of a particular conversion.

Although condominium conversion was once limited to apartment buildings, the concept has extended to other property types—even parking lots in congested metropolitan areas are sold by the parking space. The success of a condominium conversion depends on the adaptability of the building to the form of ownership. In most cases, the building and all of its components must be in the best possible condition for the property owner who is doing the conversion to achieve the greatest possible return on their investment. The property owners must also consider the fact that a condominium is a long-term financial commitment for the buyer—a prospective owner is usually more selective than a prospective renter. It's important to understand that investors think about selling their assets even at the time they are buying them—they need to perform *due diligence,* which ensures that the offering statement does not misstate or omit pertinent information during the examination of a property. Owners understand the properties they're investing in and the investment classes they intend them to be. In fact, owners should set goals for the property as soon as possible. They determine the projected sales price they might obtain from another investor or converter and whether doing the conversion themselves would be most profitable or even possible, considering their skill sets. Market conditions may require the reverse as well.

Demolition for New Development. Demolition may seem to be an easy alternative, but it can be very expensive. The cost of demolishing a building along with the cost of building a new one increases the necessity for the new structure to generate a high level of income. In some cases, a proposal to demolish a building—even if it is in serious disrepair—can lead to a public outcry and tarnish the image of the new structure. For instance, if a site is listed in the National Register of Historic Places, demolition of the building is prohibited. The decision to demolish an old building and replace it with something new requires thorough review of more than the financial aspects. The impact on the neighborhood and the possible loss of goodwill are also important considerations. In addition, the new building would need to conform to today's building codes and standards; that is not always required with minor remodeling of existing buildings.

Cost-Benefit Analysis

Since changing a property always involves costs, the amount and extent of the costs depend on the scope of the changes. Establishing a new accounting procedure, or other operational change, might only require training of staff and replacement of certain software—regardless, these have measurable costs. Rehabilitation and other structural changes are costly and can cause interruption of part or all of the rental income while the work is done. Even a recommendation to maintain the status quo has to be justified financially.

In order to determine whether a specific recommendation will improve the property's income, a *cost-benefit analysis* will need to be conducted, which involves the evaluation of each alternative to ascertain which would yield higher levels of NOI and cash flow than the property would yield if left unchanged. Recovering the costs of making the change, plus any financing, is also an issue. Clearly, the benefit of increased NOI and property value must outweigh the cost if a recommendation is feasible. To determine this, the *payback period* will need to be evaluated—the amount of time for the change to pay for itself. The cost-benefit analysis should also show the potential increase in property value from the improvement. (Exhibit 5.4 shows an example of a cost-benefit analysis.)

Conclusions and Recommendations

Finally, while the conclusion and recommendations may be sound and easily undertaken, property owners will ultimately make the final decision based on their personal financial goals, desired holding period, or other factors. Determination of the highest and best use, however, is a necessary exercise that, while perhaps not immediately implemented, will make small changes or improvements that may help guide future decisions.

Management plans can be long and complex, so there are certain ways to make the document easier to follow. For instance, recapping the major conditions that affect the property and including a summary of the primary recommendations are helpful ways to make the document clear and concise. Essentially, the management plan should include the rationale for specific changes and the expected results, along with a clear statement of the anticipated

EXHIBIT 5.4

Sample Cost-Benefit Analysis Calculation

The real estate manager of a 30-year-old apartment building discovers that residents in the neighborhood tend to pay higher rent for apartments with new kitchen appliances. While the refrigerators and ovens in the 50 units at the subject property are as old as the building, they still operate well. However, new appliances and built-in microwave ovens are standard equipment in comparable buildings nearby. If replacing appliances will cost $2,000 per apartment, or $100,000 for the entire building, suppose further that the improvement will allow an increase in rent of $50 per apartment per month and that the property historically has had 90% occupancy (45 leased units out of 50). The payback period, ROI, and increase in property value would be calculated as follows:

$2,000/apt. × 50 apts. = $100,000 total cost of improvements
$50 additional rent × 45 leased units = $2,250/month additional income
$100,000 total cost ÷ $2,250 per month
= approximately 44 months (payback period)

$2,250/month × 12 months = $27,000 additional annual income as NOI
$27,000 increase in NOI ÷ $100,000 improvement cost
= 27% return on investment (ROI)

$27,000 increase in NOI ÷ 0.10 (cap rate) = $270,000 increase in prop. value
$270,000 increased value – $100,000 improvement cost
= $170,000 net increase in value

The calculation assumes the improvement cost is paid in full by the owner or from reserve funds accumulated for the purpose. Whether a 44-month payback period is reasonable or feasible depends on the owner's expectations of the property. The possibility of a higher occupancy rate may reduce the payback period to less than 44 months. Operating expenses may also decrease because of lower repair expenses, which may reduce the payback period even more. The owner also benefits from a cost recovery deduction for the improvement (depreciation), which reduces the owner's tax liability on the income from the property.

On the other hand, if the owner financed the improvement cost, the debt service on the loan would reduce the total annual revenue, the increase in property value, and the owner's return on investment. The payback period would increase.

long-term financial performance—the effect on the bottom line. The main objective is to be sure the owner understands the reasoning behind the management plan. Highlighting this information in an *executive summary* at the beginning of the document (instead of placing the summary at the end of the report) will help guide the owner through the document. Recommendations that relate to only one area of the property's operation may not require a complex management plan. A market analysis may suffice to assess the condition of a property and recommend maintaining status quo. However, any proposed change, including a change in rental rates, requires a cost-benefit analysis.

SUMMARY

The management objectives of each owner for each asset will always be unique, but a well-written management agreement and management plan will spell them out. Both documents are integral to defining how the property should be managed and the responsibilities for both the real estate manager and the property owner; they should be considered carefully and in great detail to ensure the future success of the business relationship. Since the management agreement is a formal contract, it should clearly outline the real estate manager's responsibilities and the owner's obligations, while authorizing the manager to operate the property on the owner's behalf.

It's important to remember that the owner is ultimately responsible for the property. The real estate manager must know how to assess a property's potential and how to explain that assessment through a management plan. Evaluation of the data on the region, the neighborhood, and the property itself forms the basis for an analysis of the property's current market position. Assessment of the property's structural integrity, operating history, rent levels, and other factors indicate whether change is necessary to bring the property in line with market demand. Every change proposed to improve profitability involves a cost, which must be evaluated. Altogether, preparing clean, well-organized documents is essential for maintaining a strong sense of professionalism and establishing the foundation for a professional career in real estate management.

CHAPTER 6
Financial Management

Financial management goes beyond simple recording and reporting. It includes well-informed income and expense projections in the form of operating budgets and analyses of any variances. These reports serve as a basis for analyzing the efficiency of property operations and help to drive profitability. In a world of fiscal transparency standards and competing institutional asset investors, real estate managers are being asked to adopt business practices from the financial services industry. Though it may sound challenging, operators are assisted by technology to streamline decision making and operations, enhance performance, and optimize investor returns. With the quickly growing popularity of revenue management models, even more data points are available for analysis beyond the traditional operating reports.

Income and expenses must be promptly and accurately recorded in order to relay the financial status of the property to the owner. For most rental properties, cash receipts and expenditures relate to one of three categories: (1) normal day-to-day operations (recorded in the income statement); (2) reserves (that may include capital improvement costs); or (3) security deposits (recorded in the balance sheet).

Funds received and disbursed should be recorded in a property management software solution—a business intelligence system that integrates property tasks, compiles property data to analyze asset performance, and produces reports to be shared with the property owner(s). Upon review of receipts and disbursements, there may be operational items that need to be changed or improved—these actions will help increase the *net operating income (NOI)*.

EVALUATION OF OPERATING FUNDS

For any income-producing investment, the measure of its success is the amount of return to the investor. For rental real estate, the most important measures are NOI and the cash flow that results from efficient operations. NOI and cash flow are derived from many contributing factors and events.

The Cash Flow Chart

There are specific terms used by the real estate management industry to identify the various types of income and expense relative to cash flow. The following chart shows the relationship between income and expenses:

Cash Flow Chart

Gross Potential Rental Income
+/-	Gain/Loss to Lease
–	Vacancy, Concessions & Collection Losses
=	Effective Gross Income
+	Miscellaneous Income
=	Total Income

Operating Expenses
| – | Operating Expenses |
| = | Net Operating Income (NOI) |

Other Cash Transactions
–	Annual Debt Service (Interest and Principal)
=	Before-Tax Cash Flow (this is the amount usually disbursed to the owner after deduction of a minimum bank account balance)
–	Income Tax
=	After-Tax Cash Flow

The owner's assessment of the property's investment return is usually based on before-tax or after-tax cash flow. The following sections define the components of cash flow.

Gross Potential Rental Income

The maximum income, regardless of occupancy, the property can earn from rent is its *gross potential rental income*—not to be confused with *gross potential income (GPI)* which is the absolute sum based on 100 percent occupancy. It is a statement (or financial inventory) of the amount of income the owner would receive if the building were fully leased at their current rental rates and all tenants paid rent in full, on time, and without offset. It does not indicate income actually received. Once established, this figure remains fairly constant from month to month. The only factors that affect gross potential rental income are changes in rental rates or in the space available for rent.

Changes in rental rates occur most commonly when leases are renewed or when new residents or commercial tenants move in. Changes in the leasable space are more complex. Older buildings may have storage and other areas that are unleasable. Yet, if those areas can be made leasable, the income they generate may be listed as additional rental income and contribute to the GPI at that time. For example, in an older office building, the maintenance department may currently store supplies and equipment in space in the basement that originally contained offices. While the space may no longer be usable for offices, it may be leasable to current tenants as space for storage of their supplies and records. If the space is converted to leasesable space, any scheduled rental income from the space should be itemized as additional rental income or included in miscellaneous income. Alternatively, the conversion of a basement apartment into a laundry room reduced the building's leasable footprint; however, a common area, unleasable for occupancy was formed. Any revenue from card- or coin-operated washers and dryers would be reported as ancillary income.

New developments often have a model unit, which is classified as unleasable during this time. Although models are usually in move-in condition, they are considered unleasable since they are not generating revenue and are not readily available for move-in. Model units are not typically in place when demand outpaces supply.

Gain/Loss to Lease. The amount of income gained or lost due to rental rates being higher or lower than the maximum market rents (or GPI) is *loss to lease*. This measurement is important when evaluating a property in a rising market to project future rent increases. For example, consider an apartment building that has 10 leases. In 2007, they all rented at $750. At the start of the 2008, the market rent (GPI) rose to $1,000. However, only six of the leases were up for renewal at the start of 2008. Those six rented for $1,000. The other four under the old lease continued to rent at $750. As a result, the loss to lease comes out to $250 per month for each of the four leases. The opposite can happen with gain to lease—if the existing rents are *greater* than market rents.

Vacancy, Concessions, and Collection Loss. The actual rent received is rarely equal to the gross potential rental income. Vacant space produces no income, and rents not collected represent lost or delayed income—both reduce the rent collected. In the cash flow chart, *vacancy and collection loss* is subtracted from gross potential rental income to indicate the actual amount of rental income for a given reporting period—usually a month. Most real estate managers list vacancy losses and delinquent rents separately. When finally paid, delinquent rent is added to the income category and not considered a true loss of income, whereas nonpayment of rent *is* a true loss of income. Although vacancies represent a loss of income for the period of time they remain vacant, they optimistically do not represent a total loss. Instead, vacancies simply reduce gross potential rental income until they become occupied.

Effective Gross Income. Subtracting the vacancy, concessions, and collection loss amount from the gross potential rental income yields the *effective gross income* of the property.

TWO TYPES OF VACANCY

1. **Physical vacancy** is the percentage of units (apartments, office suites, store spaces) that are unoccupied but are available for lease.
2. **Economic vacancy** is the percentage of units that are not producing income. In addition to physical vacancy, economic vacancy includes the following:

   - *Space that is leased but does not yet produce income.* A resident may rent an apartment in August, but the rent payments may not begin until October. Commercial space is often leased in an unfinished condition (tenant improvements must be completed in order to occupy the space); rent payment (which may include reimbursement of tenant improvement costs) usually begins after construction is complete and the tenant moves in.

   - *Delinquencies.* If a resident or commercial tenant is behind in rent payments, the unit or space is classified as occupied, but it is not producing income.

   - *Leasable space that is used for other purposes or is otherwise unleasable.* Spaces used as models for leasing purposes, manager offices, or storage space; apartments provided as compensation to staff members who live onsite; and apartments or commercial spaces that are not in fit condition to be leased or occupied.

Miscellaneous Income. Although the cost of rent provides the vast majority of income, most income-producing properties receive some additional or ancillary income. Income derived from sources other than scheduled rent, e.g., coin-operated laundry equipment, vending machines, late fees, is categorized as *miscellaneous income* (or *unscheduled income*). Other related sources of income include installations (e.g., *air rights,* interior building wiring), leased storage space, storage lockers, parking or garage rental, and express shipment drop boxes. Unscheduled income may also include previously unpaid rent that is recovered after a tenant no longer occupies the rental space, usually after the matter has been turned over to a collection agency or an attorney. In addition to these unscheduled payments, *pass-through operating expenses*—common area mainte-nance (CAM) and taxes that the owner charges to the tenants—are taken into account as miscellaneous income.

For commercial properties, any miscellaneous items are classified as scheduled income in a separate line item since these expenses are estimated in the budget and are paid by tenants as "additional rent." Delinquent operating expense reimbursements are treated the same as "base rent" in most commercial leases; therefore, a commercial real estate manager can take action in the same manner as they would for base rent delinquencies. Altogether, miscellaneous income may be generated for the property, but on the whole, it is a very small amount in comparison to the income derived from the rental of tenant and resident space.

Total Income. Adding miscellaneous income to effective gross income generates the total income of the asset. This figure should match the total amount collected (gross receipts) during the reporting period. In this respect, the effective gross income total can help verify the accounting for the rent and other receipts from miscellaneous income during the accounting period. Effective gross income—which can vary substantially from the gross poten-tial rental income for the property—is the amount that is available to pay building expenses, annual debt service, and a return on the owner's investment.

Operating Expenses

Any expense associated with products or services required in the operation of the building are the property's responsibility to pay. Everything related to maintaining the condition of the property and providing services to its occupants (with the exception of debt service) fits into the category of *operating expenses*. Such items include payroll, office supplies, maintenance, repairs, groundskeeping, util-ities, decorating, and security. Owner expenses such as insurance, real estate taxes, and fees for legal and accounting services are also considered operating expenses, and they are passed through to the tenants. (The section on accounting discusses categories of expenses in more detail.)

One objective of tracking operating expenses is to calculate how much of the effective gross income remains after payment of the bills; keeping this figure at a consistently high level is important. Real estate managers and owners compare operating expenses as a percentage of effective gross income to industry statistics—a measure of the effectiveness of the financial management of the property.[1]

Net Operating Income (NOI). The remainder, after deducting *Operating Expenses* from *Effective Gross Income,* is the NOI—an objective measure of the financial performance of the asset. Overall property value is a ratio of NOI and capitalization rate; therefore, higher NOI produces greater property value. Maximum NOI is achieved through optimization of income while controlling expenses. Any variance in effective gross income, operating expenses, or both will cause NOI to vary. As part of management services, operating expenses are paid from NOI.

Annual Debt Service (ADS). An owner's performance evaluation of a property does not end with NOI. The *annual debt service (ADS)* obligation of a property—the amount required to repay the mortgage—is deducted from NOI. Although this amount is a recurring expense, it is not an operating expense. An owner will want to know if a property will generate enough cash to service the debt and provide a satisfactory return on their investment. In some instances, real estate managers handle the payment of debt service for the owner—other owners prefer to make those payments themselves. Determining who makes the debt service payments is a point subject to negotiation in developing the management agreement. (More information on the management agreement is explained in Chapter 5.)

---

1. The IREM annual *Income and Expense Reports* are good resources for comparing expenses to other properties.

Cash Flow. The amount remaining after subtracting debt service and capital expenditures, leasing fees (for commercial properties), etc., from NOI is the *cash flow* (Exhibits 6.1 and 6.2). When the required debt service payment exceeds the amount of NOI, the cash flow is negative. Cash flow is the owner's before-tax income and one measure of *return on investment (ROI).*

Two important payments are made from the cash flow of the property. These are contributions to the (1) *reserve fund* and (2) *personal income taxes. Reserve funds* are monies set aside to accumulate for future use; *capital expenses* that are passed through to tenants are included in operating expenses and reduce NOI. However, capital

---

EXHIBIT 6.1

Calculating Cash Flow

The cash flow chart may also be presented as shown here. As indicated, some of the expenses are market forces, while others are owner decisions. This more detailed format lists loss items separately and accounts for pass-through expense reimbursements (typical for commercial properties) and reserve funds.

	Gross Potential Rental Income
+/–	Gain/Loss to Lease
–	Vacancy and Collection Loss
=	**Net Rent Revenue**
+	Miscellaneous Income
+	Expense Reimbursements
=	**Effective Gross Income (EGI)**
–	Operating Expenses
=	**Net Operating Income (NOI)**
–	Annual Debt Service (ADS)
–	Reserve Funds and Capital Expenses
=	**Before Tax Cash Flow**
–	Income Tax
=	**After-Tax Cash Flow**

MARKET FORCES

INVESTOR DECISIONS

EXHIBIT 6.2

Description for Calculating Cash Flow

Gross Potential Income (GPI)	Maximum amount of rental income a property can produce when 100% of the property is leased 100% of the time at full-market rents
+/– Gain/Loss to Lease	Loss due to rents being less than the GPI, OR the gain if existing rents are greater than market rents
– Vacancy and Collection Loss	Physical and/or economic vacancies that include available but unoccupied space, or the loss from concessions or space not available for lease; and collection losses of delinquent and/or uncollectible rent
= Net Rent Revenue	Difference between GPI and losses due to below-market rents, vacancy, and delinquencies
+ Miscellaneous Income	Income from any source other than rent (e.g., parking, coin-operated laundry)
+ Expense Reimbursements	Pass-through operating expenses to the tenant, (e.g., real estate taxes, insurance, or common area maintenance [CAM])
= Effective Gross Income (EGI)	Net rent revenue plus miscellaneous income and reimbursement for expenses
– Operating Expenses	Costs associated with operating the property (e.g., real estate taxes, salaries, insurance, maintenance, utilities, and administrative costs)
= Net Operating Income (NOI)	EGI less operating expenses
– Annual Debt Service (ADS)	Annual payments of principal and interest on a loan
– Reserve Funds and Capital Expenses	The property may be required to add reserves for replacement, leasing commissions, and tenant improvements expenses, or capital improvements expenses above the before-tax cash flow line
= Before-Tax Cash Flow	Amount usually disbursed to the owner after deduction of a minimum bank account balance
– Income Tax	Calculated and paid by the property owner
= After-Tax Cash Flow	Measure of the property's financial performance, which determines the ability to generate cash flow through its operations

expenditures for improving vacant space for occupancy would be below NOI and only affect cash flow. The owner's requirements and the property's tax situation determine these items. For example, homeowners' associations (e.g., in condominiums) are required by law to maintain replacement reserves—institutional owners typically do not accumulate reserves.

A property owner generally calculates and pays its income tax. Depending on the management agreement, the after-tax cash flow received by the owner may be the same as cash flow. In fact, if the owner has no debt on the property, or if the annual debt service (ADS) is paid directly by the owner and a reserve fund is not maintained, cash flow is the equivalent to NOI.

RETURN ON INVESTMENT (ROI)

Investment return may be expressed in dollars (cash flow) or as a percentage. The percentage rate is often referred to as *return on investment (ROI)* or *cash-on-cash return.* The percentage of ROI is calculated by relating the annual NOI from the property to the dollar amount of the owner's initial cash investment. The formula follows: NOI ÷ initial cash investment = percent return.

If an investor purchases a property with $100,000 down and the property produces an annual NOI of $10,000, the result is a 10 percent return.

$$\frac{\$10,000 \ (NOI)}{\$100,000 \ (initial \ cash \ investment)} = 10\% \ (return)$$

The same formula can be used to calculate ROI based on pretax or after-tax cash flow. This is a very basic description of the calculation of ROI. For many real estate owners, the calculation is more complicated; such calculations are studied extensively in the IREM courses on *Investment Real Estate Financing and Valuation.*

Other Operating Fund Considerations

The amount of the annual debt service depends on how much cash the owner used to purchase the property and the terms of the mortgage loan. The property owner may ask for an evaluation of the loan terms—based on current rates in the market—to consider whether the owner or the property could benefit from refinancing the debt. Fiduciary responsibilities to the owner include evaluating alternatives and making recommendations to increase an owner's return.

Depending on the current market, an owner may be able to refinance an existing loan at a lower interest rate, for a longer term, or for a larger or smaller principal amount. Sometimes refinancing will lower the amount of periodic debt service payments, thereby increasing the before-tax cash flow and producing a higher return on the owner's investment. Taking equity out of one property allows the investor to diversify holdings and perhaps purchase a an additional property for the management portfolio. Conversely, some investors prefer to be more conservative and keep the equity in their property as high as possible. Therefore, it is extremely important to know the owner's investment style.

Regardless of the property's price and whether the owner purchased the property with cash or borrowed funds, the property's NOI will be the same. The constancy of the NOI of an income-producing property, therefore, makes that sum a definitive measure of the property's market value. Because of that constancy, the value is easily measured against that of the property's competition as well.

Property Valuation. Maximization of NOI, regular repayment of debt service, and satisfactory return on the investment while maintaining or improving the physical property will increase the likelihood of a management agreement renewal. The level of NOI represents more than the owner's return on investment—it directly affects the *value* of the property. It's important to have a continued focus on the greater success of the properties. Do not ignore required maintenance or raise the rent strictly in pursuit of increasing NOI in order to acquire a management agreement renewal.

One method of calculating the estimated market value of income-producing real estate is the *income capitalization approach.* It is important to note that cap rates can be acquired, which can be obtained by talking to various brokers—in that case, they can be subjective and generalized. Actual cap rates can be based on the NOI and sales price of a recent sale, among other methods.

Using the income capitalization approach, estimated market value (V) is calculated by dividing the annual net operating income (I) by a *capitalization rate* (R) as indicated in the equation that follows. The capitalization rate or *cap rate* is a decimal constant.

$$\frac{I}{R} = V, \text{ or } \frac{\text{Net Operating Income (NOI)}}{\text{Capitalization Rate}} = \frac{\text{Estimated}}{\text{Property Value}}$$

As an example, if the cap rate is 10 percent and the annual NOI of a property is $100,000, the property's estimated market value is $1 million ($100,000 ÷ .10 = $1,000,000). The same property valued with an 8.5 percent cap rate ($100,000 ÷ .085) has an estimated value of $1,176,471. The lower the cap rate, the higher the value. The higher the cap rate, the lower the value.

Conversely, if a neighboring property sells for $2.4 million and has an NOI of $200,000, the cap rate can be determined ($200,000 ÷ $2,400,000 = 8.33 cap rate). Using the IRV formula, if two of the three numbers are available, the third number can be determined. If a property is similar in type, size, amenities, etc., using 8.33 as a cap rate to value, the similar property would be a fair estimation of its value.

Investors and brokers use cap rates to determine the potential return that a property will produce. An owner whose goal is to preserve value has a much different (usually lower) expectation of a return on investment than one whose goal is capital appreciation.

The cap rate for a specific property depends on the property type, recent sales of comparable properties in the area, and market conditions, including interest rates. Variations in the cap rate have major effects on value—which declines as the cap rate rises.[2] Cap rates are determined by the market, not the investor. Therefore a real estate manager can influence value only by improving a stabilized NOI, not by adjusting the cap rate.

When the same cap rate is used in a comparison of similar properties in a market area, the property with the highest annual NOI will have the highest estimated market/property value. If the NOI of a property decreases and the cap rate does not change, the property value will decrease—this is in addition to the reduction in periodic income resulting from the lower NOI. On the other hand, any factor that helps to increase NOI also increases property value. For example, a rent increase of $100 per month on one leased space equates to an additional $1,200 annually to NOI. Market and/or property value is calculated based upon 12 months of revenue. At a 10 percent cap rate, that increase in rent improved the property's estimated market value as follows:

$12,000 ($100 × 12 months = $1,200 ÷ .10 = $12,000)

IMPACTING PROPERTY VALUE

The following demonstrates a dramatically positive financial impact that the real estate manager wields in impacting the value of a property:

For example, a 200-unit apartment building with an NOI of $500,000 and a capitalization rate of 8% yields a value of $6,250,000. A rent increase of $10 per month each month from each resident will boost the value of the property 4.8% ($230,000/$6,250,000) to $6,555,000.

---

2. The cap rate is also considered an indication of the risk involved in an investment. The higher the cap rate, the riskier the investment.

Income Tax. Real estate managers may have no involvement whatsoever in the tax paid on the income generated by a managed asset. However, due to the growing complexity of income taxation and its effect on real estate ownership, a basic understanding of taxes is needed. Income taxes on profits from real property owner-ship usually are levied against the individual investor's personal income. Stated very simply, if an owner's taxable income from a property is $10,000 and that amount is subject to tax at a 28 percent rate, the amount of tax owed is $2,800 ($10,000 × .28). Assuming a before-tax cash flow of $15,000, the after-tax cash flow would be $12,200 ($15,000 – $2,800). Because each individual's tax obliga-tions are different, only an estimate of *before tax cash flow (BTCF) can be calculated.* Professional tax accountants and attorneys can best advise an owner regarding the taxes on investment income and the resulting after-tax cash flow.

Reserve and Security Deposit Funds. The operating funds of a property that determine NOI are usually the most extensive and require the most attention, but reserves and security deposits also need continual monitoring. While operating funds may not always be in an interest-bearing account, reserve funds sometimes depend on regular earnings for part of their value. Depending on various state and real estate licensing laws, security deposits must be maintained and accounted for separately. In Oregon, for example, security deposits must be recorded, but they can be sent to the owner as a return on their investment. In that case, the security deposits are listed as a liability on the balance sheet. It is critical to know the different federal, state, and local licensing and accounting laws.

Reserve Fund. A *reserve fund* is money regularly set aside to pay future expenses. If this money comes from the income of the property, it is deducted from NOI. A reserve fund is commonly used to pay for major capital expenditures (e.g., boiler or roof replacement). Regular operating expenses are generally paid from monthly receipts.

The reserve fund can be kept in an interest-bearing checking or money market account. If the reserve fund earns interest, some real estate managers use that interest to accumulate funds for operating expenses that are not paid monthly. Real estate taxes and insurance premiums are often due only once or twice a year. Prorating the amounts and accumulating funds on a monthly basis means the money will be available when the payments are due, and cash flow will remain fairly constant from month to month. Any payments for operating expenses made from the reserve fund should be recorded as such.

Specific amounts deposited into the reserve fund for *capital improvements* can be a set percentage of effective gross income or NOI. Because deposits to the reserve account are usually for a predetermined purpose—such as replacing major equipment in five years or remodeling apartments according to an established schedule— the periodic payments into this account can be budgeted as a set amount. With commercial properties, reserves are sometimes paid by the tenants through their operating expense reimbursements and are to be used for major capital expenditures. There is an obligation to account for those funds to the tenants who may have contributed. For example, if the funds are not spent (or not entirely spent) in a predetermined period, the owner may need to return those unused funds to the tenants, depending upon the specific lease language.

Developing a reserve for *capital expenditures* usually requires accounting for the funds on a capital expenditure report and a ledger. The expenditure is paid as a check drawn on the reserve account. It is important to note that the accumulation of reserve funds reduces the amount of cash available to the owner from the income of the property. Because of this, an owner may be reluctant to allow the accumulation of such funds.[3] There also may be different perspectives on the adequacy of reserve funds and their disposition. The availability of reserve funds is extremely important

---

3. It should be noted that money put away for reserves still represents profit and is taxable to the investor.

and subject to negotiation in establishing the management agreement, or as a requirement in tenant leases.

Security Deposits. Residents and commercial tenants usually pay a security deposit as a guarantee of their performance of the terms of the lease (payment of rent, preservation of the property, etc.). Many states regulate the maintenance of security deposits. Some require property owners to hold the deposits in trust or in a separate bank account that is established and maintained exclusively for security deposits. Many states and municipalities require property owners to pay interest on the amount held and may require that security deposit funds be held in an interest-bearing account. Such laws also commonly stipulate the rate of interest to be paid. The interest rate is typically low enough that earnings on the security deposit account exceed what the owner owes to the resident or commercial tenant, with a small amount of additional income provided.

In some states, residential properties incur rigid penalties when these requirements are not scrupulously observed. In other states, legislatures are slow to act and landlords have frequently been required to pay slightly higher interest to tenants. If the state does not require the segregation of these funds, landlords may use them as operating capital, and that is often ample compensation for the difference; however, *commingling* of security deposits with operating funds is not recommended.

For tax purposes, the interest the account earns is reported as income to the owner if it is not distributed to the tenants. To reduce (or eliminate) the owner's tax obligation on the interest, checks to residents or commercial tenants might need to be issued annually with the tax distribution reported to the Internal Revenue Service (IRS) and to the tenants.

Knowledge of current tax laws, application to such funds, and implication to an owner is a fiduciary responsibility of real estate management. Even if the amount of interest owed is relatively small, the cumulative amount owed to all tenants could require the owner to pay much higher income taxes if the account is not properly maintained.

ACCOUNTING FOR INCOME AND EXPENSES

One of the main responsibilities in real estate management is collection and deposit of rents and other regular property income into a checking account maintained exclusively for the payment of property operating expenses. Any monies intended for security deposits or property replacement reserves are deposited into a separate account that is not used for operating expenses. This basic fiduciary responsibility is routine but very important because misappropriation or errors can have drastic and long-lasting effects. It is important to understand how to properly account for income and expenses for licensing, tax, and lease requirements, while staying in line with the owner's preferences. Records of income and expenses must be accurate because these records are the basis for disbursing funds to the owner and filing income taxes. For obvious reasons, these records must also be consistent to avoid duplications and omissions, verify budget projections, and explain variances.

Accounting Systems

Based on the management agreement, a specific chart of accounts and other documents to record receipts and disbursements using the basic accounting systems and designated method of accounting for the property can be created.

Chart of Accounts. The best way to ensure accuracy and consistency in accounting is to establish a *chart of accounts* (Exhibit 6.3), which usually has account numbers or codes for specific categories of income and expense. No chart of accounts is definitive—most buildings have unique features that require separate categories, entries, or subentries. Generally, the type of property and its size affect the scope of a chart of accounts.

Depending on the level of detail desired, income and expense categories can be grouped under general headings or subdivided further. A detailed chart of accounts usually provides account codes for security deposits, reserve funds, and debt service payments. The chart can identify *all* income and expense items for a property since specific capital expenditures may also have separate account codes. Real estate managers use this information not only for purposes of accounting, but also for reporting to the owner and others as well as for preparing accurate budgets. In fact, some real estate managers who are developing a chart of accounts for a new property seek advice from professional accountants who help ensure they identify all of the separate accounts that a specific property needs.

EXHIBIT 6.3

Common Categories for a Chart of Accounts

Operating Income	**Operating Expenses**
Rents	Management Fee and Administrative
Miscellaneous Income	Costs
	Payroll and Related Expenses
	Utilities (Gas, Electricity, Telephone)
	Cleaning
	Maintenance and Repairs
	Supplies
	Miscellaneous Services
	Security
	Groundskeeping
	Water and Sewer
	Rubbish Removal
	Snow Removal
	Interior Painting and Decorating
	Recreational Amenities
	Real Estate Tax
	Advertising and Promotion
	Insurance

These major categories are usually divided into subaccounts to facilitate tracking of specific income and expense items.

Accounting Methods. Regardless of the type of accounting system used, one method of accounting must be agreed upon to ensure consistent, accurate, and easily understood financial records and reports. The entire accounting and reporting system usually conforms to one of the following two methods: (1) *cash-basis accounting,* which records income when it is received and payments as they are made, and (2) *accrual-basis accounting,* which records income when it is *due* and expenses when they are *incurred*, but the records may not reflect actual receipts and disbursements. Some real estate managers use a modified cash system in which expenses that are not due monthly (insurance, taxes) are accounted on an accrual basis. When using such a mixed system, the records of NOI should be adjusted to reflect the partial accruals.

Income Categories

For residential properties, the only distinction between income sources may be rents, utilities (billed to residents), and miscellaneous income. For commercial properties, tenants often pay one or more amounts in addition to *base rent* each month. Certain charges may be categorized as *additional rent* if the owner passes all (or part) of the real estate taxes, property insurance, and common area maintenance (CAM) or operating expense costs to the tenants. *Tenant improvements (TIs)* are charged back to the tenant (sometimes with interest) may also be categorized as additional rent.

Where leases for retail space require payment of *percentage rent,* such income would be accounted separately from the base rent. If tenants are charged for parking, a separate income category would be warranted; this is especially true if parking space is leased to non-occupants of the building. Some items discussed earlier as sources of miscellaneous income (e.g., rents or fees from telecommunications installations or storage spaces) may be itemized separately, especially when the amounts are substantial.

MAJOR SOURCES OF INCOME FOR COMMERCIAL PROPERTIES

Revenue

- Base rent
- Percentage rent
- Parking income

Other Cash Transactions

- Debt service
- Reserves
- Capital improvements
- Leasing fees

Expenses

- Utilities
- Repairs and maintenance
- Insurance
- Property taxes
- Management expenses
- Common area maintenance (CAM)
- Extra services

EXPENSE CATEGORIES

Although amounts and types of expenses vary by property, the real estate management professional recognizes some common expense categories. Every real estate management company defines expenses in its own way or by the owner's request. Some major categories might have to be subdivided to adequately account for the operating expenses of a specific property. In addition, property owners sometimes request unique expense categorizations. It's important to understand and consistently apply the management firm's standard categorization of expenses and then adjust them as needed to accommodate the owner's needs and wishes.

Management Fee and Administrative Costs

The compensation paid to the managing agent may be a percentage of the effective gross income of the property, a flat fee, or a combination of the two. When a combination fee is used, the flat fee is usually a stated minimum, and the actual fee paid is the greater of the two amounts. The minimum fee assures compensation for management if the effective gross income is below expectations. *Administrative costs* cover supplies, postage, and other common expenses associated with operating an on-site office. At times, the management company may also charge some of these office expenses—if they can be segregated by property—to the owner for reimbursement. Nonstandard charges such as fees for tax preparation are usually listed as administrative costs.

Payroll and Related Expenses

Payroll and benefits may be listed as a single item, but the various deductions and distributions usually require separate accounting for wages or salaries, withholding taxes, benefits, and the various employer contributions required by state and federal governments for Social Security, Medicare, and unemployment taxes. Because of the complex accounting, it may be easier to list each of these items as a subaccount under payroll. As an alternative, payroll may be established as a subaccount in the appropriate operating expense category on the basis of the employees' duties (e.g., administration, maintenance, and groundskeeping). In such cases, subentries would be made for salaries, benefits, and taxes. Ultimately, the specific listing for payroll (and any chart of accounts category) should be determined by the management company's and owner's preferences. For instance, some owners may prefer the payroll category to be separately recorded as subcategories of administrative, marketing, maintenance, or management. The most important point is to be consistent.

The payroll schedule can skew monthly reports and the monthly flow of cash through the accounts of the property. Management firms generally receive rental income 12 times a year, on the first of every month, but they rarely use a monthly payroll, and a weekly payroll is often impractical. Paying employees biweekly (26 times a year) yields 10 months with two pay periods and two with three pay periods. To avoid such variations, most real estate managers commonly use a semi-monthly payroll system or they budget actual pay periods per month.

A *semi-monthly payroll system* pays employees twice a month—usually on the 15th and the last day of the month. That system balances payroll distribution against rental income. Because rent is commonly collected on the first of the month, activities during the first week of the month usually center on processing incoming checks and issuing late notices for unpaid rents. The middle of the month is usually less active from an accounting standpoint, so a semi-monthly payroll system can help to ensure steady bank balances, a monthly payment to the owner that is fairly constant, and a manageable schedule of activities in the accounting department. A semi-monthly payroll may require additional computations for employees paid by the hour because the number of workdays per pay period varies, but the savings that result from preparing payroll only 24 times a year instead of 26 may offset the additional work. Some commercial properties hire outside vendors for all property services and, therefore, have no payroll expenses at all. The cost of property management services is borne by the property management firm itself.

Insurance

Insurance premiums come due on varying schedules, although semi-annual and annual payments are most common. This category is usually limited to insurance relating to the property. Employee medical coverage, workers' compensation, and employment insurance taxes (Social Security, Medicare, unemployment) are accounted as payroll expenses. The types of insurance usually included in this category follow:

- **Fire insurance.** Protects the policyholder against all direct loss or damage to the insured property from fire.
- **Extended coverage (EC).** Usually purchased as an addition to fire insurance—covers loss from specific perils such as windstorm,

hail, explosion, aircraft, vehicles, smoke, riots and civil commotion, and water damage from fire fighting.

- **Flood insurance.** Available to any property that is located in a community that participates in the National Flood Insurance Program (NFIP).
- **Earthquake insurance.** Features a high deductible, which makes this type of insurance useful if the entire property is destroyed, but not useful if the property is merely damaged. Rates depend on location and the probability of an earthquake.
- **Terrorism insurance.** Signed into law on December 26, 2007, as the Terrorism Risk Insurance Program Reauthorization Act (TRIA) of 2007. The law provides for a transparent system of shared public and private compensation for insured losses resulting from acts of terrorism.
- **Boiler insurance.** Pays for any damage resulting from a boiler malfunction.
- **Property damage insurance.** Protects against liability for damage to the property of others that occurs on the insured property.
- **Bodily injury insurance.** Protects against liability for damages arising out of injury or death occurring on the property.
- **Employment practices liability insurance (EPL).** A type of coverage that protects businesses from the financial consequences associated with a variety of employment-related lawsuits such as charges of racial or age discrimination, sexual harassment, wrongful termination, or noncompliance with the Americans with Disabilities Act. EPL insurance also helps protect businesses against legal dismissals that flare up between employees and third parties, such as vendors or customers.
- **Special form insurance.** Previously referred to as *all-risk insurance*—covers damage from any cause that is not specifically excluded from the policy. This type of policy includes most property and liability coverages offered as separate policies—some states require that liability coverage be a separate policy.

- **Rent loss insurance.** Protects the owner from loss of income resulting from damage that makes all or part of the property unleasable.
- **Owner, landlord, and tenant (OLT) liability insurance.** Covers claims against a property owner, a landlord, or a tenant arising out of injury to a person or persons on the property.
- **Umbrella liability insurance.** Provides additional liability coverage beyond the limits of the basic liability policy.
- **Automobile insurance.** Purchased for service vehicles owned by and operated for the property and to protect the property owner from liability incurred as a result of operating these vehicles.
- **Fidelity bonding.** Protects individuals against financial loss that might result from dishonest acts of another specific individual. Though usually obtained from an insurance company, this is not an insurance policy as such. It is a three-party arrangement called a *surety*. A management firm usually purchases fidelity bonds for its employees—specifically, those who handle money. The bonds would not be an operating expense for the property unless they are maintained for site staff that the property owner employed.

Some properties may need additional insurance coverage because of special conditions; more favorable premiums may be obtained by insuring several properties under one *blanket policy*. The best practice is to consult with an insurance agent who specializes in the type of property in question.

REAL-TIME DATA AND REPORTING

While the organization of accounting departments and their extensions into the field may vary by company and property type, the accounting software will be the main source for generating both financial (external) and managerial (internal) reports. Contemporary property management software has produced a change in expectations because the software makes possible the generation of real-time reports from multiple locations. It is now assumed that new data will be input immediately, and accuracy is expected on an up-to-the-minute basis. The features of such software make it possible for real estate managers, site managers, and company executives to have instant access to all permitted information.

In the past, when administrative staff controlled the flow of data, they also controlled the generation of reports. If data entry staff fell behind in entering payments, for example, they would just delay generating a delinquency report until everything was caught up and the deposits were in the bank. Such delays are no longer considered acceptable; those who can access information, even from thousands of miles away, expect all data to be collected and entered as it is received.

An even more recent trend has property owners accessing real-time data about their properties. Web-based access to property information can be granted as needed and desired to owners, their asset managers, and virtually any stakeholder in the investment. Some real estate management firms actually use this as a differentiating factor in promoting their business. A property owner's choice of a real estate management company may be influenced by the ability to generate instant reports or by having 24/7 access to data online.

Financial Reporting Requirements

Property owners have varying needs for financial reporting, and real estate managers must be flexible in generating financial statements to meet those needs. In daily practice, real estate managers are exposed to financial reports from four general sources:

- External reports generated by a property owner's accounting professionals, including financial statements and tax returns
- Reports generated by another property management firm, by the owner of a property if it is self-managed, or sometimes by a court-appointed receiver or bank

- Reports generated by the real estate management firm, both for internal analysis and for reporting to the property owner
- Forecasts prepared by brokers for a property under management or under consideration for purchase by a potential or existing client

Typically, real estate managers collect property-operating data in great detail. It is organized and categorized, and then reports are provided at the level of detail needed by the particular user. Whether historical data is intended for external financial reports or for internal managerial reporting, the collected data is the same— it is just organized differently based on the type of report being generated.

The accounting department in most real estate management firms is charged with preparing financial reports for the property owner—usually monthly or as agreed to between the owner and manager—to meet contractual requirements. The type of statements, methodology, and frequency are determined by the owner, along with whether reports are delivered directly to the owner or to the asset manager responsible for the account.

A real estate manager must be able to understand the differences in financial reporting from various sources and to modify the statements into a format that allows for analysis of the property. In general, the real estate manager plays two roles in financial reporting. He or she may:

- Analyze reports and draft a cover letter that explains salient factors of the period's operations, including variance explanations
- Prepare supplemental managerial reports to include with the financial reports

External Reporting

Reports for external parties tend to give an overall financial picture, focusing on the figures themselves. They provide a historical representation of the performance of a business, describing how a property has performed in the past. Preparing financial reports for external use is part of financial accounting. Financial accounting is a system of classifying financial transactions that documents a company's financial position in the form of a balance sheet and an income statement (external reports). These condensed external reports are sent to the various stakeholders in the property, including lending institutions, the IRS for tax purposes, and stock-holders and other types of owners. They often include a narrative portion with a summary that describes how the owner's goals and objectives for the period have been achieved. The narrative report should be supported by the following:

- Financial monthly and/or annual reports or statements
- Summary of cash receipts and disbursements
- Budget variance report
- Capital improvements recap
- Income statement

The most fundamental financial statements shared with external stakeholders are the balance sheet and the income statement. The periodic management report also is often accompanied by a rent roll that provides details of lease arrangements with all tenants to date as well as vacancies. However, the content of these reports should always be tailored to satisfy the owner's requirements.

Internal Reporting

In general, reports for internal use include more detail about specific financial transactions and the manager's assumptions about a property. Internal reports use accounting data in a format that allows the user to arrange the data for specific analyses and to forecast performance. They are based on historical or forecasted information and address past performance, current data, or future expectations. The real estate manager uses this information from the past, evaluates it in terms of current market conditions, and projects future performance.

While the information in internal reports should be complete, they do not always have to follow a strict format. Some of the reports provided to external stakeholders are also commonly used internally as part of managerial accounting. Some common reports used internally are listed below and are sorted by property type:

Type of Report	Residential	Office	Retail
Rent Rolls	✓	✓	✓
Vacancy Reports	✓	✓	✓
Delinquency Reports	✓	✓	✓
Accounts Payable, Receivable	✓	✓	✓
Percentage Rent Reports			✓
Tenant Sales Analysis Reports			✓

Rent Roll. While the rent roll is perhaps one of the most popular reports for real estate owners and managers alike, there is little agreement on exactly what it should contain. Most property management software programs have at least one rent roll report that discloses information to varying degrees. In some cases it is a report on unit occupancy; in others it schedules out accounts receivables. The rent roll almost always lists data relevant to the specific resident/tenant or unit/suite when vacant (rent, size, lease commencement and expiration, date vacated, etc.).

Vacancy Report. A vacancy report lists and describes the property's unoccupied space, whether in square feet for commercial space or by unit in the case of multifamily or condominium units. In many cases, it will calculate the accrued loss of rent due to vacancy (economic vacancy) and the number of square feet or units vacant (physical vacancy). Vacancy reports may also include such information as the number of days a particular space has remained vacant or when the apartment will be market ready and re-leased.

Delinquency Report. While a rent roll may display balances due, it does not necessarily show the period for which rent has been unpaid. A delinquency report displays the amount due, the detail of what is unpaid, and the number of accounting periods for which a balance has remained unpaid.

Accounts Payable. Unpaid invoices are a liability of the property owner, and the amount of money owed to vendors must be properly disclosed in financial statements. The accounts payable aging statement may summarize all unpaid invoices; or it may be a detailed schedule of each invoice not paid, the period that it is past due, and why it was not paid on time. Significant delinquencies in accounts payable should be pointed out to an owner in the cover letter to the financial statements. In addition to these financial statements, the accounting department usually includes a copy of all relevant reconciled bank statements.

Accounts Receivable. The statement may be very detailed, as in the delinquency report, or it may just summarize balances due and the period over which they have remained unpaid. A real estate manager must be alert to informing the accounting department or designated individual to write off rents that are unpaid for an extended period. Some companies establish a policy that any account unpaid over a specified period—perhaps 90 days—is considered a bad debt and deducted from accrued rent revenue. In most real estate management circumstances, especially multi-family properties, eviction proceedings will be well underway for residents or tenants that have reached that level of delinquency.

BUDGETING

Budgeting is not an exact science. The actual income and expenses of a property rarely (if ever) conform precisely to budget projections. A budget is a tool; it is the working guide throughout the budget year. Real estate managers use it to establish the priority of spending (based on the income the property produces and the expenses incurred) and to estimate cash flow. The budget helps minimize the variance of the property's NOI and assess the property's cash position at a given time. When an unexpected expense creates a cash shortage, the budget can guide the evaluation of alternatives for meeting the expense.

Several types of budgets exist. Real estate management commonly uses three: (1) operating budgets, (2) capital budgets, and (3) long-range budgets.

Operating Budget

The most commonly used budget is an *operating budget* that lists the principal (or regular) sources of income and expenses for the property, usually on a monthly basis. The gross potential rental income listed in the income and expense reports for the property should be fairly constant from month to month. Every other item of income or expense for the property is added to or subtracted from the gross potential rental income to calculate NOI. The NOI reflects any variance in individual entries. Therefore, even though gross potential rental income may be a fixed amount, the NOI and cash flow can vary substantially. A budget permits better projection and monitoring of income and expenses.

Aside from showing the sources of income and expenses for a property, a budget indicates *when the transactions are expected to occur.* Differing monthly amounts allocated for heat and air conditioning throughout the year reflect seasonal variations in energy consumption. Advertising expenditures for an established apartment building may be minimal for most months, so the greatest part of funds allocated for this expense are divided among the months of highest expected leasing activity. On the other hand, a

---

TYPES OF BUDGETS USED IN REAL ESTATE MANAGEMENT

1. Operating (annual)
2. Capital
3. Long-range

A separate *marketing budget* is usually prepared each year (an extension of the annual operating budget) as well as during lease-up of a new property or following rehabilitation of an old property.

new development or a property that is undergoing extensive rehabilitation may require a large advertising budget divided equally throughout the year to reflect the intensity of the leasing activity.

The budget is the starting point for considering alternatives for paying unanticipated expenses. If winter weather is exceptionally cold and snowy, higher fuel consumption generally increases the fuel expense for the property. Greater demand for fuel usually leads to price increases, and that, coupled with increased consumption, can devastate a fuel budget. Energy providers may also provide alternatives. A budget plan at a fixed rate may be offered. However, at the end of the billing cycle, any overages may be billed and the budget must account for that.[4]

Other increases in season-related expenses, such as snow removal, can have a significant effect on cash flow.[5] Snow removal companies typically offer two choices: (1) paying per occurrence or (2) contracting a monthly set rate throughout the season. However, there is a risk on the part of each party to the contract. If the contract for is set for a monthly rate and it is a dry year, the cost will be more than if a per-occurrence plan was chosen.

When such extra expenses conflict with projections made in the budget, review other projected expenses to see if another budgeted expense can be postponed temporarily—or omitted altogether for the year. Those changes will offer a way to offset part or all of the extra weather-related expenses. In accordance with the terms outlined in the management agreement, notify the owner of any action proposed or taken.

---

4. Energy companies will make allowances for agreements that are to their advantage. For example, they may offer a lower rate to buildings that are willing to switch from gas to oil reserve tanks if demand is too high, or in hotter climates with air-conditioned buildings, they might consider charging lower rates if residents or tenants are willing to endure short "shut-offs" during peak usage.

5. For example, online statistics are provided by regional meteorologists that state the average number of snowfalls with accumulations of two inches or more that will require plowing, but the forecast for the upcoming season is for unusually heavy snow.

Annual Budget. The *annual budget* is the most common form of operating budget. There are two kinds of annual budgets: (1) historical and (2) zero-based. To prepare a *historical budget*, review income and expenses from previous years. A *zero-based budget* consists solely of projections—it ignores past operating expenses. The annual budget projects the whole year's income and expenses for each account. If any departures from normal operations for the upcoming year are anticipated, e.g., temporarily high vacancies because of remodeling, the budget should account for them as well.

Possibly one of the most valuable aspects of this annual exercise is the presentation of the proposed new budget to the owner. It offers a natural opportunity for the owner to discuss the past performance of the property and adjust individual budget items as he or she previews the coming year. By reviewing each item in the budget, explain how anticipated income and expenses may affect the property's performance. Gross potential rental income, vacancy and collection loss, and effective gross income categories will reflect planned increases in rents. An increase in staff size or wage adjustments will affect payroll expenses. Before the budget is implemented, the real estate manager and property owner must agree on and review each line item in detail.[6]

Monthly Financial Statement. The budget is often developed in greater detail by allocating an amount for each line item on a month-by-month basis, as shown in the *monthly financial statement*. Some items divide easily into 12 equal parts because they do not change from one month to another, while others vary substantially from month to month based on seasonal and other factors. Projecting the income *when it is expected to be received* and expenses *when they are expected to be paid* is important. If a property normally incurs an expense in March and pays it in May, budgeting for that expense in March will result in variances for both months, and the variances

---

6. The annual budget preparation is also the perfect time to discuss major renovation projects or needed repairs with the property owner(s) because these items affect the overall cash flow.

will require explanation. In addition, these variances cause the cash flow to change significantly.

Quarterly Budget Updates. Essentially, the annual budget serves as a point of reference. However, actual income and expenses can differ significantly from such a budget as the year progresses. To compensate for such differences, *quarterly budget updates* might be prepared, which reflect adjustments to the original projections made in the annual budget. These modified budgets can be more accurate than the annual budget because the projections are not so far into the future. In addition, such quarterly budgets cover the approximate time of one season, so their projections of seasonally affected income and expenses can be more accurate.

In some cases, owners of commercial properties might ask for additional forecasts for five or even 10 years in addition to the required annual budget. However, many owners do require a periodic monthly reforecasting. In general, budgets are intended to be the real estate manager's best forecast of revenue and expense. They are not a wish list of items that the real estate manager would like to see happen. Those "what-if" scenarios are appropriate for internal analysis for strategic planning, but they are not budgets that should reflect the manager's forecasting techniques.

Capital Budget

Because one purpose of a reserve fund is to accumulate capital for improvements, a *capital budget* is prepared to show how much to set aside in the reserve fund on a regular basis. In principle, this simply requires calculating the cost of the improvement and dividing the total by the number of months before the improvement is to be implemented, then factoring in interest income that the account will earn.

However, if funds are accumulated over a period of years, consider inflation. If the interest earned on the accumulating reserve is not substantially higher than the rate of inflation, the anticipated total accumulation will not meet the actual cost of the improvement.

Furthermore, the cost of materials may rise faster than the inflation rate, so a larger monthly allocation will be necessary to assure a reasonable match between the amount of reserve funds and their anticipated use. Capital budgets include leasing commissions, tenant improvements (TIs), major maintenance, and improvements or additions to the property.

Real estate managers who work for institutional owners approach a capital budget differently. These owners rarely accumulate reserve funds. Rather, their capital budgets reflect anticipated expenditures for specific capital improvement projects, TIs, and leasing commissions. Some owners may have required reserves for these that are paid monthly to the lender. The budget would then account for the expense to be paid when incurred, and reflect the reimbursement from the reserve account at some future point. Properties with heavy leasing and TIs may require an accounting of reserve account balances on a monthly basis and in the operating budget as well.

Planning for the replacement of major items should be an exercise performed as part of the budget process, regardless of whether the owner sets aside funds for that purpose. All items, from pumps and motors to roofs, have typical lifespans. Skilled engineers, maintenance technicians, and vendors can provide this information and the current costs of replacement or major repairs. Ownership and management should have a conversation early in the relationship to discuss how capital improvements and TIs will be handled. For example, the following two questions must be answered:

- If there is no established replacement reserve fund, will additional funds be made available?
- If loans will be required, is there sufficient equity?

If needs are to be ignored or delayed, the consequences of deferred maintenance should also be a part of this discussion. It is extremely important to understand the owner's goals and objectives. Asking the previous questions is an excellent way to discover how ownership intends management to perform in the long term.

Long-Range Budget

Use of a capital budget often leads to the development of a *long-range budget* that illustrates the relationship between operating income and expenses over five or more years in the life of a property. The level of detail and precision is less in this type of budget than in an annual budget because projections cannot be as accurate for the longer time involved.

A long-range budget can show the owner what to expect over the time the investment will be held. It can illustrate the anticipated financial gain from a rehabilitation program, a new marketing campaign, or a change in market conditions. Long-range budgets illustrate expected income, expenses, and sources of funding. Long major projects may require the owner to make extraordinary cash contributions or financing arrangements in the early years of the holding period. Ideally, the owner will recover these extra contributions in the later years of the holding period, after the income from the property stabilizes at an amount greater than it was when the property was purchased—or when the changes were implemented.

SUMMARY

The success of an income-producing property is measured by the amount of money it generates and the return to its investors. A property's performance is accounted through detailed financial reports and accounting statements. This complete and multifaceted aspect of management involves establishing and maintaining thorough and accurate financial records for the property and for individual units, residents, or commercial tenants. Every dollar of income and expense must be accounted and categorized based on its source or destination as identified in a chart of accounts. The accounting records are the basis of the financial reports provided to the owner each month. Additionally, those records will help in developing budgets to predict future income and expenses. The main objectives are to maximize NOI and minimize variances between actual and budgeted income and expenses. Altogether, the various budgets are among the most useful documents developed for clients or the owners.

A budget is a living, breathing document that should be adjusted accordingly to ensure a property's success. Like with any roadmap, there are obstacles that will be encountered. Remember to communicate effectively and communicate often. This way, even if the property is not positioned for success at year end, all parties will understand why and be in a position to better plan for success in the forthcoming year.

7 | Staff Management

Real estate managers have many titles for the jobs they fill and the job descriptions vary accordingly. Rarely does a single real estate manager perform all of the tasks inherent in these responsibilities; nevertheless, it is the manager's duty to ensure that all of the following work (listed in no particular order) is accomplished:

- Correct and maintain any fire/life/safety issues including regularly scheduled audits and inspections
- Develop a maintenance management program
- Develop an emergency procedure plan[1]
- Establish rents that make the units or spaces marketable by knowing the competition
- Market and prospect for tenants for vacant premises
- Develop and implement a resident or commercial tenant retention program
- Collect rent and other fees, properly account for these funds, and prepare long- and short-term budgets
- If authorized, pay any expenses the property incurs
- Manage employees of the management firm and on-site staff
- Develop the property management plan
- Communicate effectively with the property owner
- Maintain compliance with all applicable laws and regulations

Real estate managers can accomplish these responsibilities in three ways: (1) hire staff to work on site, (2) assign employees of the management firm to fulfill on-site work, or (3) contract with others to provide the necessary workforce. The real estate manager

---

1. A good resource for developing an emergency procedures plan is the IREM publication, *Before and After Disaster Strikes: Developing An Emergency Procedures Manual, 4th Edition* (2012).

may serve as a bridge between the site personnel (maintenance, on-site leasing, and site administration) and the employees of the management firm (accounting, marketing and leasing, and clerical workers). Generally, the real estate manager is the supervisor of all of these individuals and report to a senior or executive property manager in the management firm.

The relationship between the real estate manager's goals and the goals of the property owner are the foundation of the relationship between the real estate manager and the staff. The employees must understand the goals and work toward fulfilling them by cooperatively applying their abilities. They must believe that meeting these goals is a worthy endeavor and that they are treated fairly as part of the team's overall success or failure. Employees must also understand the relationship between the real estate manager and the owner and the way those goals relate to each other; they must also understand how individual efforts contribute to the success and value of the property. Ultimately, the real estate manager's success truly depends on how well he or she trains the staff in understanding the goals. Inspiring and instilling the desire to serve clients as they would want to be served will make or break the success of the property.

STAFF REQUIREMENTS

For a single property, hiring on-site staff is usually most beneficial. Employees of a management firm may provide services to more than one property—their services to a particular property are part of the contractual arrangement with the property's owner. Outside contractors may perform all types of work, which most often requires specialized skills, equipment, or specific licensing. To manage a property, the execution of necessary tasks requires cooperation among on-site staff, management firm employees, and contractors. Real estate managers should assign each specific task to one or more of these groups.

On-site Staff

The type of property, its size and layout, and the number of residents or commercial tenants determine how much work is done on site and how large a staff is needed. Real estate managers of residential properties may have to respond to residents around the clock. For example, office building managers provide services to tenants and their employees during business hours, while cleaning and other custodial tasks are typically done after hours, usually in the early evening. Large shopping centers require staffing not only while stores are open for business, but also after business hours for security and custodial maintenance.

While all properties require on-site work, many are too small to justify a regular part-time or full-time staff member. If a property requires sufficient maintenance and repair work to occupy one or more people full-time, hiring skilled staff is usually the most economical approach. However, an individual with a single skill (e.g., carpentry or plumbing) is usually not hired on a full-time basis. Large properties that include complex operating systems are more likely to employ skilled personnel to maintain these systems.

For small properties that require only occasional repairs—amounting to less than a day's work—having one or more contracts for skilled labor as needed is generally a better choice. A contract laborer—hired through an employment agency—usually earns a higher hourly wage than a full-time employee; however, a *contract for labor as needed* means that money paid is for specific work done and actual hours worked. The payroll taxes and forms for the contract laborer are completed by the employment agency—eliminating extra paperwork and expense for real estate managers and management firms. Another benefit is that contract laborers do not require training, and the employment agency normally handles any employee-related performance and/or disciplinary issues. A higher wage might be required in hiring a contract laborer; however, the overall cost may be about equal.

THE EMPLOYER OF ON-SITE STAFF

Whether the owner or the management company is the employer of on-site staff is an important question that relates to the assignment of risk, hold-harmless provisions in contracts, etc. The issue should be negotiated beforehand and should be documented in the management agreement.

On-site staff members may technically be employees of the property owner rather than of the real estate manager, which is often the arrangement when an individual real estate manager contracts directly with an owner to manage a single property. However, the real estate manager or other employees of the management firm may actually hire, train, supervise, and terminate the on-site staff in addition to processing their payroll. This sometimes raises questions as to who is the true employer of on-site staff—the property owner or the management firm? Even though a management agreement may stipulate that the owner is the employer of the on-site staff, the U.S. Department of Labor may take the position that they are employees of the management firm because of the circumstances of their employment. Regardless of who employs the on-site staff, their wages are paid out of the operating funds of the property.

On-site staff members normally work only at one site. However, if a property owner or a management company has several buildings that are near each other, staff members may be assigned to all of their buildings and not just one of them. In such situations, the labor cost of work performed may be charged to the respective properties on an hourly basis, or a worker's total compensation—per month or per year, including both wages and benefits—may be allocated on a percentage basis to each property to account for all hours worked.

The most common on-site work is maintenance, but many other duties at a property may require part-time or full-time staff. If the property has its own office, it may warrant an office manager or full-time clerical worker. In large properties, front desks must employ staff when the building is open—if not around the clock. Larger luxury apartment communities have door attendants and concierges. High-rise office buildings usually have lobby attendants, day porters, and security guards. Major shopping centers and enclosed malls may offer information or stroller rental services to customers in addition to providing personnel to clean the common areas and security for the commercial tenants, their employees, and their customers. Having a large staff may necessitate employing supervisory personnel, such as a director of operations or services manager, all of whom report to the real estate manager.

Employees of the Management Firm

The size of a management firm and the range of services it offers depend on the extent of its portfolio. Management firms often begin as two-person enterprises—they usually start as an independent management business with a few clients and most likely hire a second person to do clerical work. Initially, the clerical worker may only work part-time depending on the workload—it might not be enough to warrant full-time employment. The clerical employee of a new management firm may be responsible for several office activities, such as processing correspondence, answering the telephone, accounting and record keeping, payroll, balancing bank accounts, and making bank deposits. As the firm secures more management contracts, additional employees may be hired—a full-time administrative assistant and then, perhaps, a property accountant. As the size of the firm's portfolio increases, a greater demand for specialization of staff members' roles becomes necessary. Specialization reduces the number of daily interruptions of one specific assignment by an unrelated task that has the same or greater priority. However, one individual often performs numerous unrelated tasks, especially in small firms with limited economic means.

Two questions must be continually asked regarding the size of the management firm's staff: (1) Is it the right size to give every client timely and accurate service? and (2) Is it adequate to perform its own administrative tasks?

When a firm's portfolio is small, one or two employees in addition to the real estate manager will be able to provide tenant services, client services, and routine office administration. However, if the management firm expands, or if clients require additional services at some point, compare the cost of additional staff to both the service requirements of the firm's clients and the needs of the management firm. There is almost always an imbalance in the amount of staff and work required. Management firms can rarely afford to have too many staff on board awaiting new business; they most likely suffer the reverse—too much work for the staff in place. The number of staff members and their level of specialization within the management firm depend on the following eight factors:

1. **Number of properties the firm manages.** A newly established management firm usually starts out with few accounts, so the expense of a management-support staff may be neither justified nor feasible. The founding real estate manager initially does most of the work. With more accounts, however, additional site managers may need to be hired to handle the day-to-day management of individual properties. Site managers can be assigned by property type, owner, geographic proximity, number of units, or square feet of space. The central office may employ administrative, accounting, or even maintenance staff to relieve the site managers of some of their responsibilities.

2. **Types of properties in the portfolio.** Some management firms specialize in specific types of properties. However, a firm with many diverse property types in its portfolio may have divisions for each property type; in that case, each division is likely to have its own specialized (or dedicated) staff as well as leasing and marketing personnel. With mixed-use communities—consisting of retail, residential, commercial, and other

types of properties—real estate managers are essential. These property types require different skill sets. In the past, real estate managers have been specialists in only one property type. Generalists who are skilled in all property types are more and more in demand. Individuals who are capable of successfully managing the dynamic of an urban village and maximizing the performance of each product type are highly successful.

3. **Size and tenancy of managed property.** Managing and interacting with tenants in each phase of the cycle of tenancy requires significant work, so actual and potential numbers of tenants affect the size of the firm's administrative and support staff. The potential number of tenants is based on the number of existing units in each property that is managed or the capacity for its square footage to be subdivided into leasable spaces. The frequency of turnover and the total number of units or square footage actually occupied influence the size of the marketing and leasing staff as well as the size of the accounting department staff. A property of substantial size may require the assignment of full-time firm employees to that property alone, even though they may perform their duties at the management firm office and not on site.

4. **Number of clients the firm has.** Just as the potential and actual tenant population influences the size of the firm's staff, the number of owners served influences the management firm's reporting, accounting, and administrative workload.

5. **Level of service required.** Clients may have unique needs for which the management firm must allot time. Some property owners—institutional owners in particular—may request or require that their reports conform to their standard formats, and the management firm may have to send multiple reports to various investors or partners. Many require the management firm to use a specific software package, or even input the data into the institutional owner's software. One should try to ascertain how much involvement the owner expects to have. That is, some institutional investors have asset managers who watch over and sometimes manage from headquarters.

6. **Proximity of the managed properties to each other.** A management firm that specializes in super-regional shopping centers is more likely to have a multistate or nationwide clientele than one that exclusively manages residential property. Each property may require a site manager and support staff if the properties are located in different counties or states. In an urban area where several properties are close to each other, a single real estate manager may be able to manage several properties because of reduced travel time.

7. **Size of on-site staff.** The size of the on-site staff may influence the amount of involvement the real estate manager has with the property. When a large staff works on site, more time might be devoted to that property alone, which limits the availability to manage other properties.

8. **Size and experience of property manger's support staff.** Whether working with administrative assistants and property accountants to perform some of the management duties will determine the number of properties the real estate manager can manage. The more these types of duties are delegated, the more attention will be available to focus on the task of managing the property itself.

EIGHT FACTORS THAT DETERMINE NUMBER OF STAFF MEMBERS

1	2	3	4
Number of properties managed	Types of properties managed	Size and tenancy of managed properties	Number of clients served

5	6	7	8
Level of service required	Location of managed properties	Size of on-site staff at managed properties	Size and experience of support staff

The staff requirements of a management firm can grow for many reasons, particularly in areas of responsibility not directly related to managing properties. Sometimes a mail room supervisor is necessary due to the large amount of mail that comes through a large firm. Data entry and retrieval might require an information technology (IT) specialist. Although IT specialists are not directly involved with real estate management, their presence means that real estate managers can do their job without distraction. The potential for the business of a management firm to expand is great, and the number of people it employs will grow accordingly.

In contrast, the potential for an on-site staff to expand is small—the number of people employed directly at a property rarely increases because changes made to a property are usually not significant enough to alter the size or organization of the staff. However, the addition of leasable space or changing from net leases to gross leases could create some exceptions that could lead to a change in staff size. In net leases at commercial properties, the tenant pays a prorated share of some or all operating expenses in addition to the base or minimum rent, compared to a gross lease—in which the tenant (or lessee) pays a fixed rent and the lessor is responsible for paying all property expenses (e.g., taxes, insurance, utilities, repairs). These costs are factored into the rent the tenant pays. Basically, gross leases require more work on the part of the management company, whereas net leases require the tenant to maintain their own premises.

Contractors

Because hiring employees is expensive, contracting labor for temporary or intermittent tasks can be economical. The management firm usually hires contractors—the owner may occasionally hire them—depending on whether the work is limited to one property or is needed by the firm's central office. Real estate managers might hire contract workers to work on site at the property or at the management office, or the work may be outsourced.

On-site Contract Workers. Contract workers at a site perform a variety of tasks. They often perform maintenance tasks that require special equipment or training (elevator maintenance, roof repair) or licensing (pest control). Real estate managers frequently contract seasonal services such as lawn care, snow removal, decorating, exterior painting, window washing, and even daily janitorial maintenance. If the property needs on-site security, contracting for this service can reduce the property owner's liability in the event of a crime or other incident by shifting the liability to a third-party contractor. (Chapter 10 explains maintenance contracting procedures and the liability the owner and the management company assume under the law of agency when any contractor is hired.)

The management office may employ part-time or temporary workers, especially for administrative work such as filing or accounting. Temporary employees can be contracted for a day, a week, or longer for specific assignments. Companies that specialize in providing skilled labor for maintenance, clerical, or administrative duties are more abundant in large cities, but they are also available in smaller cities.

On site or in a small firm, the real estate manager is a full-time leasing employee of the owner—or of a leasing company in charge of leasing. However, very large properties or those with high vacancy rates or frequent turnovers may benefit from a full-time leasing agent. Initial lease-up of a new or renovated property also demands full-time attention. Leasing is one real estate management task that is often contracted because leasing agents provide specialized expertise. For each successfully negotiated lease, a leasing agent on contract usually receives a commission based on a dollar per square foot of space leased or a percentage of the rental income over the term of the lease.

Outsourcing. Another approach to contracting is to *outsource* an entire function. For example, a small management firm that does not have a staff member to recruit and process job applicants may contract an outside service on an as-needed basis to perform these tasks. Management company personnel still interview and hire the individual, but the contractor prescreens applicants' resumes, narrows the field of prospects to interview, and handles all the paperwork, including the reference checks.

Other firms will take over management of all personnel operations, from the hiring process through preparation of payroll and administration of benefits, which the contracted firm provides. For a small company, the outside source can relieve an administrative burden and may expand the benefits the firm can offer its employees (e.g., medical insurance coverage) when the total number of employees is too small to form a group acceptable to an insurance carrier.

Management firms may also outsource accounting. This can be very helpful if the small firm does not have the proper or sophisticated (and expensive) accounting software programs that create reports automatically once data are entered into the program's forms.

Marketing and leasing are other functions that a firm may outsource effectively. Contracting with marketing and leasing professionals can ensure timely completion of these efforts; it can also ensure that all contacts with prospective tenants meet the firm's requirements and comply with fair housing laws. Management firms sometimes benefit from specialized outsourcing because it pays for itself quickly—the higher level of experts lease units quicker for maximum rents.

Determining Adequate Staff Size

Providing an adequate staff for a property, a management firm, or both requires careful planning and close examination of resources. The first step in this process is to list the essential tasks and estimate the time each requires on a weekly or monthly basis. The initial assessment may be very detailed, accounting for everything from the time necessary to mow the lawn to the time required to collect rent. The final compilation might resemble a budget, except that hours of work per week or per month are the primary quantitative measures rather than dollars and cents. Analysis of the resulting list should indicate how many workers are necessary for efficient operation and adequate service to the tenants and the property owner.

The size and type of the property as well as particular tenant requirements understandably influence the preparation of this list. Once all functions are noted and the average amount of time for each is calculated, the various duties can be grouped by category. These groupings may be the basis for job descriptions or for setting up the maintenance and administration departments. Use the groupings to decide how many full-time and part-time workers the property needs, as well as which tasks outside contractors may complete most economically. To be accurate, any estimate of the number of workers required must also allow for days off, sick time, and vacation days. Such time budgets may be prepared for each property as well as for the management firm. When duties are duplicated, evaluate further to decide whether the duplication is necessary or if consolidation is possible.

Once the list is completed, the payroll costs and benefits of each employee must be included in the property's budget, and adjustments to salary or benefits that the owner might require must be made for cash flow purposes. It is important to note that not all properties can afford to hire personnel solely based on this "time list." Most often, the budget is first created and payroll is then determined by the other needs of the property and/or owner. If money is tight, an owner may require that minimal staff be hired to maximize their cash flow—altogether, it is a balancing act.

HIRING QUALIFIED PERSONNEL

One of the largest ongoing investments for any property is maintaining a highly qualified and skilled staff. To build a capable, dedicated staff, pay careful attention to the recruitment and selection processes. Beyond that, investing many hours and dollars in continual training and development is an essential component in maintaining a high level of service for the managed properties.

Recruiting Applicants

Qualified candidates can be found by creating online job postings, employing staffing agencies, utilizing certain social media websites, seeking personal referrals, or promoting current employees. There are plenty of websites available for posting a job. Some websites cater to specific industries, while others assist potential employers in gaining quick responses for easy-to-fill administrative jobs. There are even websites specifically created for jobs within certain regions or states; other websites post jobs nationwide.

For specific real estate management jobs such as portfolio managers, directors of property administration, associate property managers, and even on-site residential managers.[2] There are many ways to recruit highly qualified candidates. With the demographics of the industry and employee turnover rates, real estate management firms have been building their own workforce by creating relationships with community colleges, tech schools, and universities to offer internships and manager-in-training programs.

Online Job Postings. Online employment ads generate quick responses, especially if they are effective and posted on popular websites, in which case, employers may receive hundreds of resumes from candidates. Some of the most popular websites include CareerBuilder, Indeed, SimplyHired, and Monster. Posting fees may or may not be involved. Some websites base the posting fee on a maximum cost-per-click (CPC), which is the highest amount paid for a click on the job posting. The more spent on the job posting, the more the traffic will be directed to the posting. Other websites simply offer a basic flat rate for a job posting; the rate is based on the length of time the posting stays visible online.

In general, many applicants will be over- or under-qualified for the position, and filtering out the most qualified candidates can be time consuming. To facilitate the screening process, the job posting

---

2.   *Careers.iremjobs.org* is a good source for finding qualified candidates through posting jobs, searching resumes, and tracking activity.

should describe the duties of the job and required qualifications. It should instruct applicants to submit a resume, work history, or other pertinent information that applies to the job.

Social Media. Social media is not only used as a recruitment and networking tool, it also helps to promote real estate management firm in many ways—especially by displaying the brand and logo. In order to be successful with job postings via various social media platforms, it's important to develop content that helps candidates learn more about the organization. It's important to educate the staff about the social media outreach and invite them to participate in ways that will improve the image of the real estate management firm.

Staffing Agencies. In order to save time *or* in situations of hiring director- or senior-level personnel, employing a well-known and reputable staffing agency is a good option. In other situations in which time is of the essence, a staffing agency can quickly gather a selection of qualified temporary workers. For example, in residential student housing, temporary workers might be needed between school semesters when students are signing leases or moving into and out of apartments. Understanding the staffing agency's screening process is important to ensure that they find candidates with the specialized skills required for the position. Although working with an agency spares the time of conducting interviews, consider the agency's fee, which is sometimes a percentage of the annual salary for the position filled.

Internal Promotion. Promotion within the company is an effective way to retain and increase the value of excellent employees. Some people believe that promotion from within doubles the cost of training because the person who is promoted and the successor must be trained simultaneously. However, promotion can be highly rewarding and is often more efficient even though the initial training expense can be slightly higher. Internal promotion is not only excellent for morale, it's also a great motivator for employees to know there is room for growth within the company. Another

WHAT NOT TO INCLUDE IN A JOB DESCRIPTION

A well-written job description consists of more than a laundry list of the tasks and responsibilities the job entails—it reflects a sense of priorities. The following list provides a few ideas to keep in mind when writing a job description:

- Describe the job itself, *not* the *person* in the job. It is easy to fall into the trap of writing about the person who currently performs the job, but it is essential to describe what the position requires.

- It is illegal to indicate specific gender, race, religion, national origin, age, disability, or other potentially discriminatory characteristics in a job description. For example, referencing a specific gender such as sales *man* in the job title or requirements is illegal.

- Avoid adding strict requirements that could eliminate suitable candidates. Try not to include excessively stringent requirements or a wish list for the perfect candidate because that will eliminate qualified candidates from the job pool. Use flexible requirements instead. For example, consider substitutions of education for experience and vice versa.

- Do not rely solely on a job's history when putting together a current job description. Focus instead on what the job *needs* to be in light of the property and the owner's current needs and long-term objectives.

benefit is that the promoted employee is already familiar with the company and most likely understands the new position quite well. If time allows, the person promoted may be able to train their successor, which reduces the demands on the trainee's supervisor. In addition, the newcomer enters a lower-level position, a situation that provides room for their individual growth within the company rather than fostering a need to seek outside opportunities.

Personal Referrals. Personal referrals from current employees of the company or from acquaintances are also valuable resources. Such prospects usually have some knowledge of and a genuine interest in the company, and are most likely capable individuals. However, be careful not to depend too much on personal referrals because they might not attract a diverse workforce or provide a fair workplace. Other sources for referrals are through professional activities. Membership in professional organizations can provide many contacts that allow other professionals to keep up to date on local business activities—including who is working for what company and how well those people are doing. Established professional relationships can help locate the right person for a position and quickly check their credentials.

Unsolicited Applications. In addition to a company's active recruiting, the property or the management firm may occasionally receive unsolicited resumes and applications. Examine these applications when they arrive—even if no positions are available. Information sent in this manner is often evidence of an applicant who has sound qualifications and a sincere interest in working for the property or the firm and who may even have researched the property or firm in advance of applying. If such an applicant appears to have the proper credentials, keep their resume or application on file for two to three years.

Selecting Employees

Regardless of how a prospective employee is recruited, all candidates should complete an *employment application form,* which organizes and standardizes the information needed to make the hiring decision. A personal interview is necessary before making a final decision on employment. In addition to showing if the candidate is capable, interviews help in ascertaining if the applicant is compatible with the requirements of the job and willing to work toward the goals of the owner or the management firm. Individual applicants should be evaluated based on the requirements for the particular position.

SAMPLE INTERVIEW QUESTIONS FOR CANDIDATES

The overall goal when developing interview questions is to find the right candidate for the job—someone who is trustworthy, outgoing, and passionate about what they do. The following lists examples of questions that will help reveal certain behavior types:

- Tell me about the one thing outside of work of which you are the proudest.
- Tell me about the most frustrating experience you've had in the workplace.
- You've been assigned to a project development team, what do you think will be your biggest asset to the team?
- What has been your greatest success in your current or previous job?
- What do you feel is unique about you and makes you the best candidate?
- What strengths do you possess that we haven't discussed?
- Tell me about a time when you had to motivate someone. What did you do and what was the result?
- If money were no object and you could follow your passion, what would that be and where would it take you?
- What makes you sad or troubled about the world today? What makes you hopeful about the world today?

Verify Information. Before making a formal offer, verify the employment application information. To acquire all the information needed, have applicants sign a separate waiver—to be copied and sent to former employers—that releases previous employers from liability for information given in references. Request a copy of the applicant's driving license and obtain a copy of their driving record if they are going to have to use a car in the performance of their duties.

Verifying information provided on job applications can be a time-consuming activity, and the information gathered may be

---

SAMPLE INTERVIEW QUESTIONS FOR SUPERVISORS

One of the goals when conducting an interview is to determine whether the responses display a personality type or potential value system that closely mirrors the ideal candidate. The following lists additional questions that can be asked for supervisory positions:

- Describe your management style.
- We often serve as the intermediary between tenants and owners. Describe a time when you had to ensure the satisfaction of both parties.
- Real estate managers wear many hats. Explain your methodology in mastering these many roles.
- Describe the general responsibilities of an onsite manager, facilities manager, or property manager.[1]
- Describe your ideal supervisor.
- Describe your ideal subordinate.
- How would you provide an atmosphere in which you would support others' ideas, feelings, and concerns?
- Provide an example of when you had to deliver negative news and how it was received.
- Describe a time when you suggested improvements and how (or if) they were adopted.

---

1. If candidates are new to these positions, this question would allow real estate managers to correct inaccurate assumptions and better explain the specific roles so the candidates know exactly what the jobs entail.

---

incomplete or inaccurate. Privacy laws require employers to safeguard personal information that applicants supply. Using an employee-screening service, which has more resources available to it, has the advantage of distancing the employer from liability related to the screening process.

Formal Job Offers and Rejections. The formal offer of employment should always be formalized, even after an offer is made and accepted over the phone or in person. Generally, within three days of hiring, the new employee and the employer must complete an *Employment Eligibility Verification form (Form I-9),* which verifies the employee's identity and right to work in the United States. Employees can present a number of documents to verify their identity and right to work. Employers are required to retain I-9 forms in the employee's personnel file for three years after the date the person begins work or one year after the person's employment is terminated—whichever is later. Applicants who are not offered the job should promptly receive rejection letters as a matter of business goodwill, but not until after the selected candidate is employed and performing the job.

Ensure Nondiscrimination. Although some reasons for selecting one candidate over another are subjective, the promise of capability combined with demonstrated reliability are usually the main factors in selecting a new employee. Certain outside factors should never influence the compensation offered to an applicant, a current employee, or any other decision that affects an applicant

---

CONTENTS OF AN EMPLOYEE MANUAL

As a standard practice, all employees should be required to sign a statement acknowledging receipt of the employee manual. The following lists some of the basic contents of a items in an employee manual:

- Company description and history
- Company policies and procedures
- Employment rules
- Employee benefits
- Department and company organization
- Safety and security policies
- Customer relations
- Ethics
- Hiring and orientation policies

The manual should also include a policy that requires any employee to take any conflict with their employer to binding arbitration instead of immediately going to court.

or employee. Title VII of the *Civil Rights Act,* which is enforced by the United States *Equal Employment Opportunity Commission (EEOC),* prohibits discrimination against employees and applicants for employment. Various state and local laws may also prohibit discrimination in employment, and their requirements may be more stringent.

The importance of nondiscrimination in the workplace goes beyond legal compliance. People of all races and creeds own and rent property. To provide owners and renters with superior service, the staff of the property and the management firm should reflect the diversity of the community. The owner and the management firm should provide diversity training to the property staff. The ability to work with people whose backgrounds are varied is an asset of incalculable worth. To stay up to date on the laws that apply to all types of work situations, including hiring, firing, promotions, harassment, training, wages, and benefits, visit *www.eeoc.gov.*

EMPLOYEE ONBOARDING

All new employees should receive training and orientation regardless of their competence or familiarity with their new duties; this is also known as *employee onboarding,* which is a comprehensive approach to bringing in new hires that goes beyond simple orientation. Onboarding plans are intended to make new employees familiar with the overall goals of a management company or specific property and support them as they embark on early projects in an effort to achieve success.

The ultimate payoff is to reduce turnover and encourage workers to stay with an organization for a longer tenure. Since every company has a unique culture and particular procedures, new employees should be properly introduced to the work environment as quickly as possible. An employee manual stating the company policies reinforces an orientation program. An employee manual should include but is not limited to the following:

- **General rules of employment.** Hours of work, paydays, holidays, sick leave, vacations, etc.
- **Company's policies affecting internal and external activities.** Public relations, ethics, employee attitudes, promotion from within, discrimination, sexual harassment, etc.
- **Information about the company.** A brief history, a statement of objectives, and an organizational chart.
- **Other policies and procedures as required or needed.** Proprietary information, confidentiality, fiduciary responsibilities, etc.

Once employees are established in their jobs, schedule regular performance reviews and conduct them as promised. These sessions should be structured to help employees increase their value to the firm. They are also a great opportunity to discuss any deficiencies or performance corrections that may be needed. Businesses commonly review employees' performance at least once a year. In addition, new employees may receive employment reviews after their probationary period, or the first three months. A review early in the period of employment can be an opportunity for both employer and employee to reaffirm their employment decisions—or to agree that the decision was not right and go their separate ways.

Employees adapt to their new work surroundings and obligations at their own pace. Depending on the job and the individual, some employees require as much as a year on the job before their productivity reaches the level the employer expects. Conversely, the employer may realize early that an employee is incapable of doing the job assigned.

A comprehensive review of the employee's performance may indicate that his or her talents lie elsewhere—refer to the recommended performance appraisal methods in the next section. Review of the job description may also reveal that the work is too much for one person to accomplish. Additional training or a transfer may be a way to retain an employee who shows promise but is not qualified for the job they were hired to do.

RETAINING VALUABLE EMPLOYEES

A talented and dedicated staff is an employer's most valuable resource. Developing qualified staff requires great effort, and continually rebuilding a staff because of turnover is extremely expensive. An employer can minimize personnel costs and increase the value of individual employees by retaining responsible, dedicated people. Appropriate compensation, open communication with employees, and consistent encouragement of individuals to grow in their jobs are factors that facilitate employee retention.

Performance Appraisal Methods

One of the main components of retaining valuable employees is through appraising their work performance. A few of the most effective and widely used methods utilize the following three components: (1) graphic rating scale, (2) weighted checklist, and (3) management by objectives. These are just a few ways of determining the strength of the staff and evaluating and reviewing their performance. Essentially, through the review process, employees learn areas in which they have improved or in which they still need improvement. Such a review is meant to help motivate employees.

Graphic Rating Scale. There are a variety of ways to gain honest and constructive feedback from employees based on their performance appraisal. Using the *graphic rating scale* method, there is an appropriate place on a scale for each task listed. A typical scale has a five-point rating: 1 is significantly below standard, 3 is standard, and 5 indicates performance significantly above standard. A comments section is typically included for providing additional information about the employee's performance in each dimension.

Weighted Checklist. Using the *weighted checklist* method, the appraiser is given a list of statements and checks the items on the list that describe or apply to the employee. Some items may be weighted higher than others to arrive at an overall tabulated result. This system is limited because each appraiser may interpret statements and words differently.

For example, the checklist might have the following items:

- This employee is a team player.
- This employee arrives at work on time.
- This employee is a good leader.

Management by Objectives. A process in which employees help set objectives for themselves is known as *management by objectives (MBO),* which defines what they intend to accomplish within a given period. The employers and employees mutually agree on the goals and objectives. When employees are involved in setting goals, a higher level of commitment and performance can result. Employees clearly understand goals they helped to set, and that fosters an increased sense of accomplishment and dedication to the company.

Compensation

Pay and benefits are the tangible rewards of dedicated service. Compensation must meet market levels to keep employees satisfied. It must also offer employees security and incentives to strive for greater rewards.

Wages. The federal *Fair Labor Standards Act (FLSA),* which the government revises from time to time, regulates the minimum wage per hour and the maximum number of hours employees can work per day and per week in positions that are paid an hourly wage. If the maximum hours per day or cumulative hours per week exceed those prescribed, the employer is required to pay overtime—standard wage plus 50 percent. In addition, employers are required to pay employees for *all* hours worked in a workweek, including time worked in the workplace, time spent traveling as part of the job, training, and work performed at home at the employer's request or with the employer's permission. While employers must follow the minimum wage law, market demands generally require a higher wage rate to recruit qualified employees. Other incentives such as double-time pay for working on holidays may also be necessary.

To be *exempt* from the Wage and Hour Regulations of the FLSA, a position must meet several specific tests. Among them are supervision of others and performance of office work directly related to business operations. Determining whether an employee is exempt from overtime requirements under the FLSA has long been problematic because the rules were confusing. Under the rules put into effect in July of 2009, the U.S. Department of Labor (DOL) issued specific guidelines for determining exempt status, including salary level. In addition to hourly workers, real estate managers working in the corporate setting whose annual salary is less than a certain dollar amount ($47,476) must be paid overtime when they work more than 40 hours in a workweek—in the past, the hours per day or per week maximum did not affect exempt employees. The new rules also spell out the duties that define the roles of exempt employees.

Employers should schedule salary adjustments regularly, budget them routinely, and administer them fairly. Reliable, dedicated employees will continue to provide quality service if their good performance is noted and compensated. One incentive to excellent performance—and cost-consciousness—is to link a portion of the employees' compensation directly to the employer's annual profit. Instituting such programs places more ownership on an employee because they now have a "personal" stake in how well the company fares.

Employee Benefits. If the employer's goal is to retain employees, it's important to have a benefit plan that gives a sense of value to employees' jobs and increases their economic security. Typical employee benefits might include but are not limited to the following (listed in no particular order):

- Relocation assistance
- Medical, prescription, vision, and dental plans
- Health and dependent care
- Retirement benefit plans, pension, 401(k), or 403(b)
- Life insurance, employee, and dependent health insurance

- Disability insurance
- Car allowances or company cars
- Stock options
- Savings programs
- Paid vacations and holidays

Depending on the type, some of these benefits are based on seniority or level of responsibility, and their distribution is often complicated by the effort to avoid or defer tax payments on them. In addition, some employers provide accommodation and enhancement benefits that include employee assistance programs such as smoking cessation or weight loss. Employees want stability in their jobs; therefore, it's essential to provide a benefit plan to retain valuable employees.

Federal Programs

The United States government requires employers to participate in federal programs that provide for workers if they are terminated, retire, or become disabled. Those programs are presented in the sections that follow.

Federal Unemployment Tax Act (FUTA). FUTA and various state unemployment programs are intended to ensure compensation if an employee is laid off or terminated. The employer alone makes the contributions, and the amount or rate is based on the number of employees and the number of claims made. Usually minimum and maximum amounts are paid—on a per-employee basis and related to the employer's history of layoffs. The federal government collects the FUTA taxes, but the state usually administers the unemployment compensation.

Worker's Compensation. Employers must also provide *workers' compensation insurance* to compensate employees in the event of a work-related illness or injury. Employers purchase the insurance through the state or from a private insurance company. As a rule, firms with five or more employees must be covered, although contractors with even one employee must also buy coverage.

Social Security/Medicare. In addition to these employer-paid programs, workers collect Social Security and they may collect Medicare benefits when they retire. Funds for these benefits are collected and administered under the *Federal Insurance Contributions Act (FICA),* and the employer and employee contribute funds equally based on the employee's income.

Communication

Clear communication with employees is a basic and valuable retention tool. Many employees' only source of information about their company is their coworkers. Their reliance on such news source creates the potential for damaging rumors to spread. To avoid such rumors and their consequences, employers should disseminate information that affects the business in a timely manner and explain it fully. News of particular significance—that is, items that the press may publicize favorably or unfavorably—should be released to all employees at the same time it is released to the press—or even beforehand to avert speculation.

Companies might use a Facebook page, a blog, an e-mail update, an intranet site, or a newsletter to communicate with their staff. Employees welcome recognition of service anniversaries, promotions, and personal news items about their fellow workers along with news about the company's activities. Management most often publishes and controls these communications. However, they should be directed to all employees, and the writing style should be friendly and personal.

Central to the communication program of any company is the policy manual or manuals—previously mentioned in this chapter. This material provides all employees a reference to consult for information on company benefits, work hours, and minimum performance standards for particular procedures. Individual departments may institute policy or procedure manuals for the tasks they perform, but all employees should receive some definitive source of information regarding their relationship within the company.

Unfortunately, grievances are a natural part of life and work. Misunderstandings can result in the loss or dissatisfaction of reliable employees if the employer does not address their concerns promptly and sincerely. An open-door policy for airing work-related problems can preserve an excellent working relationship if it prohibits recriminations against those who use it. An open-door policy allows employers to examine their working relationship with their employees. If employees belong to a union, the union contract usually outlines specific grievance procedures. Maintaining good relations with the union can make the process more workable.

Managers should expect all workers to use their skills and talents to the maximum in their work. They should treat all coworkers with respect regardless of the tasks they perform or whether their position is that of a supervisor or a subordinate. Managers should openly welcome dialog on grievances because it leads to opportunities to take corrective actions or make improvements. Employees who feel they have a voice and are really heard are more likely to have an increased sense of investment and commitment to the firm.

Promoting Morale

Effective communication is only part of an overall program to maintain employee morale. Developing teams for managing properties, having a mentor program within the company, and helping employees interact with one another on a positive level helps to foster good morale among employees. Recreational activities among coworkers should also be encouraged. Employees who are dedicated to their jobs yet balance their hard work with recreational activities—and can differentiate between the appropriate times for each—usually have a positive attitude toward their careers. Company-sponsored baseball teams, golf outings, and bowling leagues are common pastimes among coworkers. The cost of such sponsorship may be very little—a set of matching T-shirts is a nominal investment to foster employee enthusiasm.

Managers should expect excellent performance of every employee, and they should compensate their employees for such performance. However, occasional thanks for a job well done is also important to an employee. Dedicated employees want to know that their employer appreciates their work and that their efforts contribute to the organization's success. An expression of gratitude, whether oral or written, can add greatly to good morale.

Continual Training

In the normal pace of business and family life, time is rarely available for additional training or education. As a result, formal education for many employees ends with high school, trade school, or college. As an incentive to continue learning, many employers institute education reimbursement programs for their employees. The rules and incentives for these programs vary greatly, but the benefits to the employer can be substantial.

In addition to formal course work, many associations and corporations sponsor seminars and courses in aspects of real estate management as well as other disciplines such as accounting, maintenance, and human relations. Seminars that teach management and interpersonal skills foster both personal and professional development. Before sending employees to any workshops or seminars, the employer should investigate the cost and quality of such programs. The size of a company and the resources available to it determine the extent to which it can offer such educational programs.

Developing Talents

While a job description is a valuable reference for both employer and employee, it can hinder the employee's progress if interpreted too narrowly. The job description should define the basic functions of a position but should not set limits on what the person performing the job can do. Employees commonly desire definite boundaries to their duties. However, boundaries can limit more than the number of hours that an employee must work—they also permit employees to concentrate only on the minimum the employer expects them to do. While boundaries help create a sense of security, they can also be stifling—people begin to think they are in a rut at work. In establishing boundaries, balance is important. If workers resist change too much, their department can stagnate and hinder a thriving business. However, if they pursue every new opportunity and ignore fundamental procedures, the department or company can flounder from lack of direction. In other words, allowing the employee some latitude to be creative and try new ideas provides more opportunity for career development and growth for both the employee and the company.

Most job descriptions gradually change as a business evolves, so workers must increase their knowledge to be able to keep up the pace. As previously mentioned, communication and training enable workers to grow with the demands placed on the business—so does encouragement. If an employer encourages employees to undertake new tasks, and if they are legitimately capable of mastering the work, they will be productive workers. In such cases, the employer may not have to hire additional staff in order to expand its operations. The employees also gain if they develop more self-confidence and can base their sense of security on their own growing abilities.

EMPLOYEE DISCIPLINE

Those new to managing staff might struggle with the issue of establishing disciplinary action when it is needed. The most common mistake is ignoring a problem—doing so will have a domino effect. Assuming the problem will "get better" by ignoring it will most likely cause the problem to get worse, while also losing the respect of other employees. Addressing issues early will assist in maintaining a professional work environment.

In spite of the efforts an employer may make to retain valuable employees and to develop their talents, situations unfortunately occur in which employee discipline becomes necessary. When an employee disobeys a firm's policies, the employer has the following three steps to take: (1) warn the employee and remind them of the policy, (2) establish disciplinary action, and (3) finally, dismiss the employee. *Discipline* implies reform, and *dismissal* precludes the possibility of reform. Choosing which action to take depends on the infraction involved. The desired result is the same regardless—the employer hopes to remedy or undo any damage from the employee's actions and to prevent any recurrence.

Supervisors sometimes are not properly trained in conflict management, dealing with difficult people, or even approaching an employee who is having issues.[3] From time to time, reputable managers will take a look at their own performance and evaluate how they are doing as supervisors and make corrections, too.

Employment Policies

The *employee manual* should state company policies regarding employee behavior, discipline, and termination. Even small companies must have some form of employee manual or list of procedures and policies that is presented during the onboarding process to establish the general guidelines of the company's expectations of their performance. Employees should sign a statement that they have received and understood the company's policies. Most work rules are absolutes, and they should be easy to enforce.

Progressive Discipline

Some of the most vexing disciplinary problems are a result of minor disobedience. The circumstances that require discipline can provoke anger, but employers must restrain their anger. It is important to preserve impartiality and respect for the employee. When a supervisor learns about or witnesses an infraction, they should write down what is known about the incident and interview

---

3. The *IREM White Paper on Leadership Development: Conflict Management* is a great resource for employers needing to learn how to deal with conflict in the workplace.

the employee regarding the matter. Any required disciplinary action should take place as soon as possible after the offense, and the matter should be discussed in private. Accusing an employee of wrongdoing in the presence of coworkers neither rectifies the problem nor serves to rehabilitate the offending employee. Moreover, other employees who witness the exchange between supervisor and subordinate may lose respect for the employer.

Although the employer should establish a thorough and impartial system of discipline, writing a comprehensive set of disciplinary measures to cover every possible circumstance is impossible. Regardless, the employer must deal with all employees individually and fairly, based on the nature of the incident. To ensure fair treatment, all comparable incidents should be handled similarly—that is, disciplinary measures should be applied consistently.

The employer should establish a system of *progressive discipline* to provide ample opportunity for the employee to change or correct their behavior. Such a system usually involves (1) oral warnings, (2) written warnings, (3) probation, and (4) termination. The first three steps are discussed below. The employer should carefully document any disciplinary action against an employee—even a verbal action.

1. **Oral Warnings.** The number of notices (warnings) given to an employee regarding a particular problem depends on the type of infraction. One or more conversations calling attention to company policy and asking for the employee's commitment to eliminating the problem may be all that is necessary if an employee is repeatedly late for work or regularly extends their lunch period beyond the allowed time. As mentioned, such conversations should be documented in the employee's file.

2. **Written Warnings.** A written memorandum copied to the employee's personnel file would be the next step. Some undesirable behavior may require a written notice from the beginning. This is particularly appropriate if an employee's failure to follow company procedure is causing problems for others on

the staff. For more serious infractions, a disciplinary meeting should be attended by a third party—preferably a member of management. This person can attest to the conversation held, agreements reached, and the accuracy of any memorandum placed in the employee's file.

3. **Probation.** Sometimes a period of *probation* is necessary. Probation gives the employee a fixed amount of time to overcome the work-related problem. It allows an employer to monitor and report on the employee's improvement. During probation, the supervisor should remind the employee that being on probation might affect their next performance review. If the employee corrects the problem before the next performance review, canceling the probation officially (in writing) may be appropriate. The supervisor should inform the employee that if the problem is not corrected, their employment will be terminated. Regardless of how the disciplinary action is set up, pay and benefits should remain intact during a probation period.

EMPLOYEE TERMINATION

The typical American employee no longer makes one place of business a lifelong workplace, as was common with previous generations. Seven to 10 company changes and four or five career paths are common. Turnover is a way of life because of resignations, corporate takeovers, layoffs, and changing client needs. When change occurs, employees should never feel they are just another commodity. Whether an employee retires or resigns or whether the employer must lay off or terminate the employee, such a departure is always stressful for both parties. Nevertheless, dealing with such matters is a part of managerial responsibilities.

Facing a Layoff

When income decreases or expenses increase, or if tenants or clients are lost, a layoff may be the only way to counter the financial shortfall. Whether permanent or temporary, a layoff can be devastating to the employees and their families. The stress on those who remain will increase; they will be concerned about their job security and might have to perform additional work without additional pay. The personal feeling of responsibility and the work to salvage the business exact a high toll. To be effective and lessen problems, organize all the details ahead of time. Severance packages, layoff letters, explanations of benefits, and all other relevant documents must be prepared. Making corporate outplacement services available to departing employees will soften the blow and offer compassionate support to help former employees.

The most valuable assistance involves being direct with employees about the condition of the business and giving them as much warning as possible about the economic situation. Before notifying any employees, however, the employer must review the personnel list to preclude discrimination against any group because of the layoff.

Dismissing an Employee

The most extreme action an employer can take against an employee is *termination.* In many states, employment is *at will,* meaning that either the employee or the employer may terminate the relationship at any time for any reason (with or without cause). Exceptions to this are anti-discrimination (protected classes), anti-retaliation (whistle-blower) statutes, and specific contractual arrangements, including collective bargaining agreements.

A primary concern for the employer is protection from an unjust termination suit, so termination is usually a last resort. Employers should seek advice of legal counsel before adopting specific employment policies—especially those regarding unacceptable (i.e., dangerous) behaviors and their consequences.

In implementing discipline and termination procedures, the employer must be sure to administer their system consistently. Discrimination claims are based on misconceptions and disparate treatment of differently situated individuals. To avoid susceptibility to such claims, the employer must carefully document all disciplinary actions and terminations. Prior to taking any action under a policy, the employer should review their files for any past instances of similar conduct, and where similar conduct has previously been the subject of disciplinary action or termination, the employer should administer its policy to preserve uniformity.

Before terminating an employee, the employer should thoroughly document the event or behavior prompting dismissal. Documentation should concentrate on the work performed (or not performed), not on assumptions regarding its cause (e.g., substance abuse). The meeting during which an employee is to be terminated should also be attended by a third party—a member of management—who can attest in writing to the conversation between the supervisor and employee. Third-party attendance aids in preparing a defense if the employee should later file a lawsuit for discrimination or wrongful termination.

While terminated, employees are usually entitled to collect unemployment compensation—unemployment benefits may be denied in certain circumstances. A dismissed employee could sue the employer for denied unemployment compensation or for damages based on discriminatory or other unfair practices by the employer. To avoid such a suit, an employer should establish and fairly apply a policy of progressive discipline and carefully record reasons for dismissal.

EMPLOYER LIABILITY

Understanding the potential liability involved in the role of employer is important. Employers may reject applicants or terminate employees who pose a direct threat to the health or safety of others in the workplace. In real estate management, the workplace includes not only the managed property, but also the property of residential and commercial tenants, as well as the latter's employees and their customers, and even the management employee's coworkers.

Apart from the problems that arise directly from an employee's actions, the potential exists for legal action by others. If a pre-employment background check would have revealed a prior conviction for a felony (e.g., assault), the employer of an individual who assaults someone on the job could be sued successfully for *negligent hiring.* If an employee who exhibits dangerous behavior on the job (e.g., showing a weapon, making or carrying out threats of harm) is allowed to repeat the behavior and someone is hurt, a lawsuit could be filed based on *negligent retention.* If training and oversight of an employee is inadequate and an incident results in injury to another person, employee, tenant, or visitor, the employer could be sued for *negligent supervision.*

Criminal background checks and drug testing are some of the tools available to help prevent and reduce problems caused by employees, but none will ensure the absolute prevention of harmful acts by others. In terms of firing an employee, paper trails and documentation are critical. In the courts, real estate managers may need to provide support for their actions. To ensure that behavior, policies, and procedures are all accurately and professionally presented, a clear documentation of all procedures will keep the manager on the right path.

SUMMARY

In real estate management, good relationships with employees are central to maintaining good relationships with tenants and the property owner. All staff members, whether supervisors or subordinates, are colleagues and should always work toward fulfilling the owner's goals for the property. The size of a management firm's staff depends on the specific attributes of the properties managed as well as the attributes of other properties in the firm's portfolio. People who work at a property may be employees of the management firm or sometimes of the property owner. In some cases, contractors may be hired for specialized work. Regardless of who hires them, all workers must perform their duties harmoniously and cooperatively.

A wise selection of staff members is as crucial to successful real estate management as it is to any other business. The key to hiring superior employees is searching for qualified candidates who possess the appropriate skills and are willing to share the goals of the manager of the property. Continual training and encouragement to pursue additional education fosters individual productivity. Such programs are good investments when companies can afford to implement them.

Employers can retain employees by treating them fairly, respecting them, and regarding them as colleagues. This includes providing fair compensation and benefits. Honest communication and genuine concern should be at the forefront of employer-employee relationships. It is essential to consider how effectively the supervisor communicates with his or her staff. Communicating through e-mails or other alternative methods is, without a doubt, the quickest and most reliable method of communicating. By balancing communication with the staff between e-mails, phone conversations, and face-to-face meetings, the stability and security of the relationship is enhanced.

8 | Marketing and Tenant Retention

Regardless of the type of property being managed, the principles of resident and tenant relations are essentially the same. In fact, the *cycle of tenancy* is common to all properties. The current tenants once started out as prospects who were attracted to the property for one reason or another. Some tenants eventually move out, but satisfied tenants may refer others to the property. When leases expire, the tenants' satisfaction with the location, appearance, and structural integrity of the property are important factors in their decision to renew the lease. However, tenants are less inclined to move out of a property after specific programs are implemented that are designed to retain them. This chapter explores all phases of the cycle of tenancy, along with the skills and dedication required of the real estate manager.

UNDERSTANDING THE MARKET

Marketing real estate is different from marketing other types of products and services. Obviously, real property is immovable, so altering it to meet market demands is difficult and expensive. Specific features of a property may limit the size of its market and the number of its potential tenants. Therefore, real estate managers (or leasing agents) must thoroughly understand the property's features before identifying the market, and concentrate promotion in media appropriate to that market. Careful study of the limitations on the market before initiating a marketing program will reduce the time and expense required to produce results.

Four primary factors limit the potential market: (1) property type, (2) size of the rental space, (3) location, and (4) rental price. *Property type* limits leasing agents who need to determine whether they are marketing store space to merchants, office space to businesses, or apartments to people looking for a place to live. Each of these property types requires a different marketing approach.

The second limiting factor, *size of rental space,* narrows the range of potential tenants for a specific store, office space, or apartment. For example, the number of employees and size of equipment help determine the square footage needed for the office space. For commercial properties, supermarkets must have 50,000 or more square feet of space—some require 100,000 square feet—while a gift shop usually requires 2,000 square feet or less. In terms of residential space, members in a household and their income generally define the size and layout.

Location, the third limiting factor, also relates to the type of property. Specific features, such as access to transportation and proximity to local attractions, define the market as well. Shopping centers can seek tenants nationally, but rental housing and office space generally attract prospective tenants from the surrounding neighborhood or region. On the other hand, a time-share condominium in a resort area may attract residents from all parts of the country or the world, depending on what they can afford, which leads to the fourth limiting factor—*rental price.* Any particular level of rent will attract only those in the market who are able to afford the rent and are willing to pay it.

Once the general characteristics of the tenant profile become evident, real estate managers can examine what will attract the greatest number of prospects to visit the site. The effort at this

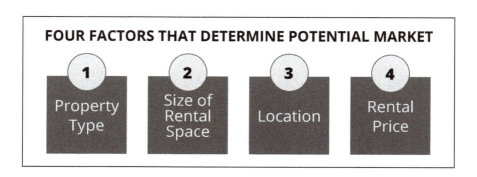

FOUR FACTORS THAT DETERMINE POTENTIAL MARKET

1 — Property Type
2 — Size of Rental Space
3 — Location
4 — Rental Price

point is to make the market aware of the property's existence, its advantages, and its available space. It is important to ensure that the property will lease up quickly by choosing the medium and message that will generate the most responses—the greater the number of responses, the larger the number of prospects. Many types of media are available to market a property, but when selecting media, consider two key elements: (1) reach and (2) frequency. *Reach* applies to the specific audience exposed to the medium, and that should be the largest possible number of prospects who mirror the target market. The *frequency* is the number of times the ad appears in the medium.

By its nature, a new property attracts attention. Its location, size, and state of completion invite curiosity. In this regard, a new development benefits from the free publicity it receives simply because it is new. People's natural inquisitiveness can be further encouraged with specific advertising. On the other hand, an older property may not generate much curiosity, but compared to a new structure, an established property may have fewer vacancies to fill.

New residential properties usually have impressive model units that contain furniture and accessories, which should reflect the market and ideal tenant (Exhibit 8.1). Model units also help prospects

---

EXHIBIT 8.1

Residential Model Unit Reflecting the Market

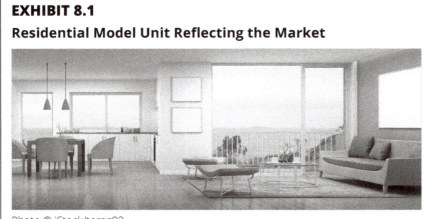

Photo © iStock/terng99

envision the space as their home. While the furnishings of a model space should suit the target market, the furnishings themselves should not be the focus of attention—they should subtly enhance the space, not overshadow it. Oftentimes a prospective resident may request a viewing of an unfurnished, vacant unit in order to fully envision the space without the model decor (Exhibit 8.2). When leasing office or retail space, models are rarely a factor in obtaining tenants. These spaces will typically be marketed in a *vanilla shell* condition—walls ready for paint, floors ready for flooring, and a restroom with standard finishes.

DEVELOPING A MARKETING PROGRAM

The first step in developing a marketing program is to consider the costs of advertising and promotion in order to quantify how much money is available because an advertising program generally requires its own budget. The second step is to determine whether (and to what extent) to use an advertising agency. Although more common with new construction because of the extra expense

---

EXHIBIT 8.2

Vacant Residential Unit in Ready-to-Lease Condition

Photos © Avanath Capital Management, LLC

involved, real estate managers typically hire advertising agencies to promote very large developments or a group of properties under one ownership. When considering an advertising agency, verify the extent of the services desired, the precise cost of those services, and the length of time the contract will last. The costs for these services may include but are not limited to the following:

- Signage
- Social media
- Website development
- Print media:
  - ○ Brochures, letterhead, forms, and business cards
  - ○ Direct mailings and press releases
- Broadcast media and billboards
- Events and networking
- Locator services and referrals

A comprehensive marketing program includes a variety of media, and it should never exclude existing occupants. Funds should always be specifically allocated to retaining occupants, which is explained later in this chapter.

After assessing the budget and costs, the final step is to utilize the information that is uncovered from the market analysis to determine the *target market*—the ideal tenant, who might be interested in renting at the property. For example, the target market for residential properties is usually composed of a particular age group or income bracket, matching the current resident profile. For commercial properties, certain tenants will be targeted in the attempt to achieve the desired image and tenant mix for the property.

The sections that follow explain the different advantages and disadvantages of promotional methods that help target a certain market. These methods involve *developing a theme*—a concept that is reflected across all marketing efforts, conveyed through a name, logo, design, fonts, color scheme, etc., and appears in signage, brochures, and the property website. This theme functions as branding that sets the property apart from its competitors.

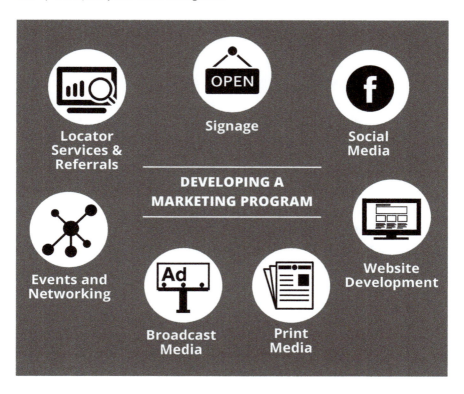

Signage. Every property, whether it has vacancies or not, should display a well-designed and easy-to-read sign that is one of the first things a prospect will see. Good signs identify the site, show the name of the managing agent or firm, and have information on how to obtain rental information. Basic signage is durable and requires minimal maintenance, while providing a continual, cost-effective form of advertisement. Although the response to on-site signage is promising, it also has an understandably limited effectiveness. Only people passing the property will notice the signs, and they may already know the information, which is why signage alone is not adequate—other forms of advertising should accompany it. Marketing signs and other promotional gimmicks, such as brightly colored banners, tall flags, or balloons, are sometimes used throughout a property or near a specific vacancy to immediately grab attention (Exhibit 8.3).

FIVE GENERAL TYPES OF SIGNAGE

A building's signage conveys a certain impression about the property. The property name, logo, or other symbol used to represent the property should appear consistently in all signage to maintain the *unified theme.* The following lists the five types of signage:

1. **Identification signs** are typically located at the entrance and include the permanent identification sign (*monument sign, keystone entry sign, pylon sign*) showing the property's name.
   - High-rise buildings—an engraved plaque may be coordinated with the building exterior
   - Commercial properties—signs placed on or above doors to indicate entrances, exits, and unit or suite numbers or special rooms (e.g., leasing office, laundry room)

2. **Directional signs** guide visitors and tenants to their destination in the building. Buildings that have numerous entrances may have signs directing visitors to the main entrance. Off-site directional signs lead prospects to the building and to the on-site office. These types of signs contain few words and may use arrows to indicate direction.

3. **Informational signs** convey messages and should be kept to an absolute minimum. Certain warning signs are legal requirements that mandate the posting of safety information, such as swimming pool rules, emergency procedures, handicap signs, and fire exits.
   - Temporary signs—occasionally used to warn tenants about a malfunction (wet floor or wet paint); should be immediately removed once the problem is corrected
   - Handwritten signs—usually mismatched; detract from a building's overall image

4. **For-Lease signs** indicate available space and provide leasing contact information. These signs are usually placed inside vacant spaces or at key entrances to the property.

5. **Project signs** introduce a site prior to and during construction and may include a rendering of the property, square footage, availability date, names of the developers, and leasing contact information. Anchor tenancy may be listed for retail space in an effort to attract specific tenants.

EXHIBIT 8.3

Examples of Residential Marketing Signage, Usage of Tall Flags

Photos ©Avanath Capital Management, LLC

Social Media. There is no form of marketing or advertising more confused, misunderstood, or inappropriately used than social media. Simply put, it's a method of communication that provides advertisers with direct access to their potential customers; however, this direct access is not a blanket authorization to commence a sales pitch. Instead, it's the opportunity to demonstrate (Twitter, Facebook, Blog) or illustrate (Pinterest, Instagram, Facebook, Tumblr) just why the property is ideal (Exhibit 8.4).

If the property has planned events centered around the holidays, great tenant functions to showcase, a seasonal special, or great reviews on Yelp, Google, or Facebook, it should be featured in whatever social media platform(s) chosen. A great aspect about social media is that it is free, but in order to maximize the overall message, it's important to create content that is easily liked, linked, accessed, and shared—start small and simple.

There are a number of third-party firms that can assist with monitoring the conversation surrounding the business in the social media sphere. Simply following, responding, and encouraging customers to communicate is key because it's a way to demonstrate

EXHIBIT 8.4

Sample Facebook Page for Residental Property

Source: Facebook, Hudson Garden Apartments

that management is available and listening to concerns. Certain responses can be predrafted so they are quick and demonstrate urgency. If the approach and messages are thoughtful, helpful, and service driven, it assists in reinforcing the property's brand and image and almost always translates to lower turnover and higher occupancy.

Website Development. Posting information online is the most fundamental resource for potential tenants and residents. Whether a custom website is maintained for a property (or company) or listed on another website, these media are relatively inexpensive and reach a wider audience. Depending on the listing, a property can be promoted as a featured listing on the homepage of other high-profile areas. Residential leasing websites such as *apartments. com, apartmentguide.com,* and *craigslist.com* advertise millions of units nationwide.

Commercial leasing websites such as *cityfeet.com* and *loopnet. com* list over two billion square feet of space. In addition, regional websites post vacancies for the local area, which allow potential occupants to search for available space using geographic parameters, square footage requirements, and rental rates, among other qualifiers. Search results include photographs, plans, detailed property information, and leasing contact information. Most websites include a virtual tour to view a revolving image of the interior or exterior of a property.

Also popular with consumers are sites such as *Hotpads.com*, *Zillow.com*, and *Trulia.com*, which allows users to access a more information-based search. Rather than the typical sales pitch with click bait, *Zillow.com* provides more of a research tool to allow users to access neighborhood information, rent comps, and additional data before making a decision on whether or not to sign a residential lease.

Creating a custom website and maintaining the information on it requires specialized design skills and involves either a flat rate or ongoing costs, whether it is for a property management company or property (Exhibit 8.5). Certain designers might charge as low as $400 and as high as $2,000, depending on the features and style used. Some website designers are also experienced in logo design

---

EXHIBIT 8.5

Custom Website Design for a Property

Source: ©The Lodge at Peasley Canyon

and might have other specialized skills that can be used in the overall marketing of the property. Common features in property websites are links to applications for housing that include easy payment of application fees, and maintenance requests.

Print Media. Certain publications accept display ads that are larger and more expensive than typical print ads. Display ads are usually placed in apartment guides or commercial guides that are distributed free of charge—especially in major cities. Real estate managers of office buildings can advertise in magazines, journals, bulletins, and monthly newsletters directed to a specific industry—for instance, the medical field. For shopping centers, specific publications directed to general retailing audiences, as well as to specific types of retailers help gain prospects. Display ads are most helpful during initial lease-up of any type of property and are very effective for inviting a broader audience to visit a new or renovated building.

As with many industries, the need for print media and advertising is slowly fading. More and more service providers are switching to online or hybrid in-print and online platforms that allow clients and customers to obtain the maximum return on advertising investment possible. Online advertising allows for greater exposure, interactive, and virtual tours, as well as enhanced tracking tools to better understand what works and what does not. In fact, many real estate owners and operators are switching to online only for their marketing collateral.

While they are used far less, some newspaper ads are still placed in certain markets. Newspapers with larger circulations periodically publish a special section on real estate that appears in a magazine or tabloid format including information on properties, neighborhoods, property owners, real estate brokers, developers, and managers, and appeals to numerous readers. The real estate manager must weigh the appeal and potential success of advertising in these special sections because they usually carry an added cost.

Brochures, Letterhead, Forms, and Business Cards. The most detailed piece of advertising for a property is usually printed in a *brochure* with colorful and appealing, high-quality photos that fully describe the property and rental space. Brochures are usually available to hand out to prospects, and they can be mailed to those who inquire by phone or be distributed to local businesses for employee break rooms, etc. For residential properties, brochures should include sample floor plans with photos of the model spaces. For shopping centers, they should include a plot plan, traffic statistics, consumer demographics, and sometimes aerial photographs of the site and the neighborhood. Office building brochures should have information about the amenities and nearby facilities along with photos. Depending on the particular company, brochures can also list the name of the management company and their contact information.

To minimize costs, before a brochure is designed, consider how long it will last. For example, a design that allows updating information on rent prices will help a brochure last several years. The same primary design elements (logo, typeface, and graphics) should be used to maintain the consistency and general theme. To design a brochure, various design software programs allow businesses to easily customize the software as needed. Depending on the budget, the cost differences must be weighed between purchasing the design software and contracting a graphic designer.

Coordinated business cards, forms, documents, and company letterhead maintain a unified theme and branding for the company or property. Such printed forms should contain the same font styles, logo, and graphics. They work together to establish the reputation of a property as being on the cutting edge or more modern compared to other properties that might appear older and out of date.

Direct Mailing and Press Releases. If legitimate prospects for a particular property can be identified, a direct-mailing campaign may be profitable, but identifying prospects can be problematic.

While producing, printing, and mailing an ad is costly, preparing or purchasing mailing lists is usually even more expensive. Most purchased lists are ineffective for reaching rental space users directly; however, lists of brokers who represent tenants (or *tenant reps*) are useful for leasing office, retail, and industrial space. Because of the costs involved, direct mailing is not a primary means of promoting rental real estate, but it can be effective if sent to a targeted market and followed up with a personal contact. Much of this is effectuated in today's market via eBlast and other commercial marketing sources that generate and send e-mail solicitations to target audiences.

Press releases are sent to real estate editors of local newspapers as well as broadcast media outlets in the form of direct mail or e-mails. When sending press releases, be sure they are newsworthy items for local publications and broadcast media. For example, information about a new development or a property that has undergone substantial rehabilitation can lead to rental inquiries at virtually no cost. The presentation should be clean, attractive, and free of errors. Including the following items in a press release will help attract an editor's attention:

- The name and phone number of the person to contact should be at the top of the page.
- The release should be short—two pages double-spaced at most; one page is preferable.
- The first paragraph should include the "who, what, when, where, and why" and should be kept as short as possible.
- The subject should be a legitimate news item, not a veiled advertisement.
- Photographs should be sent whenever possible.

Press releases should be maximized for their publicity and public relations value, even though they do not replace the effectiveness of advertisements. Developing a relationship with the real estate editor of the local newspaper can be beneficial—especially when announcing events, such as grand openings or the reopening of a property.

Broadcast Media and Billboards. Real estate managers occasionally use TV or radio commercials to lease a new residential development or to promote tenant businesses in large shopping centers. TV commercials are extremely expensive because both production and airtime costs are high. The cost of airtime is usually much lower for local channels than for network television, and the advertisement can target a specific market based on the particular channel's programming. Radio promotion is primarily useful for residential space, although office and retail space may benefit from advertising on all-news or business stations or programs. For instance, Saturday or Sunday afternoon radio commercials may effectively direct drivers to open house showings. In some aspects, radio has advantages over television—it is less expensive and serves narrower target markets compared to certain TV stations.

Another advertising option on a larger scale is through use of billboards, especially for new or renovated properties. Billboard messages are concise; they announce the location, type of space, and projected occupancy date of the property. The size and content of billboards are influenced by the volume and speed of traffic passing the sign, based on its location—whether an intersection, a highway, or a public transportation station. Since billboard advertising is expensive, it is important to simply announce that space is available for lease and provide basic contact information.

Events and Networking. Unlike advertising, public relations (PR) refers to any form of promotion that is not paid for, such as press releases and word-of-mouth endorsement. PR helps increase awareness and build the image of the property in a cost-effective way. Clearly, creative public relations can affect the target market at a fraction of the cost of advertising. In fact, some experts say that consumers are five times more likely to be influenced by editorial copy than by advertising. Special events such as a Halloween Trick-or-Treat through the property or even an Easter Egg Hunt at the site will generate news and attention. Another important way to help build clientele and expedite leasing is through membership and active participation in professional organizations and social networking events they might host. This allows real estate managers to make use of business and professional contacts. For example, attending annual conferences and participating on committees and boards are ways to increase this interaction. Many associations offer opportunities to teach their courses throughout the country and internationally.

Locator Services and Referrals. Real estate managers must budget their use appropriately when relying on locator services and referrals because both services require compensation. Locator services are more common in the apartment market, and they often assist people who are relocating into the area. They provide a centralized listing of available rental space and usually offer their services directly to the prospect. However, the property owner whose space is rented usually pays the fee—typically a percentage of the first month's rent.

For commercial markets, leasing agents and real estate brokers provide a similar service to owners and prospective tenants through referrals. These representatives seek out prospects if they work for an owner. If they are tenant reps, they search for office, retail, or industrial space that meet the prospect's criteria. The broker's fee (leasing commission) relates to the negotiated rent. In a soft market, the owner of the leased space pays the fee. In a tight market, the tenant may have to pay the commission. Commercial brokers and leasing agents are often part of a network. (The local Commercial Board of REALTORS® provides a gathering place to exchange information.) Many have multiple-listing services and mechanisms for distributing flyers on available properties to their members. They may refer properties or prospects to other brokers if they are unable to match a commercial tenant to a particular space. In such situations, a reciprocal arrangement may be made regarding commissions if a lease is arranged.

Referrals are excellent sources of prospects for any type of property. Happy residents and tenants actively discuss their satisfaction with friends and business associates; this can be encouraged by offering referral incentives, which should be carefully evaluated in terms of what to offer and the costs. A rental discount is usually an attractive incentive to offer; however, other incentives may be more effective for a residential property. The most popular forms of incentives include cash payments, rental discounts, gift certificates, or improvements to the leased space (new appliances or fixtures). Before instituting a referral incentive program, investigate any legal limitations on tenant referrals or compensation for them. Certain restrictions may relate to real estate licensing requirements—some states may prohibit monetary incentives.

Marketing and Branding

In today's social atmosphere, branding and messaging is more important than ever. From helping a company establish their presence in a market or submarket to repositioning or launching a new property, there are many reasons to create a brand, and crafting a catchy or creative logo and tagline is just part of it. Presenting the brand to customers and clients on and off site can make business more successful and also enhance occupancy.

There are three primary types of branding that occur on-site or across a portfolio, and each is directly related to the identity of the entity: (1) owner or ownership group, (2) management company, and (3) the physical asset.

The Property Owner's Branding Goals. Depending on an owner's goals and objectives, they may seek to advertise their name or brand at the site. While this tends to be more common with an owner/operator, it is not uncommon with investment groups or funds seeking to garner attention as an area expert—perhaps as they seek out off-market investment opportunities in a particular market or submarket. Additionally, it can help with fundraising if the group is active in the marketplace and looking to grow their investor base. There is no better way to evaluate the relationship between physical and financial oversight than to walk the property. Seeing the owner's name and logo at the property level shows investors and customers that the owner stands by their product.

LIFESTYLE BRANDING

A secondary brand that has emerged in recent years is the lifestyle brand, where a company will launch a brand that is specifically tailored to meet a niche market. Historically, this has occurred in the hospitality sector with companies like the Marriott with their flagship Marriott brand, luxury JW Marriott brand and business-minded Courtyard by Marriott brand.

Multifamily companies such as Avalon Bay have three tiers, starting with Eaves, then Ava, and ultimately Avalon. Other regional/national players such as McKinley and Laramar have launched brands focusing on smaller, localized assets in specific markets. While McKinley has launched their Hyde Park brand in Tampa, Florida, Laramar has launched their "local" brand in Los Angeles that caters to a niche property type and allows them to market their brand to a specific "lifestyle" renter.

The Management Company's Brand. The management company stands to benefit greatly from marketing their brand on site. Collateral can be proudly displayed in the interior and exterior common areas to identify the management company and direct interested customers and clients to contact the company for additional information on both their services or space available. The properties truly represent a physical "resume" of the management services, so through effective messaging and branding, it helps to ensure that the management company stands out as the local market expert. It's important to understand the owner's position on displaying the management company's marketing on site. Placing items such as signs, banners, decals, stickers, flags, or other materials in public view can help drive customer and client traffic to both offices—leasing/management and corporate—all while adding additional elements of excitement to the property's marketing opportunities. Benefiting from the management of a physical asset, there is great potential leverage for current successes into future third-party management opportunities.

The Property's Brand. It is not uncommon for a property to undergo a repositioning project that will include a physical upgrade or overhaul, along with a name change. If a property has been owned for an extended period of time and an ownership group is looking to boost returns, it is also common for the rebranding to take place in accordance with said renovation efforts. A property might suffer or benefit from a name attached by a local, regional, or national developer. Unless the name and/or brand has changed when the renovation efforts start, which include physical upgrades and improvements, they can sometimes be lost on the market. Successful property brands will garner an appeal on their own, often tying into the local community, a neighborhood, or region. Branding the site is increasingly common and critically important in today's world, where local lifestyle elements are sometimes the key to additional revenue and income streams.

It's important to consider the property branding in conjunction with other on- and off-site marketing in order to ensure the property branding efforts do not just coexist but truly cooperate to maximize the overall marketing and branding efforts outlined in the property's marketing plan.

Offering Marketing Incentives

The list of incentives and concessions that an owner can offer to new tenants is endless. Incentives to lease residential space tend to center on amenities such as free cable television, a lower security deposit, or interior decorating (paint, wallpaper). However, the choice of incentives should not detract from the property's image or reputation. If possible, concessions should be aimed toward enhancing the property after a resident vacates, so that incentives do not lower NOI or decrease the property's value.

Leasing incentives are typically offered to prospective tenants for office, retail, or industrial space. Examples include upgrading the tenant improvements or reimbursing part or all of their moving costs. For shopping centers, a modified percentage rent or caps on pass-through expenses may be granted. Market conditions as well as how desirable a particular space is to a particular tenant (and how desirable the tenant is to the owner) are considerations in offering such incentives.

Concessions. In areas with high vacancy and a poor economy or a large amount of new competitive space, offering *concessions*—free rent for a month as a marketing incentive—is common. Free rent is a costly concession for an owner to make; the reduction in NOI reduces cash flow and property value. However, if the market is poor and competitors are offering rent-free periods, the owner may have no choice but to offer such a concession.

Offering an incoming tenant a period of free rent technically reduces the amount of income derived from the rental space. However, the impact of this concession on property value and long-term income is not as great as a straightforward reduction of the rent—provided the rental space is priced competitively. When a financial concession seems necessary, the real estate manager and owner must strive to minimize the negative effects of the concession on NOI. At the same time, if a concession is not offered, the damage to NOI may be more severe.

Effective Rent. Real estate managers should understand the concept of effective rent in order to evaluate the ramifications of a rental concession accurately. *Effective rent* is the cumulative rental amount collected over the term of a lease expressed as an average monthly rental (residential) or an annual rate per rentable square foot (office, retail, and industrial). If a lease term is 12 months— more common in residential than commercial leasing—the effective rent is the total rent collected during the 12-month period.

When one month's free rent is given as a concession, the effective rent is equal to only 11 months' total rent. Averaged over the entire lease term of 12 months, this total is less than the quoted rent for the space per month—even though the full monthly amount is collected in each of the 11 months. However, a period of free rent is actually preferable to reducing the quoted rent because that may reduce the effective rent for many years—not just one. For commercial properties, everything is part of the negotiation process and effective rent and *net present value (NPV)* of the entire package must be considered, including *time value of money* since leases tend to be longer.

Exhibits 8.6 and 8.7 demonstrate this concept. The impact of lowering quoted rent is magnified when seen in the context of the whole building or property—more important; it reduces NOI and property value.

Measuring Marketing Effectiveness

The effectiveness of each marketing effort (or advertisement) is measured in terms of the number of prospects who come to the property, the cost to reach them, the number of prospects who become residents or commercial tenants, and the length of time the space remains vacant. The amount of advertising needed depends on the occupancy level and location of the property. If the property is fully leased and no move-outs are expected, no advertising is necessary. However, most large buildings have continual turnover; therefore, continual advertising is essential. A prominent location may generate enough walk-in traffic at a residential property to reduce the advertising needed—less prominent properties may require significantly more promotion to achieve sufficient rental traffic. There are no set rules to determine how much advertising an individual property needs, but thinking of advertising as an investment underscores its monetary value. The return on this investment is finding a qualified tenant to fill a vacancy as quickly as possible.

With that in mind, advertising expenses can be calculated in terms of the *cost per prospect.* For example, $100 might be spent

EXHIBIT 8.6

Residential Rent Concessions and Effective Rent

Assume the quoted rent for an apartment is $840 per month and the lease term is one year (12 months). The impact of one month's free rent on effective rent would be as follows:

Quoted rent	$840/month
Expected effective rent	$10,080/year ($840 × 12 months)
Actual effective rent	$9,240/year ($840 × 11 months)
Average rent collected	$770/month ($9,240 ÷ 12)
Amount of rent loss	8.3% ($840 ÷ $10,080)

Note that if the quoted rent were reduced to $770 per month, the effective rent would also be $9,240 ($770 × 12 months). Either way, the loss of income is more than 8 percent. However, the impact of the rent reduction is greater going into the future.

Suppose greater operating expenses necessitate a rent increase of 5 percent in the second year of the lease. The impact of the increase in rent would be as follows:

Rent increase in second year	5%
Increase applied to original quoted rent	$882 ($840 × 1.05)
Effective rent for second year	$10,584 ($882 × 12)
Increase applied to reduced rent	$809 ($770 × 1.05 = $808.50 rounded to $809)*
Effective rent for second year	$9,708 ($809 × 12)
Second year loss (additional)	8.3% ($882 – $809 = $73 ÷ $882)

Reducing the quoted rent in the first year results in even less increased rent in the second year—an additional 8 percent loss of potential income. In order to increase the second year's reduced rent to the quoted rent (from $770 to $882 per month), a 14.5 percent increase would be necessary. Few residents would be willing to renew their leases under such conditions. That could result in another period of vacancy, and the owner might have to offer another concession to lease the apartment again.

Because lowering quoted rent can cost so much income, prudent management of real property often includes promotion of carefully planned nonmonetary concession packages.

---

*The number is rounded because rent is not quoted with cents.

EXHIBIT 8.7

Commercial Rent Concessions and Effective Rent

Suppose the base rent for 1,000 sq ft of office (rentable area), retail (gross leasable area), or industrial space is $18.00 per sq ft per year. On a three-year lease with three months' free rent, the effective rent for the lease term is calculated as follows:

1,000 sq ft × $18.00 = $18,000 annual rent × 3 years = $54,000 total rent due

$18,000 annual rent ÷ 12 = $1,500 monthly rent × 3 months = $4,500 free rent

$54,000 total rent – $4,500 free rent = $49,500 total actual effective rent ÷ 36 months = $1,375 actual effective monthly rental income

$1,500 monthly rent – $1,375 actual effective monthly rent = $125 (more than 8% lost income)

On a square-foot basis for the three-year term, the base expected rent of $18.00 would be effectively reduced to $16.50 ($1,375 × 12 months ÷ 1,000 sq ft).

If the base rent were reduced to $16.50 per sq ft instead of giving three months' free rent, the total effective rent for 36 months would still be the same: $49,500. However, if the lease were renewed for another three years at a 4 percent increase, the total effective rent for the new lease term would be only $51,480 ($16.50 × 1.04 × 1,000 sq ft × 3 years) as opposed to $56,160 ($18.00 × 1.04 × 1,000 sq ft × 3 years), a difference of $4,680. In order to achieve the equivalent total effective rent of $56,160 for the new lease term, the reduced rent would have to be increased 13.5% ($56,160 – $49,500 = $6,660 ÷ $49,500).

This example presents the basic method for arriving at effective rent for commercial space. However, it does not take into account the time value of money—a valuation concept usually applied in calculating effective rent for leases that have a term of more than one year. A calculation of effective rent incorporating the time value of money would produce a rental rate per square foot lower than the stated $16.50.

In addition, owners may extend the lease an equal number of months on the back end of the lease to account for the free rent at the beginning. In this example, the lease term would be three years and three months, or 39 months. In effect, the owner is still only obtaining three full years of rent.

to advertise in an industry-specific publication to fill a vacancy in an office building. Because very few vacancies exist in the community, 10 prospects respond to this ad, and two of them are intent on signing a lease for this $800-a-month office space. The $100 investment certainly would be a value at a cost of $10 per prospect. The number of strongly interested prospects was two out of ten, making the prospect-to-tenant ratio five to one. This ratio is called the *conversion ratio.* The advertising cost, selected medium, and length of time before a new tenant is found must be evaluated in relation to the resulting conversion ratio to determine the effectiveness of a particular marketing campaign. In other cases, the conversion ratio is used to evaluate a leasing agent's talents and performance against those of their peers.

Real estate managers commonly use a *traffic report* to record what attracted a prospect to visit the subject property. The example shown (Exhibit 8.8) is for a residential property; a traffic report for an office building would record similar information with the prospects' space needs indicated as ranges of square footages. By evaluating traffic reports, the effectiveness of different marketing methods can be determined. The most effective approach is the one that produces the most prospects at the lowest cost per prospect in the least time. Today, automated software solutions help take the traffic report a step further by providing solution-specific phone numbers that are customized to fit a specific advertising method. For example, Zillow, Facebook, and Google are used, each number would be different. These numbers, once dialed, are tracked in the database and both site-level and off-site supervisors are able to access this information in real time to understand where most leads are coming from.

Using Sales Techniques

Since prospects usually become tenants only after visiting the property, certain sales techniques should be used to persuade prospects that they are receiving the best value to accommodate their needs. Sometimes the rental space may sell itself, but regardless

EXHIBIT 8.8

Sample Weekly Traffic Report (Residential)

Property _____ Week of _____ Prepared By _____

	Mon	Tue	Wed	Thu	Fri	Sat	Sun	Total
Nature of Inquiry								
Telephone call								
Visitor								
Time of Inquiry								
Before noon								
Noon to 5 p.m.								
After 5 p.m.								
Referral Source								
Classified ad								
Display ad								
Billboard								
Drive-by								
Telephone directory								
Word-of-mouth								
Direct mail								
Television								
Radio								
Internet website								
Apartment locator service								
Current resident								
Prior visit								
Apartment Desired								
Studio								
One-bedroom								
Two-bedroom								
Three-bedroom								
Other								

Weather conditions _____

Comments _____

_____

_____

of the condition of the available space, there is no guarantee. Real estate managers and leasing agents should master the following four fundamental leasing tactics:

1. Know the features of the property thoroughly.
2. Get acquainted with the prospect.
3. Show the features of the property thoroughly.
4. Close the sale.

All four are critical—the last is most important of all and must go beyond the obvious. For example, if prospects who are considering an apartment mention that they have children, simply saying, "There is an elementary school in the next block," is not enough because the prospects are probably already aware of the school. Instead, leasing personnel should be able to volunteer detailed information about the school that goes beyond knowing the location. In fact, they should be thoroughly familiar with the neighborhood (schools, shopping, transportation, etc.) so they can answer specific questions as well as describe the setting in which the property is located.

A leasing agent who shows office space should be able to discuss features and businesses in the vicinity that may be of use to prospective office tenants and their employees. Examples are the proximity of business-to-business services such as attorneys, commercial banks, restaurants, health clubs, and public transportation. Information about the trade area population, traffic counts, and the competition (or lack of it) should be available for retail prospects. While answering questions and engaging in conversation with a welcoming, warm demeanor, the leasing agent will soon get acquainted with the prospect.

Multifamily property owners use tools such as LRO (lease rent options) or YieldStar® to set prices based either on market activity or trends or portfolio-wide occupancy. These tools, though intended to maximize revenue and occupancy to fit an owner's goals and objectives, can be quite confusing for a prospect. The rent is customized to a specific point in time and as a result, the next prospect can sometimes receive a more or less favorable price quote for the same unit. In any case, the technology best demonstrates the need for a blend of old-school market expertise: knowing the competitors, their product, and their rates and strong sales skills. Things do not always go over well when the leasing agent's response is "well, that's what the computer says." Computers and software can help so much in this business, but face-to-face interaction at application and move-in time are absolutely essential for building rapport and creating a favorable customer experience.

When it is time to show the space for lease, appearance is everything. Most prospects assume that models represent the best that the property has to offer and that any apparent defects in the model will be magnified in the rental apartments. The following are a few guidelines for showing model apartments:

- Use an apartment(s) with a less-desirable location or layout because the most desirable apartments are the easiest ones to lease.
- Be sure the model(s) is easily accessible from the leasing office.
- Clean and inspect the model on a daily basis.
- Use decorations that accentuate the best features of a unit and its layout.
- Be sure the furnishings used reflect the income level of the target market and are appropriate for the size of the unit.

For residential properties without model units, the condition of the vacant spaces is as important as the condition of a model would be. At all times, an assortment of vacant apartments should be in *market-ready* condition—thoroughly clean with all improvements made. These apartments should be inspected daily to ensure there are no issues when shown to a prospect that might pose objections to leasing. An inspection checklist for a residential property typically includes the following:

- All walls and ceilings should be freshly painted, including closets or shelving.
- Carpeting should be freshly shampooed; burns or stains should be removed or the carpeting should be replaced.
- All windows should be washed inside and out.
- Windowsills, ledges, and shelves should be wiped clean.
- Light fixtures and switches should be in working order.
- The temperature should be set at an appropriate level for the season.
- The kitchen should be immaculate with all appliances clean and in working condition.
- Bathrooms should be spotless—watch for dripping faucets, stains, and tub and tile grout that should be replaced.

Extremely good leasing agents will be able to close the sale after conducting the property tour and showing evidence that the apartment meets the needs of the prospect. Most often, the prospect will be ready, but just needs a little push to start the application process.

Approving a Prospect for Tenancy

Diligence is necessary to ensure that the prospect can and will pay the rent, care for the property, and be a cooperative resident or tenant. Most of the qualification process involves financial history, but it should include other pertinent credentials as well. For residential or small commercial properties, the prospect usually supplies the information on a rental application form. A credit bureau can verify information about current loans, activity on credit cards, payment history, and delinquent debts. Appropriate consumer reporting agencies, such as tenant-screening and reference-checking services, can provide other types of information, such as an applicant's rental history. Managers may ask residential prospects to pay a fee for such a credit check, and they customarily leave a refundable deposit to reserve the space until the credit check is complete. However, some states require real estate managers to supply the prospect with written criteria (screening criteria) before the prospect completes an application and pays a fee. The screening criteria are based on credit reports to be obtained by making phone calls to verify employment history.

For larger properties, there is access to more advanced web-based screening services that help determine—within a matter of minutes—whether the applicant should be accepted or declined. The criteria notify prospects of the types of factors the real estate manager will be investigating for the fee paid. After reading the criteria, the prospect can decide to pay the fee or walk away if they know that they might not qualify for some reason. Another tool for screening a prospective tenant is the criminal background check, which can be secured through most tenant-screening companies. When the prospect is approved, the initial deposit should be applied toward the security deposit rather than the rent, and if any amount is due, the remainder of the security deposit should be collected when the lease is signed.

In compliance with the Fair Credit Reporting Act, prospects that are denied a lease based on a credit report must be notified in writing of the adverse action. A residential rental application should request the prospect's current and previous addresses so both property owners can be contacted. The information they can provide about the prospect as their resident is not available anywhere else. To establish creditworthiness for commercial tenant prospects, financial statements, federal tax returns, etc., should be used for the entity legally responsible for paying the rent. (Qualification of tenants is discussed in Chapter 11 for residential and Chapter 12 for commercial, office, and mixed-used properties.)

Owners and real estate managers are not responsible for implementing the Customer Identification Program of the U.S.A. Patriot Act. However, they should verify the applicant's identity and citizenship or immigration status because of the risk associated with renting to a terrorist and because of the increase in identity theft. Real estate managers routinely require photo identification in the form of a driving license; federal (green card) or state-issued identification; and foreign passport. The tenant's file should include a copy of the identification record.

The prospect's Social Security number (SSN) or individual tax identification number (ITIN) is another required critical piece of information. Issued by the Internal Revenue Service (IRS), ITINs are available to noncitizens who need to report income for tax purposes but are not eligible for SSNs. The Gramm-Leach Bliley Act, which became effective in July 2001, requires property owners and managers to safeguard personal and financial information collected from prospective tenants and to dispose of it properly to protect against misuse and identity theft. The information collected during the screening process must be kept in secure files and must be properly destroyed when appropriate.

RETAINING TENANTS

The most important element in keeping tenants satisfied with their choice of rental space is to let them know that their business is valued. Thinking of and treating tenants as customers, rather than simply rent payers, fosters the notion that they are valued. Rent is usually a major expense for tenants, and for that, they expect the components of the building to operate properly and efficiently and the property as a whole to be pleasant, comfortable, and secure.

Building a business relationship with residents or commercial tenants requires months or even years, especially if the real estate manager is new to the site and some of the tenants have been there for several years. Any dissatisfaction with the previous manager or management firm must be dispelled. Tenant dissatisfaction can be very damaging in terms of current occupancy and the property's future reputation. Real estate managers can rectify legitimate concerns such as deficiencies in service; however, regaining the respect of the tenants may be extremely difficult if service was substandard for a long time.

Welcoming New Tenants

The efforts to retain tenants begin before they move in. Between the time that one resident vacates a unit and another moves in, the property staff should inspect the premises to make sure all components are operating and are properly installed. Thorough inspection and repair at this time will avert dissatisfaction on the part of the incoming resident. If a repair cannot be completed until after move-in, tell the new resident approximately when the task will be finished. Commercial property owners may lease vacant space as is, or they may completely gut the space to allow for new tenant improvement construction, in which case additional factors, such as specifications having been met and occupancy permits, may come into play.

Incoming residents and commercial tenants should receive a handbook that outlines the rules and regulations of tenancy as well as a list of important names and phone numbers. The handbook should define emergencies and non-emergencies. Management and staff of residential properties in particular may receive calls at any time of day or night, unless guidelines are provided. Although a resident should never be dissuaded from calling about a problem, they should be able to distinguish a repair that can wait from one that is a true emergency.

Handling Requests

Residents and commercial tenants at times request improved services or products, and those requests should not be considered as complaints. Although some tenants may think the motto, "The customer is always right," grants them the privilege to make outrageous requests or demands, most understand the limitations involved in operating a property. All requests should receive responses as quickly as possible. However, requests that are particularly complex may require research, and the real estate manager should advise the tenant of that fact and when an answer may be expected.

Not all requests can be granted, and delaying a negative response—saying someone else must make the decision or that the request is still under consideration—may be tempting. Saying "no" is never easy, but delivering bad news as quickly as good news will gain the confidence of most tenants. Tenants are typically more concerned about receiving an honest response than about having a problem corrected immediately. They would much prefer a forthright estimate of when a problem will be corrected to a promise that will not be kept. Sometimes, hearing "I'm sorry" is all the tenant needs.

Building Goodwill with Tenants

Every communication with tenants is an opportunity to build goodwill. Special events sponsored by the property's management (e.g., a picnic or outing for a tenant appreciation day) can build morale. Residential and commercial properties can use newsletters effectively to update tenants about events on or near the site or to provide other information that pertains to all building occupants.

Another retention strategy is to perform housekeeping tasks as tenants are entering or leaving the building so they can see *what the management does for them.* Seeing the work in progress, as well as the results, tends to make that work more valuable to the tenant—*visibility adds value.*

Sending written questionnaires or e-mails to determine whether service requests have been handled promptly and satisfactorily is another way to gain tenant retention. Exit surveys can be used to find out why tenants move out and ask them what improvements to their leased premises, the building itself, or the property's amenities might have encouraged them to stay. Asking about the rent structure and the value they received is also a good idea, along with how they were treated by the manager, staff, and company as a whole. These surveys can also be provided online or via e-mail through services such as Constant Contact or Survey Monkey.

SUMMARY

Throughout the cycle of tenancy, the real estate manager's dedication to building goodwill is essential for the property to thrive. The property and its potential tenants should be examined in order to estimate the size and nature of the market to create a marketing strategy. By persuasively matching the qualities of the property with the prospect's expressed needs and wants, the prospect can be converted to a tenant. If the prospective tenant's credentials are acceptable, a written lease is executed to protect both parties to the agreement.

One of the most important aspects of tenant relations is the collection of deposits and rent. In enforcing collection policies, the real estate manager must treat all residents and commercial tenants fairly. To meet the expectations of the owner, the manager must firmly uphold the policy regarding when rent is due. If the tenant is unable or unwilling to pay, or if some other serious infraction of the lease occurs, the eviction proceedings will commence (more information on rent collection can be found in Chapter 9).

Real estate managers play an essential role in the retention of tenants; therefore, tenants' requests for repairs and services should be handled conscientiously and impartially to provide them with the best possible service. Throughout each phase of the cycle of tenancy, how the tenants are treated will have a strong bearing on lease renewals. The lease renewals should be regarded as an expression of goodwill toward the tenant and a part of the sound economic operation of the property.

9 | Understanding the Lease

Simply put, a *lease* is a legally binding contract between two parties—the owner (*lessor*) and the tenant (*lessee*)—in exchange for fixed payments (rent) for possession and stated use of real property for a specified period of time. After the marketing plan is implemented and begins attracting prospects to the site, it is necessary to develop an outline for leasing to and placing the occupants in the property. This in-house *leasing plan* typically includes a site plan of the property (preferably drawn to scale), unit numbers, and square footage dimensions. The rent schedule portion of the leasing plan outlines the current or desired rents for each space, lease expiration dates, and any concessions. The plan may also display anticipated parking counts for each occupant.

Real estate managers typically sign the lease as the agent of the owner, which is stated in writing on the contract. Regardless of the type of agreement, good management practices require a written lease, which offers greater protection to both parties. It also assures the owner that the tenant will occupy the space for a certain period and that the owner can anticipate a prescribed income for that period. In theory, no financial loss should occur because of a sudden vacancy. The tenant has possession of the space for the duration of the lease at a set rental rate. The lease may also outline procedures for rent increases, which is more common in commercial leases that have multiyear terms.

The lease should clearly delineate the property owner's and tenant's responsibilities and eliminate misunderstandings between the owner and the tenant—so both of them must understand its provisions. The real estate manager is responsible for asking new tenants whether they have read and understood the lease because any unclear provisions can be explained at that time.

Generally, a lease form that is reasonable, standardized within a property type—apartment, office space, etc., consistent with state law or any landlord and tenant acts, and suitable for all tenants— should be used. As a matter of goodwill, the lease should not contain clauses to which informed people will object or that uninformed people will ignore. When properly prepared and presented with equal emphasis on the tenant's point of view, the lease has excellent marketing value. The leasing plan should always reflect the goals and objectives of the owner. Organizations such as the Society of Industrial and Office Realtors (SIOR), the National Apartment Association (NAA), and NATIONAL ASSOCIATION OF REALTORS® (NAR®) provide lease documents through their local affiliates that are current and contain the necessary, localized disclosures and protective clauses to keep the owner and real estate manager compliant.

FUNDAMENTAL ELEMENTS OF LEASES

Numerous leases are suited for different types of rental space, but all leases should describe the *demised premises*—the leased space that is conveyed from the owner to the tenant—and state the duration of the agreement, the amount of rent, and when and how payment is to be made. The following lists the principal contents of a lease:

- **The parties.** The full legal names of the property owner and tenant are included—both of whom must sign the lease for validation.
- **Description of the leased premises.** Apartment number and address of the building for residential units, square footage, suite (or store number for commercial space), and a legal description or floor plan are included in the lease.
- **Lease term.** Duration of the lease, including the starting and ending dates, and any specific provisions regarding renewal or cancellation are outlined. If commercial leases involve construction (or free rent), they may show separate dates for occupancy and for the first rent payment.

- **Rent.** Amount of rent for each period and due date are included, which is usually monthly and due on the first of the month. For commercial leases, the lease might state the aggregate rent for the entire lease term, and includes provisions for rent increases, especially when their duration exceeds one year—nonpayment of rent is cause for termination of the lease.

- **Use of the premises.** Specific guidelines and rules for the use of space, living quarters, office space, apparel store, and any other space should be thoroughly listed.

- **Other provisions.** Lengthy clauses that detail the rights and obligations of the parties with respect to their relationship to each other, as property owner and tenant, and to the property. Responsibilities to pay specific utilities (residential) or increases in operating costs (commercial) and to maintain the property are written in this portion of the lease, along with the amount and condition for return of any required security deposit. In addition to the insurance requirements of each party, indemnification clauses are also included.

TYPES OF LEASES

The type of lease depends on the kind of property. The following lists four basic types of leases:

1. **Gross lease.** Commonly used for residential leases in which residents pay a fixed rent and the owner pays all of the operating expenses, including property taxes and insurance. Residents are usually responsible for utilities *inside* their apartments.

2. **Net lease.** Primarily used for space in office buildings, shopping centers, and industrial properties in which the tenant not only pays rent, but also assumes responsibility for certain expenses connected with the property as a whole. Itemized pass-through expenses are generally prorated based on the amount of space the tenant occupies as a percentage of the total *gross leasable space (GLA)* in the building.

3. **Percentage lease.** Sometimes used for retail properties, percentage leases include a percentage of the tenant's gross sales made on the premises. The lease usually states a fixed-minimum rent, and the tenant pays a percentage of its gross sales in excess of that amount—depending on the volume of business.

4. **Multifamily leases.** Generally similar but with only a few variations, multifamily leases offer little to no negotiation. Commercial leases, on the other hand, can vary widely—even within the same property. With commercial leases, the tenant may provide the initial draft, and its provisions may vary substantially from leases of other tenants.

LEASE NEGOTIATION

A written lease defines the rights and obligations of the office tenant and the building owner, but because of the complexity of the arrangement and a term that normally lasts more than one year, lengthy negotiations usually precede a lease signing. Real estate managers almost always participate in the negotiations. In some cases, the leasing agent may work out the details, but the real estate manager will usually administer the finalized lease agreement. As a representative of the owner, the manager will be instrumental in clarifying any of the tenant's questions and suggesting possible compromises. It should be noted, however, that any drafting of lease clauses or significant changes in the wording of a lease should be made by the owner's attorney as real estate managers are not typically authorized to perform these functions.

The starting point of negotiations is usually a proposal or *letter of intent (LOI)* from the prospective tenant, followed by the presentation of the building owner's standard lease form, which contains clauses that apply to all of the leasable space in the property. However, negotiation of each individual lease generates a unique document that reflects the relationship between the owner and a particular tenant. Many clauses require minimal discussion, but the concerns of the prospective tenant and the owner usually center on the tenant improvements and any allowances, and those are negotiated at length. Other clauses that often prompt negotiation relate to rent increases *(escalations), pass-through charges,* services, term of lease and extensions, and *tenant options.* Insurance requirements and indemnification clauses are often highly negotiated.

Standard Clauses

In developing a standard lease form, one of the owner's objectives is to minimize expenses associated with the rent received. On the other hand, the incoming tenant might want to maximize the rights and services it receives for that rent. To accommodate these differing desires, a number of specific clauses are common to leases for office space. Two commonly used clauses are (1) rent escalations and (2) pass-through expenses.

Escalation Clauses. Because a commercial lease is often in effect for several years, it commonly includes an *escalation clause* to provide for a regular increase in rent. Property owners and real estate managers write escalation clauses into a lease to recover increases in real estate taxes, property insurance, and other operating expenses over the term of the lease. Common escalation clauses follow.

Operating Expense. A lease may contain an *operating expense escalation clause,* under which any increases in operating costs are passed on to the tenants on a pro rata basis. For example, if operating expenses for a 150,000 sq. ft. building were $540,000 one year and $600,000 the next, the owner would pass the $60,000 ($0.40/sq. ft.) increase through to the tenants. The pro rata share of a tenant who occupies a 12,000 sq. ft. office would be eight percent or $4,800 per year above the prior year's expenses.

Base Year. Sometimes a lease provides for rent adjustments by referring to a *base year*—occasionally the current calendar year, but more often the first full calendar year after move-in. The base year is also a negotiable item. Once the base year is established, the tenant pays for increases over the amount of operating expenses in the base year. For example, a tenant who moved into offices in October 2017 under a five-year lease would be responsible for increases from the base year of 2018. Escalation of the base rent would take effect in 2019, 2020, and 2021, with a partial escalation for 2022 when the lease term would expire. The base year may change when the tenant renews the lease because the renewal date then becomes the base year, which might be stated as a specific rate plus accrued escalations. The property owner, with the assistance of the real estate manager, must take the property's cash flow into consideration when establishing the base year for escalations because it will be in effect for the full term of the lease.

If the property is new, the first full calendar year may not always contain the true or full services necessary to maintain the property. In this case, the operating costs may be passed through as a set maximum for the first few years, after which the base year would be determined as year two or three when expenses stabilize. Alternatively, a gross-up provision is included, whereby the property's operating expenses are increased (grossed up) to an estimate of what they would be at 95 or 100% occupancy.

Expense Stop. Another strategy is to include an *expense stop* provision, which sets a limit on the owner's expense escalations. For example, if the stop is set at $8.25 per square foot per year, the tenant must share in the increased expenses over that amount on a pro rata basis. The stop is often based on the amount of expenses for the previous full calendar year, and it may be stated as a total amount per year rather than on a per-square-foot basis.

Another term similar to the expense stop is a *"cap"* on *pass-through charges*. A negotiated cap in the previous example might be that the tenant would reimburse actual expenses, but no more than five percent over the previous year's expenses. In these examples, tenants are assured that any major swings in expenses, such as a large elevator repair billed to the tenants on a pro rata basis in one year, are eliminated and replaced with a known and capped annual increase. Caps are often included for controllable expenses such as janitorial, security, and utilities but exclude non-controllable expenses, such as real estate taxes, insurance, and snow removal in the northern states.

In most situations, operating expenses are estimated for the coming year and billed to tenants' pro rata on a monthly basis in advance. At the year's end, when the actual costs are known, adjusted amounts are billed (or credited) to the tenants—a process called *reconciliation.*

Inflation Offset. An escalation clause can also serve to offset the loss in value of the rent dollar over time due to inflation. The owner and tenant can agree to determine the increase in several ways:

1. In the initial negotiations, the parties can agree to a fixed annual increase for the duration of the lease.
2. They can declare that, at a fixed future date, rent will increase to the then-current market rate, to which both parties will agree at that future time since it will never be less than the original rate.
3. Some escalation clauses dealing with then-current market rents may contain requirements for a market analysis by a third party whose decision would be final if the owner and tenant cannot agree on the current market rent at that time.
4. They can agree to refer to a standard index, such as the *Consumer Price Index (CPI)* to determine the amount of the increase.[1]

Fixed Annual Increase. The tenant and real estate manager may prefer to agree on a fixed annual increase for the duration of the lease or on specific rates for set intervals. Annual escalations might be stated specifically, such as $10 per sq. ft. in year one, increasing to $11 in year two and $12 in year three, or as a percentage, such as eight percent per year. A lease for a very long-term rental might be negotiated to state specific increases only every three or five years.

---

1. In many areas of the United States, the CPI is rarely used as a basis for escalations in new leases because the values can fluctuate widely. Since fluctuations are less prominent in the northwestern part of the country, management firms there still use the CPI—usually with a five percent cap and a three percent floor. Older, long-term leases may still reference the CPI.

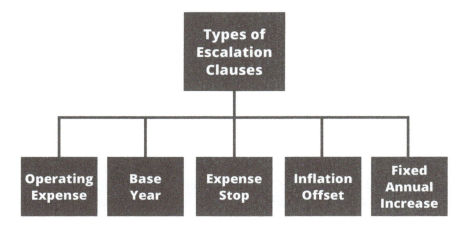

Pass-Through Charges. In a commercial lease, not all operating expenses of the property are necessarily collected in the rent. In a *gross lease,* the owner pays all the expenses of the property and must recover those costs through the rent, but that arrangement is uncommon in large office buildings. Usually the owner bills some expenses to the tenant on a prorated basis in the form of a *pass-through charge.* The pass-through charges are in addition to the base rent charged for the leased space. When the tenant pays any operating expenses directly, the lease is called a *net lease.* Three types of net leases are common, but the expenses covered under each type of net lease vary by region:

1. **Net (or single-net).** The tenant pays the smallest number of direct expenses.
2. **Net-Net (or double-net).** The tenant pays an average number of direct expenses.
3. **Net-Net-Net (or triple-net).** The tenant pays the greatest number of direct expenses.

In general, the higher the level of net lease a region uses, the lower the base rent. In other words, a gross lease for office space will state a comparatively high rent because the owner will pay all operating expenses from that rent. The *all-inclusive* rent for that space is its *base rent.* A single-net lease on that same space will state a

LEASE "NETNESS"

Net Lease Type	Also Known As	Tenant Usually Pays
Single-Net	Net	Taxes
Double-Net	Net-Net	Taxes and insurance
Triple-Net	Net-Net-Net	Taxes, insurance, and maintenance (TIM) or common area maintenance expenses (CAM)

Note: The specific expenses covered under each net lease type may vary from region to region.

lower base rent because the tenant will pay part of a certain operating expense or expenses. In the case of a double-net lease, the base rent for the space will be even lower because the tenant will pay more operating expenses. With a triple-net lease, the base rent on the space will be lowest of all because the tenant directly pays most, if not all, of the expenses. The three types of net leases are also used for industrial and retail space, and standard definitions are available for those uses; they are explained in Chapter 13.

The lease states the specific pass-through expenses the tenant will pay and the method of computing the tenant's pro rata share. The most common pass-through expenses are utilities and *common area maintenance (CAM),* in addition to real estate taxes and property insurance. Owners may pass through capital improvements in the common areas as well, particularly if the improvement reduces an operating expense (e.g., a more efficient HVAC system may lower utility costs). However, the lease must clearly state that capital improvements will be passed through and some leases may require certain capital expenses to be amortized and billed to the tenants over the life of their lease, or on the basis of the projected life of the particular improvement.

Concessions

To encourage the leasing of a space or to encourage the renewal of a lease, a *concession* is given by the owner to a prospective

THE TOP TEN OPTIONS FOR CONCESSIONS

1. Base rent reduction
2. Free rent
3. Free pass-through charges
4. Cap on pass-through charges
5. Cap on CPI-based rent escalation
6. Percentage rent adjustments
7. Tenant improvement allowance
8. Options
9. Lease term
10. Other restrictive or financial provisions

tenant. The concession usually provides a monetary incentive but may not reduce the quoted rent. Concessions may be in the form of free or reduced rent for a specified period, financial assistance with moving from the former location, payment of penalties for breaking a former lease, or payment for above-standard tenant improvements. A concession can also be an advance of funds that allows the tenant to invest in certain improvements or incur other costs initially and pay the money back to the owner over the term of the lease. This permits the quoted dollar rent per square foot to stay as high as the market will bear. Concessions might be greater at certain times—for example, when the supply of available office space exceeds demand.

Tenant Options

Prospective tenants or current tenants negotiating a lease renewal may seek other *rights*. In a lease, an *option* is the right to obtain a specific condition within a specified time; the option is often written into a lease as a formal addendum, or addition. Except for situations in which a cash payment to the owner is involved, options always benefit the tenant rather than the owner, who is understandably reluctant to grant them. However, the property owner may need to grant options so a property can be competitive and reflect market conditions. Option clauses usually require the tenant to notify the owner of their intention to exercise the option within a certain number of days of the lease expiration. Failure to provide such notification may void the tenant's rights.

Option to Expand. A tenant that anticipates growth may bargain for an *option to expand* that requires the owner to offer additional space at a stated time in the future—often at the end of the lease term. Except in very soft market conditions, owners rarely grant such options because they can mean the expansion space will be vacant for some time before the option is exercised. In other cases, the anticipated expansion space might be temporarily occupied by another tenant, and that could require additional costs moving them to another space.

Right of First Refusal. As an alternative to an option to expand, the owner may offer a *right of first refusal,* which gives the tenant first choice to lease contiguous space or other space in the building *only* when it becomes available—the lease clause usually specifies the area.

Right of First Offer. Another possibility is for the property owner to grant a *right of first offer,* which gives the tenant the right to be the first to make an offer when and if a specific space becomes available. If the subject space is leased to an existing tenant at the time the owner grants the first-offer right to the tenant who requests it, the availability date can occur at several times:

1. When the existing tenant does not exercise any renewal options it may have for the space
2. When the existing tenant does *not* have a renewal right, the property owner first actively markets the space for lease to third parties, which often occurs within 12 months prior to the scheduled expiration date of the existing tenant's lease
3. When the property owner first receives an unsolicited preliminary offer or request for a proposal from a prospective third-party tenant to lease the space

An owner may also give a right of first offer on unleased new space; this takes place when a building is under renovation or construction, the delivery date is uncertain, and marketing has not begun. The tenant that holds the right of first offer usually has a short time after receipt of the owner's availability notice to exercise that right.

Option to Renew. Sometimes a tenant may seek an *option to renew* on the same terms and conditions as the original lease. However, owners are disinclined to grant such renewal options for several reasons. First, a multiple-year lease usually does not account for all possible market changes during its term—even with escalations still in effect, the actual rent may remain below the market rate. In addition, a renewal option does not guarantee that the tenant will remain. When granted, such options usually refer to a rent adjustment to an increase to be agreed upon or to market rates current at the time of renewal.

Option to Cancel. Under some circumstances, a tenant may seek an *option to cancel* or a *termination right,* which grants the tenant the right to cancel the lease before its expiration—sometimes upon certain stated circumstances—and, if granted, usually requires a financial penalty. For example, if government regulations change and a tenant's current use violates those regulations and it can no longer sustain its operations, the tenant's termination right would be exercised.

LEASE RENEWAL TECHNIQUES

Lease renewals are very important in the overall economics of property performance. Renewing the lease of an existing tenant is usually more profitable than finding a new tenant for the space for the following several reasons:

- Renewal eliminates the rent loss that occurs when a new tenant does not move in as soon as the current tenant moves out.
- The expense of finding a new tenant—marketing the space—is saved.

- The cost of improvements related to a renewal is usually less than the cost of preparing the space for a new tenant.
- The current tenant is a known quantity—payment history, level of respect for the property, and the other tenants—and evaluating prospects entails the investment of time and money.

Only tenants who are satisfied with the property and the service they receive will renew their leases. In this regard, every contact with the tenant is an indirect renewal effort.

The reasons for not renewing a lease are beyond a real estate manager's control. Market conditions usually change during the lease term, rents may go up or down, and vacancy may increase or decrease. Lease expiration usually requires negotiating new lease terms unless the lease that is expiring contains an *option to renew* that already has specified terms and conditions of renewal. The starting point of negotiations may be whether the parties are willing to renew the lease, and the conclusion may be whether the proposed terms are acceptable. The following lists some principal bargaining points:

- The amount of any rent increase
- The length of the new lease term
- The extent of repairs, service, and rehabilitation that are conditions of renewal

Both parties usually expect the rent to increase, but the exact amount may be subject to negotiation, depending on market conditions. Renewal terms are more likely to be negotiated for commercial leases, and the negotiations may be as comprehensive as for a new lease.

To facilitate lease renewals, two basic administrative tasks will be performed: (1) generate a list of all tenants' lease expiration dates based on the property's rent roll, and (2) contact the residents or tenants directly when leases are about to expire. If possible, speaking to the tenant face to face is the best and most direct approach. Otherwise, contacting them via letters or e-mails is effective as well.

The timing of renewal negotiations should be adequate for tenants to make their decisions and for the manager to find replacements for those who decide to move. For residents, a notice of 60 to 90 days in advance of lease expiration is expected. For commercial tenants with long-term leases, renewal negotiations may begin a year or more in advance. Note that market conditions will often dictate how far in advance the manager should begin working on a renewal. In a soft market, tenants will be contacted much earlier than the standard notice period in an effort to minimize turnover.

Other Lease Issues

Commercial building owners are increasingly responsible for installation, operation, and maintenance of telecommunication risers and cabling in their buildings. The lease document should address the risks that accompany this responsibility, which include the tenant's insurance, operating expense pass-throughs, escalations, and system failures.

Deregulation of electric and gas utilities means volume users can purchase directly from low-cost sources; however, the electricity and gas will continue to be delivered via the existing local distribution systems. Owners of buildings whose tenants use large amounts of electricity may purchase power to sell to their tenants. Commercial tenants may choose to purchase their own power directly, and leases need to accommodate these changes in their utilities provisions. In addition, pass-through common area charges may be affected.

Some tenants' leases may need to address regulatory compliance. Disposal of hazardous waste materials is an issue when health professionals lease space in medical office buildings. Additionally, a separate clause should specify the owner's and tenant's responsibilities for compliance with the Americans with Disabilities Act (ADA)—including provisions for indemnification of either party from liability for costs arising out of the other party's noncompliance. For instance, nonprofit organizations that provide a real property tax break may contain lease clauses that require the owner to pass the savings onto that particular tenant or all of the tenants in the building.

RENTAL COLLECTION

As with all other aspects of tenant relations, tact, diplomacy, and goodwill are essential to the collections process, but it's important to also be firm in requiring payment of rent on the date it is due. Real estate managers pay operating costs, taxes, and other property expenses out of the rental income, and expenses accumulate daily.

Timely collection of rents is imperative for timely payment of the property's bills. In addition, some portion of the manager's compensation is usually a percentage of the total rent collected, and any decline in that amount reduces the income. These two concerns—(1) operating expenses and (2) personal compensation—are incentives to collect the full amount of rent on time.

Rent Due Date

The advance payment of rent is an accepted practice—leases with federal agencies are exceptions because the federal government always pays one month in arrears. Monthly rents are usually due on the first day of each month, although some are due on the lease date. To streamline accounting, rent collections, and payment of the property's expenses, all leases should have rent due on the same date. To accomplish this effectively, the first month's rent should be prorated for tenants who do not take possession on the first of a month.

Most tenants pay their rent on the date it is due, but inevitably, some will be late. Three significant reasons for not tolerating any delay in rent payments follow:

1. Rent is one of the tenants' largest expenses, and each day's delay increases the chances that the tenant will not pay the whole amount for that month.

2. Acceptance of a partial payment increases the tenant's obligation in the following month, and the tenant's financial situation may not improve.

3. Most leases require payment in full on the first, and habitually accepting late payments may compromise the property owner's right to require timely payment and to evict a tenant for nonpayment.

Late Fee and Delinquency

Most real estate managers and owners expect payment in full by the first of the month, and they impose *late fees* as a reinforcement of their policy. Late fees may be a residual source of income for management, but the delay in receiving the rent and the time spent accounting for the fees tend to cancel any expected benefit.

A small late fee actually encourages late payment because such a policy has an inherent grace period associated with it. For example, if management imposes an extra charge for payments received on the sixth of the month or later, the tenant has no compelling reason to pay the rent until the fifth.

If late fees are used, they should be large enough to encourage prompt payment. Some municipalities limit the maximum late fee that a property owner can charge on residential rent, and this must be a consideration as well.

Back rent is a debt, and collection of back rent is subject to the requirements of the Fair Debt Collection Practices Act. Statutes always control delinquency, collection, and eviction rights and procedures. It's important to be familiar with and understand the laws and the practices that govern these matters. Local law may be more favorable to residents and commercial tenants than to property owners, and the laws in nearby municipalities may differ from each other.

In terms of facing delinquency, encourage payment on the first day of each month. Keeping that simple policy justifies distributing notices of delinquency very early in the month, followed by a personal contact soon thereafter if payment is not received.

Collection System

All residents and commercial tenants should have a clear understanding of the rental collection policy before signing the lease. Be careful not to compromise any of the owner's legal rights by presenting a policy that is more lenient than the law requires. It's important to explain the policy in a firm manner that does not jeopardize the extension of goodwill toward the tenant.

A series of forms is the basis of a good collection system. A notice should be delivered to the resident or commercial tenant on the first day the rent is delinquent; it should be a strongly worded but a friendly reminder. The check may be delayed in the mail, so the reminder notice should simply state that the rent has not been received and ask the tenant to contact the office about the matter.

Eviction

If the resident or tenant does not respond to the reminder notice and the rent is still delinquent, the next step is to send or serve an eviction notice or such other notice as state or local law may require to initiate eviction.

Eviction is ejection of a tenant from the leased premises by the property owner. It is a drastic measure. It can result in the forcible removal of the tenant's possessions from the premises if the tenant refuses to move out. State laws governing eviction vary widely, but most provide for the property owners or their attorneys to serve eviction notices or notices to cure a lease violation within a specified period. Municipalities frequently have laws concerning evictions and tenants' rights as well.

Eviction Notice. This notice should be a demand that the tenant pay the rent within a specified period or vacate the premises within that same period. State and/or local laws prescribe the time allowed, the form, how the notice is served to the tenant and the content of the notice. If the law permits a late fee, the notice should state that amount.

By law, such a notice may automatically terminate the lease, so the manager must understand its effect. In some states, an owner may accept a partial payment of the amount due without compromising the notice or the owner's right to bring suit for the whole amount of the delinquency. In some jurisdictions, accepting a partial rent payment may preclude collection of the total amount that is in arrears. Because an error can lead to the owner's or the real estate manager's liability to a tenant, an attorney must be consulted to determine the requirements of state and local law.

Eviction Proceedings. If a tenant refuses to pay all the delinquent rent specified in the notice or violates the lease in some other way and fails to cease or cure the violation within an allotted period, eviction proceedings can be initiated. The management agreement should expressly grant the real estate manager discretion to evict tenants or specify a procedure for obtaining the owner's approval. An eviction should never begin without the owner's approval.

In the case of *nonpayment,* if the tenant has not responded to the demand for payment within the time allowed, the real estate manager must file a complaint with the court. The complaint prompts the court to issue a summons to appear in court. A third party, such as a sheriff or private process server, delivers the summons. If the summons and complaint cannot be delivered personally to an occupant, state or local laws will specify alternate procedures, which *must be followed exactly.* Sometimes a notice may be affixed face-up on the front door of the premises or in another conspicuous place.

The complete form usually includes an *affidavit of service*—a sworn statement that the notice has been properly served—which the process server completes. This affidavit is then presented in court. The form must be completed and delivered *exactly* as stipulated by the legal procedures specified in it and by state and local law or court rule, or it may be ruled invalid.

Any procedural inconsistency, if the notice is served impartially, may permit the tenant to avoid the eviction—necessitating a complete restart of the process—or leave the tenant with a claim for a countersuit. The tenant should not be harassed, intimidated, or denied access to or use of the rental unit or specific services—such actions can also be cause for a countersuit.

In court, the judge may give the tenant an opportunity to pay the rent, but state or local law determines whether the property owner has a legal obligation to accept the rent. However, if the tenant offers to pay, the judge may direct the owner to accept payment. If the tenant cannot pay, the judge will usually render a decision or award judgment in favor of the owner—for possession, rent due, and (possibly) court costs. As part of the judgment, the tenant will be given a date by which to vacate the premises. If the tenant does not yield the space by that date, state and local law dictate further procedures.

Other Eviction Types. There are two reasons for eviction: (1) monetary, nonpayment of rent, (2) and non-monetary, breach of a lease covenant. Examples of non-monetary eviction involve keeping a pet when the lease stipulates that no pets are allowed (for residential properties), or manufacturing products in space leased for use as offices (for commercial properties). In addition, the owner may terminate a tenancy without stating a cause if the tenant has a month-to-month lease—this is a *no-cause action,* not an eviction. It's important to understand the differences between the two types of evictions and the owner's right to terminate a month-to-month lease because they involve different procedures.

Evictions can be expensive even though the fee can be negotiated with an attorney. In the best circumstances, an eviction may require months to complete. Some states allow tenants to claim retaliation for an eviction if the tenant has complained about certain deficiencies or other matters prior to the eviction. Every such lease violation should be documented thoroughly or be reviewed by an attorney before any eviction process is initiated.

The best way to minimize the need for an eviction is to be diligent in selecting tenants, perform credit checks, and verify credentials for all prospects before they sign leases. Although the staff of a property must be diligent and prompt in taking action when rent is late, or if tenants fail to respect any section of the lease, the most effective means of maintaining harmony on the property is to give tenants the respect they deserve. If the staff treat residents and commercial tenants properly and professionally, give them prompt service, and respect their privacy, the great majority will faithfully observe the requirements of the lease.

Security Deposits

In addition to rent payments, almost all leases require a *security deposit* that the resident or commercial tenant pays in advance and the owner holds to ensure the tenant's performance under the lease. The amount of the security deposit is often equivalent to one month's rent, although it can be any amount for commercial properties. Residential properties are governed by the Landlord Tenant Law in the specific state and there are often stipulations on the security deposit.

Real estate managers should not permit tenants to apply the security deposit to the last month's rent, especially if damage occurs to the premises, excluding normal wear and tear—the deposit will not cover both repair expenses and the rent. The deposit must be large enough to be an incentive to the tenant to take care of the premises, but that does not always necessitate the equivalent of one month's rent. On the other hand, a leased residence that includes furnishings has greater potential for damage and warrants a larger security deposit.

If the tenant fulfills all the obligations of the lease, the security deposit should be returned within a reasonable time after the tenant moves. However, the deposit should be held until damage charges can be itemized and deducted. The turnaround should be finished quickly so the space can be made market ready imme-diately. If feasible, inspection of the unit in the tenant's presence on the last day of the lease is helpful in explaining the need for damage or cleaning charges.

SUCCESSFUL LEASING

Leasing success depends on staff members having a shared commitment to the goals determined by property ownership and management. A variety of staff members may perform leasing activ-ities, including the real estate manager and on-site leasing agents for residential properties and on-site leasing agents and leasing brokers for commercial properties. It is important to remember that the staff must work as a team to achieve the leasing objectives. An on-site leasing staff member performs full-time leasing duties for the property. For on-site staff, a professional dress code should be established and should coordinate with the property's image or theme. It is important to minimize the chance of the staff member failing. It's also important to establish clear job descriptions that detail the scope of tasks, and these responsibilities should be developed and shared with the staff. Initial and ongoing training should be provided for the staff so that they are familiar with the leasing goals for the property.

It is also important to encourage the leasing staff to perform well by learning what motivates them. Some employees are driven by awards, contests, letters of recognition, and public acknowledgments. Other staff members might be concerned with power-related motivators like a tough challenge or increased authority. Money-motivated employees will be inspired by the potential for increased compensation. Bonuses and incentive plans are always successful when motivating most staff members. Nonetheless, all leasing staff members should be recognized and rewarded for their successes—such as an increase in occupancy rate or a decrease in turnover.

SUMMARY

The leasing plan should always reflect the goals and objectives of the owner. A basic lease displays different components that are suited for different types of rental space. The core of the lease describes the duration of the agreement, amount of rent, and when and how the payment is to be made. After the marketing plan is implemented and attracts prospects to the property, an outline for the lease plan should be developed, and should include a site plan of the property, unit numbers, and square footage dimensions, along with the rent schedule that outlines the current or desired rents for each space, lease expiration dates, and any concessions. Real estate managers should always anticipate and also participate in lease negotiations. Whether or not a leasing agent works out the details, real estate managers represent the owners and are instrumental in suggesting possible compromises and clarifying the tenants' questions.

10 Managing the Physical Asset

Managing the physical asset for the property owner is a key to superior presentation and optimal function because it preserves—and sometimes improves—the condition and value of the property. Regular cleaning and repairs are necessary to keep tenants and residents comfortable and to ensure safety. Maintaining curb appeal and appearance are two of the easiest things to do, yet they are so often overlooked. The following lists the benefits of a comprehensive maintenance program:

- **Tenant retention and curb appeal.** If the property is flawless and the building components are in good working condition, tenants will be comfortable in their surroundings and their satisfaction will result in a lower vacancy rate. The owner will have less expense for turnover of rental space because tenants will be inclined to renew their leases. With a well-established maintenance program and attention to detail, properties with exceptional curb appeal help entice customers and keep them coming back. Increased curb appeal also attracts a better caliber of tenants, which over time increases the value of the property and reduces turnover rates.

- **Reduced operating costs.** Maintenance and repair costs may be a large part of a property's operating expenses, but investment in maintenance and repair may reduce other operating costs such as utilities, rubbish removal, and insurance premiums. These investments may also have an equally good effect on some other functions or expenses—for example, removing graffiti promptly deters further graffiti, thereby reducing costs. Rental income increases due to increased tenancy in a well-maintained property. Therefore, it's important to investigate and uncover cost-reducing measures that pay for themselves over time that will produce indirect savings and improved income.

- **Preservation and enhancement of property value.** After a comprehensive maintenance program is established, the property's value is preserved and enhanced during the course of regular operations. Deferred maintenance causes the greatest loss an owner can suffer on a real estate investment. Even if a fire or natural disaster consumes the property, the owner can usually regain the financial investment if the property is properly insured. However, there is no insurance against neglected maintenance.

Safety is also a critical issue. If an injury occurs because of neglected maintenance, the financial repercussions could be severe, even with liability insurance in place. Regular maintenance and repair reduces potential hazards and provides a safe environment for residents, on-site staff, prospective tenants, visitors, businesses, customers, and employees.

PROPERTY SYSTEMS IDENTIFICATION

When a new or an experienced real estate manager takes over a new property, learning what systems are present and where they are located will be the first step in the maintenance program. For example, site plans should list the following locations (including but not limited to):

- Mechanical rooms
- Fire hydrants
- Electrical panels
- Catch basins
- Water shut-offs
- Drain clean-outs
- Fire risers
- Lock box locations
- Irrigation controllers
- Apartment number sequence
- Laundry rooms

Although the list can be endless, merely documenting the existence of the various systems will save time and resources. Both large and small properties benefit from visual aids and lists, especially when employees change or when new vendors arrive on site to service the property. Such lists also help the maintenance process operate more smoothly and efficiently.

Once the inventory of systems is established, maintenance falls into the following five categories:

1. **Custodial maintenance** establishes the day-to-day cleaning and upkeep that should be a part of every property's ongoing program to retain value—and retain tenants and residents. Most property owners have high expectations concerning the appearance of their investment.

2. **Corrective maintenance** involves the ordinary repairs that a building and its equipment require on a day-to-day basis.

3. **Preventive maintenance** is a program of regular inspection and care to avert problems or at least detect and solve issues before major repairs are necessary.

4. **Deferred maintenance** is ordinary maintenance of a building that is *not* performed at the time a problem is detected. If left unchecked, deferred maintenance will eventually diminish the use, occupancy, and value of the property, and it will cost more to correct in the long run, resulting in *physical obsolescence—* which is aged property due to general wear and tear.

5. **Cosmetic maintenance,** a type of preventive maintenance that enhances the property's aesthetic value, should also be a large part of regular inspection because it aids in the future development of the property by maintaining an up-to-date appearance.

Regulatory compliance sometimes demands specific maintenance procedures and related activities. For example, some locales require fire drills that include evacuating all tenants and property staff from the building twice a year. Elevators, boilers, required postings, *material safety data sheets (MSDS),* and smoke alarms are just a few areas that are regulated by some form of government authority (more details are explained later in this chapter).

Inspections and monitoring of some equipment may be necessary to safeguard the environment from potentially hazardous emissions; this is more likely for industrial than other types of properties. Maintenance for regulatory compliance is not necessarily

OBJECTIVES OF MAINTENANCE

- Accomplishment of the owner's goals
- Tenant satisfaction
- Higher tenant retention
- Lower operating costs
- Optimal function of the property
- Maximized property value
- Safety of employees, invitees, and occupants

separate from the listed maintenance categories—most regulatory compliance activities fall into the preventive or the corrective maintenance categories. Establishing and enforcing strict standards for custodial and preventive maintenance can significantly reduce corrective and deferred maintenance, enhance value, and safeguard the health and safety of residents and tenants.

SCHEDULES, INSPECTIONS, AND MAINTENANCE TASKS

In the effort to minimize monthly operating expenses, owners sometimes unwisely have cleaning and maintenance work done only when absolutely necessary or in an emergency. On any property, it is inevitable that some deferred maintenance is evident, but too much will eventually result in excessive, costly repairs as well as a loss of value. For example, not heeding the manufacturer's recommendations for maintaining a motor may temporarily delay the expense of a service call or replacement parts. However, excessive wear on the motor from lack of maintenance can lead to temporary loss of service from the motor and perhaps premature replacement, which will eventually cost much more than timely maintenance. Neglecting day-to-day maintenance significantly shortens the life span of major appliances and other real estate components such as HVAC equipment, furnaces, and roofs; the useful life of such equipment could be 15–25 years, but it could be significantly less if neglected.

Because of budget constraints, some deferred maintenance might have to be tolerated. When this occurs, list the deferred maintenance in order of priority and incorporate it into the list of routine maintenance procedures. That way, the staff can gradually reduce the list of deferred projects while they keep pace with ongoing maintenance. However, when deferred maintenance is a major factor in an owner's lack of cash flow, disclosing these items and suggesting a systematic program for repair—whether such repair can be funded with a property's cash flow or with an owner contribution—can serve multiple purposes and have positive results. These include increased tenancy, which increases cash flow; increased cash flow produces more income with which to continue these repairs, and the cycle continues until the asset is functioning as it should. It's important for real estate managers to be honest with the property owners, regardless of whether funding is available to correct deficiencies. For instance, newer real estate managers may hesitate to report to their owners that the roof needs to be replaced. However, not disclosing such a need can lead to drastic consequences—it's also contrary to the IREM Code of Professional Ethics.

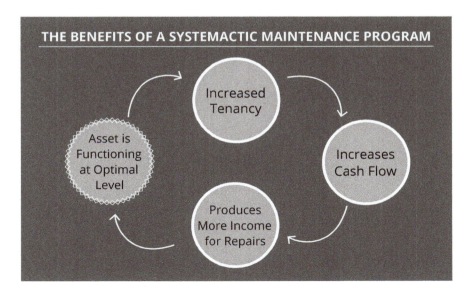

Schedules and Inspections

Planning is the first step in any maintenance operation. This starts with a list of every component that requires maintenance, the type of maintenance required, how often each procedure is to be done, and how much time is required for a procedure. To develop this list, the condition of all functional components of the property should be surveyed. From the list, schedules for inspections and routine service should be developed. Inspection checklists contain some of the following points:

- **Leasing support.** Vacant spaces clean, tenants moving in/out, acceptance notices
- **Cleaning services.** Lobby floors and glass, mats, elevator cabs, corridors, washrooms, paper supplies
- **Security/safety.** Elevator logs, fire drill log, night access log, guard appearance, door alarms
- **Transportation systems.** Door operation, equipment ID, system plans, elevator pits
- **Building condition.** Entrances, sidewalks, caulking, exterior lighting
- **Mechanical operations.** MSDS postings, equipment log, compressor, first-aid station
- **Common corridors.** Carpeting, exit signs, lighting, elevator indicators, ceiling tile
- **HVAC maintenance.** Unit location, manufacturer, model/serial number, compressor/fan motor maintenance

A keen sense of communication with maintenance personnel is vital to ensure they maintain work schedules and handle emergency work orders promptly. Since most cell phones include a digital camera and capabilities to text message, store contact information, and send/receive e-mails, maintenance personnel can download work orders to their phones by e-mail or from a web browser, and they can photographically document equipment repairs or damage in a unit. Service providers are increasingly becoming more sophisticated as well. For instance, some roof maintenance contractors allow customers to access the contractor's database to view actual satellite images of the customer's roof, and see all of the locations of each repair that occurred that month or year. Having such capabilities allows access to information on specific service reports showing exactly what was repaired, how much it cost, and any recommendations for future repairs. Asking service providers for information about their technological equipment and resources will help learn new ways to improve the management of the clients' investments.

Inspection Reports. Scheduling inspections and cleaning is crucial. Some building components (lobbies, corridors) require daily cleaning or maintenance, while other components (fan motors) need only periodic maintenance to function optimally. However, areas like the rooftop may only require annual (or semiannual) inspection. Assemble these considerations in a master maintenance chart and use them to establish a regular and efficient pattern of inspection, cleaning, and repair. An *inspection report* (Exhibit 10.1) usually lists all of the major components of a property (e.g., grounds, foundations, exterior walls, electrical system), with numerous sub-entries under each major component. For example, transformers, circuit breakers, fuse boxes, wiring, wall plugs, light switches, and light fixtures might be subentries under "electrical system." Space is provided to record the condition of the component, specific work to be done, an estimate of the cost of the work, and timing of re-inspection or whether an item is targeted for repairs in future budgets.

For residential properties, laundry rooms, recreational facilities, or other amenities would be added items for inspection along with appropriate subentries. A separate form will be used for inspection of apartment interiors, including individual rooms as items and appliances and fixtures as subentries. An office building form would include restrooms and other employee (or public) facilities—light wells or atriums, equipment rooms, fire escapes, and office interiors. Most real estate managers use separate forms for

EXHIBIT 10.1
Sample Property Inspection Report

Property _____

Inspected by _____ Date _____

Item	Condition	Repairs Needed	Est. Next Cost	Inspection
Grounds				
Foundations				
Exterior walls				
Roof				
Gutters and downspouts				
Windows and casings				
Lobby				
Common areas				
Elevators				
Stairways				
Boiler or furnace room				
Air-conditioning plant				
Electrical system				
Plumbing				
Gas lines				
Fire safety equipment				
Garbage disposal area				

This example includes most of the *major* categories of items inspected. Mechanical rooms, storage areas, and parking facilities are other items common to all types of properties. In actual use, an inspection form is customized for the property, including numerous subentries under each of the items listed here. Condition might be noted as good, fair, or poor (definitions should be included to ensure consistent evaluation, or items might be marked as okay or not okay), with the latter meaning an item needs attention.

the building exterior and interior since it is just as important that they inspect the exterior as frequently as they inspect the interior common areas. A separate janitorial survey may be used to review the level of cleanliness of entrances, public areas, lobbies, restrooms, and their components. Inspections of vacancies can be recorded on a form that also serves as a work order to prepare the space for leasing renewal. Inspection of a shopping center includes examination of the surrounding area and access to the property, along with parking lots, signage, and vacant and occupied stores. Take note that not all inspections are completed by maintenance techs. In some organizations, inspection work orders are created to be performed by leasing and/or management staff as a way of documenting that the area was inspected—even when a formal report may not be required.

Maintenance Schedules. Inspection reports are coordinated with a maintenance schedule to ensure timely follow-up. The *maintenance schedule* (Exhibit 10.2) usually lists specific tasks and their frequencies. It may also provide spaces for assignment of specific

---

EXHIBIT 10.2

Sample Maintenance Schedule

Date _____

Property _____

Project	Frequency	Date
Patch parking lot and other concrete	Once per year	
Clean windows	Twice per year	
Inspect and oil exhaust fans	Once per quarter	
Clean gutters and downspouts	Once per year or after heavy rains	
Inspect and test fire safety equipment	As needed, at least monthly	
Recharge fire extinguishers	Once per year	
Inspect common area lighting	Once per week	
Clean or replace HVAC filters	Once per month	
Polish chrome and brass in lobby	As needed	
Wax lobby floors	Three times per year	
Prune hedges	Twice per year	
Touch up exterior paint	Twice per year	
Touch up interior paint	As needed	
Vacuum swimming pool	Twice per week	

Parking lot striping and changeover between heat and air conditioning are examples of other items that such a schedule might include.

personnel and a specific time of the week, month, or year for completion of the task. Preventive maintenance of equipment is usually addressed on a separate schedule that lists each piece of equipment and its location on the property, with columns for each month of the year so the maintenance supervisor can indicate how often work is to be done.

The organization of inspection reports and maintenance schedules depends on the design of the structure and its surroundings, the individual components that require service, and the availability of personnel qualified to do the work. The maintenance supervisor must integrate all of these factors into a logical and efficient program for maintaining the property. Certain types of software can expedite the scheduling process while also documenting specific maintenance activities and helping maintain adequate inventory of parts and supplies. Detailed budgets that document such services, their timing, and cost can be downloaded as spreadsheets and disseminated in multiple forms to fit the specific needs of any property type.

Establishing effective schedules may take time and experimentation, especially for an older property whose service records are incomplete. However, a new property should have a complete set of owner's manuals and manufacturer's recommendations that can facilitate development of an equipment maintenance program. In an effort to be paperless, it would be wise to bookmark or save the locations of manuals and important electronic documents for easy access.

Consider the specific timing of some maintenance activities—groundskeeping and custodial maintenance in particular—so residents or commercial tenants will be aware that the work is being done. In fact, such tasks become part of a tenant retention program. Seeing ongoing property maintenance gives tenants a sense of added value for their rent dollars, i.e., visible is valuable. On the other hand, some tenants and even residents prefer that these tasks be completed in silence, so to speak, to minimize inconvenience and noise issues.

Custodial Maintenance

Custodial maintenance (or *janitorial maintenance/housekeeping*) is the process of keeping the building clean for residents, commercial tenants, prospective tenants, and visitors. This element of custodial maintenance is most noticeable because it directly relates to residents' or tenants' sight and smell; it is the simplest form of corrective maintenance. The typical daily or weekly tasks also establish a pattern for inspecting every part of the building, which over time will help in avoiding deferred maintenance by discovering a need for more extensive corrective maintenance. Whether the task is performed by an employee or outside service providers, the mere frequency of the visits can help be the "eyes" on site when the real estate manager is away from the property.

Quantifying the level of traffic that passes through each section of the building will also help to schedule custodial maintenance. Some areas of the building may require hourly attention—others may require only an occasional spot inspection. Nevertheless, the custodial maintenance schedule should list all rooms and sections of the common areas in the building so they will be inspected regularly and kept clean. This list should include equipment rooms and supply closets, which might seem unusual because they are hidden from the public, but a well-organized supply room saves staff time when seeking parts and supplies and helps protect stored materials. Maintaining an orderly supply room also reminds staff of the wide-ranging importance of cleanliness throughout the property. The following sections describe some of the areas of a property that require frequent custodial, as well as corrective, maintenance.

Walks, Driveways, Parking Areas, and Grounds. The schedule of custodial maintenance duties for the property grounds depends partly on the time of year. In winter, all driveways, parking lots, and sidewalks must be free of ice and snow. Doormats must be inspected and cleaned regularly. In the spring, especially after the snow melts, the grounds should be cleared of litter that accumulated beneath the snow. In the summer, keeping the lawn mowed and weeded and taking care of flower beds will add greatly to the *curb appeal* of the property. The staff should look for serious cracks in the concrete or asphalt pavement and patch them if necessary; at the same time, they should remove weeds growing in these gaps and pick up any litter around the area. Bushes, shrubs, and trees should be watered and pruned regularly, and they should be replaced if they are dead or dying.

Exterior Walls and Components. The level of traffic around the outside of a property and the exterior finish of the building determine the frequency of custodial maintenance. In addition to cleaning dirt from the outside walls of the building, staff should regularly clean signs, light fixtures, touch up paint on interior and exterior areas, and fix all surface finishes; all of this aids in maintaining the overall aesthetic of the property exterior. Flowers, signage, and benches help "freshen" the look of the property—all evidence of having attention to detail and pride in managing the property.

Windows and Casings. Cleaning all of the windows and window casings of a building may or may not be done routinely depending on their location. Being in a high traffic area, windows in the lobby should be washed daily because they become the dirtiest and they are the first windows seen by everyone; they also reveal much about the overall cleanliness of the establishment. The interior and exterior of other windows may require cleaning semiannually or annually. Trained window washers will usually be contracted to clean window exteriors for high-rise buildings.

Interior Walls. Some interior walls may require frequent painting or cleaning, which can be time consuming and costly. To avoid that, maintenance staff should choose paint with a satin or semi-gloss finish, which is ideal for walls that need to be cleaned regularly. However, a satin finish should not be used where there are wall imperfections because it will make the imperfections more apparent. An eggshell finish is the most popular paint option—even though it lacks the shine and easy-to-clean surface of a gloss finish because it masks imperfections in the wall and is the easiest to apply in a single coat.

Elevators, Lobbies, and Other Common Areas. Elevators and lobbies require daily cleaning. Brass, mirrors, or other metallic surfaces need regular polishing, and floors need periodic refinishing. Corridors require the same level of attention, especially in high-traffic areas. Buildings that have lobby information desks have the advantage of personnel in attendance to keep those areas free of litter or report their condition to the appropriate personnel.

Amenities. People are attracted to amenities such as swimming pools and fitness centers. At the minimum, these areas require daily attention because of health, safety, and sanitation requirements. Most real estate managers contract for swimming pool maintenance because they must be vacuumed frequently, and chlorination or other chemical treatment levels must be monitored. Periodic testing of water samples may be required by law. If the facility supplies towels, staff must collect and wash them. Locker rooms and showers must be cleaned and disinfected frequently. Since these areas can be high-injury zones, frequent safety inspections and correction of faulty equipment, slippery surfaces, and other components are critical to preventing liability to the owner and/or the real estate management company.

Corrective Maintenance

Corrective maintenance is required for the following reasons:

- Improper installation of a building element
- Use of improper component
- Functional obsolescence of a component
- Improper regular maintenance of a building element

Parking lot lighting is a perfect example of needed corrective maintenance. Over time, older light fixtures lose their ability to illuminate to the proper specifications. Correcting to the proper illumination for safety reasons would require that the fixture or the bulb be replaced—possibly to an even more energy-efficient compact fluorescent fixture or bulb.

Filling a pothole in a parking lot is another example of corrective maintenance. A deficiency is being corrected that is present either due to lack of proper preventive maintenance or because of specific incidents that need immediate attention. Routine inspections of inherent functionality problems may uncover other components that need correction.

Preventive Maintenance

Ensuring reliable functional performance and extending the useful life of building components defines *preventive maintenance*. For comfort, safety, and efficiency, all parts of the building must be regularly inspected and maintained. The number of maintenance personnel and their levels of skill and training will indicate how much of this work outside contractors should do. For reasons of safety, equipment availability, licensing requirements, and special skills involved, contractors should perform some types of preventive maintenance. The following sections discuss some components of properties that require regular preventive maintenance.

Walks, Driveways, Parking Areas, and Grounds. Most sidewalks, driveways, and parking lots are finished with asphalt, brick, or concrete. The effects of traffic, vibration, water freezing in winter, and extreme heat in summer cause these materials to crack. Regular patching or resurfacing will extend the life of these surfaces significantly, prolonging the need to replace them entirely. Parking lots have to be re-striped periodically to mark parking stalls and fire lanes. Landscaping that has been neglected may have to be redesigned to be more aesthetically pleasing. Lawns may require reseeding or sod replacement in the spring to restore areas where grass has died.

As an extension of preventive maintenance, grounds should be inspected especially during or immediately after high winds, severe thunderstorms, or heavy and prolonged rains. During storms, shrubs are easily uprooted, branches can be torn from trees, and signage and property lighting can be damaged; such issues require prompt attention to avoid potential hazards to people and vehicles.

Foundations. Building foundations should be inspected periodically for evidence of water penetration, settlement, cracks, and other signs of deterioration. To prevent further deterioration, staff should correct problems when they are discovered. When problems are severe, professional engineers should be consulted.

Exterior Walls. Preventive maintenance of exterior walls depends on the construction or finishing material. Because of repeated freezing and thawing, cracks can develop in the mortar of brick walls, and *tuck-pointing*—the periodic replacement of mortar—becomes necessary. It is recommended that brick exteriors also be sealed routinely to ensure water tightness. Painted exterior walls should be examined for cracked or peeling paint—occasional touch-ups will protect a painted surface, but complete repainting will eventually be necessary. Wood surfaces should be inspected for splintering, decay, and insect damage caused by termites, carpenter ants, etc. It is often possible to replace portions of a wood surface without completely refacing the building. To prevent re-infestation, a professional contractor must exterminate insects before repair work begins. Concrete walls must be checked for cracks or chipping. Glass curtain walls should be examined for stability and to detect cracks or other damage.

Roof. A roof endures extremes of heat, cold, and moisture. Over the years, an owner may have a building reroofed many times. Severe weather may weaken areas of the roof, necessitating occasional patching. The surface of the roof should be routinely inspected for wear. Roof inspections should be at least annual, and a qualified roofing contractor should usually accompany the manager. A *thermal scan* may help identify problems that are not visible to the naked eye—areas of heat loss due to absent, inadequate, or wet insulation.

Antennas and satellite dishes may be installed on the roof to provide communications and television services. These require little or no ongoing maintenance, but suggesting that the contractors who install these items use the owner's roofer—to ensure roof penetrations are roofed-in and sealed properly—may be a wise policy to enforce. Installers must take care not to compromise the integrity of the roof system at any time. These areas should be carefully checked when inspecting the roof. If the roof system has a current warranty, any work performed on the roof by others must be completed in a manner that will not void the warranty.

Roofing Alternatives. Two major alternatives for roofing surfaces can lower costs and save energy: (1) reflective roofs and (2) green roofs.

Reflective Roofs. *Reflective roofs* generally lower costs because they reduce roof surface temperatures by preventing the sun's heat from transferring into the building; as a result, they help downsize air-conditioning equipment. In fact, a reflective roof can even extend the roof life by reducing the amount of thermal shock that occurs on the roof's surface.

Green Roofs. The other alternative is *green roofs,* which are basically extensions of an existing roof that require high-quality water proofing, root repellent, and drainage systems to support systems for growing plants. There are two types of green roofs: (1) *intensive roofs,* which are thicker and can support a wider variety of plants but are heavier and require more maintenance, and (2) *extensive roofs,* which are covered in a light layer of vegetation and are lighter than an intensive green roof. The following are a few general advantages of green roofs:

- Absorb rainwater to reduce runoff that would otherwise collect pollutants
- Reduce urban heat
- Protect the roof from UV rays and other types of deterioration
- Double the roof's life expectancy
- Filter carbon dioxide and pollutants out of the air

The Environmental Protection Agency (EPA) estimates that green roofs can save up to 25 percent of the building's annual energy costs, and the Federal Energy Management Program (FEMP) has found that green roofs also double the roof's life expectancy—equating to a savings of $8 to $10 per square foot. Obviously, the decision to establish a roofing alternative will be discussed with the owner during the management agreement and planning process to examine the maintenance involved in more detail. (The management plan and agreement are explained in Chapter 5.)

Gutters and Downspouts. Many buildings have exposed gutters and downspouts. These prevent the accumulation of water on the roof and protect the exterior walls from excessive water flow. Gutters usually have to be replaced as often as the roof. They should be inspected frequently, especially after heavy rains, and they must be kept clear of leaves and other accumulating debris. Some residential buildings have gutter guards and rain barrels at the end of their drain spouts, and others may have rain gardens. However, regular inspection is always important as a preventive measure.

Windows and Casings. In addition to cleaning, windows require maintenance of their moving parts and frames. The maintenance staff may have to install separate storm windows in the autumn and remove them in the spring. When windows need replacing, double-paned windows should be investigated because they may serve as their own storm windows; such windows are more applicable to residential properties. They are energy efficient in all seasons and require less maintenance. Governmental rebates may even be available for replacing windows, installing insulation, and adding other energy-saving upgrades on residential and commercial buildings. Any such inducements that might benefit an owner in cost-saving measures, tax rebates, or both. Newer office buildings usually have windows that do not open, and older buildings are often retrofitted to prevent the opening of windows to prevent injury in the case of high-rise buildings.

Elevators. Contract for elevator maintenance and work with the contractor to develop the system that is most efficient for handling the volume of traffic in the building. A typical elevator inspection form includes information on door opening/closing speed, alarms in the cabs, acceleration/deceleration, and the general smoothness of the ride. The elevator contractor will provide preventive maintenance such as lubricating parts, inspecting cables, and cleaning the rails. Inspections and testing by governmental authorities will be required on a regular and ongoing basis. Placards for emergency contacts and telephone, intercom systems, or emergency alarms (depending upon the type of elevator system) must be present and in good working order at all times.

Strategies can be made to protect the building's elevators from improper use. While not specifically preventive maintenance, such strategies can minimize damage and prolong an elevator's life. To discourage use of passenger elevators for freight, and vice versa, the freight elevator should be separate from those for passengers. However, in buildings that lack a freight elevator, passenger elevators must serve as freight elevators. The risk of damage to passenger elevators used for freight warrants a creative approach. One possibility is to reserve one of the passenger elevators for freight use and make it accessible only to appropriate personnel who have a key. When using that practice, pads should be provided for the elevator walls and designate a particular time of day when the elevators may be used for moving freight. This will avert disruption during periods of peak traffic. Another possibility is to load furniture on the top of the elevator cab rather than inside. The ability to do this depends on the system in place (elevator cab construction, door controls, etc.).

Stairways. No matter how they are constructed, stairways require close attention because they are frequently the site of accidents involving injuries. The most common challenge is keeping stairways free of debris. Step surfaces show wear over time, and this alone can be a potential hazard because the surface (tread) is no longer smooth or level. Stairs should be inspected for any loose or deteriorating steps. Stair edges should be clearly marked if it is difficult to distinguish the surfaces of successive steps. All stair-wells should have adequate lighting for emergencies as well as for normal use; they should have handrails that are easy to grasp and are securely fastened to the wall or staircase. Stairway maintenance also includes fire escapes, which must be kept free of debris to serve as escape routes during emergencies. Inspections to ensure that the fire escapes are working properly should occur regularly.

Heating, Ventilation, and Air-Conditioning (HVAC) Equipment. Controlling the climate in buildings is an ongoing challenge. In addition to controlling temperature, HVAC equipment regulates humidity, supplies fresh air to the building, and removes stale air. Regulating all of these conditions requires a system of controls and precise monitoring of each room or floor in the building. A malfunc-tion or error in programming this equipment can cause tenants extreme discomfort. Maintenance staff may be trained to clean and replace filters, lubricate portions of the mechanical equipment, or monitor thermostat settings. However, most real estate managers usually contract maintenance and repair of HVAC equipment unless the size of a property justifies the skilled labor needed for that work. Local ordinances may require licensing of boiler opera-tors. Heating and air-conditioning systems usually require special maintenance for start-up and shutdown when the seasons change. It is important to note that the HVAC system of most buildings will be one of the most expensive components. Therefore, regular preventive maintenance will prolong the system's life, lessen the need for costly repairs, and save dollars in the long run.

Electrical Network and Plumbing. As demand for electrical service grows, it must be monitored to determine if the capacity in the building can meet that demand. In particular, prospective commercial tenants should be asked about their electrical require-ments to determine whether the building can accommodate them. An existing building can often be retrofitted for the electrical and network cabling required for computers and their adjunct equip-ment. However, that may be a major undertaking that warrants retrofitting the entire building, rather than only one tenant's leased space.

The maintenance supervisor should regularly inspect all electrical wiring and all electrically operated pumps and motors. All property staff should know the location of transformers on, or near, the property, the location of the transformer identification number, and the contact information of the electric utility company. The main shutoff switch should be identified, and employees should know its location in the building and the circumstances that warrant disconnecting the property from its power supply. Licensed personnel should make any changes in the wiring and appropriately document those changes.

Plumbing should be inspected regularly. Work required to clear drains, repair leaks, and otherwise maintain the integrity of the system should be done immediately. Residential properties usually have more plumbing fixtures than any other property type. Consequently, they have the most plumbing problems. To minimize service calls and reduce the amount of toxic drain cleaner released into the environment, residents should learn responsible and proper use of plumbing fixtures. It would be wise to give commercial tenants information to use to educate their employees about proper garbage disposal—and what not to put into sinks or toilets. The main water shutoff valve should be clearly identified, and employees should know its location in the building and the circumstances that warrant its use.[1]

Gas Lines. Only trained personnel from the gas company should perform the maintenance of gas lines. Maintenance staff should be alerted in case there are gas leaks, and to report them to the proper authorities while initiating appropriate emergency procedures. If the property is equipped with a primary shutoff valve and the gas

---

1. Managing septic systems where sewer systems are not available in the local area entail a whole host of inspections and maintenance, requiring staff to be well versed in their overall management—and with the various city, county, or state regulations that may govern such systems.

company provides instructions on how to use it, that information should be conveyed to the employees.

Co-generation Equipment. Maintenance staff may be responsible for certain routine tasks on properties that produce electricity using a co-generation plant—also referred to as combined heat and power (CHP) plant—which uses a heat engine or a power station to simultaneously generate both electricity and useful heat. This is one of the most common forms of energy recycling; however, authorized contractors must perform most preventive and corrective maintenance. These systems can include wind power, solar power, and other energy-producing sources; if present, such systems require maintenance by qualified personnel or contractors.

Fire Prevention and Safety Equipment. To minimize the threat to life and property from fire, everyone in the building should be informed about fire safety procedures, make sure that the associated equipment is functioning properly, and verify that all equipment meets local fire codes. All fire exits and fire doors should be marked clearly and kept free of obstructions. Proper operation of fire doors, alarm systems, fire escapes, fire extinguishers, and interior sprinkler systems should be verified at least once a year. Certificates of inspection may be required, and maintenance may have to be contracted.

Most jurisdictions require the installation of smoke alarms. Batteries must be checked and replaced in smoke detectors that are not connected to a central system. Some jurisdictions even require supervised fire drills, especially for multistory office buildings. Regardless of requirements, routine drills should be provided for all property personnel, residents, and commercial tenants detailing the way to summon the fire department and to evacuate the building.

An outside service must recharge and tag fire extinguishers as prescribed by the manufacturer. In the United States, fire extinguishers are classified by the extinguishing material they contain.

ADDITIONAL CONSIDERATIONS FOR FIRE SAFETY

Thousands of buildings catch fire every year, and thousands of people lose their lives in those fires. Real estate managers must know how to minimize the risk of fire and, in the event of a fire, how to properly react to minimize injuries and property damage.

- A fire prevention and safety program may start with a call to the local fire department. An inspection of the site by the fire department will identify potential fire hazards and equipment that must be installed or upgraded to comply with safety standards or codes.
- Lights in exit signs must be inspected regularly to ensure they are functioning. Installing emergency lighting that automatically turns on in a power failure in corridors and stairwells may be advisable—some jurisdictions require it.
- Sprinkler systems are often installed in building common areas and leased premises.
- Fire extinguishers and smoke alarms should be installed in common areas.
- The local fire department may also help to prepare a fire safety training program for on-site staff and tenants.
- Advice from the fire department and occasional fire drills help to ensure the appropriateness of an evacuation plan, such as:
    - Knowing where the nearest exits are located
    - Touching a door with the back of a hand before opening it
    - Staying near the floor for fresh air
    - Closing doors when possible to contain the fire
- Annual smoke alarm testing should be a standard operating procedure for residential managers.

The extinguishers should be placed by class according to the combustibles nearby.

Most real estate managers commonly install type ABC (dry chemical) extinguishers because they are effective against all types of fires. Fire-suppression systems in computer rooms may contain halogenated compounds (Halon) that are similar in action to carbon dioxide (CO_2) gas.

Pest Control. An ongoing concern among real estate managers is the control of insect pests and other vermin. Most properties contract for a regular extermination service, and many states require licensed pest control operators. The frequency of the exterminator's visits depends on the severity of infestation, the season, and the locale. Cockroaches are ubiquitous and particularly difficult to exterminate. Other troublesome insects are termites, carpenter ants, and fire ants. Because these insects burrow into foundations and wooden beams, they may be noticed only after they have done extensive damage. Larger rodents such as rats can infiltrate sewer lines and nest in walls, causing numerous other problems and damage as well.

To eliminate an infestation, fumigation may be necessary. However, if only one leased space is fumigated or sprayed after a tenant has vacated, the pests may not die—they may merely relocate to adjoining spaces. To ensure complete extermination, the exterminator should spray the entire building, or a large section of it, at one time. Properties whose tenants include restaurants or food stores are especially prone to vermin infestations. However, local health departments require most food stores and restaurants to spray periodically for pests.

Since mice, rats, and cockroaches thrive in unsanitary conditions, the most effective way to exterminate them is to remove their food sources. Residents and tenants should be informed about the proper frequency and method for disposing of garbage on the premises. If no place is available outside the building to maintain dumpsters, garbage must be stored inside the building. The garbage room (or storage area) should be inspected regularly—cracks in the walls and other types of damage provide conduits for pests to spread throughout the building. To control odors and inhibit bacterial and fungal growth, routine cleaning and disinfection of the garbage room are mandatory. The garbage room should be insulated from heat, especially if the room is near the furnace or boiler. Good lighting and painted walls encourage tenants to keep the room clean and facilitate the detection of insects on the walls. Regardless of where garbage is stored, a program to sort trash for *recycling* may also help control pests by concentrating the organic garbage in fewer containers; recycling of paper, glass, metals, and plastics is mandatory in some states.

Bed Bugs. Beginning in the late 1990s, particularly in the United States, bed bugs made a startling resurgence. Although the exact cause is not known, experts suspect the resurgence is associated with increased resistance of bed bugs to available pesticides, greater international and domestic travel, and the basic lack of knowledge regarding control of bed bugs due to their prolonged absence.[2] With this increase of bed bug infestations, several states introduced legislation to mitigate this pest. The law in some states requires real estate managers to disclose existing or past problems with the bugs as well as address how to remedy the problem with the pests and who will pay for it.

Property owners are required to pay for the extermination of bed bugs if detected. However, if tenants and residents do not cooperate with the extermination efforts, they could be held responsible for subsequent treatment costs. In other states, real estate managers of larger apartment buildings are required to provide pamphlets to tenants detailing preventive methods and other information on bed bugs. Bed bug infestations are required to be exterminated as soon as they're discovered—if immediate action is not taken, fines up to $300 per infested bedroom and/or $1,000 per infested common area could be enacted.[3]

Wildlife. Insects are not the only pests that cause disturbances. In many areas, squirrels, bats, birds, and other wildlife can also become "pests" and can cause serious damage to the outsides of

---

2. The Centers for Disease Control and Prevention (CDC) and the U.S. Environmental Protection Agency (EPA) have developed information that highlights emerging public health issues associated with bed bugs and additional information regarding safety and treatment in dealing with this pest.

3. Monitor social media to learn if resident or tenants are talking about bed bugs on the property. Since extermination can be quite costly, and it's difficult to pass the expense onto the tenants/residents, some leases include a policy they will charge the tenant for extermination if they are detected more than a certain number of days after occupancy.

buildings. Campus-style commercial and residential properties are particularly vulnerable. In certain situations, animals can also be hazardous to people—through scratches, bites, and disease transmission. As the habitats available for animals diminish, encounters with wildlife increase. Federal and state laws protect most wildlife species and their management; therefore, proactive measures should be taken to eliminate food sources and discourage habitats that attract animals. If certain issues exist, seek advice from wildlife rehabilitators, other wildlife experts, or animal control on additional ways to deter wildlife.

Deferred Maintenance

Deferred maintenance is the practice of postponing maintenance activities such as repairs on real property (or infrastructure) and personal property (or machinery) in order to save costs, meet budget funding levels, or realign available budget monies. The failure to perform needed repairs could lead to asset deterioration and ultimately asset impairment. Generally, a policy of continued deferred maintenance may result in higher costs, asset failure, and in some cases, health and safety implications. Real estate managers who take over the management of a property sometimes find that deferred maintenance exists, and a plan should immediately be put in place for a resolution.

OTHER ASPECTS OF MAINTENANCE

Regulations enforced by local, state, and federal governments establish minimum standards for the safety of employees and building occupants and affect many maintenance procedures. Laws governing minimum standards change frequently, therefore it's important to stay abreast of new laws and court interpretations. In addition, properties must comply with current environmental regulations, and compliance with maintenance practices relates to the safety, health, and well-being of tenants.

Safety

The Occupational Safety and Health Administration (OSHA) of the U.S. Department of Labor establishes job safety standards and is authorized to conduct inspections and to cite businesses for violations. OSHA standards should be made aware by real estate managers, especially those that apply to activities on the property. Unsafe work practices should be identified and employees should be provided with the proper equipment and knowledge for correct use. Appropriate and approved protective devices for equipment and personnel—shields on power saws, safety glasses, and rubber gloves, etc.—must be readily available.

Various chemicals and other materials used on site, such as cleaning products may include potentially combustible, flammable, or toxic substances. Personnel who work with such chemicals should be aware of the specific hazards and wear protective gloves and other appropriate equipment. Product labels identify the hazards and indicate how to treat persons who are exposed to the materials as well as how to dispose of the products and their containers properly. A material safety data sheet (MSDS) accompanies chemicals purchased in bulk in drums.

Temporary barriers or fencing should delineate construction and other work areas. The barriers should be clearly identified with signage, and they should be locked to prevent unauthorized persons from entering. Even such tasks as mopping and waxing lobby floors require clear delineation and signage to minimize the potential for slip- or trip-and-fall accidents. Even training employees on the proper use of ladders and how to bend and lift large items properly can help prevent accidents and injury.

Protecting the Environment

Understanding proper ways to handle and dispose of wastes ensures safety, compliance with regulations, and preservation of the environment, yet waste disposal is only one aspect of environmental protection. Many materials once considered safe for use in buildings have been found to be harmful to humans. The U.S. EPA and state and local governments have enacted regulations to protect people and the environment. It's important to know whether harmful materials are present on the property and whether they are potentially hazardous in their current state. The presence of hazardous materials can lower the property's value, even if the materials do not pose a threat. Liability for leaving such materials in place or for removing them has received considerable attention.

The following lists some hazardous materials that can be found in buildings:

- **Asbestos.** A fibrous mineral used in buildings prior to 1981 for flooring, insulation, and fireproofing. In 1989, the EPA issued a final rule banning most asbestos-containing products, but in 1991, this regulation was overturned. However, its use *is* banned in new flooring felt; rollboard; and corrugated, commercial, or specialty paper. Only licensed contractors can assess the condition of asbestos-containing material (ACM) in a property to determine its *friability* (how easily it crumbles). Only they can remove it *(abatement)* or maintain it in place *(containment)*. "Popcorn" ceilings in residential buildings are an indicator of asbestos. It may not be illegal to rent an apartment or commercial space with popcorn ceilings or asbestos-containing ceiling tiles, but it is important to disclose that these surfaces must not be disturbed in any way, shape, or form, and if changes to such surfaces are required, they must be performed by licensed contractors.

- **Radon.** A colorless, odorless, tasteless gas that occurs naturally in the radioactive decay of radium and uranium. It became a problem with the advent of energy-efficient buildings that allow only minimal transfer of air between the building's interior and the outside. If high levels of radon exist in a building, a qualified contractor can identify the sources and recommend ways to seal them or better ventilate the building. Some jurisdictions require carbon monoxide detectors.

- **Polychlorinated biphenyls (PCBs).** Chemicals in electrical transformers that are relatively harmless if left undisturbed. However, if a PCB-containing transformer leaks or burns, lethal *dioxin* gas may be released. Local or state law may require removal of PCBs during rehabilitation. An authorized hazardous waste hauler must transport transformers that contain PCBs to a licensed location for disposal. The property owner may be liable for any PCB contamination caused by the transformer, even after it has been removed from the property. However, when the utility company owns the transformers, which is often the case, it has the burden of responsibility for correcting transformer-related environmental problems.

- **Chlorofluorocarbons (CFCs).** Chemicals that contain two types of halogens—chlorine (Cl) and fluorine (F)—are being phased out and replaced with similar compounds that do not include chlorine atoms. Many were banned when the United States signed the Montreal Protocol. Newer refrigerant chemicals are not always compatible with existing air-conditioning systems, but it is possible to modify the equipment to use them. Information on refrigerant chemicals and equipment modifications and costs is available from the American Society of Heating, Refrigerating, and Air-Conditioning Engineers (ASHRAE).

- **Lead-based paint.** A type of paint used in housing built prior to 1980 that poses a serious lead-poisoning hazard to resident children. Its use in the United States was outlawed in 1978. The hazard may be abated by removing the paint (dipping removable components in chemical strippers); encapsulating it by covering painted surfaces with other materials (installing wallboard); and replacing painted window frames, doors, balustrades, and other easily removed components. Only qualified contractors should perform abatement work and disposal of the hazardous waste. By federal law, the property owner must disclose the presence of lead-based paint to potential buyers, residents, and commercial tenants.

- **Formaldehyde gas.** A foaming agent once used in foam insulation and still present in adhesives used in making pressed-wood products. Its presence in a building can be harmful. Manufactured homes are most susceptible to high levels of formaldehyde gas because of the amount of pressed wood and the type of insulation in them. Although formaldehyde gas will dissipate eventually, removing some of the formaldehyde-containing materials or increasing interior ventilation to hasten the dissipation and eliminate harmful effects may be necessary.

While *indoor air quality (IAQ)* problems can arise in any type of building, office buildings are the most susceptible. That is partially because their centralized HVAC systems serve such a large space and partially because they are built new or retrofitted as entirely enclosed systems (the windows cannot be opened), which results in poor air circulation. Contaminants, including *volatile organic compounds (VOCs)* and bacteria, can be distributed throughout the building, causing occupants to experience headaches, dizziness, drowsiness, nausea, and other symptoms of *sick building syndrome (SBS)*. *Legionella* bacteria, which can grow in fouled water-cooling towers, are the cause of *Legionnaires' disease* (an often fatal respiratory infection). As yet, there is no federal regulation of IAQ, but ASHRAE established IAQ standards in the early 1990s that have since been formalized as Standard 62-1999; they continue to evolve. The standards specify minimum ventilation rates and IAQ that are acceptable to human occupants.

Mold or mold-like substances can exist in rental homes, condominiums, apartments, and commercial buildings. Water damage, leaks, improper ventilation, lack of proper temperatures, and other moisture intrusions or seepage are the primary sources of mold growth. Mold may adversely affect human health. However, it appears that the effect of mold on humans is short term rather than long term—removing the mold removes the effect. Not all mold that grows in buildings is "the toxic mold" that has sensationalized this subject. When mold is detected, actions to remediate the problem should be initiated promptly. A qualified contractor should remove the mold and repair the damaged area. Straightforward, informative communication with building occupants will help diminish the perception of mold hazards and minimize the risk of liability for the property's owner and manager.

Many older buildings used to maintain their own fuel supply for their boilers, usually in storage tanks on the premises. The threat of contamination of groundwater by *leaking underground storage tanks (LUSTs)* has led to regulations requiring inspection and replacement of tanks that are still in use—those no longer in use may have to be removed. The presence of extra pipes may indicate a forgotten underground tank. If an abandoned tank is found on the premises, the alternatives for making it completely safe are to remove it or to fill it with cement. Always contact the local authorities regarding the legally correct procedure to use when dealing with environmental issues.

Controlling Energy Consumption

Not only are energy-saving features appealing to tenants, they can also function as a marketing tool to entice tenants who are concerned about the environmental performance of places where they live and work. Managing energy usage is an ongoing aspect of maintenance, and energy savings reduces operating costs and increases potential profit for the property. *Energy conservation* is a way to ensure comfort and reduce fuel consumption.

Basic Energy Conservation Programs. Some energy programs cost very little to implement. For example, a simple reminder to residents and commercial tenants to report leaky faucets can reduce wasted water and fuel, or implementing a policy for the cleaning staff to turn off the lights after cleaning a room can save an enormous amount of electricity. Installing occupancy sensors and timers for lighting in common areas that are not fully occupied (e.g., restrooms, conference rooms, private offices, and even supply closets) can have a dramatic impact on a building's energy reduction. For example, a typical 100,000 sq. ft. office building can save more than $14,000 a year by installing occupancy light sensors.

DISPOSING OF FLUORESCENT BULBS SAFELY

It is important to note that all fluorescent bulbs contain extremely small amounts of mercury that can potentially be harmful to people and the environment if they are not disposed properly. If a bulb breaks, it is important to reduce mercury vapor exposure by having people and pets leave the room while the room airs out for about 10 minutes, shut off the HVAC system, and thoroughly collect all of the broken materials for disposal in an airtight container.

As an alternative to sensors and timers, something as simple as replacing conventional incandescent light bulbs with compact florescent lights (CFLs) can have long-lasting energy-saving results. Although the cost of CFLs is higher than the cost of regular incandescent bulbs, the life expectancy of CFLs is 10 times greater, and they use 75 percent less energy.

Adjusting thermostats throughout the building (especially in office buildings that have central HVAC systems) is another simple example of reducing energy costs. By setting the temperature a few degrees lower during the heating season and, similarly, a few degrees higher during the cooling season, it will create substantial energy and cost savings. Many residential buildings also have central HVAC systems, and these can be adjusted similarly. It is important to keep in mind that the temperature should satisfy the residents' and/or tenants' comfort levels. Local ordinances may dictate thermostat settings during certain hours of the day or night or require certain levels of heating (or cooling).

Other Energy Conservation Tactics. In certain situations, controls can be installed on existing equipment depending on age; however, other circumstances require replacing systems with new equipment. A *retrofit* is the replacement of an old building component with a new, energy-efficient one—installation of a new boiler, for example, especially one carrying the ENERGY STAR® label. Retrofitting can be very expensive, but the installation will eventually pay off, especially if the component was already due for replacement. Although the payback may take years, retrofitting can become a strong competitive advantage if energy costs soar; it can also increase the value of the property (lower expenses increase NOI) if NOI is normally used to calculate value.

The following examples provide a condensed list of other energy conservation tactics:

- Low-flow shower heads can reduce consumption of water and fuel
- Motion or infrared sensors for parking lot lights can reduce electricity consumption without compromising security
- Combination timer thermostat on a boiler can match high-water temperature with peak demand
- Routine cleaning and oiling of machinery results in better performance, longer life, and lower energy consumption
- Dual-flush toilets (low- and high-water flushes) can save water consumption
- Frequent inspections of the property and routine maintenance are essential to prevent energy waste

It's important to learn about the energy consumption of a property, billing procedures used by utility companies, and energy control devices available in the market. Be aware of nonprofit organizations, such as the U.S. Green Building Council, which offers a Leadership in Energy and Environmental Design (LEED) certification—an internationally recognized green building certification system. The IREM Certified Sustainable Property (CSP) is another valuable certification that is an attainable, affordable, and meaningful recognition program for all property types.

The goal of energy management is to strike a balance between the initial cost of an energy-saving device or program and the amount of time before it pays for itself. Reducing expenses in this manner also improves NOI and adds to the property's value. To optimize energy conservation, real estate managers should think creatively about energy costs and usage.

Maintaining Property Security

Successful maintenance programs contribute to a building's security. Preventing crime in buildings will always be a difficult task—especially since many crimes do not result from forcible entry. Being complacent about security measures will create greater opportunities for crime. Therefore, regular inspections and thorough preventive measures are the best defenses against crime at any property.

Some real estate managers and property owners may consider a security staff or surveillance equipment crucial, but before making such an investment, the issue of liability should be considered. The presence of a security force or monitoring equipment—or the promotion of these services when marketing the property—may be construed as a security guarantee. If that guarantee fails, the owner or real estate manager could be liable. Despite this risk, security personnel are crucial for certain property types—especially office buildings and shopping centers.

Whatever security program is in place, staff should continually monitor to make sure the program functions exactly as planned. The following lists some basic action items to be shared with staff (and tenants of commercial properties):

- Doors that lock automatically should not be propped open for long periods of time because most crimes in apartment buildings result from entry and fire doors being propped open.
- Maintenance staff should replace burned-out light bulbs as soon as they discover them so that areas at night are visible.
- High priority should be given to repairing any component that may provide access to the property.
- Be sure that overgrown shrubbery is frequently trimmed to help eliminate potential hiding places.

In the aftermath of September 11, 2001, security tightened espe-cially for large commercial properties, which has caused real estate managers to be more alert to the threat of terrorist acts, such as bomb threats, dangerous air pollutants (including biological and chemical agents), nearby hazardous materials spills, and other inci-dents. Real estate managers should work with local authorities in planning for emergencies while also staying abreast of alerts issued by the various governmental authorities. In this context, greater scrutiny of prospective tenants and of current tenants' activities is also warranted. The U.S. Department of Homeland Security iden-tifies an *active shooter* as an individual actively engaged in killing or attempting to kill people in a confined and populated area. In most cases, active shooters use firearms, and there is no pattern or method to their actions or selection of victims. Finding and presenting such information from various agencies to staff and tenants helps educate them to situations that may be unfamiliar and that would not otherwise be at the forefront of their minds.[4]

MANAGING MAINTENANCE WORK

Since the real estate manager and the property owner are respon-sible for choosing the most effective method of maintaining the property, it's important to find qualified personnel to do the work and keep records of the work performed.

Staffing Choices

Real estate managers can find personnel to do maintenance work by either hiring on-site staff, using management firm employees, or by working with contractors.

On-site Staff. Hiring on-site staff is a customary practice and an effective way to quickly provide custodial and preventive main-tenance. The size of the building usually determines the number of people and the range of specialized skills required. However,

---

4. For more information about how to deal with an active shooter, read the *Journal of Property Management* article, "The Aftermath of Workplace Violence: Taking Control of the Situation" (Sep/Oct 2013, Vol 78, No. 5).

it is important to note that on-site staff entails payroll expenses, human resource personnel, training, supervision, and an added liability to the owner and property management firm—all of which carries with it a large responsibility to manage. Essentially, real estate managers who are well qualified to lead, inspire, manage, and motivate employees will succeed in their daily duties.

Management Firm Employees. When providing nonroutine maintenance to a managed property, the management company will bill the property owner for labor and parts in addition to the regular management fee. With such an arrangement, disputes can sometimes arise between the real estate manager and the owner regarding the amount of extra charges. If the management company provides maintenance services, negotiating a totally separate fee or billing arrangement may be more appropriate. In addition, real estate management companies must be relatively competitive with the cost for services that could be provided by an outside contractor. However, slightly higher fees may be justified if tenants recognize the speed with which items are repaired or cleaned. Better service will help maintain higher occupancy and increased revenue in the long run. Added consideration must be given to increases in insurance rates for those who perform manual labor as opposed to general office work.

Contractors. For maintenance that requires specialized skills or licensing of those who do the work (e.g., elevator maintenance), contractors may be used in addition to, or in place of, on-site staff. Regular janitorial services might also be contracted, as well as independent security agencies that provide on-site security officers on contract.

All contractors should be properly insured, and if their particular duties require licensing, verify that their licenses are current. Janitorial, security, and other contracted personnel who will work on site for extended periods should undergo pre-employment criminal background checks. Contractors should be required to show proof that they have adequate and appropriate insurance, such as workers' compensation, and to supply several references—all of which should be checked.

Before choosing contractors to perform certain jobs, draft precise *specifications* for the work describing details of the job, materials to be used, any special equipment or tools required, and potential time constraints that may apply. Contractors will then be invited to *bid* on the job either informally or as a formal *request for proposal (RFP)* process, which requires the bidder to provide written specifications for services. The contractors will submit *quotations* that state their analysis of the job, the time it will take, and the cost. After receiving the quotes, the contractor who will provide the necessary level of quality for the fairest price is selected. In some instances, stating a firm price is impossible, especially if a job (elevator repair, for instance) could take on a different character after the work begins.

The contractor may submit an *estimate* showing known costs (for parts) and specific rates to be charged for variable components of the job, an hourly rate for labor, and mileage charges for travel—also known as time and materials or T&M. Contractors or management companies typically use specific written contracts for technical or repetitive maintenance services; they may use purchase orders or work orders for work not covered by a contract.

It's in the best interest of the real estate manager to develop and maintain positive relationships with the contractors that service the properties on a regular basis. Contractors can provide advice and help with cost-saving measures. Walking the property with these providers (such as a landscape contractor) frequently or at least once per year can uncover needs that may not have been identified during normal weekly or monthly servicing. Face-to-face or phone conversations help develop such relationships and can possibly clear up confusing details more efficiently than with e-mails or text messages.

Record Keeping

Whether the maintenance work is done by on-site staff, employees of the management firm, contractors, or a combination of the three, the record-keeping requirements are essentially the same.

Work Order. Each specific maintenance or repair activity should have an individual *work order* (Exhibit 10.3) that indicates what, when, and who will do the work. Work orders are usually e-mailed directly to contractors from work-order programs such as Corrigo, which promotes mobility with wireless work orders. Most companies receive invoices through a service and never handle paper

---

EXHIBIT 10.3
Sample Maintenance Work Order

Work Order Number _____Assigned to _____
Property _____Date _____
Maintenance required _____
_____
_____
Location on property _____
Maintenance performed _____
_____
_____
Materials used _____
_____
_____
Time required/cost of labor $ _____
Cost of materials $ _____
Total $ _____
Maintenance performed by _____
Unable to complete because _____
_____
_____

This is a generic example. For work to be done in an apartment, a work order form would include spaces for the resident's name, home and work phone numbers, the presence of a pet, and whether permission to enter the unit has been received, as well as whether the resident is to be charged for the work and the reason. A commercial property work order would also include tenant contact information. Work done is usually charged back to commercial tenant. Space on the form may also be included for the tenant to acknowledge the completion of the work. Some real estate managers combine this form with a *maintenance service request* form.

invoices. After the job is done, the worker should complete the work order and return it to the real estate manager or the maintenance office.

Maintenance Service Request. Tenants and residents usually complete a *maintenance service request* to initiate work to be done in their leased spaces. A staff member may also fill out the form when a request is phoned to the office. Most properties provide this form on their websites to be completed online.

The service request form should identify the tenant and the leased space, include contact information, and describe the work requested. Space should be available for the tenant to sign the form and grant permission for staff to enter the leased premises to determine the priority of the task. Some maintenance systems include an e-mail confirmation to the tenant of the work performed and any cost to be charged, along with a request for the tenant's response as to whether the work was satisfactory.

An expanded form might include space for information about parts, scheduling, and actual work done, along with space for the maintenance worker to sign the form when the work is complete— or a space to make notes about a return visit if the repair could not be completed at that time. Such an expanded form effectively combines the service request with the work order form.

Work Log. Most real estate managers use a *work log* to record maintenance jobs on a cumulative basis. Some keep a master work log for all property staff and contractors that list what has been scheduled and the cost of the work (Exhibit 10.4). Supervisors may ask staff members to maintain a separate log record of assigned tasks and time allotments. The worker can check off the work as it is completed, indicating the actual time required, and reasons for any time variances (or if a task is not completed, the reason).

Some residential properties keep records of maintenance by the apartment (e.g., a list of when the carpet was last changed). It is also important to keep all documentation on competed service

EXHIBIT 10.4

Sample Maintenance Work Log

Order Number	Location	Description of Work	Time	Date	Assigned To	Completed	Cost

The information displayed in this form is usually sufficient for most purposes. The location column may be used to identify the space and the resident or commercial tenant, or separate columns can be created for this information. Columns may be added to track other details such as the amount of time to do the work, purchase order numbers, additional work to be done, and when the work was inspected.

requests that explains when the request was completed, what the request entailed, and how long it took to complete. Documentation is extremely important for rare occasions when issues are raised in court by individuals claiming they were discriminated against due to their inclusion in a protected class in the timing, quality, and/or attitude of the workers in resolving maintenance issues.

Purchase Order. Staff members who are not directly involved with maintenance might complete a *purchase order* for supplies or equipment; this record has a direct effect on maintenance efficiency. A purchase order should show the following items:

- Name of the vendor
- Date of the order
- Kind, quantity, and price of each item ordered
- Delivery date
- Terms of acceptance
- Any substitutions (if they are allowed)

Purchase orders help monitor inventory levels and ensure an adequate supply of replacement parts. Tracking inventory through purchase orders can prevent purchasing too many or too few supplies and spare parts—both situations are costly. Overstock represents cash that is not available for other uses, and having too many parts on hand can lead to pilferage by employees or tenants, or the potential for damage while being stored.

Inadequate inventory is also expensive, especially in terms of the staff time involved in making a special trip to purchase a part. Some companies require maintenance workers to come to the workplace with their own tools and supplies, which removes the need to track the inventory of supplies.

Inventory Control System. To verify inventory levels and track the frequency of restocking, develop an *inventory control organization* that provides for each item to be recorded as it is removed from inventory, and for the remaining inventory count (item total) to be reduced. Regular review of the list indicates what needs to be restocked and when. There are numerous software programs available specifically for property management firms to manage their overall maintenance program and work-order-request systems. Some programs even allow the user to incorporate requests directly into the inventory, accounting, purchase order, and invoicing systems.

SUMMARY

Managing the physical asset of a property involves more than simply cleaning and repairs. A good maintenance program antici-pates malfunctions and schedules regular examination and care of building components. More than anything else, appearance is the best marketing tool for any property. Custodial maintenance can optimally be scheduled by monitoring traffic flow through various parts of the building, and by making sure the maintenance staff know how often inspections are required under various conditions. Most importantly, preventive maintenance lowers repair costs and helps deter crime by ensuring that door locks, alarms, and strategic lighting in parking lots and stairwells are operational.

Meeting the terms of OSHA regulations is a must because it helps to provide a safe working environment—especially because maintenance and repair of equipment pose risks and hazards to staff. Staff should also understand the proper procedures for safely disposing items that carry a variety of chemicals—especially those used in cleaning supplies. If hazardous materials are on the premises, the staff should know the proper procedures for handling them in order to comply with federal, state, and local environmental regulations.

Establishing a habit and practice of keeping accurate records is an integral part of managing the physical asset. Using purchase orders and inventory controls saves the owner the costs of excessive or inadequate inventory. Clear and concise records are necessary for tracking specific maintenance work and when (or whether) it is completed. Real estate managers should always be attentive to and watchful of chronic maintenance issues and try to get to the root of each problem. As an industry, real estate managers do not want to become notorious for just treating the symptoms and not the disease.

Altogether, property maintenance of an owner's asset, regardless of size or type of property, is under the authority of the real estate manager and is one of the most comprehensive and important functions in property management. Without an adequate product to rent or sell, there will be no renters or buyers—and thus no revenue for the owner. While this chapter provides an overview of some building components and their specific maintenance needs, keep in mind that no two properties are alike. Knowing all of the ins and outs of a property is the only way to develop a proper maintenance program to enhance the property's longevity.

11 | Residential Properties

Few aspects of real estate management are as complex and multifaceted as the residential sector. Residential, of course, includes both single-family (houses and condominiums) and multifamily (apartments and condominium associations). As a career, managing residential property offers some of the greatest opportunities simply because of the diversity and number of properties available to manage. Being new to this industry, it's important to be prepared for the dynamic, ongoing evolution of what it means to manage real estate. This chapter specifically examines the details involved in managing residential property as opposed to other property types.

Professional real estate managers provide services for the following residential property types:

- Multifamily housing (apartment buildings)
- Government-assisted housing
- Military housing
- Common interest realty associations (CIRAs)
    - o Condominiums
    - o Cooperatives
    - o Planned unit developments (PUDs)
- Single-family homes
- Manufactured housing (mobile home parks)
- Senior housing
- Mixed-use developments
- Student housing

RENTAL HOUSING

From high-rise buildings to single-family homes, rental housing is in use 24 hours a day, meeting the housing needs for all the residents. This continuous occupancy tends to increase the demand for highly skilled professional management, maintenance, and repair. When people rent a space, they expect management to provide specific services such as yard work, window cleaning, and snow removal. If service is inadequate for any reason, the property manager might inevitably become a representation of the problem to the resident—residents have an emotional as well as a monetary value attached to their apartment. For this reason alone, having superior customer service skills is essential in addition to proficiency in the administrative functions of managing residential properties. Because the rental income of the property is usually the basis for the real estate manager's compensation, efforts must be focused on maintaining the highest levels of occupancy, without sacrificing the quality of the resident. Satisfied residents are always more likely to renew their leases.

Management of residential property requires specific applications of the principles of real estate management already outlined in this book. The personal nature of the use of leased space makes special demands on the property's staff. The following sections discuss characteristics of rental housing that make its management challenging, unique, and rewarding.

Multifamily Housing (Apartments)

Gone are the days when apartments were seen as nothing more than an affordable place to stay. Today's renter has many options and is able to choose a site and location that best suits their lifestyle. Additionally, the apartment industry offers much more in terms of concepts, design, size, and features that appeal to everyone from the millennial or senior looking to downsize or the career-minded professional with concierge needs. Newer apartments usually have standardized floor plans, appearing in the types of amenities built into the individual units and the building, or the property as a whole.

Although new buildings are generally more popular with renters, there are some renters who prefer a specific period architecture or "vintage" property type, especially in urban areas. Location, size, age, and amenities make every apartment building unique, and the challenge of managing those apartments is recognizing and accentuating the positive characteristics to create a more appealing residence and enhance the property's value. The oversight and management involved in multifamily housing requires carefully selected, qualified on-site personnel who can execute on the owner's management plan and enforce lease terms.

Apartment Types. With land values on the rise, many real estate developers are forced to explore high-density projects, especially in major cities. As developers build upwards, this creates more *high-rise buildings*. Buildings 10 stories and taller are considered high-rise buildings; however, the classification varies by region. Some larger high-rise buildings can contain hundreds of apartments and can house thousands of residents; they can also contain a variety of recreational amenities such as fitness and business centers, tennis courts, community rooms, swimming pools, saunas, and hot tubs. The availability of parking on decks or in underground garages connected to the building might be another amenity. Most high-rise buildings have a continuously staffed front desk, concierge, or they may have all-night attendants or security staff on duty when the on-site office is closed. Some high-rise buildings might include retail space on the ground floor for convenience stores or newsstands.

Mid-rise apartment buildings, a type of multiple-unit development that has five to nine stories, exists in both cities and suburbs. These buildings may include the same types of amenities as high-rise buildings—some might have central lobbies, mailrooms, or fitness centers. Mid-rise buildings in urban areas usually do not provide parking, but their counterparts in small cities and suburban areas usually do.

Low-rise buildings consist of one to four stories and may contain ten or more apartments within a single structure. Some have elevators; those without elevators are called *walk-ups*.

Garden apartments, another type of low-rise building, are often located in suburban areas where land is comparatively less expensive and developers have more leeway—some garden apartment communities occupy several acres. In some cases, a separate building may house laundry facilities, the management office, or recreational amenities. Appealing landscapes and quieter surroundings are part of the attraction of suburban garden apartments as compared to a downtown, urban area.

The two main factors in distinguishing different types of properties are (1) building height and (2) configuration. If land is relatively cheap, the developer can more easily construct shorter buildings and spread them out over a larger area. If land is expensive, developers construct taller buildings in order to get more apartments onto the land. The number of apartments in relation to the land area is referred to as *density*:

Number of apartments ÷ Land size = Density

Apartment Management. The architectural design, construction, location, and size of multiple-unit apartment developments affect the complexity of managing them. For instance, high-rise apartment buildings include sophisticated elevators, centralized HVAC equipment, and other systems that require specialized maintenance. Large garden complexes offer a different set of management challenges because they have more spacious lawns and separate systems and equipment in each of several buildings. Small apartment buildings usually provide few extra services and facilities and consequently are less management intensive. However, those structures are sometimes older, and their general maintenance may be time consuming. In addition to the physical upkeep, the number of properties in a portfolio influences administrative time. If all the units in one building are owned by a sole proprietor, the preparation of an operations report on 300 apartments may be a relatively light exercise. On the other hand, 300 apartments in 30 individually owned 10-unit buildings will require the same type of reporting magnified by nine.

Government-Assisted Housing

When part of the rent payment or other considerations impacting rent comes from a governmental body, the residential type is considered *government-assisted housing*. In some cases, the interest rate on the mortgage is subsidized for some government-assisted housing types. Unlike conventional housing, *subsidized housing* has unique marketing and leasing requirements, some legislative and regulatory, due to the nature of the property type. *Public housing,* on the other hand, is generally owned and managed through a local or state governmental agency. As a rule, governmental housing subsidies are either resident- or property-based (explained in more detail later in this chapter).

Private investors usually own rental property in which a subsidy is provided. The common forms of real estate ownership—partnerships, corporations, and REITs—also apply to subsidized housing. The owners' desire for a fair return on investment (ROI) is the same as in conventional housing; however, a portion of the ROI in subsidized housing may result from additional tax advantages granted for (1) development, (2) leasing part of the property to residents eligible for housing subsidies, or (3) leasing to the local housing authority. Special loan arrangements involving lower debt service payments also increase the return so the investment is competitive with conventional housing. Another common arrangement is for the developers and investors—looking for a tax break—to build the complex and sell it to the housing authority or to a nonprofit (religious or charitable) organization that specializes in subsidized housing.

Resident-Based Rental Assistance. The *Section 8 Housing Choice Voucher Program,* a part of the Housing Assistance Payments Program, was authorized by the Housing and Community Development Act of 1974, which provides nationwide rental assistance to low-income families, seniors, and disabled individuals. Public housing agencies (PHAs), which receive funds from the U.S. Department of Housing and Urban Development (HUD), locally administer housing choice vouchers.

The individual or family who receives a housing voucher is responsible for finding a suitable housing unit in properties that accept such vouchers. The PHA then pays the subsidy directly to the property owner on behalf of the participating renter. The renter pays the difference between the amount subsidized by the program and the actual rent charged by the owner—usually limited to 30 percent of the renter's adjusted monthly income. In some cases, PHAs have extensive waiting lists of prospective renters for certain properties. The voucher program has provisions that outline resident and owner responsibilities.

In addition to the traditional resident screening by property owners, HUD permits PHAs to screen applicants to define and verify acceptable documents, which is also a major challenge for real estate managers. To simplify this time-consuming task, *Enterprise Income Verification (EIV) systems* are extremely helpful for this process. The EIV system is a federal database that provides the information needed to verify a resident's income—federal wages, quarterly unemployment compensation, monthly social security, and supplemental security income benefits. In 2010, HUD mandated that owners and agents use the system to reduce subsidy errors. Since the EIV system is closely monitored and protected by the Federal Privacy Act, it can only be used by authorized persons; it requires a signature agreeing to the rules and strict accessibility guidelines, ensuring the privacy of information.

A PHA may choose to use up to 20 percent of its voucher funding to implement a project-based voucher program to provide rental assistance for eligible families who live in specific housing developments or units. After one year of assistance, a family may move from a project-based voucher unit and switch to the PHA's resident-based voucher program when the next voucher is available—meaning that the resident can therefore choose where they live. A PHA may commit to pay project-based assistance for a term of up to 10 years, subject to availability of funding from HUD. In some locations, a PHA's payment standard (the amount paid by the housing authority from the federal subsidy received through HUD) will not support the asking rent of an apartment home. This is especially concerning for owners who like to work with the Section 8 program, but are forced to subsidize the difference between their asking rent and the PHA payment.

Project-Based Rental Assistance. Section 8 *Project-Based Rental Assistance* is also available directly from HUD. With this program, HUD makes up the difference between the rent that a very low-income household can afford and the approved rent for an adequate housing unit in a multifamily project. Eligible renters pay rent based on their income. HUD originally provided such project-based assistance in connection with new construction or substantial rehabilitation of existing structures. In addition to these Section 8 programs, many other federal housing programs exist. For example, the *Section 202* and *Section 811* programs cover supportive housing for seniors and the disabled, respectively. The U.S. Department of Agriculture, Rural Development, administers other housing programs that might include rental assistance for those who meet their qualifications.

Federal housing programs are often subject to the availability of funds, and the government may modify requirements for participation—by property owners and low-income residents—from time to time. In some cases, certain programs could be discontinued, but aspects of it do not change immediately because of the long-term commitments involved.

Subsidized Housing Management. The need for effective management for subsidized and public housing creates a demand for real estate managers who are skilled in balancing the interests of all the parties involved:

- Owners
- Governmental agencies
- Residents—who receive subsidies
- Residents—who do not
- Citizens' action groups
- Resident associations

In addition to understanding the principles of real estate management, one should thoroughly understand all of the applicable local, state, and federal regulations. For example, to continue to receive housing benefits, residents of subsidized housing must be recertified periodically by the real estate manager. If dealing with subsidized and public housing, it's important to understand the role and structure of the governmental agencies involved and the way they must work within budgets that are limited because of lower-rental income. Under most federal, state, and local housing programs, an extensive series of forms and reports must also be submitted, which is often time consuming. If the reports are improperly completed, the governmental agency will not send compensation until the reports are correct.

Managers of subsidized housing have a specialization that extends beyond the ability to work with governmental agencies. Their interactions with residents are often more demanding than in other housing types because the objective of assuring the residents' comfort has additional social, political, and fiscal dimensions. In subsidized housing, real estate managers must establish lines of communication to overcome a multitude of barriers—ethnic, economic, social, and linguistic. In addition to maintaining peaceful coexistence at the property, the improved relations that result from their efforts help the community and society at large.

Low-Income Housing Tax Credit (LIHTC). In 1986, President Ronald Reagan signed into effect the Tax Reform Act of 1986. This marked the birth of the federal low-income housing tax credit program. Throughout the past 30 years, the program has helped house more than 13 million people. In short, a federal tax credit used to develop affordable housing can be claimed over a 10-year period. This allocates $1.25 per capita to state agencies for use in incentivizing the development of low-income residential units. The program places great emphasis on compliance and, as a result, the management companies who choose to include LIHTC in their portfolios typically employ a compliance director or department to review resident files and income certifications to ensure compliance with the state or local agency's agreement.

Military Housing

In 1996, the *Military Housing Privatization Initiative (MHPI)* bill was passed to help the military improve housing conditions for their service members. The fundamental goal of the legislation was to partner with private-sector financing, expertise, and innovation to provide necessary housing faster and more efficiently. With the military housing privatization act, the Department of Defense (DoD) provided safeguards against any disruption in the flow of rental payments in the event of base closure, downsizing, or deployment. Military personnel receive a stipend for housing called the *Basic Allowance for Housing (BAH)*. When private housing is created or converted on the site of the military post, the BAH is released directly to the housing manager. Unlike civilians, military personnel cannot voluntarily end their employment, but they can be redeployed as the need arises. In a time of war, deployment from the base may sorely challenge the real estate manager's ability to turn over the residences for new prospects. This market offers many unique challenges and rewards, but not without its share of unique operational issues.

Senior Housing

As people age, housing that suits their needs and lifestyle becomes increasingly important. Many considerations influence the type of senior housing—some retirees are more concerned with social and recreational activities while others might require more hands-on medical care. Housing options range from aging in place to full-scale assisted living. Of course, many alternate housing choices are available between the two extremes. When residents age in place in conventional rental housing, real estate managers are usually confronted with a changing occupant profile, which would require spending more time with the residents, altering the building services or building components, and being more aware of services within the community. Purpose-built senior housing requires managers, their vendors, and their partners to broaden their skillset to include knowledge of recreational amenities; food service; transportation options; and social, psychological, and medical services.

There are two primary types of senior housing communities: (1) regular rental spaces and (2) *Continuing Care Retirement Communities* (CCRCs), also known as buy-in communities. Both types of senior housing are designed for healthy seniors looking for security and living an independent lifestyle. However, residents of CCRCs typically pay a substantial entry fee—usually a six-figure amount—which establishes an ownership interest in a community with available nursing services. In addition to the entry fee, a monthly service fee (in essence, rent) is paid by the resident for services rendered by the community.

Regardless of the types of senior housing communities, managing these establishments involves a greater diversity of services and greater interaction with residents and their off-site families. For the most part, offering a variety of amenities and services keyed to seniors' needs is likely to attract and retain a growing, stable, and appreciative category of residents. Associations such as the National Investment Center for Seniors Housing & Care (NIC) offer valuable resources for real estate managers working in senior housing. NIC provides research, data, and various publications for this growing market.

Student Housing

In the past 15 years, a niche has developed in the student housing market—luxury student housing. These newer developments, characterized by high-end amenities and high-priced rents, are located just off campus, but close enough to serve as student housing to neighboring campuses. These properties try to provide some aspects of dorm life without the parental tone, by hosting social and student-oriented events.

The types of amenities available for these developments include resort-like swimming pools with cabana and lounge, high-speed Internet, fitness centers, gaming rooms, large clubhouses for socializing events, laundry services, and granite countertops in kitchens. Some student housing is rented by the bed, rather than the unit, and strangers are placed together as they would be in campus dorms. For example, a typical unit has three to four beds with each bed priced from around $925 to $1,335 per month and includes utilities. These residences present a new set of challenges for real estate managers, who must market buildings to multiple audiences through multiple channels, while still providing exceptional customer service.

Another challenge is appealing to a greater number of audiences other than the final name on the lease. There are three constituencies: (1) students, (2) parents, and (3) college administrators. The manager must be creative in promoting the property. Using social media to publicize the property is a good starting point. It is important to keep a focus on pleasing the parents, who want to know that the building is safe, secure, and clean.

Establishing connections with local colleges and universities is essential. Once their support is gained, it'll be easier to attract residents through their housing offices, which often provide information on off-campus housing options. Due to the nature of the luxury status of student housing, it's essential to respond quickly to maintenance requests. Most properties provide a 24-hour turnaround in fixing any issues on the property. Managing properties catering to students requires patience, creativity, and resourcefulness.

SELECTING QUALIFIED RESIDENTS

When selecting qualifying prospects for residency, many responsibilities are involved. Before establishing a lease—regardless of the housing type—the following questions should always be asked about the prospect:

- Does the prospect have sufficient resources to pay rent and their other financial obligations?
- Will they pay the rent on time?
- Will they respect the privacy and property of others?
- Will they maintain the rental space?

The answers to these questions are usually provided on a *rental application form* (Exhibit 11.1). With the exception of financial or even criminal background data, verifying some of this information may be difficult. Inquiries pertaining to prospective residents' behavior must be made cautiously and without any bias—a decision that can be perceived as discriminatory can lead to liability. Understanding local, state, and federal fair housing laws is of the utmost importance in selecting residents. (Resident selection will be discussed in more detail in this chapter.) However, whether state law requires it or not, it's a good management practice to inform residents of the items for which they will be screened, prior to the screening itself. For instance, in the state of Oregon, if a screening fee is accepted to cover the cost of the resident screening, the law requires that property management provide prospects with written criteria first, so they will have an opportunity to decline or accept.

Fair Housing Laws. Since the adoption of the *Fair Housing Act* in 1968, HUD held a lead role in its administration. Today, fair housing laws at all levels—federal, state, and local—effectively prohibit housing discrimination on the basis of race, color, nationality, sex, religion, age, family status, or mental or physical handicap. It is unlawful to refuse or to fail to show an apartment, to supply rental information (e.g., rates), or to rent an apartment because of an applicant's protected status. It is also unlawful to impose different terms or conditions, such as extending different privileges in regard to the rent of an apartment or in providing services based on a resident's protected class.

The interpretation of fair housing laws has been strict—partly because few people overtly say to a prospective renter, "I will not rent this apartment to you because…." Even an unwitting breach of the law can result in a discrimination lawsuit—an event that can end a career and result in a substantial monetary fine. One of the most common discriminatory practices involves *steering*—which includes dissuading a prospect who inquires about available property from living at a particular site, encouraging them to look elsewhere, or hiding known vacant spaces from them.

EXHIBIT 11.1

Information Requested on a Rental Application Form

Property/Lease Information
- The space to be rented (street address and apartment number)
- Rental rate (dollars per month)
- Duration of the lease term (if applicant approved)
- Amount of security deposit or other fees

Applicant Personal Information
- Name and Social Security number (SSN)—or federal individual tax identification number (ITIN)—of principal applicant (and all adults who will sign the lease)
- Name(s) of all other occupants, including minor children
- Description(s) of any pets (if allowed)

Applicant Residency Information
- Current address and phone number
- Name and phone number of current property owner or manager—address (if different from applicant's)
- Duration of current tenancy and rent amount paid
- Reason for moving
- Same information for prior residence

Applicant Employment Information
- Current place of employment (company name and contact info), job title, years with the company, immediate supervisor(s), and salary
- Same information for prior employer

Applicant Financial Status
- Institution names and account numbers for bank savings and checking accounts, credit cards or charge accounts, and other outstanding loans, such as car payments or student loans
- Whether the applicant has ever filed bankruptcy

Other Information
- Identification of any requisite deposits or fees to be paid at the time the application is completed (e.g., for processing the credit check) and their refundability
- A statement of authenticity of all information provided and authorization to verify it—including credit and criminal background checks
- Applicant signature
- Spaces for initials of staff who process the application and the date

A standardized rental application form ensures the uniformity of information requested from each applicant, avoids the possibility of discrimination, and facilitates verification of the data for a rental decision.

Occupancy standards vary by state and local jurisdiction, check with the state and local ordinances, or consult with an attorney before establishing occupancy standards or guidelines. Once the occupancy standards are established, they should be uniformly applied as a standard to all applicants. It's important to maintain consistency in all phases of relationships with prospects and residents, especially when upholding the spirit of the law.

When preparing the lease, it's important to understand the difference between a private occupancy restriction and a local building code. Most cities have local building codes that impact occupancy standards; however, building codes may not be appropriate and should not be relied on for setting a proper private housing occupancy standard—as they are customarily used in determining occupancy for single rooms and studios. In addition, while many state and local fair housing enforcement agencies try to persuade housing providers to adopt occupancy policies that may allow more than two persons per bedroom, most of these agencies are not acting pursuant to any established law. Always be aware that those states may accept familial status complaints based on a two-person-per-bedroom limitation, and be sure to check with an attorney to avoid a familial status complaint based on occupancy standards.

Fair housing law also applies to marketing materials. Advertisements should never include words or images that indicate or imply any limitations or preferences in the rental of apartments—or sale or other transactions related to housing. Some state and local jurisdictions may publish lists of words that rental advertisements may *not* use. As a rule of thumb, describing the specific property being rented, as opposed to the *type* of resident being sought, is an acceptable policy for such advertisements. For example, it is acceptable to state that this is a nonsmoking building, but it cannot be advertised that only nonsmokers are welcome. Additionally, it may be interpreted that having policies against certain behavior directed solely towards children can be discriminatory. For instance, posting a sign that says, "No children allowed on the lawn," could be discriminatory against *familial status*. If the lawn is a concern, the sign should simply state, "Please stay off of the lawn," and it should apply to all residents.

Fair housing laws are always subject to change, particularly as states and local jurisdictions enact their own rules and courts adjudicate discrimination lawsuits. Local requirements are often more stringent—they may include additional protected classes (e.g., sexual orientation)—and the most stringent law in place is at the local level. Two ways to remain informed on these important laws are to (1) consult with an attorney and (2) read on the subject of fair housing.[1] Because these laws are constantly being expanded, real estate managers are responsible for staying up to date on the local, state, and federal fair housing laws.

Rent-Paying Ability. A prospect's past payment record, sources and amount of income, and level of indebtedness are the main considerations in determining rent-paying ability. The amount of rent as a percentage of the individual's income is not by itself a definitive indicator of an individual's ability to pay rent. The size of a household and the number of its members who are employed affect the amount of money available for rent.

Most occupants of rental housing pay their rent from current income. Use of reserves or proceeds from financial investments is not common. The resident who loses a job may soon be unable to pay the rent because they do not have enough cash in reserve to meet living costs for an extended period. In times of financial difficulty, some real estate managers accept proof of significant assets.

Income Sources. Examining prospective residents' sources of income to verify their ability to pay rent is fair and necessary. Factors to consider are the length of time a worker has been in a position with a company, the amount of income and frequency with which it is paid, and the nature of the employer's business. Individually, these factors may not qualify or disqualify a prospect, but taken together, they can be a good indicator of personal financial strength.

---

1. For a good resource on fair housing, visit *www.fairhousingfirst.org.*

- **Duration of employment.** The longer someone has been in a position, the stronger the probability of the prospect's job security.
- **Amount of income.** Although the amount of rent as a percentage of income can be used to estimate the prospect's ability to pay the rent, that is not the only deciding factor. In addition to wages or salary, ask the prospect about other financial resources (e.g., alimony, child support, bonuses, or commissions).
- **Frequency of payment.** Knowing how often the prospect is paid can be helpful in predicting the timeliness of rent payments, especially since renters usually pay rent from their current income.
- **Nature of the business.** The changing economic climate from decade to decade proves that there are no guarantees for job security—anyone can be laid off at any time. Because the prospect most likely works in or near the community, basic information about the company and its reputation is easily available.

Review of these factors may cast a favorable light on a prospect, but none of them indicate whether they manage money wisely. A large family with limited means may be very frugal, while someone with a large income and a secure position might not. Just as verification of sufficient income is important, so is checking the applicant's payment record for loans and revolving credit programs. Regular and timely payments signify responsibility and ability to manage money.

Credit Reports. Real estate managers generally hire credit bureaus or consumer reporting agencies to conduct the financial investigation of an applicant. The resulting credit report includes information on bank accounts, credit card debt, outstanding loans and judgments, and bankruptcy filings that can help determine how much of a prospect's income is already committed. Credit bureaus give individual consumers a credit score based on their credit activity. Many real estate management firms require that prospects meet a minimum credit score in order to qualify for a lease at properties they manage. Businesses are willing to provide a reputable credit bureau with accurate information because they may rely on the credit bureau for information themselves or they may foresee a use for the service. With a credit bureau's well-known reputation for maintaining confidentiality and for being a reputable organization, they know precisely what to ask without inadvertently requesting information that cannot be shared. Keep in mind that using a third party to check credit shifts the real estate manager's responsibility at lease initiation.

Regardless of how the information is acquired, the *Fair Credit Reporting Act (FCRA)* requires that the prospect be advised that their credit is being checked. A standard rental application form usually includes a statement that the prospect—by signing the form—authorizes the property owner to verify the information provided. The FCRA also requires written authorization to investigate any other aspect of the applicant's background—e.g., occupancy history, employment, and criminal record. Applicants who are rejected based on a negative credit report must receive written notification of the adverse action. The letter must include four major areas: (1) give names, addresses, and phone numbers of all consumer credit reporting agencies that provided information; (2) state that the agencies only provided information and were not involved in the rental decision; (3) advise the applicant of their rights to obtain additional information from the credit reporting agency; and (4) provide a consumer statement describing their position.

Respect for Property and Neighbors. Real estate managers are permitted to inquire about a prospect's rental history—whether they maintained the properties in which they lived and displayed the required respect for the "quiet enjoyment" of the neighbors with whom they shared the dwelling. However, that is difficult to verify. The information is usually beyond the scope of a financial investigation, although other local firms may be engaged to perform such background checks. Such firms may also scan public records for evidence of evictions and checks returned because of insufficient funds. It is extremely important not to invade a prospect's privacy.

Length of residency is additional evidence of reliability. A succession of moves may imply instability, while long-term occupancy tends to indicate that the prospect is dependable. Keep in mind, however, that in an active market with substantial new construction, a succession of moves may only indicate a prospect's search for the best rental deal.

OTHER LAWS THAT AFFECT RESIDENTIAL RENTALS:

- **Americans with Disabilities Act (ADA).** In compliance with the ADA, residential rental properties must have certain public accommodations in their design and construction such as curb ramps, parking access aisles, elevators and lifts, or a combination of these elements.

- **Residential Lead-Based Paint Hazard Reduction Act.** For apartment buildings constructed before 1978, it is a requirement to give renters (1) a disclosure form detailing the presence of lead-based paint; (2) a government pamphlet on lead paint hazards; and (3) a copy of any existing reports that describe lead paint hazards at the property.

- **Megan's Law.** The sexual assault and murder of seven-year-old Megan Kanka in 1994 sparked the federal government's enactment in 1996 of House Resolution 2137 (called Megan's Law), which requires disclosure to the public of the presence of convicted sex offenders (names and addresses). This information is available through the local police department and online *(www.nsopw.gov).*

- **USA PATRIOT Act and Executive Order 13224.** Executive Order 13224 of the PATRIOT Act prohibits any business, including real estate professionals, from entering into business relationships (e.g., leases) with entities identified on the Specially Designated Nationals and Blocked Persons List (SDN). The order applies to both residential *and* commercial properties.

It's also important to note that a complete criminal history may not be given if the prospect intentionally failed to list a previous address. Check carefully for gaps in the prospect's rental history and ensure that background checks and collections are handled by a vendor specialist. Failures in these areas have led to expensive lawsuits and serious crimes. Although taking the extra time to check on the background of prospective residents can seem time-consuming, in the end it's beneficial to secure a lease with trustworthy and responsible people.

Rental Agreement

The lease protects the resident's as well as the property owner's interests. In an attempt to dispel any negative connotations of the word *lease,* management firms sometimes call a residential lease a *rental agreement*. The lease for any rental property is based on the intended use of the space and any special provisions for that usage. Residential leases by nature are not complicated, but they must include certain provisions and clauses discussed in the following sections. Some states require residential leases to be written in "plain language" because they might require preapproval of the lease, and violators may face stiff penalties.

Lease Clauses and Provisions. Printed lease forms include specific clauses that define the leased space, govern the payment of rent and handling of security deposits, and state the responsibilities of and the relationship between the property owner and the resident. These forms usually include various protections for both parties. The clauses listed below are especially important:

- Parties to the lease
- Term of lease
- Condition of premises
- Non-refundable fees
- Pet policies
- Right of reentry
- Subleasing
- Services and utilities
- Rules and regulations
- Landlord-Tenant Laws:
  - Security deposit amount
  - Late fees and other charges
  - Insurance requirements
  - Reasons for eviction

Parties to the Lease. The lease should state that all of the signers are responsible for paying the rent and fulfilling the lease agreement. In some situations such as college student housing, having unrelated individuals sign separate leases may be appropriate. While having multiple leases for one rental unit may seem cumbersome, it facilitates changes in occupancy. Having an individual lease for each roommate makes it easier to evict one resident who is irresponsible or behind in paying rent. That arrangement also prevents friends of the residents from becoming long-term guests.

Lease Term. While no standard *lease term* for residential property exists, one year is the usual period; six-month or month-to-month terms are also common. The length of the term is often based on what is popular in a given market. In most markets, a written lease that lasts at least one year covers residential units that command high rents.

Establishing the term of the lease has advantages and disadvantages. When a lease is signed, the rent is probably the highest the market will bear at the time for the space leased. If market demand rises during the lease term, the owner has essentially undersold the space. If the market declines, the resident has agreed to a rent that may exceed the rate for comparable space.

Other circumstances may also justify a modified lease term. For example, a prospect who needs to find a place to live during the winter and an owner who wishes to fill a vacancy during that period are both limited in their options because little turnover occurs in winter, especially in northern regions. If a qualified prospect is found, a 16- or 17-month lease may benefit both the owner and the resident even though the period is unusual. The longer lease term would preclude the unit becoming vacant the following winter, and it would protect the resident from having to move again in the cold.

Condition of Premises. Prior to a resident's moving into an apartment, a *statement of condition* is a reflection of what a real estate manager notes during their inspection. Incidental damage may be noted so a new resident will not be charged for it on move-out. Some residential leases spell out the resident's responsibilities for maintenance within their leased premises—e.g., cleaning carpeting once a year, keeping appliances clean and in working order, not keeping hazardous substances other than appropriate cleaning aids, etc.

The statement of condition also includes information about what charges for damage the management will assess at move-out and what it considers to be normal wear and tear. The overall purpose of the statement of condition establishes the state to which the resident is expected to restore the apartment at the time of move-out, in order to receive their full deposit without offset.

Non-Refundable Fees. Depending on state law, some properties allow the collection of cleaning and move-in fees that help offset the expenses incurred for turnover. If this fee is charged, some states require that an itemization be provided to the resident detailing how the fee was used (or will be used). On the other hand, some residents think because they paid a cleaning fee, they can leave the apartment in worse condition than they ordinarily would. While such fees may cover the cost of turnover carpet cleaning or other turnover expenses, there can be an inherent list of dos and don'ts that come with them as well.

Pet Policies. Regardless of the property owner's decision of allowing pets in the units, a *pet clause* is necessary.[2] The lease can establish thorough guidelines that specify what's allowed and what's not. Alternatively, pet policies may be stated in a separate *pet agreement* that the pet-owning resident signs, or the policies may be listed in the resident's handbook (discussed later in this chapter). The provisions in a pet agreement may just reiterate local ordinances, but if they are a stipulation of the lease or of house rules, they are easier to enforce. Guidelines often set limitations on the

_____

2. Fair housing laws apply for people with disabilities (or emotional dependency) that require a service animal. They may not be denied housing because of a "no pets" policy.

type, size, and number of pets allowed—requirements should be listed for damage deposits, use of leashes, and cleanup of animal wastes—and reiterate legalities related to licensing and vaccinations (Exhibit11.2).

Separate agreements may also state an amount of monthly "pet rent" that has been established for each pet, which essentially allows owners to collect a premium for the inevitable wear and tear that a pet can cause on an apartment. Although a pet policy may appear harsh when itemized and listed in an agreement, remind the resident that these measures are similar to advice given by pet associations and humane societies. In addition to protecting the owner's property, these policies safeguard the pet and protect all residents of the property.

Right of Reentry. The resident is entitled to *quiet enjoyment* of their leased space, free from disturbances by others and by the management. However, the property owner is granted the right to enter an occupied apartment to make repairs, provide agreed-upon services, and show the apartment to prospective residents and others—subject to certain limitations, which should be specifically stated in the lease. For ordinary repairs, obtain written permission to enter the premises; notification requirements may be prescribed by law. In case of emergency, the property owner can enter regardless of whether granted admittance. Real estate managers typically inspect apartments to review maintenance issues, to ensure the proper functioning of smoke alarms, and to check the overall cleanliness of the apartment at least once or twice per year. Frequent inspections that lack a specific purpose could be construed as harassment, which violates the resident's right to their quiet enjoyment of the property.

Subleasing. In certain cases, prospects request inclusion of a *transfer clause* that allows the resident to break the lease without penalty in case of a job transfer. If that is the case, request documentation from the resident's employer to that effect. On the other hand, a prospect who is renting while also looking to buy a house may

EXHIBIT 11.2

Items for Developing a Pet Policy

Type and Size of Pet. State the type of animal and specific weight and height requirements to exclude extremely large dogs or exotic animals.

Number of Pets. Specify a maximum number of pets to preclude residents from having too many animals.

Pet Deposit. Similar to a security deposit, the pet deposit (for each pet) should be sufficient to cover any damage to the leased space or the property.

Pet Registration. Require the pet owner to register each pet with the manager of the property. This links a specific pet to the deposit and verifies the number of pets on the premises.

Leash Requirement. To encourage residents to take extra care with their animals and not allow them to roam, state that all dogs must be kept on a leash when outside.

Cleanup. Require pet owners to clean up after their animals. Many communities have passed such ordinances, and this should be a policy of managed residential property as well.

Vaccinations and Licenses. Require proof that all animals have appropriate vaccinations and licensing as required by law. Neutering or spaying may also be required.

Insurance. Require pet-owning residents to carry renter's insurance that includes liability coverage. For example, dog bites may be covered but not other animal-related injuries, and property damage by a pet may be excluded.

Prohibited Areas. Indicate where animals are prohibited on the property—for example, the sandbox in a children's play area or the swimming pool and surrounding area.

Animal-Friendly Areas. Identify animal-friendly areas of the property, such as a designated dog-walking area with signage.

ask for a *home purchase clause* that similarly allows the resident to break the lease in the event a purchase transaction is closed before the lease term ends.[3]

The lease may also contain a *sublet clause,* which states that in order for the resident to vacate the premises before the end of the term, the resident must find a suitable replacement to sublet the space for the remainder of the lease obligation. The replacement resident must be approved and the resident or the subtenant must pay for the credit check. In the event of a job transfer, the employer may use its resources to help find a subtenant, or it may pay, on the employee's behalf, a negotiated penalty for breaking the lease without finding a subtenant. If the subtenant defaults, it's the responsibility of the original resident to pay for the remainder of the lease.

Services and Utilities. Residents are usually responsible for payment of utilities, such as gas and electricity, for which the utility provider bills them directly. The lease should state specifically what utilities are the resident's responsibility. This is especially important if residents pay for their own heat, water, and sewer. If some utilities are charged to the property owner, such as a boiler providing heating for the entire building, a system for prorating such expenses—based on apartment square footage or some other generally acceptable formula—may be implemented. Some residential properties include utilities in the rent.[4]

Rules and Regulations. To guarantee the safety and protection of residents, their rights, and the physical integrity of the property, a set of rules and regulations should be distributed to residents in the form of the a *resident's handbook*. In addition to reiterating information from the lease, the resident's handbook states specific policies regarding trash disposal, laundry room, common

---

3. Federal law is set out in the Servicemembers Civil Relief Act, enacted in 2003 to amend the Soldiers' and Sailors' Civil Relief Act of 1940, which provides specific rights relating to renting and leasing obligations.

4. This is a common practice in older buildings in which the apartments are not individually metered or for ease of payments for luxury student housing.

area amenity use, and permissible or prohibited furnishings. To encourage residents to abide by these rules, residents should sign a form accompanying the handbook stating they understand the rules. The lease should also contain a clause stating that the resident understands and will abide by the house rules. To make the house rules more acceptable, they can be called policies rather than rules and regulations—positive statements are more readily accepted than a list of what is not allowed. Exhibit 11.3 lists some items that a resident's handbook can include. Certain items that are not covered specifically as lease provisions should be listed in an addendum and incorporated into the lease by reference.

Compliance with Landlord-Tenant Laws. Most if not all local jurisdictions have laws that affect the rights of residents; known collectively as *landlord-tenant laws*, they state the rights and obligations of owners and residents and detail what either party can do if the other does not comply with the lease or the law. Landlord-tenant laws usually govern issues that the lease clauses or policies (rules) for the property address. In particular, they define *habitability,* regulate the handling of security deposits, set the maximum late fee, state provisions and requirements for subleasing, explain insurance requirements, and specify procedures for eviction.

Certain locales also have *rent control laws* that set a maximum on the amount of rent that an owner can charge or the maximum allowable increase on renewal or both. Rent control is a concept that some metropolitan areas see as a way to maintain affordable housing, but it does not benefit owners or residents over the long term. If rent is held below what the market will bear, the income of the property may not be adequate to maintain it properly. The result will be a greater concentration of poorly maintained residential space; properties that are not maintained lose value. Depressed property values reduce municipal income because of the lower real estate taxes they yield. Since it reduces or precludes the potential for financial success, rent control also discourages new construction.

EXHIBIT 11.3

Typical Information Listed in the Resident's Handbook

In general, the resident's handbook should be useful and welcoming. Information about the neighborhood such as schools, shopping, public transportation stops, and places of worship will help orient newcomers. Other appropriate additions might be sources for personal services such as barber and beauty shops, dry cleaners, and nearby restaurants, cinemas, and amusement parks, along with local social service agencies. The followings lists the general items listed in the handbook:

• Rent due date and treatment of delinquencies—dealing with late payment and other fees
• Purpose of the security deposit and conditions for its return
• Limitations on occupancy by visitors and persons other than those named in the lease
• Limitations on parking by residents and visitors
• Pet agreement conditions
• Limitations on particular furnishings
• Use of laundry room, pool, and/or gym, etc.
• General upkeep the resident should perform, such as replacing light bulbs when necessary
• Contact information for emergency maintenance
• Utilities that are the residents' responsibility
• Insurance residents are expected to carry
• Map of exit routes for evacuation procedures
• Notice of renewal, nonrenewal, or termination of the lease
• Inspections of the unit before move-in and after move-out
• The right and conditions of the property owner(s) to enter residents' premises with or without notifying them
• Subletting rules
• Grounds for eviction
• Other limitations on residents' actions

The handbook can also include information regarding proper care of built-in appliances such as ovens, refrigerators, air conditioners, furnaces, or thermostats. Such instructions can avert damage or minimize wear on the appliances. Other suggestions, particularly those pertaining to energy conservation—replace air-conditioner filters regularly, keep windows and doors closed in the winter, or when operating the air conditioner in the summer—will reduce the resident's utility bills or the owner's expenses for master-metered fuel.

Rental Forms and Other Resources. Local associations like IREM or the National Apartment Association (NAA) exist in most states. These associations provide rental housing forms that comply with the latest and most up-to-date landlord-tenant laws in the area. Certain forms, such as regular leases, screening criteria, lead-based paint pamphlets, pet policies, and late notices, can be purchased in bulk and used as main forms for the property. Some associations also allow these forms to be completed online, with a subscription, so as to eliminate the need to purchase a stock of forms that may later be out-of-date when new laws or regulations are implemented. Either way, associations do most of the leg work to help eliminate the need to create or monitor such forms for their legality.

Resident Retention

There are many creative ways to have strong resident retention program through a solid marketing strategy that might have been established for a new residential property, or for a new initiative when taking over an existing property. Along with having good resident relations and maintaining great upkeep on the property, gaining lease renewals is the ultimate goal.

Encouraging Lease Renewals. Residents whose leases are nearing expiration should be contacted two to three months before the expiration date. Some real estate managers send out a new lease, while others simply send a renewal notice stating any change in the rent and noting any specific changes in terms and conditions of the prior lease. Hand delivery of a renewal lease or a follow-up visit is a way of showing residents through personal contact that their tenancy is valued. However, personal interaction with a resident does not have to be limited to lease renewal time. Frequent, but respectful interaction with residents almost always results in a more positive experience for both parties, making the renewal process more pleasant and meaningful.

Unit Improvements. Even though residents generally anticipate a rent increase, they may protest it. Because of the potential for reaction, focus on lease renewal as the time to improve the unit. Upgrading is a sound business practice and can be an incentive for the resident to renew. Upgrades can include items such as new appliances or painting a few rooms. In fact, improvements might actually be necessary to keep the unit competitive in the market if the resident does not renew the lease. The following lists three main benefits to improving a unit as part of a lease renewal:

1. **Good resident relations.** Even if the improvement is not necessary for the resident to commit to a new lease, the extension of goodwill strengthens the relationship with a good resident. If the improvement alone wins the renewal, it is most likely a cost-effective means of keeping the unit leased. The cost is usually equivalent to or less than one month's rent. If the improvement averts a rent loss because of temporary vacancy, it also averts the expense of advertising and marketing. Always remember that residents are customers—they are more likely to stay if they have a good relationship with the staff.

2. **Increased property value.** A comprehensive program of individual unit improvements increases the value of the property as a whole, which may lead to higher income both in the short term and in the long term. The investment may increase the resale value of the property by much more than the actual cost of the improvements. In the short-term, this can help to save on turnover expense and vacancy loss as well.

3. **Tax benefits.** Apartment upgrades can be tax deductible in one of two ways. An improvement that will increase the value of the property and will endure for more than one year may be depreciable over several years. On the other hand, the cost of repairs done to preserve the integrity of the property may be deductible as an operating expense for the year in which it is paid.

COMMON INTEREST REALTY ASSOCIATIONS

Properties in which individuals own dwellings, along with a shared interest in so-called common areas, are called *common interest realty associations* (*CIRAs*). Examples are condominiums, cooperatives, and planned unit developments (PUDs). Managing CIRAs is different from managing residential rentals because of the ownership structures involved.

Managing Condominiums

A *condominium* is a multiple-unit residence in which the units are individually owned. The word "condominium" literally means "joint dominion," where the domains (homes) are arranged together in a single property. An individual who owns a unit in a condominium development actually owns the space bounded by the floor, walls, and ceiling of a particular unit (or townhouse) but does not own the land that it sits on.

Managing condominium associations can be a difficult venture for newer real estate managers who are not accustomed to managing associations. Since the owners of each unit have a stake in the decisions made about the property through the Board of Directors, the real estate manager will commonly become the go-to person for any conflicts, essentially becoming a quasi mediator between the two groups.

Common Area. The rest of the property—hallways, lobbies, grounds, and any other part of the property not individually owned—is referred to as the *common area.* Individual owners technically own a percentage of the common area, and this percentage is usually based on the square footage of their living areas compared to all of the living area in the building. It may also be based on the desirability of the individual unit; irrespective of square footage, some units will have higher values because of various amenities and, therefore, represent a greater percentage of the entire property value. However, common area ownership is *undivided,* so no owner can claim a particular section of common area as their own.

Condominium Association. State law requires that condominium unit owners form a not-for-profit corporation comprised of all the individual owners, the *condominium* or *homeowners' association,* which discusses and acts on common concerns of the property. All owners are association members with a board of directors elected from among the membership. Among the board of directors, the association members elect individuals to serve as officers. A large association may have a president, vice president, secretary, and treasurer, while a smaller association may combine responsibilities. The remaining board members, who are not officers, are at-large members. The condominium board is responsible for managing the property and normally hires or contracts professional management.

Ownership of a condominium does not mean that the owner must live in the unit. An owner may move out but not want to sell the unit. As an investment, the owner may lease the unit to someone else whose rent payments ensure that the mortgage and monthly assessments will be covered. In fact, some people invest in condominium units solely to lease them to others. Since renters have no vested interest in the condominium, they cannot participate in the association, so having a large proportion of a condominium's units occupied by renters can pose problems. The renters of these condominium units might feel they have no voice in how the property is managed or maintained and, therefore, may be reluctant to come forward when there are issues that could affect other renters or homeowners. In addition, lenders might be more reluctant to finance a condominium purchase if more than a certain percentage of the units are not owner occupied, which is an issue that should be addressed by the condominium association.

Governing Documents. In addition to hiring and communicating with real estate managers, the condominium association upholds and fulfills the tenets of the *governing documents,* which usually include the following items:

- **Declaration.** Commits the land to condominium use, provides for the association's creation, defines the method to determine each owner's share of expenses, and outlines the relationship between the individual owners and the association. The declaration is effectively the constitution of the association.
- **Bylaws.** Provide specific procedures for handling routine matters, whereas the declaration establishes the broad administrative framework for the association. The bylaws detail procedures for the following items:
  - Accounting
  - Maintenance of common areas and individual units where the unit owner is responsible for repair and maintenance within their unit
  - Election of officers and their duties
  - Votes by the association members
  - Collection of assessments
  - Other administrative business
- **Unit deed.** The document that legally transfers to the purchaser the title of a condominium unit and its undivided portion of the common areas.

Two other documents relate to the establishment and operation of a condominium: (1) the *articles of incorporation,* which state that the condominium association is a corporation under the laws of the state and (2) the *house rules and regulations*, which are the guidelines for day-to-day behavior on the premises and for settling disputes that may arise. Although many rules are common among condominium properties, each association is likely to establish their own unique rules that might cover anything from pets to noise to parking.

Assessments. The bylaws or a separate document usually specify the percentage of the property owned by each unit owner by taking into account the amount of living area—and possibly the desirability—of each unit. These percentages are the multipliers used to calculate the monthly *assessment* paid by each owner, which is used to pay the operating expenses for the whole property—common-area services, maintenance, and management.[5]

The regular assessment collections must also factor in the *reserve funds*, which can be used to pay for anticipated and unanticipated capital expenditures. If a capital expenditure is required and reserve funds are not sufficient to pay it, or if the association chooses not to deplete reserves to pay the expense, a *special assessment* will be necessary to defray the cost.[6]

Timeshares. The *timeshare* is a specialized form of condominium found mostly in resort areas. As the name implies, the owner has the right to occupy the unit for a specific period of time. There are several ways to set up a timeshare condominium. In order for the owner to have an actual share of property and its accompanying tax advantages, they might cooperatively own a percentage of a condominium unit. In other words, a person who owns one month's possession of one unit every year may own 30/365 of a unit. On that basis, a 100-unit building could have 1,200 or more owners.

Fractional Ownership. Similar to the idea of timeshares, *fractional ownership*—sometimes called private residence clubs—divides a property into more affordable segments for individuals and also matches an individual's ownership time to their actual usage time. Unlike timeshares, fractional ownership often allows a longer time on the property and a greater chance of property appreciation, while offering the same rights as any other real estate purchase. Although the cost of a fractional property is quite a bit higher than that of a typical timeshare, it is still less expensive than whole ownership of a luxury home in the same location.

---

5. For example, if the board determines that operating expenses for the whole property are $6,000 a month and the bylaws state that the owner of unit 6B owns five percent of the property, the owner of 6B will pay the association at least $300 every month.

6. For example, if the property needs a new roof and $30,000 of that cost will not be paid from the reserves, the owner of unit 6B (who owns five percent of the property) will be required to pay a special assessment of $1,500.

Managing Cooperatives

Cooperative ownership differs from condominium ownership in that the *cooperative* incorporates itself to purchase or build a multiple-unit dwelling and issues shares in the corporation to represent the proportion of ownership of the entire property. A single mortgage covers the entire cooperative property, and shareholders receive a *proprietary lease* that entitles them to occupy one unit. This traditional ownership structure is common, and unit owners can pledge their shares in the cooperative corporation as collateral for a loan. The proprietary lease is assigned to the lender—the transaction is recorded in the land records—and the lender obtains a *recognition agreement* from the cooperative corporation. Under the agreement, if the borrower or unit owner defaults on their obligation to the cooperative corporation, the corporation will give the lender an opportunity to cure the default before the cooperative forecloses on the unit.

Managing a cooperative differs from managing a condominium in several ways. Residents tend to be long-term, highly stable, and consistent. Decisions for the cooperative are made by a board, which is comprised of shareholders in the corporation. However, cooperative boards can be more active than condominium boards, and they sometimes enforce greater restrictions on the property. The board must interview and approve new residents. It may have the right to approve or deny improvements to units. The board may stipulate that all sales of shares must be on an all-cash basis, and it might state that only shareholders can reside in units, that is, they cannot be bought as investments and leased to others.

Planned Unit Developments

The residential *planned unit development* (*PUD*) combines the concept of the conventional neighborhood subdivision with characteristics similar to condominium ownership. Most residents purchase their dwelling, the property, and an undivided share of the common area—roads, parks, and recreational amenities— within the PUD. The residents pay a monthly assessment to maintain the common areas. The assessment may also pay for lawn care, snow removal, and other services for individual units.

A developer normally designs a PUD as a single entity before ground is broken, much as the plans of a building are completely drawn prior to construction. Unlike a single building, however, the PUD may be constructed in stages over several years. A character- istic of PUDs is that the developer pays as much attention to the location of open space as to the placement of buildings. Although open spaces are emphasized, land is used more intensively than in conventional subdivisions because townhouses and multiple-unit dwellings are more common than single-family homes. This con- centration of land use particularly benefits the following three groups:

1. **The developers.** The profit margin on land resale is higher, both because a PUD has more living units per acre and because careful planning of the development as a whole makes it aes- thetically attractive.
2. **The community.** More real estate taxes can be collected per acre.
3. **The residents.** Assessments for common area services are minimized because of the large number of residents per acre and because the intensive use of the land reduces the amount of common area to maintain.

A PUD is a departure from conventional residential zoning; there- fore, the term planned unit development also refers to a special zoning apparatus that permits the undertaking. Because it is a unique zoning form, public officials can be heavily involved in the site plan review and may play a key role in determining the nature and shape of the PUD.

In addition to dwelling types that may range from detached houses to rental apartments, a very large PUD may include retail and service facilities if such facilities are not immediately accessible from its location. In most cases, a homeowners' association comparable to that of a condominium governs the PUD. However, the developer may be more prominent in the homeowners' association of a PUD, especially if the property has rental units.

Since only property owners can be association members in PUDs that have both privately owned and rental residences, renters do not have a voice in the association. The collection of assessments for common area maintenance would be the major responsibility of the real estate manager. In fact, the association may rely on them to create the assessment structure, which might entail a variety of separate collections including standard assessments, special assessments, rental security deposits, and rents. Maintenance services provided may encompass landscaping as well as general upkeep and repair of apartments, building exteriors, roads, and amenities.

The Role of Real Estate Managers Working with CIRAs

While the homeowners' association governing a small number of units may manage the property on its own, larger properties require full-time supervision, which is usually why a real estate manager is hired—or retained as a consultant. Unlike rental property, condominiums and cooperatives have no effective gross income; PUDs may have some rental income as previously mentioned. Their monthly assessment collections are based on anticipated expenses, including management fees and funds for reserves. Because of this, compensation for management is usually a fixed monthly amount, which is prorated into the owners' monthly assessments. However, separate fees may be negotiated for specific additional services or for attending after-hours board meetings.

Owner Relations. Because each encounter between a staff member and a resident is an encounter with one of the property owners, all management employees must understand their relationship to the owners. Their efforts to extend goodwill should not compromise the agreement between management and the board of directors. Because the residents actually own the property, they may think the staff is at their service for any maintenance or repairs in their individual units. However, owner-residents usually have to pay separately for such services. Depending on the management agreement, the residents may have to call an independent service of their choosing or pay the association to have the work done by staff. To be fair to the other unit owners, the individual owner must reimburse the association for an employee's work on an individual unit. As a convenience, some properties can provide service in individual units at no extra charge to residents. However, the association members must agree that such a benefit is worth higher assessments for everyone.

Working with a Board of Directors. Each year, the association usually elects a board and new officers, or it may have an annual election with staggered multiple-year terms to ensure consistency of the board's decisions. The meetings are usually after-hours in one of the resident's units or in an office or common room on the premises. Because the board meeting is also a gathering of neighbors, the agenda may yield to tangential discussions. Sometimes complications can arise when disputes occur among the owners, board of directors, and real estate manager.

By virtue of living in the same building or property, the proximity of the board members encourages frequent meetings. Real estate managers are required to attend *some* meetings. However, the amount of time spent at these meetings can often be minimized if the management agreement includes an hourly fee for attending meetings.

While the board makes management decisions, the real estate manager might be the one who carries out those decisions, which sometimes requires mediating differences of opinion among the board members. Real estate managers are probably better qualified to decide which course of action to take. However, management decisions may provoke dissent because some board members might consider the manager's viewpoint biased. Because these differences of opinion can be extremely frustrating, it would be smart to have the board hold the president responsible for communicating with the real estate manager; that will help prevent conflicting demands and bombardment from several owners at once.

Maintenance. As owners of the property, the residents will be especially attentive to maintenance of the building and grounds. While a rental property must be sold as a whole, the units in a condominium (or PUD) or the shares of a cooperative may be bought and sold independently. Rental property can tolerate some deferred maintenance for a limited time without losing value. However, once the owner decides to sell a rental property, they must correct its deferred maintenance to assure the highest sale price possible. In contrast, any deferred maintenance of a resident-owned property, whether in a particular unit or in a common area, lowers the individual unit or share value. The real estate manager may occasionally have to remind the board or the president of that fact, especially when a repair is extremely costly. Because resident-owned properties are investments and resale potential is paramount to the resident-owners, it's important to be aware of a heightened demand for custodial maintenance. It is especially important to work diligently with the association to ensure that adequate funds for maintenance of the property are budgeted and sufficient funds are in reserve.

Fiscal Affairs. The assessments paid by unit owners are primarily to cover the operating costs of the property that they own in common—insurance and utilities. These costs must be kept under control to minimize the residents' individual assessments. However, assessments should not be so low that a provision for reserves is lacking. Low monthly assessments usually result in requirements for special assessments every time the property needs a major repair. If only one or even a few residents do not have the money available to pay a special assessment when it is levied, the necessary work may be jeopardized. For this reason alone, accruing an adequate reserve fund through the regular assessment is important.

Encourage the board to develop ample reserves since it's in the owners' best interests to preserve the value of the property as a whole and to enhance it. Prospective buyers recognize the value of a large reserve and will be more inclined to pay a higher price for a condominium or PUD unit or shares of a cooperative because of it.

As a rule, a homeowners' association can apply for tax-exempt status under the Internal Revenue Code in the following four situations:

1. A prescribed percentage of its gross income comes from unit owner assessments.
2. A prescribed percentage of its expenses are for managing, maintaining, and caring for common areas.
3. All of the units are used as residences.
4. No part of the net income benefits any individual member of the association.

Some sources of income, such as interest earned by reserve funds or fees received for special use of amenities are not exempt under any circumstances, especially since tax exemption protects the principal of the reserve fund. If the association does not have exempt status, the IRS could construe that the reserves collected as part of the assessment are the association's profit, and it could tax them accordingly. Periodically consult a tax specialist for updates on rules governing tax exemption of a homeowners' association. It is always good practice to keep up with changes in state laws regarding different types of common-interest realty associations.

OTHER RESIDENTIAL PROPERTIES

There are plentiful variations on traditional rental and ownership arrangements; they include single-family homes, manufactured housing (mobile home parks), military housing, and senior housing. Few real estate managers work exclusively with these types of properties, but they represent a large part of the housing market. In some localities, one of them could be the dominant type of housing.

Managing Single-Family Homes

A *single-family home* is defined as a house that has its own entry. Townhouses are also classified as single-family homes because, by definition, they share a common wall but have private entrances. A single-family home requires a smaller financial commitment than a multiple-unit dwelling—the percentage required as a down payment is often lower, and owners usually resell a house more quickly and easily than a larger property. Some first-time real estate investors start in this manner. Those who buy a house to live in when they retire and retain their original house as a source of rental income make up another group of investors. There is also a trend in the growth of vacation homes, which are rented out when the owners are at their primary residence. Because these investors may live far away from their rental properties, they often seek professional management services.

Since houses used as rental units are rarely next door to each other, they can generally be more time-consuming to manage. If an owner demands a level of maintenance that exceeds what can be required of the resident, the general upkeep of the premises can be as time-consuming as it is for a larger property. Marketing and leasing require more time because of the amount of travel to the individual units. In all likelihood, each rental house in a management company's portfolio will be individually owned, and reporting to numerous owners is required—many of whom do not live nearby.

In essence, real estate managers can end up doing the same, if not more, work for single-family home management as for a 12-unit property. Despite these seeming disadvantages, some real estate managers have marketed their skills exclusively to the single-family home rental market with great success. In fact, a house usually commands more rent than an equivalent-sized apartment due to the value placed on greater privacy, more accessible parking, and a private yard. Another benefit is that some owners allow residents to take care of the lawn and other yard work, further reducing extra maintenance tasks from the real estate manager's end.

Managing Manufactured Housing Communities

Manufactured housing is usually built at a factory and, depending on its width, is transported to the installation site in halves or as a whole. At the site, final assembly and connection of the home to gas, electrical, water, and sewer facilities takes place. In most cases, zoning laws prohibit manufactured housing in neighborhoods of conventionally built houses. For the most part, manufactured housing is found in areas zoned for *mobile home parks.* Residents of these communities generally own their homes, but they rarely own the land. They pay an access charge for the utility connections and maintenance of community roads and amenities. However, residents are responsible for maintaining their homes and private yards, and the utility company bills utilities directly to residents of the manufactured housing community. At other times, the community may serve as a distributor and bill residents for the utilities they use.

A manufactured housing "condominium," which is popular in resort areas, is an arrangement in which the owner purchases the lot in addition to the manufactured housing unit and pays an assessment for community services and amenities. The form of management for a manufactured housing community depends on what is managed. Community owners may contract with real estate managers to lease lots, collect rents, manage park staff, and supervise the placement of homes on lots in the park. The real estate manager might be responsible for maintaining a clubhouse or other recreational facilities, supervising an activities director, or overseeing any other special services the community offers.

MAINTENANCE ISSUES FOR RESIDENTIAL PROPERTIES

Maintenance for residential properties is usually more intensive compared to other property types because of the amount of wear and tear of having residents 24/7. Once maintenance is required, the resident must be informed prior to staff entering the premises—failure to inform before entry is interpreted as trespassing in a court of law. Certain local or state ordinances require that a written notice be given a certain number of hours before entering a unit. Entry without advance notice is *only* permissible in case of emergency or a malfunction that threatens the property or general safety. In these specific cases, some jurisdictions require that a note be left in the premises indicating that the property was entered and the purpose (the emergency).

Unit Preparation

After a resident moves out and before another moves in, management has an opportunity to do extensive maintenance and repairs in a vacant apartment—sometimes specifically for marketing purposes. To minimize vacancy periods and maximize rental income, all units must be attractive and all components must be operational. Even though a vacancy that lasts a month or more reduces income, it can provide significant time to paint and repair the unit. New residents should walk into a unit that is in superior condition, not only for their satisfaction as a customer, but also to avert future service calls.

If the time and resources are available, the staff should inspect a vacant apartment as often as possible, perhaps even as much as every day, depending on circumstances. In relation to weather, inspect for frozen pipes after a snowstorm or water leakage after a rainstorm. Periodically inspect for signs of a break-in or vandalism, depending on the location. As the staff inspects and repairs vacant apartments, a unit make-ready report (Exhibit 11.4) is a useful guide to help verify which units are ready to be shown or to be inhabited by a new resident. During the move-in and at the move-out of a unit, accompany the resident for inspection. In doing so, a combination move-in/move-out inspection form will most likely be used since it has spaces for signatures for both the manager and resident. This form documents the unit condition and its acceptance by the resident at move-in, and it helps minimize disputes regarding condition at move-out—if the real estate manager needs to retain part or all of the security deposit to cover the cost of repairs.

EXHIBIT 11.4
Residential Unit Make-Ready Report

Property _____ Date _____

Unit _____

Date vacated _____ Date to be occupied (if known) _____

Initial inspection by _____ Date _____

Checklist Before Move-In	Special Instructions
Check that all plumbing in unit (toilets, faucets, etc.) works properly. Make sure no leaks or drainage problems are present.	
Check all appliances (run dishwasher once on each cycle; check for proper operation of refrigerator, disposal, range). Make sure all appliances and kitchen cabinets are clean.	
Inspect all windows and screens (no breaks in either). Verify that all sliding components work correctly and easily. Clean out tracks of all windows and sliding glass doors. Clean inside of all windowpanes.	
Check painted surfaces for chipping, peeling, discoloration, and stains. Determine whether repainting is necessary.	
Check all walls for holes, seams, cuts, cracks, and nail pops.	
Check Venetian blinds for proper operation and clean them.	
Check flooring (all floors cleaned and waxed, parquet block floors or wood strip and asphalt tile included; vacuum carpet).	
Clean bathroom(s) (tub, toilet, basins, vanities, mirrors, medicine cabinets, wall and floor tile).	
Verify that all towel bars, toilet paper holders, and soap dishes are secure and clean. Check tile in bathroom(s) for cracks or other flaws.	
Make sure that all baseboards, cabinets, shelves, electrical outlet plates, and smoke detectors are properly installed and secure.	
Verify that thresholds and metal strips are installed properly where needed.	
Check that all doors close properly and that there is no rubbing or warping. Check that all locks and keys work properly.	
Check that all vents and registers are properly installed.	
Check heating and air-conditioning units to verify that they are working properly. Clean or replace air-conditioning filter.	
Make sure all lighting fixtures work properly and have new bulbs.	

Final inspection by _____ Date _____

Approved by _____ Date _____

Maintenance for Common Area Amenities

Common area amenities are unique to each residential property and require special care and attention. While the foregoing maintenance considerations are specific to rental properties, condominiums or cooperatives—especially older properties converted from rental use—may have similar facilities and similar requirements for maintenance. For instance, manufactured housing communities and PUDs have road repairs in addition to maintenance of amenities, and all properties that provide parking must maintain the parking lots or garages.

Laundry Rooms. The laundry room is a perfect example of an amenity that should be as clean and inviting as the rest of the property. Maintenance of the room itself is a management responsibility, which is why it should be regularly inspected for wet or soapy floors that can cause a fall, air ducts and drains that might clog with lint, and trash that can accumulate in the area. The regular maintenance of the washers and dryers is often contracted to a company that specializes in this service, and the cost is paid out of the revenues from the machines.

Storage Areas. Storage spaces not attached to the units are usually located in a common area, often in the basement. Typical storage spaces are enclosed by wooden or wire floor-to-ceiling partitions that the resident can secure with a padlock. Storage spaces should be protected from seepage, flooding, mildew, and vermin.

Swimming Pools. Many larger developments offer indoor or outdoor swimming pools for residents and visitors. Although these can be a great attraction, pools also pose a serious danger. To minimize the risk, post and enforce rules for pool use that include hours of access. The maintenance staff must monitor the chlorination (or other chemical treatment) level and regularly vacuum the pool. For reasons of safety and security, staff must periodically check fixtures such as fences, gates, and ladders.[7]

---

7. There are a number of laws regarding the proper type of covers on drains and other requirements, such as showing water depth with clearly marked depths affixed to the pool walls.

INSURANCE ISSUES

To avoid a financial loss from damage to the property, the best choice is to consult a capable and knowledgeable insurance expert. Unique aspects of a property require inclusion of certain provisions in its insurance coverage. For example, a residential property in an area not prone to earthquakes will most likely not require earthquake insurance; however, insurance for property along the California coast must include this type of coverage. Likewise, a condominium association would not require insurance to protect against the loss of rent in the event of damage to its building, but the insurance of a rental property should include rent loss coverage. In fact, the mortgage holder may require such protection. If the building sustains a physical loss, insurance covering the building will pay to restore the premises. During restoration, however, the property may be partially or completely uninhabitable, resulting in little or no income. Rent loss coverage provides some income to the owner during restoration and thereby reduces the prospect of foreclosure.

Types of Insurance

Two main types of insurance are common for residential properties:

1. **Actual cash value (ACV).** The least expensive leaves the owner the most vulnerable since it pays a claim based on depreciation (from use) of the original value of the item. The amount may be substantially below the cost of replacement—for example, a desk listed for $1,000 might be valued at only $700 under ACV coverage.

2. **Replacement cost coverage.** Pays the cost of the new or equivalent replacement item. For example, the desk listed at $1,000 when purchased three years ago and is priced at $1,700 today would be reimbursed at the current cost. Naturally, the premium for this type of coverage is higher.

An option for lowering the premium cost is to carry a *deductible,* which is a certain amount the owner agrees to pay before insurance pays for any of the claim. This practice benefits both the insurance company and the property owner. The owner pays a lower premium, and the insurer does not have to investigate or pay small claims. A deductible may be $500, $5,000, or $5 million—depending on the circumstances, policy, and negotiated terms. The deductible may apply per occurrence, per building, or per year.

Most insurance policies for damage to a property have *fire insurance* as their basis. That is especially important for residential properties because of the unpredictability of a fire starting in a private residence. There are often careless causes, such as cigarettes left smoking, stoves that were never turned off, and outdoor grills or candles that were not carefully put out. Fire protection itself is not enough, nor will fire insurance necessarily pay for fire damage under every circumstance. It might pay for direct loss but not for related smoke and water damage. Greater protection is provided by adding *extended coverage* insurance, which usually encompasses damage from specific perils. Coverage is still limited, however, and broader coverage may be desirable.

A *special form policy* is more comprehensive because it includes most of the coverages commonly obtained as separate policies, and pays for anything that is *not* named as an exclusion—anything can be excluded. Special needs can be accommodated by paying additional premiums for specific add-ons, such as boiler coverage or water damage.

Insurance for acts of terrorism may be included in a policy or offered as an endorsement for an additional premium. For most residential properties, with the exception of those in potentially vulnerable locations—urban centers or near military installations—insuring against acts of terrorism may be a questionable expenditure. Advice of the owner's insurance agent can be helpful in this regard.

In certain cases, real estate managers may need to do some research to find out about the land or area to obtain the proper coverage. For instance, some real estate managers have worked on properties that were located in a flood zone and did not have the proper coverage when it was needed. However, most management agreements state that it's the owner's responsibility, rather than the real estate manager's, to obtain insurance.

Choice of Insurance Packages

Each residential property usually requires a unique insurance plan to maximize coverage, especially since the level of coverage and type of policy vary with the insurance carrier. Insurance for one property may come from several different insurance companies, and numerous *endorsements* or *riders* may ensure protection against particular circumstances that the basic policy does not cover.

Possibilities for endorsements are unlimited. If the property has a rare sculpture on its grounds, an endorsement may be added to the basic policy to insure against theft of or damage to that particular piece of art. To obtain the best possible coverage for the lowest premium, carefully calculate the costs and benefits of each type of additional coverage (endorsement). An owner of several properties may be able to group them together under a single *blanket policy* at a reduced overall premium. In this way, one or two higher-risk properties might be included in the package at a lower rate than they might otherwise receive, which is especially critical for properties that run close to break even, helping reduce the overall expense ratio of the property.

Administration of such complex insurance coverage is also complicated. Real estate managers usually have the responsibility of filing claims and ensuring that premiums have been paid—although some owners elect to do this work since they are named as the primary insured party. However, as the owner's agent, the real estate manager will act in the owner's place with regard to the property. For this reason, the owner should agree to list the real estate manager as an additional named insured party on all policies; that will protect the manager and expedite the handling of claims when contacting the insurance company.

Physical damage to the structure is only one type of risk that owners and real estate managers must guard against—*liability* is another. In particular, if an individual is injured or dies on the premises, the real estate manager or the owner may be deemed liable, which is determined in a court of law, usually in response to a lawsuit. The expense of court time and the prospect of a judge or jury awarding damages to a plaintiff make liability insurance essential.

Liability insurance protects the owner from financial ruin. It pays the expense of defense against the claim and, if the owner is ruled liable, it pays the settlement. The premium for liability coverage is usually a flat rate per $100,000 of coverage. Additional coverage may be obtained by carrying *umbrella liability insurance,* which is a separate policy that will pay claims that exceed the basic liability coverage. Because the owner is not the only possible defendant in a liability suit, the real estate manager should be identified as an additional named insured party in the owner's liability insurance.

Regardless of the amount of insurance or the types of coverage a property owner carries, the owner's insurance only protects the property, the owner, and the real estate manager. The residents' personal possessions are not covered. For this reason, the real estate manager should encourage all residents to carry renter's or homeowner's insurance—depending on the nature of their residency.

SUMMARY

Managing residential property is particularly challenging but can also be rewarding. Each property has the potential to create unique situations that require specialized management skills. For instance, government-assisted properties require additional administrative paperwork and compliance with legalities with a heightened awareness of laws. In all rental properties, real estate managers will always work with an owner, but this basic concept becomes more complex when dealing with CIRAs and homeowners' associations since the residents *are* the owners.

Whether working with a conventional or government-assisted property, face-to-face contact with staff and residents are important factors in retaining them. Staying up-to-date with local and state laws as well as national news is essential in maintaining a strong awareness of the property, location, and any outside factors that could affect the residents and staff. Developing the ability to recognize trends in the changing world of residential properties is one of the best ways to become a successful real estate manager.

CHAPTER 12 | Office Buildings

Commercial real estate consists of all nonresidential property types, including: office buildings, shopping centers, research and development parks, warehouses, and buildings designed for medical and other professional services. These are the types of commercial properties professional real estate managers most often manage. Two of the most striking distinctions between managing commercial and residential buildings are (1) the length of the initial lease term and (2) the complexity of rent payments. While it's true that residents can remain in one apartment for many years, the tenant's initial commitment is usually one to two years.

This chapter specifically focuses on the realm of office buildings, which is a unique type of commercial property that has special management requirements. Office tenants can expand their leased premises, relocate to a more favorable location within the building, or downsize—which usually doesn't occur at a residential site unless the number of occupants changes.

Even the property analysis for office buildings is completed according to class of structure. Tenant selection, rent determination, and lease negotiations also require special consideration. Due to their differences from other commercial property, this chapter details the unique management requirements of office buildings.

PROPERTY ANALYSIS

The concentration of high-rise buildings within a community has come to be known as the *central business district* (CBD). Some of the largest cities have seen the development of multiple business districts both within the cities and in their surrounding suburbs. The high price of land and increasing congestion of the CBD fueled that development, along with the availability of business services that are concentrated in CBDs.

While skyscrapers may dominate a city's skyline, numerous smaller buildings also require full-time management. High-rise buildings represent only a fraction of the office buildings that require and deserve professional management.

When a building owner and real estate manager or management firm sign a management agreement, they must examine the property objectively to discern its marketable qualities. The manager must learn how the tenants, prospects, and others in the market perceive the property in terms of desirability. It's important to be very realistic about the property's place in the market. For this reason, the integrity of the property should be studied, and the first procedure in this assessment is to examine the building for the purpose of classifying it.

Class of Structure

Although no definitive standard defines what constitutes a specific class of office building, many publications and industry experts commonly refer to three classes of office buildings: Class A, Class B, and Class C. Age and obsolescence are the two prevailing issues in building classification. An older building has the potential to be notable and appealing, but only if it can accommodate current business needs. If a building cannot be retrofitted for advanced office systems (e.g., wireless technology) or if the space cannot be configured for efficient use by current standards, the class—and therefore the economic potential—of the building is likely to decline.

Class A. These buildings attract the most prestigious tenants and command the highest rents in their areas. They have outstanding locations and accessibility. They are usually newer structures with the latest high-quality amenities such as conference rooms, concierge services, and fitness centers with state-of-the-art systems.

Exceptionally well-renovated older buildings in the best locations are often categorized as Class A as well. A complete-service staff—including full-time maintenance and security personnel—is generally available in Class A buildings.

Class B. These buildings attract the widest variety of tenants because the rents are average for the area. The amenities and finishes are fair to good and the systems are adequate. The rents may be lower for many reasons such as the building being older, the location being less desirable, and the building offering fewer amenities.

Class C. These buildings attract tenants who need functional space, and rents are usually below average for the area. These buildings are older and reasonably well maintained, and they could possibly have been Class A or Class B at one point in time. Their amenities,

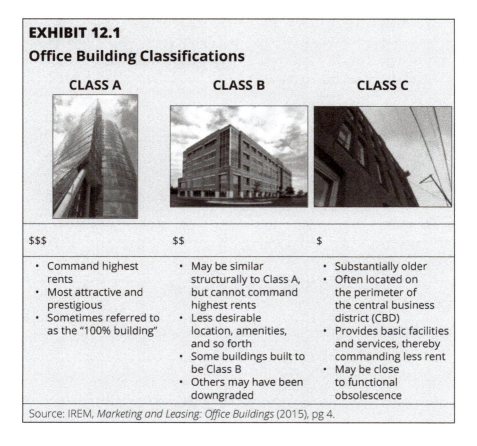

EXHIBIT 12.1

Office Building Classifications

CLASS A	CLASS B	CLASS C
$$$	$$	$
• Command highest rents • Most attractive and prestigious • Sometimes referred to as the "100% building"	• May be similar structurally to Class A, but cannot command highest rents • Less desirable location, amenities, and so forth • Some buildings built to be Class B • Others may have been downgraded	• Substantially older • Often located on the perimeter of the central business district (CBD) • Provides basic facilities and services, thereby commanding less rent • May be close to functional obsolescence

Source: IREM, *Marketing and Leasing: Office Buildings* (2015), pg 4.

finishes, and systems may be below current standards and may exhibit some degree of functional obsolescence or deferred maintenance. They may be located on the perimeter of the CBD, and their rents may appeal to those tenants who are most sensitive to price.

The classification of a building is an estimate at best. Visualizing the differences between Class A and Class C buildings is easy, but the distinctions between Class A and Class B buildings can be subtle. Regardless, the building classification can be useful to convey the desirability of the building in general terms.

Criteria for Classification

Not surprisingly, the criteria that influence building classification are those evaluated by prospective tenants as they select office space to lease—current tenants also review these criteria when they consider renewing their leases. Thirteen factors are involved in classifying the types of office buildings; most of the factors are interdependent, but examining them separately illustrates their relationship and importance:

1. Location, location, location
2. Accessibility and parking
3. Management
4. Prestige and amenities
5. Appearance
6. Lobby
7. Elevators
8. Corridors
9. Office interiors/efficiency of usable space
10. Building services
11. Mechanical systems/communications technology
12. Tenant mix
13. Sustainability

Location. The desirability of an office building is largely measured by its proximity to other business facilities, but it can change over time as one section of a city becomes more popular than other sections. Evidence of this is recorded in the history of most large cities. As the CBD develops, most of the buildings on the two main streets are Class A. With each block that is farther away from the main intersection, the property values and prestige decrease— even though the buildings may still be Class B. Some locations on the perimeter of the CBD may become less desirable because the expansion is in the opposite direction, which is an example of *economic obsolescence*. What was once a Class B building may now be Class C solely based on the location.

The effects can reverse as well. As growth of the CBD continues, the surrounding areas might become popular because they offer relatively inexpensive land and opportunity for expansion. If so, occupancy rates will increase once the buildings in the area have been rehabilitated or the land has been redeveloped. This will lead to an increase in income and an improved property classification.

Buildings developed outside the CBD can also be Class A. Companies often leave the city because land prices, business taxes, and rents are lower in the suburbs, which generates demand for offices in the outlying regions, resulting in the development of *office parks*, or business centers, near airports, major highways, malls, and other suburban attractions. Population growth in the outlying suburbs also provides a large pool of workers and customers from the local area. Another factor that influences the desirability of a location is the attractiveness and cleanliness of neighboring sites. If an office building is well constructed and maintained, it could be considered a Class A—especially if its surroundings are attractive and clean.

Besides the attraction of the CBD or a similar suburban location, the presence of a major corporation can influence suppliers and other associated businesses to locate nearby or in the same building. A major bank may attract investment counselors, brokers, and accounting firms to the site. Likewise, a bank that works closely with large businesses may consider proximity to its major customers when choosing a site.

The desirability of a location because of prestige or convenient access can overshadow most other factors. A strategic location near transportation, within walking distance of major business and financial centers, or adjacent to government services can make a 100-year-old building in sound condition as desirable to a prospective office tenant as the newest construction.

Accessibility and Parking. The ease of accessibility to transportation strongly affects building classification because workers must have an efficient and quick way to reach the office. Office buildings served by several transportation alternatives (buses, commuter trains, elevated and subway rapid transit lines, and highways) generally have greater value because employers benefit from the availability of a larger labor pool.

The availability of parking is also a consideration of accessibility. In general, buildings in CBDs cannot offer as many parking options as those in outlying regions; however, buildings centrally located in large cities usually do not require as much parking as those in suburban locations because of the availability of public transportation. If land in CBDs is available, parking areas are generally located underground or even above the office building itself since land is at a premium. More and more employers are offering incentives for employees to use public transportation or other eco-friendly alternatives to single occupancy vehicles.

Management. The quality of a building's management is invaluable. Business people are aware of the influence management has on the appeal of a property and the efficiency of its services. Most office buildings have on-site management personnel, while smaller properties may have management based at another location.

The level of maintenance is a direct indicator of the professional dedication to the property. A well-maintained building with quality wood, polished floors, clean washrooms, dust-free cornices, and general tidiness is more attractive to current and prospective tenants. A prospect that discovers anything less will select a property that is better maintained. Upkeep of mechanical systems and the extent of building security are also indicators of management quality. The overall effectiveness of management influences demand for space in the building and contributes to the reputations of the firms whose offices are located there.

Prestige and Amenities. Image and reputation are important factors in business, and location can enhance prestige. For instance, an ambitious lawyer may want an office in the same building as the city's leading law firms or at least in the same area. The directors of a financial institution will want it to be in the most desirable building in the financial district or as close as possible to such a center. Therefore, the building with a prestigious address and reputation ranks high on the scale of desirability.

Although much of the prestige may stem from location alone, the building's ownership, reputation, management standards, and customer service can enhance its status. Building size contributes significantly to prestige. A building that is prominent in the city's skyline may command higher rent because it offers the most prestigious views of the city. A large building can also include extensive and state-of-the art amenities that further enhance the site's prestige.

Appearance. Two main physical attributes affect an office building's desirability: (1) architectural design and (2) exterior appeal. Multistoried office buildings are often uniformly cubical or rectangular masses of glass, steel, and stone that lack distinguishing external features, but architectural creativity can give newer buildings distinctive visual appeal. Attractive older buildings may be retrofitted so they can support today's high-technology uses. Buildings designed by famous architects like Frank Lloyd Wright or Frank Gehry most definitely add to the prestige and overall appearance of the structure.

Exterior maintenance contributes to the building's overall impression and attraction. Fresh exterior flower displays, polished entrance doors and signage, and sparkling windows add visual appeal and welcome tenants, prospective tenants, and other visitors. The general curb appeal contributes greatly to property class. But class does not apply only to the physical appearance, it also includes the overall cleanliness.

Lobby. The appearance, floor plan, lighting, pleasant smell, and overall mood of a building's lobby help establish the general character of the building. The entrance to any building is part of the setting in which each tenant's business is conducted. A lobby that appears outdated, worn, or neglected detracts from an otherwise attractive building. It's important to pay attention to the primary services that the tenants, employees, and visitors expect from a lobby as well. An updated, well-maintained building directory and unobstructed access to elevators or stairs are essential.

Elevators. In multistory office buildings, elevators are vital—each additional story increases the demand for efficient and rapid service. Several factors influence the perception of elevator quality—location is one of the most important. The desirability of space in the building will decrease if tenants, employees, and visitors have to walk a long distance from the main entrance to the elevators and then walk an equally long distance to their destinations after they arrive on the appropriate floor. Such inconvenience and perceived inefficient use of space create negative impressions of the building and its accessibility.

The appearance of elevator entrances and interiors can also affect the perception of the office building as a whole. Passengers expect adequate lighting, proper ventilation, understandable controls, and well-maintained floor coverings in an elevator. To create the illusion of a larger space, a mirror or other reflective surface on the back wall of the cab is sometimes helpful. Any lessening of aesthetic and maintenance standards in the elevator can raise doubts about the quality of the building's tenancy and may even provoke questions about safety in the minds of the elevator passengers.

The two most important standards of elevator service are (1) safety and (2) speed; however, for passengers, speed includes more than travel time in feet per minute. They judge the amount of time their elevator trip takes from the moment they press the call button to the moment they arrive at their destination. The time spent waiting for the elevator to arrive and the number of stops it makes en route usually influence the perception of quality more than the actual rate of movement. Sometimes, depending on the character of the building, background music can offer a pleasant mood, while other buildings showcase their modern status by installing voice indicators for floor stops.

Corridors. The general decoration and details throughout the corridors should fit the occupants of each particular floor, while also maintaining a subtle, pleasant, and clean appearance. It's important for certain floors and specific companies to have the freedom to express their company image and logo. For example, a design firm would most likely incorporate modern and updated colors in their corridors, while a law firm would display more neutral tones and subtle décor. Most important, staff must diligently maintain corridors in immaculate condition, and up-to-date signage should be clear, yet discrete and consistent in appearance throughout the building. Although allowing full-floor tenants to have some license in designing their elevator lobby area, it is important on multi-tenant floors to have a consistent look and quality from the ground floor lobby up through the upper-floor corridors.

Office Interiors. Office suites are usually configured initially or reconfigured later to accommodate new tenants' needs and aesthetic choices. Desirability depends less on existing interior design than on alternative floor plans and the efficiency of the usable space—discussed later in this chapter. Numerous factors can limit possibilities for changes.

The size and number of windows in a given space and their relative locations often determine the size of the offices. In newer buildings that have expansive windows, the spacing of the *mullions*—vertical bars that separate the panes of glass—usually determines the placement of the walls. Sometimes it's evident that interior walls are formed in line with the mullions and not directly in the middle of a pane of glass.

Other factors that can limit changes are the existing lighting, the depth of the space from the corridor to the outside wall, the width of the space between supporting columns, and even the view. Older buildings have more load-bearing columns that limit the efficiency of use and the flexibility of the space. Newer office buildings with sophisticated engineering usually have wider column spacing or even lack of visible supporting columns, which permits numerous alternative configurations and more efficient use of space.

In addition to layout, the perception of interior quality depends on decoration, wall finish, light fixtures, illumination, and ceiling height. Prospective tenants will judge all of these on their conformity or lack of conformity to the office interior that is available in the most prestigious building or space in the market. As with any other property, rental value of office space is ultimately based on what else is available in the market and what might better suit a tenant's needs. In fact, some offices may be leased as-is, which affects the price and desirability. In other offices, each new tenant has the option of overhauling the interior to their own specifications, and in that case, the condition of the suite may not have any effect on price desirability. On the other hand, needing to spend less money might influence the tenant's desire to lease the space.

Building Services. Prospective tenants judge an office building by the quality and variety of the available services included in the rent. Most important among these are custodial or janitorial services, security, prompt response to service requests by on-site maintenance personnel, after-hours access to the building, availability of after-hours HVAC, and HVAC maintenance.

Some office buildings provide special amenities for tenant use, such as conference rooms with extensive audiovisual equipment and exercise facilities. The presence in the building of retailers, such as stock brokerage firms, restaurants, banks, drugstores, and newsstands that serve the needs of employees, are also an asset. In some parts of the United States, office buildings may include a concierge or even daycare services, which could possibly be services provided by other building tenants. The selective tenant who is shopping for office space or simply considering a move takes note of these amenities and their direct or indirect costs, but for the most part, the availability of amenities frequently influences the prospect's decision.

Mechanical Systems. Advances in office technology have increased demands on electrical wiring and HVAC systems. The mechanical systems are often a crucial consideration in a prospective tenant's search for space to lease. Tenants increasingly request more power and bandwidth to support the growing use of video conferencing and other bandwidth-intensive applications. To keep pace with this demand, buildings continue to acquire smarter information systems that require more room for ducting and wiring. Newer buildings usually have state-of-the-art systems that can keep pace with user demands. They incorporate computer controls into the electrical and HVAC networks to monitor and regulate energy usage, and they include advanced wireless telecommunications systems.

Owners and managers may consider buildings that do not meet the infrastructure demands of new technology for retrofitting. However, many buildings—even relatively new ones—cannot easily be retrofitted to accommodate the many technological advances. In some cases, the costs of retrofitting may be prohibitive. In other circumstances, the design of the building may preclude an efficient or cost-effective retrofit. In fact, some buildings cannot be retrofitted at all. This functional obsolescence is one reason Class A buildings become Class B or Class C despite good locations and high management standards.

Tenant Mix. Image and reputation are crucial elements in business, and fellow tenants in an office building can enhance (or detract from) these qualities. For this reason, both the prospective tenant and the real estate manager of the property closely examine the *tenant mix* in an office building. A prospective tenant guards against other tenants who might not contribute positively to their reputation, or they avoid locations near direct competitors.

The principal tenant in the building usually governs the overall tenant mix. For example, if the major tenant is a bank, other financial enterprises—investment and mortgage bankers, brokerage firms, and accounting services—will seek space in the building because of that tenant's reputation in its industry. The name of a major tenant is often applied to the building, and that can further encourage a particular type of tenant to lease space or discourage a major competitor.

Tenant mix is more vital to retail properties, but it's important to be wary of prospects whose businesses may detract from the property's image and reputation. Such a tenant may have a negative effect on the businesses of other tenants, which can result in a decline in the property's reputation and income.

Sustainability. In today's age of efficiency, it's not just building owners and real estate managers who are focused on conservation. The *Better Buildings Initiative* was developed specifically for commercial properties because they use about 20 percent of the energy consumed in the United States. In this incentives-based program, national housing and real estate associations have supported the government's plan to provide more generous tax credits and more incentives for owners who undertake costly retrofits on existing properties. Many programs exist for improving the building's performance, but the two major organizations are (1) the U.S. Green Building Council (USGBC), which offers a LEED Certification, and (2) ENERGY STAR, which is a joint program of the U.S. Environmental Protection Agency (EPA) and the U.S. Dept of Energy (DOE).

Leadership in Energy and Environmental Design (LEED) Certification. The USGBC, a nonprofit organization, offers a _LEED certification_—an internationally recognized green building certification system. This certification provides building owners and real estate managers the understanding needed to implement practical, environmentally friendly building design, construction, operations, and maintenance solutions. It leads real estate managers and owners to examine their building lifecycle patterns and even to go beyond the building into the neighborhood and local communities. The LEED certification is a performance-based system—designed to be comprehensive in its scope and simple in its operation—that offers earnable credits. There are four rating levels, including: Certified, Silver, Gold, and Platinum. These levels indicate a varying level of utility resource efficiency, using less energy and water, but also resulting in reduced greenhouse gas emissions. Tenants often seek out LEED-rated buildings to satisfy customer or client demands, fulfill a corporate goal, or simply to be on the forefront of ecofriendly efforts. Gaining this certification involves an elaborate process, but its overall goal is to increase the importance of sustainable development and its practice nationwide.

ENERGY STAR. The ENERGY STAR program was created to help the public save money while protecting the environment through energy-efficient products and practices. In its early initiatives, ENERGY STAR focused on creating specific products (such as dishwashers, refrigerators, and washing machines) that reduced greenhouse gas emissions, but it then expanded to cover the development of commercial and industrial buildings. This program functions much like the LEED Certification, where a rating system is in place that scores the building's overall energy usage and performance. With the highest rating of 100, a building must score at least a 75 to be eligible to display the ENERGY STAR label. In earning and displaying the ENERGY STAR label, the real estate manager is highlighting the building's achievements to the public by showing current and prospective tenants that the building has met strict energy efficiency guidelines.

IREM Certified Sustainable Property (CSP). The IREM (CSP) certification is an attainable, affordable, and meaningful recognition program for all commercial properties. The certification gains recognition for properties not covered by the previously mentioned programs, while extending sustainability across the real estate manager's portfolio. This certification is a good way to start a sustainability initiative from scratch, if necessary. The following lists the prerequisites for office buildings:

- At least 25,000 sq. ft.
- At least 18 months since substantial completion or repositioning
- At least 75 percent occupied
- Smoke-free property
- In compliance with all environmental laws
- Commitment to respond to an annual IREM survey on sustainability

The CSP allows real estate managers to train their staff on sustainability and resource efficiency, while also marketing the property's sustainability success.

TENANT SELECTION AND CRITERIA

Just as an office tenant anticipates being in a building for several years, the real estate manager should seek tenants who can and will commit to a long-term relationship. The following lists four major criteria to consider for the prospect's type of business and company reputation:

1. Financial stability
2. Long-term profitability
3. Space requirements
4. Service requirements

The value of an office building is based partly on the business reputations of its tenants. The prospect's business should be compatible with the mix of tenants already in the building, and its reputation should enhance or at least reinforce the reputation of the building as a whole.

Financial Stability

Investigating the credit of prospective tenants is often easier compared to checking residential prospects because the basic information about the tenant's financial stability is usually public information. Ultimately, the property owner is responsible for reviewing and accepting or rejecting the financial condition of a tenant, but it's the real estate manager or leasing agent who gathers the information. A prospective tenant should complete an application that lists the following basic items:

- Type of business
- Length of time the tenant has been at its current address
- Previous address
- Principals of the business
- State in which the business is incorporated (if a corporation)
- Location of the home office (if a branch office)
- Type of space the business is seeking
- Names of its bankers
- Credit references (usually vendors)

Financial statements, such as the Dun & Bradstreet credit rating (a leading source for commercial credit rates), local chamber of commerce or business organization, and the prospect's bankers and suppliers are good sources of credit and financial information.

Long-Term Profitability

When determining the long-term profitability of the prospective tenant, it's important to gather information on the company's history. Consider the number of years in business, along with the company's financial success. Requesting a prospective tenant's business plan is not an odd request—especially if it's a relatively new business venture. In fact, large multinational firms can potentially face bankruptcy just as suddenly as smaller firms.

Regardless of the company's size or reputation, every potential tenant should be closely examined on a consistent basis. Investigate how the business is constituted as a legal entity by requesting articles of incorporation. In addition, confirm the authority of the person who will be executing the lease and that he or she is authorized to do so. When appropriate, seek legal advice for the necessary procedures for checking the *Specially Designated Nationals And Blocked Persons (SDN) List* as provided by the U.S. Department of Treasury.[1]

Space Requirements

One of the most complex issues of tenant selection is deciding whether the building has adequate space for a specific prospect. Efficient use of space is crucial, and some prospects may not qualify as tenants simply because the available space cannot be designed to comply with their requirements. The following three factors must be considered in determining whether the available space is suited to a particular prospect:

1. **Configuration of the available space.** No guarantee exists that a prospect currently occupying 10,000 sq. ft. of space can operate efficiently in the same amount of space in a different building. Exterior walls, window placement, columns, elevator shafts, and stairwells cannot be moved or altered to suit the requirements of individual tenants. Those structural elements usually determine the size and configuration of the building's floor plate (rentable floor size) and, thus, determine whether a specific space can be configured to meet a prospect's needs.

2. **The nature of the prospect's business.** Depending on the type of organization, it may require many executive offices, which are usually located along exterior walls of the building

---

1. The SDN is a list of individuals and companies owned or controlled by, or acting for or on behalf of, targeted countries. It also lists individuals, groups, and entities, such as terrorists and narcotics traffickers, designated under programs that are not country specific. The assets of these individuals are blocked and U.S. persons are prohibited from dealing with them.

because the lighting and view are signs of prestige. However, it's becoming increasingly popular to have an open-space concept for offices that are laid out for natural light to permeate the entire space, while the private offices are stationed in the interior of the space. Regardless, corner offices for senior executives or for conference rooms are still common. On the other hand, an organization that has a particularly large clerical staff usually has less demand for perimeter space, while companies that need video recording or sound studios may need space without windows and soundproofing.

3. **A prospect's plans for future expansion.** If a company expects to grow significantly, consider how the building can accommodate that growth, especially if the prospect will need adjacent space. An allowance of about 75 sq. ft. of floor space per worker will provide a large enough area to accommodate clerical staff, along with the necessary space for cabinets, required equipment that is not part of the employee's work area, and aisles between the desks. Individual workstations with movable partitions may enclose only 50 to 60 sq. ft. of floor area. However, if the design is to include a large number of private offices, consider square footage of individual offices along with separate allowances for conference rooms. Most companies will already know the specific square footages and required floor plans.

Space needs and office configurations change as technology fosters in-house teamwork. Some companies encourage employees to work at home, which often requires less overall work space. With fewer staff members working in the office, space can be allocated for shared use by workers who come in periodically—referred to as *hoteling*—or for groups to work together on projects. Those who work in the field or at home use temporary work spaces where they can plug into the network and use the phone and other office equipment. They may also use their inside time to attend meetings, give reports, or interact with other staff members, while other times they might telecommute. These and other technology-supported strategies have affected how much space is allocated for individual employees and work functions, which is sometimes less or sometimes more.

Service Requirements

Prospective tenants always need special services to be able to conduct their business, and those requirements should be thoroughly considered in the qualification process. The following provide situations that require extra research:

- A higher level of security than is currently provided
- An extraordinary need for electrical power or HVAC
- Business hours that differ radically from those currently established for the building
- Any other service that differs significantly from standard operations.

If such factors are not given proper consideration, the building may operate at a loss because of a particular prospect's tenancy. Before rejecting a prospect outright, analyze the actual costs and the cost-benefit ratio over the long term. Deciding who will pay for the proposed accommodation (tenant/capital improvements) is one of the lease terms to be negotiated. For example, a prospect may require extensive wireless access capabilities and may be seeking an office building that has a state-of-the-art wireless system. Meeting these requirements may necessitate a large investment, and retrofitting a building for wireless technology cannot always be done successfully. However, evaluation of an accommodation is warranted for the following reasons:

1. The first installation of this kind will make a future installation less difficult or perhaps unnecessary—it can also make securing tenants with similar needs easier.
2. The prospect will most likely understand the amount of work and the expense involved in installing the equipment, and is therefore more likely to seek a long-term lease at higher rents in order to avoid repetition of this investment.

OFFICE RENT

New office space is commonly leased as *shell space*—enclosed by outside walls and a roof, with a concrete slab floor and utilities in place. The plumbing and electrical installations are unfinished, and the space has no partitioning walls, ceiling tiles, wall coverings, or flooring. Office users generally have unique requirements for the space they lease, and it is easier to design and build out an unfinished space. Construction of tenant improvements may be done according to the incoming tenant's specifications. Even a previously rented space may be gutted and rebuilt for succeeding tenants. Similar to shell space, *vanilla shell space* refers to spaces that usually have an American Disabilities Act (ADA) compliant restroom, walls ready for paint, floor ready for floor coverings, and ceiling tiles and lighting in place.

Rent is usually charged on a per-square-foot basis. It may include repayment of some or all of the monies advanced to finance tenant improvements to the leased space. Some property operating expenses—real estate taxes, insurance, common area utilities, and maintenance—may be included in the rent or charged separately on a pro rata basis. Tenants' electricity or other utilities may be metered individually, and the utility company may bill the tenant directly. Submeters may also be installed on shared utilities that determine the exact usage for a particular tenant and billed accordingly.

Measuring Rentable and Usable Space

Accurate measurement of the space is crucial to maximize rental income and the market value of the property. Three concepts are central to the measurement of office space (Exhibit 12.2):

1. The *gross area* of a building is its entire floor area measured to the outside finished surface of its permanent walls.
2. The *rentable area* of a building is the entire interior floor area *less* vertical penetrations through the floor—air shafts, elevators, and stairways, etc.

3. The office *usable area* is the rentable area *less* certain common areas that all tenants share, such as the corridors, common areas, and restrooms. It's the actual office space occupied by the tenants.

EXHIBIT 12.2

Office Building Gross, Rentable, and Usable Areas

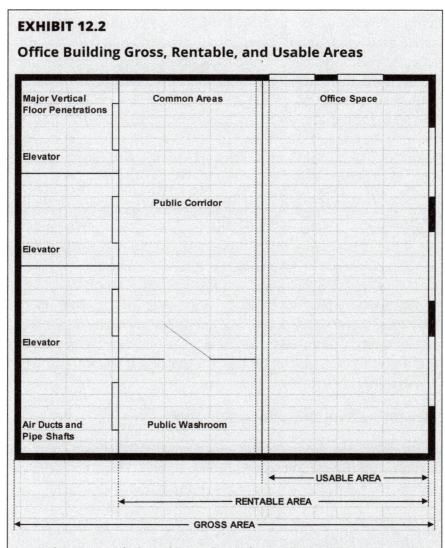

Vertical sections include each part of a window, wall, or external construction feature of an office building where the inside finished surface area varies from the inside finished surface area of the adjoining window, wall, or external construction feature, ignoring the existence of any columns.

In order to establish profitable rental rates, know how much space in the building generates revenue (rentable area) and how much of that space can actually be occupied (usable area). Accurate measurement of the rentable area is extremely important. In a building that has 100,000 sq. ft. of rentable area, a one percent error would amount to 1,000 sq. ft. If the average rent were $30 per sq. ft. per year, that one percent error would result in a loss of $30,000 in rental income each year. The resale value of the property would likewise be reduced; at a capitalization rate of 10 percent, the $30,000 shortfall would lower the property value by $300,000.

Usable Space. The *usable area* of a tenant's leased office space is the area bounded by its *demising walls*—the partitions that separate one tenant's space from another—the interior of the corridor wall, and the interior of the exterior wall. The usable area is available for the tenant's exclusive use. This area may occupy a portion of a floor, an entire floor, or a series of floors. Although the usable area is the amount of space in the tenant's sole possession, rent is usually quoted on the rentable area.

Rentable Space. The *rentable area* of a tenant's leased office space usually includes certain common areas in addition to its usable area. In a multistory office building, the tenants on each floor pay additional rent, or common area charges, for those spaces on the respective floors. Each tenant's *pro rata share* of the common area of the floor is the percentage represented by the ratio of the tenant's usable area to the usable area of the entire floor— the sum of all defined usable areas on that floor. In addition, all tenants in an office building pay rent for their proportionate share of *building common areas*—the ground-floor lobby and any other common areas, including conference rooms, mailrooms, building core, visitor or shared restrooms, and service areas that mutually benefit all tenants.

Standardized Measurement. To avoid discrepancies, the standardized method used by the *Building Owners and Managers*

Association (BOMA) International[2] is usually adopted. The *Office Building: Standard Methods of Measurement* (ANSI/BOMA Z65.1 2010), which can be obtained from BOMA, includes definitions, illustrations, and calculations. This standard, commonly referred to as *Method B,* discusses the *single load factor method,* which is an updated calculation applied to the occupant area of each floor to determine the rentable area and is the same for all floor levels of a building.

The *International Property Measurement Standards (IPMS)* is an international standard for measuring office space that is globally accepted in the industry.[3] The recommendation for all measurements are supported by CAD (computer-aided design) drawings or BIM (building information modeling) data. There are three basic area definitions used:

1. **IPMS 1**—Comprises the overall area of the building, comparable to the gross area under the BOMA standard
2. **IPMS 2**—Represents the area of the interior of the building, segregated into eight distinct components[4]
3. **IMPS 3**—Represents the area assigned for the exclusive use of an occupier

The standard method computes a tenant's rentable area by multiplying the tenant's usable area by an *R/U ratio,* which is the rentable area of a floor divided by the usable area of that same floor. A pro

---

2. BOMA is a trade association that serves the commercial real estate building industry.

3. The IPMS standard for office buildings does not replace existing methods of space measurement. Rather, it supplements and interprets them so that people are speaking the same language when sharing measurements—they are considered an overlay to local measurement standards

4. The eight components are as follows: (1) vertical penetrations (stairs, elevator shafts); (2) structural elements (walls, columns); (3) technical services (maintenance rooms, elevator motor rooms); (4) hygiene areas (toilet facilities, shower rooms); (5) circulation areas (horizontal circulation areas); (6) amenities (cafeterias, daycare facilities, fitness areas); (7) workspace (furniture, equipment for office purposes); (8) other areas (balconies, internal car parking, storage rooms). Source: *https://ipmsc.org/standards/office.*

rata share of the building's common areas is then added to the basic rentable area to arrive at the tenant's total rentable sq. ft. The larger the R/U ratio, the greater the rent paid for the common areas. Prospects are usually more inclined to choose rental space that has the lowest R/U ratio. Older buildings usually have high R/U ratios, which is another characteristic used to classify buildings— similar to classes A, B, and C that are previously described in this chapter.

In some markets, an *add-on factor* (or *load factor*) may be used to account for the proration of the common areas among individual tenants. This may or may not be equal to the ratio between the rentable and usable areas. Some markets may establish a standard or accepted add-on factor. In other words, the R/U ratios of buildings in the CBD may range from 10 to 13 percent, but a standard add-on of 11 or 12 percent might be applied to all usable area rents in the market. This can effectively eliminate one point of negotiation on a market-wide basis. (Exhibit 12.3 is an example of an add-on factor based on the R/U ratio.)

EXHIBIT 12.3

Use of an Add-On Factor

Rentable Area	18,760 sq. ft.
Common Area	2,010 sq. ft.
Usable Area (Total)	16,750 sq. ft.

$$\frac{\text{Rentable Area (18,760 sq. ft.)}}{\text{Usable Area (16,750 sq. ft.)}} = \text{R/U Ratio} = 1.12 \text{ (add-on factor)}$$

Usable Area		×	1.12	=	Rentable Area
Tenant A:	5,000	×	1.12	=	5,600 sq. ft.
Tenant B:	4,250	×	1.12	=	4,760 sq. ft.
Tenant C:	3,500	×	1.12	=	3,920 sq. ft.
Tenant D:	4,000	×	1.12	=	4,480 sq. ft.
Total:	16,750	×	1.12	=	18,760 sq. ft.

In this sample calculation, the add-on factor is the R/U ratio. In some markets, an add-on factor that is *not* equivalent to the R/U ratio may be used.

BUILDING STANDARDS

Developing the *building standard* for finish elements throughout the building is a task shared between the real estate manager and the property owner because it defines the quantity and quality of construction involved. Some of the finish elements may include materials for partition walls near corridors and regular interior walls, as well as some of the following components that must be considered in making decisions:

- Carpeting or hard-surface flooring
- Baseboards
- Draperies or window blinds
- Ceilings
- Light fixtures
- Paint or wall coverings
- Doors and door hardware
- Keying systems

The building standard should also address electrical wiring, switches, electrical and telephone outlets, and supply-and-return air vents for HVAC, while specifying compliance with applicable codes.

The dollar amount for the *tenant improvement (TI) allowance* is also discussed with the property owner when establishing these building standards. Since this allowance is a negotiable item, it can be based on the use of building standard materials—the tenant may be responsible for any cost overruns. If materials other than the building standard are used, the tenant will most likely be responsible for the difference in cost.

Since market quality standards evolve as new materials and new technology become available, the building standards should be periodically reviewed and updated. Building codes and other relevant regulations also change from time to time. All these factors can affect building standards. For instance, the accessibility requirements of the Americans with Disabilities Act (ADA) affect both building rehabilitation and new construction, and should be a consideration in planning TIs as well.

Establishing Rates

The rental rate for a building depends on local practice and market conditions. Rent for office space is commonly quoted per square foot, either per month or per year. To determine the rent, first establish the lowest acceptable dollar amount per square foot that will offset debt service, operating expenses, and vacancy loss—and yield the owner's desired return on the investment.

If the calculated rental rate is greater than the market will bear, the real estate manager will have to examine alternatives for reducing expenses in order to lower the rent to be competitive. Otherwise, the owner may have to accept a lower return on the investment. In ideal circumstances, market conditions will allow rents to be higher than the calculated rate. The marketplace will also dictate whether and which operating expenses the owner can include in the rent or charge directly to tenants on a pro rata basis.

As with any other property, the rent that an office building earns depends on its condition and location. In most markets, higher floors and better views command higher rental rates. In terms of height, both extremes of the building will need to examined. The anticipation of high income from upper floors must often be tempered with lower expectations for office space closer to the ground. Although a high-rise office building will most likely generate a considerable amount of income from its upper floors, that amount may not be sufficient to yield a high income for the building overall.

For example, a desired average rental rate of $30.00 per sq. ft. might be calculated per year for a 50-story, class A office building. A spectacular view in this structure creates high demand for space on the upper floors, most of which can easily be leased at rates between $40.00 and $45.00 per sq. ft. per year. However, the lower floors cannot expect to command such a high rent, so space might have to be leased on those floors for rates that are at or below $30.00 per sq. ft. per year. Ideally, the income the upper floors produce should offset the lower rates achieved from the lower floors.

In CBDs, leasing ground-floor space to retailers may be possible, and that can yield additional rent. Retailers may pay higher rates for the space. Sometimes the rents for ground-floor retail space are just as high as, or higher than, the rents for the top floors.

Space Planning

A business that is seeking office space will always be concerned about the comfort of their employees and the efficient use of the space they lease. During the *space planning* process, prospective tenants require the real estate manager's assistance when determining the optimum square footage they will need. If a tenant pays for unused space, they are essentially wasting money. On the other hand, crowding too many employees into an office can easily waste the same amount of money through inefficiency.

Space planning truly incorporates the prospect's square footage requirements, organizational structure, aesthetic preferences, equipment needs, and financial limitations into the design of a specific floor plan that indicates how office equipment, rooms, and hallways will be placed in the rental space to optimize work flow. In some cases, a space planner, designer, or architect prepares preliminary drawings. Computer-aided design (CAD) equipment can quickly and economically create different space arrangements for visual purposes (Exhibit 12.4). After the lease negotiations are completed and confirmed, detailed plans are then prepared and later implemented.

Tenant Improvements

A significant point of negotiation between the real estate manager, prospective tenant, and the owner is the payment of the cost of constructing (*building out*) the tenant's space. Usually a *tenant improvement (TI)* allowance covers standard items that will be installed at no cost to the tenant. For example, installing one phone jack for every 125 sq. ft. leased, or including one door for every 300 sq. ft. If such a quantitative approach is *not* used, the allowance may be stated as an amount of money the owner will provide per square foot of leased space.

EXHIBIT 12.4

Example CAD Diagram for Office Space Planning

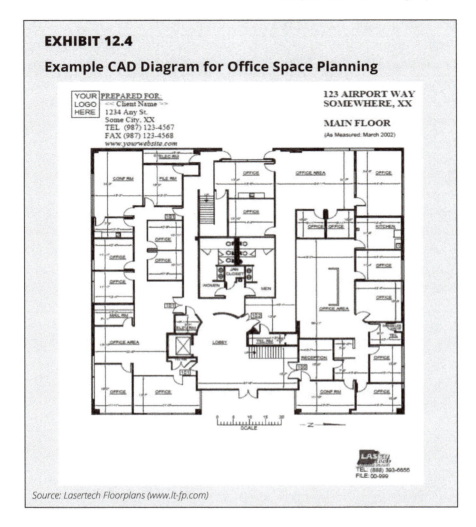

Source: Lasertech Floorplans (www.lt-fp.com)

Whether the owner or the tenant pays for construction costs that exceed the standard TI allowance depends on the market conditions and occupancy level in the building. One of four options is possible:

1. Owner pays
2. Tenant pays
3. Both owner and tenant pay a portion
4. Owner lends the incoming tenant the funds for the construction; the loan is amortized over the life of the lease and paid back with interest as part of the rent

While a loan paid back via rent is common, the tenant can also seek financing from other sources or pay for the construction outright. TIs are more frequently used as an incentive in a renter's market than in an owner's market. Because a commercial lease is usually a long-term contract, sacrifices early in the term may have lasting rewards for both tenant and owner. However, incentives that are too liberal may attract prospective tenants who are less than ideal candidates for the space, and that can burden the property with excessive expenses for many years.

It is important to note that a significant investment in TIs by the building owner at the beginning of the lease will take many years to recover—either with an amortized payback by the tenant or in higher rents. Should the tenant fail and vacate early in their tenancy, the owner may not realize any ROI, depending upon the outcome of any collection activities or negotiated termination settlement. Property owners should be cautious when investing large sums in TIs for start-up firms or firms in less than stable industries. In those instances, owners may negotiate lower rents for tenants that provide their own TIs, reducing the initial outlay of cash from the owner and reducing the risk of loss.

No matter how payment is arranged, the real estate manager and property owner will retain final authority on all construction in the office building. A construction firm is usually contracted to complete the build-out of a multitenant office building by the owner or the real estate manager working on the owner's behalf. The supervision of construction ensures that the integrity of the property's image will be maintained, which is a nice benefit for the tenant because it ensures high-quality workmanship at the lowest cost. Another benefit is that the owner's preferred contractor is usually more familiar with the building and its systems, which reduces the overall costs of construction and provides knowledgeable, realistic estimates and timing of the work so that move-in is on schedule.

In special cases, the owner (or the manager on the owner's behalf) can allow the tenant to contract for the construction. This may be the case in offices in *flex spaces*, which are single-story structures designed to facilitate different configurations that accommodate both large and small space users, as well as some non-office uses, such as lab assembly or light manufacturing. When dealing with flex spaces, the tenant must meet strict conditions, such as the owner's preapproval of plans, use of approved licensed, bonded contractors and subcontractors, and requirements for specific insurance coverages and lien releases after construction is completed.

OFFICE CONDOMINIUMS

A less common agreement involves *office condominiums*, which offer ownership of the office space as an alternative to leasing. They appeal to medical and dental practitioners, real estate firms, financial planners, entrepreneurs, and small companies that need 1,000 to 10,000 sq. ft. of space.

Not only do owners acquire equity in the property, but they are also able to project and control their costs of occupancy. Office condominiums do not offer much flexibility to expand or contract as businesses need change. Like residential condominiums, office condominiums offer different challenges for real estate managers. In certain situations, the real estate managers might serve as an association manager, which is common for condo association management.

MEDICAL OFFICE BUILDINGS

For many years, well-located *medical office buildings* (MOBs) have been considered very stable commercial real estate investments. MOBs, whose space is leased primarily to medical and dental professionals, must be modified to meet those tenants' needs for additional—sometimes specialized—plumbing and electrical wiring. Since the nature of their clients are patients who are ill, there is more exposure to blood-borne pathogens and other hazards; therefore, the services MOBs provide mandate special care in cleaning and waste disposal, and the lease must address those issues. Entrances and other common areas—including parking—must accommodate disabled and ailing individuals, and may require larger doorways for stretchers and/or unique entrances for ambulances or other specialized cars. In addition to doctors and dentists, other possible tenants within MOBs include pharmacies, biomedical laboratories, physical therapists, optical services, pain management clinics, and health maintenance organizations. For new and repositioned MOBs, excellent facility and asset management services are essential, along with specialized marketing and leasing, repositioning strategies, sales and acquisitions, and even design and development services.

For the most part, MOBs are costly to develop—TIs cost two to four times those of standard office buildings. Therefore, the TIs are amortized over longer periods, and leases typically have 10-year terms instead of the standard three- to five-year term for regular office leases. However, a benefit of working with MOBs is that tenant turnover is extremely low, especially when they reach a stable occupancy. More detailed information on MOBs and clinical facilities management can be found in the IREM publication, *Managing and Leasing Commercial Properties, Second Edition* (2016).

SUMMARY

Office buildings are a unique kind of commercial property since they are often in the CBDs of cities and suburbs. Whether a building is 100 years old or the newest 100-story skyscraper, the value of its rental space to tenants depends on its location, structural components, proximity to transportation, prestige, tenant services, management standards, and tenant mix. As office buildings continue to evolve, many current trends in office space design are the result of technological advances and environmental policies, as well as tenant needs. Long lease terms, complex rents, and tenants' desires to maximize the ability of their businesses to prosper in the spaces they rent make lease negotiations crucial to the successful management of office buildings.

13 | Shopping Centers

More often than not, shopping centers are constantly changing. With the shifts in consumer trends come new retail concepts and the need to adapt to changing demographics and consumers' needs and wants. This cycle creates opportunities for shopping center and retail property owners looking to take advantage of development, renovations, and adaptive uses occurring within the marketplace. Managing shopping centers is similar to managing office buildings in that it involves the longer lease term, a greater complexity of rent payments, and an increased involvement with tenants.

A shopping center has a unified image, and the property is planned, developed, owned, and managed on the basis of its location, size, and types of shops as they relate to the *trade area* the shopping center serves—the area from which customers are drawn. Shopping centers are classified into two types: (1) malls and (2) open-air centers—each of which is further classified into many subcategories.

1. Malls:
- Regional malls
- Super-regional malls

2. Open-air centers:
- Neighborhood shopping centers
- Community shopping centers
- Convenience centers (strip shopping centers)
- Lifestyle shopping centers
- Power shopping centers
- Specialty shopping centers (theme or festival centers)
- Outlet shopping centers

In addition to shopping centers, other retail properties and retail components can be located in *mixed-use developments (MXD),* where retail components have been added to office buildings and high-rise apartments. Just like office buildings, shopping centers are classified by their size, tenant mix, anchor tenants (main traffic draw), and their roles in the community.

PROPERTY ANALYSIS

Unlike the property analysis for office buildings, shopping centers do not involve an analysis by class structure. Instead, they are categorized according to the nature and variety of merchandise they offer and the size of their trade areas (Exhibit 13.1). The following lists the other considerations to take into account when analyzing the property:

- Aesthetic appeal
- Location
- Accessibility (proximity to public transportation)
- Availability of parking
- Additional amenities (e.g., daycare services and children's play areas)

The definitive measure of retail space is its square footage, which is expressed as *gross leasable area* (*GLA*) in reference to both the shopping center as a whole and the individual store interiors. In an enclosed shopping mall, the *gross floor area* includes the mall's GLA plus the *common areas*—courtyards, escalators, sidewalks, parking areas, etc.—that are not used exclusively by individual tenants.

Most shopping centers have at least one *anchor tenant,* such as a department store or supermarket that has large space requirements. *Ancillary tenants* occupy the smaller store spaces in a shopping center and, because of their specialization (jewelry or stationery), they attract additional customers to the center. Ancillary tenants rely heavily on the customers generated by the anchor tenant and serve to complement the product or services of the anchor. Shopping centers can be further differentiated by a variety of marketing and management strategies since they influence how each center is perceived.

Malls

Malls are more than just places to buy merchandise—they are gathering places for their communities, providing fashion, mass merchandising, entertainment, and sometimes educational activities. A successful mall usually has few vacancies and new tenants each year. New or renovated amenities such as benches, restrooms, children's play areas, and landscaping are continually evaluated, upgraded, and added. Because of a mall's size and complexity, real estate managers are constantly reevaluating the tenant mix and physical setup to make the necessary changes to remain competitive.

The very first malls were built in the 1950s, but the greater number were not developed throughout the United States until the late 1970s. Since the first malls, many generations of malls have developed. Two of those generations are the (1) regional mall and (2) the super-regional mall, which are recognized as two different types, but are both categorized within the enclosed setup.

Regional Mall. These large shopping centers have one or more full-line department stores as anchor tenants. The presence of a department store tends to attract such ancillary tenants as men's and women's apparel stores, optical shops, electronic equipment stores, and jewelers. If the anchor tenants are high-end department stores, the other tenants should offer medium- to high-end merchandise. Several stores of one type—for example, three to five shoe stores—are often located throughout these centers. The majority of *regional malls* include small fast-food outlets arranged in a *food court,* while others might also have cinemas. Regional malls contain 400,000 to 800,000 sq. ft. of GLA. Their trade area has a radius of seven to 10 miles, and they usually serve a population of 150,000 to 300,000.

Super-Regional Mall. These malls are similar to regional malls, but because of their larger size, *super-regional malls* have more anchors and ancillary tenants offering a wider selection of merchandise. They draw from a larger population base, including four or more full-line department stores and 100 to 150 small shops. Super-regional malls, as well as some regional malls (and large community shopping centers), may include separate buildings on-site called *outlots—out parcels* or *pads.* Banks, restaurants, automotive service centers, and movie theaters are also common tenants for these spaces. A super-regional mall has more than 800,000 to 3 million sq. ft. of GLA. Its trade area has a radius of 10 to 20 miles, and it serves a population of 300,000 or more.

Open-Air Malls

Although the first generation of the mall was the open-air, single-level regional mall, it became an even more popular choice for retailers and shoppers in the late 1990s. Some of the open-air malls actually became hybrids that combined the features of regular malls with lifestyle shopping centers and power shopping centers. The typical square footage of an open-air mall ranges from 400,000 to one million sq. ft. of GLA and is anchored by two or three major retailers—usually full-line department stores or other specialty stores. A major advantage of open-air malls is that the maintenance costs for the main common areas are significantly lower than regular enclosed malls—the common areas are essentially a component of the property's landscaping. Compared to regional malls, landscaping is required along with the additional maintenance for the indoor common area. The following sections provide more detail into the eight subcategories of open-air, single-level malls.

Neighborhood Shopping Center. The most common anchor tenant in a *neighborhood shopping center* is a supermarket or super drugstore—or a combination of the two. Neighborhood shopping centers usually have 15 to 25 small shops, and the ancillary tenants include dry cleaners, bank branches, beauty salons, and smaller

EXHIBIT 13.1

Shopping Center Types

Type	Concept	Sq. Ft.	# of Anchors
Regional	General merch., Fashion	400,000–800,000	2+
Super-regional	Similar to regional but has more variety	800,000+	3+
Neighborhood	Convenience	30,000–125,000	1+
Community Center	General merch., convenience	125,000–400,000	2+
Lifestyle	Upscale national chain, dining, in outdoor setting	150,000–500,000	0-2
Power	Category-dominant anchors with few small shop tenants	250,000–600,000	3+
Theme/Festival	Leisure, tourist-oriented	80,000–250,000	N/A
Outlet	Manufacturers' outlet stores	50.000–400,000	N/A

gift shops. The GLA of a typical neighborhood center is between 30,000 and 150,000 sq. ft., serving a population of 5,000 to 40,000. The neighborhood center is initially developed to provide local goods and services for the day-to-day needs of consumers in the immediate neighborhood. These centers are usually configured in a straight line or are L-shaped and do not contain enclosed walkways—although sometimes the canopies may connect the storefronts to maintain a pleasant, unified image.

Community Shopping Center. Anchor tenants for *community shopping centers* can be supermarkets, large hardware stores, or even discount department stores—sometimes a super drugstore like Walgreens or CVS. The 25 to 40 ancillary tenants frequently include apparel stores, bookstores, card shops, family shoe stores, and fast-food operations—either in-line or built in an L-shape. Community shopping centers range in size from 150,000 to 400,000 sq. ft. of GLA and usually require a population of 100,000 to 150,000 to sustain them. Community shopping centers are similar to neighborhood shopping centers, but are much larger and offer a wider range of apparel and other goods, such as home improvement/furnishings, toys, electronics, and sporting goods.

Convenience (Strip) Shopping Center. The smallest type of shopping center is the *convenience shopping center,* which usually has a convenience market anchor (such as a 7-Eleven) or other grocery store with a few small shops (two to 10 stores)—a combination gas station and food store is also common. Similar to neighborhood shopping centers, convenience centers are often designed in a straight line, and are most often referred to as *strip shopping centers.* These centers usually have 5,000 to 30,000 sq. ft. of GLA; the anchor tenant is usually open 24/7. The ideal location is on a corner or anywhere along a high-traffic street. If it is well located and fully leased, a convenience center can succeed in an area with a population of 1,000 to 2,500.

Lifestyle Shopping Center. Even though *lifestyle shopping centers* were developed in the early 1990s, the beginning of the new millennium marked a significant increase in these centers, which appear as strip shopping centers but are composed entirely of destination tenants—offering specialty shops such as beauty salons, barber shops, or shoe repair services. Lifestyle centers normally represent the upscale end of commercial development and often have a main street design with high-quality outdoor features, ranging from 150,000 to 500,000 sq. ft. of GLA. Although the community role of these centers is similar to regional malls, they provide a broader selection of high-end fashion, jewelry, and gifts—along with fine-dining restaurants and entertainment options.

The trade area may vary greatly from one center to another, depending on the local competition. For the most part, these centers have few small shops because they lack the traditional anchor tenants. These centers typically rely on customers with disposable income, versus neighborhood centers where shoppers usually buy necessities.

Power Shopping Center. A type of super community shopping center, the *power shopping center* gets its name from each anchor tenant's ability to attract customers from a wide area. Several large anchor tenants and strong, high-volume, heavy-advertising retailers occupy most of the space. Some of the following are typical anchor tenants in power shopping centers:

- Home furnishings
- Discount department stores
- Home and garden stores
- Office supplies
- Sporting goods
- Home improvements
- Toys
- Consumer electronics stores (computers, major appliances)

Power centers have GLAs ranging from 250,000 to 600,000 sq. ft. and at least four category-specific, off-price anchors—each occupying 20,000 sq. ft. or more of GLA. The trade area may extend up to 30 miles, depending on local competition—they need a minimum population of 150,000. However, power shopping centers have some disadvantages. A minor disadvantage is that there is limited landscaping. A larger problem is that most of the tenants offer merchandise that shoppers specifically seek out, rather than items purchased on impulse as seen in lifestyle shopping centers. This is an issue because power shopping centers lack the ambiance of a community shopping center or a regional mall, where the tenants benefit from surrounding businesses. For this reason, most power shopping centers have grouped together and are often located near regional malls to benefit from the nearby traffic.

Specialty Shopping Center. Also known as *theme* or *festival shopping centers, specialty shopping centers* are often characterized by a unified theme and located in a high-traffic area—tourists are the major component of their customer base. Those in downtown areas are often the result of an adaptive use of a historic building; they usually have an architectural theme based on the old design or original use of the building or location. Their uniqueness is truly their main attraction. However, specialty shopping centers do not always have an anchor tenant. Instead, the main attractions include food services; entertainment establishments; and smaller, one-of-a-kind boutiques. Specialty shopping centers usually vary in size from 150,000 to 500,000 sq. ft. of GLA. The specific use defines the trade area, and it may extend beyond the radius usually associated with centers of this size. Specialty shopping centers require an area population in excess of 150,000 to survive. A few examples of specialty shopping centers are the Faneuil Hall Marketplace in Boston and the Ghirardelli Square and Pier 39 in San Francisco.

Outlet Center. Usually located in rural areas, 50 percent of *outlet centers* consist of factory outlet stores that offer name-brand goods at lower prices by eliminating the intermediary wholesale distributor. These centers can give such large discounts because the merchandise consists of factory overruns, seconds, dated items, overstocks from other stores, and consignment purchases from manufacturers. Outlet centers have the ability to attract customers from a radius of 20 miles to as far as several hundred miles in certain rural areas, but they traditionally require a minimum population of 200,000. The square footage of outlet centers typically ranges from 50,000 to 400,000 sq. ft., but since the late 1990s, the number of outlet center developments has decreased substantially due to the industry relying heavily on the expansion of existing top-tier outlet centers. Outlet centers do not have anchor tenants, but they may be enclosed or arranged in an open-air, single level.

Trade Area Analysis

The geographic area from which shopping centers draw most of their customers is referred to as the *trade area*. The size of the trade area depends on the type of shopping center, location of competition, and other factors. The actual trade area analysis includes a *demographic profile,* which details the social and economic statistics of the population, such as size, density, growth, and decline, and its vital statistics that evaluate age, household size, education, and income. The demographic profile shows the number of people who are likely customers and their purchasing power. The analysis also includes a *psychographic profile,* which goes beyond the numbers to examine the interests and shopping habits of the people who live in the shopping center's trade area.

The trade area analysis also indicates the potential for a shopping center to succeed in a particular location. A new shopping center does not create new buying power. It must attract customers away from other shopping centers, so evaluation of the competition in the trade area is important.

Most trade areas are subdivided into three zones: (1) primary, (2) secondary, and (3) tertiary. The *primary trade area* is the immediate area around the site and accounts for 60 to 75 percent of the shopping center's sales. The *secondary trade area* usually extends three to seven miles from the site (for a regional shopping center) and accounts for 10 to 20 percent of sales. The *tertiary trade area* extends 15 to 50 miles from a major shopping center and accounts for five to 15 percent of sales. Every shopping center, whatever its size, has a trade area and trade zones—the sizes of which vary with the type of center and its location. People will usually travel only one to two miles to shop for groceries, but they will travel three to five miles for apparel and household items and eight to 10 miles to comparison shop for appliances and other major purchases.

Aesthetic Appeal, Location, and Accessibility. The aesthetic appeal of the center plays a strong role in attracting customers, particularly for regional and super-regional centers. People who shop at convenience and neighborhood centers live nearby, and proximity is their primary reason for shopping there. Small centers are not dependent on attracting people from a considerable distance, so aesthetic factors are not as critical. Larger centers must blend function and design to create a safe and attractive place to attract people. Important decorative features are architectural elements, fountains and other gathering places, lighting, seating, colors, landscaping, and flooring.

The value of one location compared to another depends on the customers' means of transportation within that trade area. Because most people who shop at large suburban centers travel by car, those centers must be easily accessible and should provide ample parking. However, being adjacent to a major thoroughfare does not guarantee accessibility—especially if traffic patterns make entering or exiting the property difficult or dangerous. Therefore, distinctive and appropriate signage to identify the center, clearly marked entrances and exits, and stop signs also contribute to accessibility.

Parking. First and foremost, parking should be convenient. When creating plans for a parking lot or garage, a great deal of preparation and a solid strategy are essential. Parking for downtown shopping centers is usually provided in multistory garages incorporated into or adjacent to the retail building; shoppers sometimes receive a discount on parking if they make a purchase.

Parking for suburban shopping centers is usually built surrounding the shopping center. The amount of land necessary for parking can be estimated in two ways: (1) local zoning ordinances specify a relationship between the size of the parking area and the size of the retail building in sq. ft. *(parking area ratio),* or (2) the number of parking spaces may be based on the gross leasable area (GLA) of the shopping center *(parking index).* The Urban Land Institute (ULI) recommends four parking spaces for each 1,000 sq. ft. of GLA for centers that have less than 400,000 sq. ft. of GLA. A center that has 400,000 to 599,999 sq. ft. of GLA should have between four and five spaces per 1,000 sq. ft. of GLA. One that has 600,000 or more sq. ft. of GLA should provide at least five spaces for every 1,000 sq. ft. of GLA.

Parking ratios and indices are merely guidelines—many other factors must be considered in developing a viable parking plan. In fact, the required parking ratios are usually included when creating the lease with major tenants. Different parking angles and varied widths of driving lanes between parking bays affect the numbers of stalls that an area can include. In addition, shopping centers must provide parking for disabled shoppers, so wider stalls and access ramps are needed near building entrances. Traffic flow, circulation patterns, and entrances and exits are other concerns.

Managing Shopping Centers

The actual management of a shopping center requires intensive work and a tireless staff. In addition to ensuring that the shopping center is up to date, clean, and safe, real estate managers will deal with the tenants and their concerns on a daily basis. Essentially, the tenants' economic survival depends on customers coming to the shopping center and visiting their stores. Competition among tenants can sometimes be intense and might result in strained relations unless the tenants are treated in a fair and consistent manner.

In addition to the physical and financial management of the property, the real estate manager will become intensely involved with the general marketing of the site and the marketing of each store. In general, real estate managers will be more involved with the ongoing activities of tenants compared to managing office buildings, residential, or industrial properties. Oftentimes, real estate managers will acquaint themselves with the actual retailing and merchandising of each tenant.

It's important to be aware of the number of shoppers that visit the site every day—depending on the shopping center, thousands of shoppers is not unusual. Such large numbers of people can lead to concerns about crime and vulnerability to other forms of criminal activity. Some anchor tenants employ their own security forces, but most shopping centers of significant size contract with a security agency to guard the premises. In many cases, real estate managers have educated tenants and their employees about ways to prevent crime and reduce criminal activity. Simple measures should be taken, such as securing HVAC systems, locking down roofs, being more cognizant of delivery schedules, and using concrete barricades. Further, information from the RAND Corporation (Research And

Development)—a nonprofit organization that helps improve policy and decision making through research and analysis—indicates traditional security approaches like installing bollards at pedestrian entrances, searching bags, and/or encouraging suspicious package reporting. Other features that increase safety include good lighting, limited escape routes, and security support from police in the surrounding community.

Tenant Selection

When choosing tenants for retail space, there are many factors that must first be weighed. Since the main goal is to attract customers to the shopping center, the ideal tenant will offer appealing merchandise in order to create synergy with the other tenants. In addition, the ideal tenant's merchandise should fill a need in the market that competing shopping centers do not meet. Requirements for store space and support services, as well as products or services that the retailer offers, must be considered—particularly as they affect where the retailer can or will be located in the center. All of these factors are in keeping with the demographic and psychographic profiles of the trade area. Real estate managers must scrutinize the retailer's reputation and financial status to determine the prospect's quality, responsibility, and ability to pay the rent—which is also relevant in keeping up to date on the ever-changing trends in the retail business and current economic conditions as part of the tenant-selection process. The following lists the main elements involved and the type of questions to ask when evaluating the retail tenant selection:

- **Retailer's reputation.** How do they treat their customers?
- **Financial stability.** Based on their financial statement, what are their liquid assets (e.g., savings account, stocks, bonds) and monthly obligations?
- **Tenant requirements.** How much space, visibility, or special needs are required?
- **Tenant mix and placement.** How would they match the types of merchandise and price lines in the existing retail space?

Retailer's Reputation. One of the most important factors to consider when choosing a retail tenant is the company's reputation. Because reputation results from public perception, learning how a retailer treats their customers is important. This is easy to ascertain for a store that is part of a franchise or chain—or from a company that is planning to move from one site to another. A visit to the prospect's present store (or multiple stores if the company is a chain) will always reveal much about the business's *customer service* practices. Observation of the treatment of other customers in the store and asking those customers about their perceptions of the store can also validate how the prospective tenant conducts business.

Another consideration is *merchandise presentation.* Obviously, a slim inventory of dusty items reveals a poor sales record, but fresh merchandise presented attractively implies the opposite. Salespeople who know their stock and present themselves well are assets to the retailer and will be the same for the shopping center in general. The level of advertising also indicates the retailer's reputation and the efforts they make to maintain it.

Most shopping centers can gain a competitive edge if they include a unique business that sets them apart from the other well-known businesses; they can quickly gain a healthy customer base strictly due to their uniqueness. Although the risks involved with a new business are greater, the rewards can often outweigh the risks. A new or developing enterprise may not have an existing identifiable reputation, but finding out how it plans to operate is not an impossible task; in fact, it's very simple. If a new company provides a clear plan of action for their new business, and the plan includes an investment in inventory and a pricing structure, they will most likely be a better prospect than one whose plans are vague. Having the knowledge base of its probable clientele and an understanding of its competition are also important, along with prior retailing and business experience.

Financial Stability. There was a time when the decision to accept a prospective tenant could be based primarily on reputation. For instance, the name Bloomingdale's was once sufficient to solidify a deal. However, in an age of buyouts and takeovers, it's important to carefully investigate the financial health of all prospects. While an established store in a chain may be doing exceedingly well, that one store may not be an accurate reflection of the success of its parent company. If the related enterprises are failing, the parent company may sell the individual store to raise funds. While such an occurrence may not affect a prospective tenant's business, any change in the ownership of a complex retailing operation increases the risks to the individual store and may create a vacancy in the shopping center.

The greatest cause of business failures is undercapitalization, which is one reason for carefully investigating new or proposed retail businesses. The costs of operating a retail business include not only rent, utilities, and maintenance of the store area, but also inventory, payroll, store design, fixtures, and advertising. For an established business, moving costs and the loss of business resulting from the move must be considered as well. Prospects should have sufficient reserve funds to be able to weather an initial lean period after they relocate. In order to gain a strong sense of the company's financial stability, request a copy of their financial statement that contains information regarding their liquid assets and monthly obligations. Obtain a Dun and Bradstreet credit report, especially when dealing with a new business. Some novice retailers expect immediate success from the day they open; realistically, it can take from one to three years to gain the level of success expected.

Tenant Requirements. The retail tenant's primary concerns are the availability of adequate space for its business, visibility of its location, and the volume of customer traffic that the shopping center generates. However, some tenants have special requirements. Food service operations have unique garbage disposal and pest control problems that must be taken into consideration.

Furniture and appliance stores require specialized loading docks. Supermarkets need large areas for short-term parking and enough space for storage of shopping carts. Most banks want to provide drive-up services for their depositors. How these unique tenant requirements can be met are topics discussed during lease negotiations. It's important to be familiar with these special accommodations to avoid making unrealistic promises during prospecting. Be aware of the specific attributes of each space, such as whether the space has the potential for certain upgrades, the size and capacity of HVAC units, and even the water pressure and grease traps for restaurant tenants.

In situations when tenants require improvements to the owner's property, it's extremely important to obtain space plans and even *as-built drawings,* which indicate the presence and location of certain utilities for future use. If that tenant is no longer at the center, the information collected from the as-built drawings will be useful or even critical for re-leasing that space. From a real estate manager's perspective, it can be frustrating when the necessary information is not readily available and it costs money to investigate the present setup.

Special services arranged for a specific tenant—beyond those normally provided—can lead to a concern for other tenants, even if the tenant pays for the special services they need. The best way to counter these concerns is by explaining positive outcomes. For example, if a movie theater in a shopping center has a last showing that begins at closing time for the other stores, the common areas leading to the theater could remain open so its patrons can exit after the show. Even if the entrances to the stores are closed and locked, tenants whose stores are adjacent to the theater may be fearful that late-hour theater patrons might damage their stores. A good way to address this concern could be to provide a security guard during late hours or until all of the patrons leave. Another option could be to limit access to a single entrance during the late hours. It might help to point out to other tenants that the theater's last showing could spark a swell in business before the stores close.

Tenant Mix and Placement. The combination of retailers and service vendors that lease space in a shopping center constitutes its *tenant mix.* A shopping center anchored by an upscale department store will attract shoppers that seek—and can afford—its lines of merchandise, whereas a shopping center anchored by a discount department store will attract people seeking bargains. The best tenant mix for each shopping center will always follow the anchor's lead. Therefore, the merchandise of the ancillary tenants should never clash with what the anchor tenants offer. To put things into perspective, a lingerie shop will probably not succeed in a shopping center anchored by a supermarket or a hardware store. Instead, a dry cleaner will most likely flourish in that type of center because it, too, serves immediate needs and conveniences.

Another consideration that relates tenant mix to merchandise is *destination shopping* versus *impulse shopping.* People usually have a specific purpose in mind when they visit an optical shop or a pharmacy in a shopping center—their search for a particular item or service has led them there. If they buy an ice cream cone in the process of going to or coming from their destination store, that is considered an impulse purchase. A good tenant mix serves both destination and impulse shoppers and increases sales of the center as a whole.

Shopping centers that have more than one anchor tenant must ensure that the merchandise each offers is a good match and is complementary to the offerings of the ancillary tenants. An effective way to create a workable tenant mix is to view the specialty shops and department stores in the shopping center as parts of one big store.

In some situations, retailers try to persuade the owner to provide them with an *exclusive use.* That means the owner cannot lease space to another tenant who provides the same merchandise or use, and if they do, penalties for the violation are usually severe. Owners, on the other hand, are reluctant to provide exclusive uses because they may preclude leasing space to another business that has the same type of use—even though such use constitutes a relatively small percentage of (or is incidental to) that tenant's overall product or service.

The placement of tenants in the shopping center is also vital. For example, shoe stores are a natural complement to clothing stores. An ice cream parlor often does well next to a sandwich shop or movie theater. When developers build new shopping centers, they pay careful attention to the placement of tenants in order to maximize their potential to attract customers through the shopping center as a whole.

Retail Rent

Rents for retail space are based on the GLA of the individual spaces. Like office spaces, stores are usually rented as open *shell space* (or *vanilla shell space*). Unlike the practice in office buildings, the tenant, not the owner, is usually responsible for completing the interior beyond the shell stage—subject to the owner's pre-approval of plans as well as other parameters. Comparatively, for office tenants, the interior work is usually a main item of negotiation with the owner prior to solidifying the lease terms.

Base Rent. Shopping center leases state rent for the space as *base rent*, or *minimum rent,* which is usually calculated on a per-square-foot, per-year basis and is commonly stated in the lease as equal monthly incremental amounts. Base rent assures the property owner a minimum income, regardless of the merchant's sales success. In addition, retailers usually pay *pass-through charges* that cover the cost of operating the center, including taxes and insurance, plus *common area maintenance* (*CAM*) charges. Shopping center leases are typically triple-net (NNN), explained later in this chapter.

Percentage Rent. In some leases, retailers may also be required to pay a portion of their sales revenue as *percentage rent.* When percentage rent is charged, the owner actually shares in the success of the retailer's store space on the property. Percentage rent is generally based on gross annual sales, but most tenants pay percentage rent monthly or quarterly—except anchor tenants, who pay it annually. Because this type of rent is based on the retailer's sales volume, the amount can fluctuate significantly from month to month, so percentage rent is usually paid *in addition to* base rent. Some retailers try to negotiate to pay percentage rent only, but owners rarely make this exception—and usually only for large establishments with high sales levels.

Since there is no universally applied percentage rent rate, it is determined by the type of business and the locale. Supermarkets have a large sales volume and low-profit margins, yet one percent of their gross sales will yield a large amount of percentage rent. On the other hand, gift shops have comparatively small sales volumes but high-profit margins, and 10 percent of their gross sales may be appropriate.

The actual percentage is always negotiated and is usually collected on sales in excess of the amount of base rent and referred to as *overage rent*. In other words, the base rent for a store could be $120,000 a year, payable in equal monthly amounts of $10,000; if the percentage rent is five percent of gross sales, the tenant's gross sales must exceed $200,000 a month before percentage rent applies ($10,000 ÷ 0.05 = $200,000). The tenant pays the greater of the percentage of gross sales or the base rent. It is best to calculate the percentage rent on a monthly basis, as opposed to annually, due to the seasonality of shopping.

According to the previous example, the $200,000 a month in sales is the *natural breakpoint*. If the store produces $250,000 in gross sales in a month, its rent will be the $10,000 base rent plus five percent of sales above the natural breakpoint—in this case, five percent of $50,000, or $2,500, meaning the total rent for that month will be $12,500. However, the prospective tenant or the owner may negotiate an *artificial breakpoint* to use as the threshold for paying percentage rent. The artificial breakpoint may be higher or lower than the natural breakpoint—a downward adjustment of the breakpoint would increase the owner's income. An advantage of an artificial breakpoint is that it can be used to accelerate payback to the owner of funds advanced for tenant improvements, lease concessions, or even in exchange for a reduced rental rate in the early stages of a new tenant's lease. However, as the base rent increases over the term of the lease, the natural breakpoint will rise accordingly. Either way, knowing the exact meaning of the lease clause and how the percentage rent is calculated is extremely important to properly collect what the tenant owes. Finally, leases typically allow the owner to audit a tenant's gross sales—annually or at some other time—to confirm their accuracy and truthfulness in their reporting.

Pass-Through Charges and Net Leases. When dealing with a *gross lease* for retail space, all operating expenses are the responsibility of the property owner, who must recover them fully in the rent. Most retail tenants have *net leases,* meaning that some expenses of operating the property are passed through to the tenant. The type of net lease the owner offers determines what the tenant pays, and pass-through charges are prorated based on the GLA of the individual store as a percentage of the GLA of the shopping center as a whole. The types of net leases follow:

- **Net lease.** The tenant pays a prorated share of real estate taxes only.
- **Net-net lease.** The tenant pays a prorated share of real estate taxes and insurance costs.
- **Net-net-net (NNN) lease.** All operating expenses including real estate taxes, insurance, utilities, CAM, and various fees are prorated and passed through to the tenant. Under a *modified triple-net lease,* which some shopping centers may use, the owner is responsible for structural (or capital) repairs to the building and for payment of management fees for the common areas.

There are numerous other—mostly regional or local—definitions of the expenses that are passed through to the tenant under a particular type of net lease, so delineation of the pass-through charges is essential when describing a type of net lease.

Major retail tenants might also negotiate with owners to set a *cap* (an *expense stop*) on certain expenses—most often on common area expenses. This ceiling assures that the retailer will pay only a certain dollar amount per year for the particular pass-through expense or expenses to which the cap applies. Unlike an expense stop in an office lease, which sets a ceiling on how much the property owner pays, a cap in a retail lease defines a limit on how much the tenant pays.

When collecting NNN (triple-net) expenses from tenants, real estate managers dealing with retail properties must consider the following critical factors:

• When a shopping center has several tenants that have negotiated caps or exclusions in their NNN charges, the recapture of expenses to the owner decreases. Having less than 100 percent collection of these expenses reduces the NOI of the center and, therefore, the value of the property.

• Because NNN charges are considered additional rent to the base rent paid by the tenant, search for service providers that offer quality services at reasonable prices. For budget planning purposes, reducing NNN costs by appealing property taxes, rebidding certain services, and shopping for new insurance will be a welcome relief to tenants. Keeping costs down goes a long way toward building tenant relations.

• Generally, pass-through costs are based on the tenant's pro rata share, but some costs can be allocated to each tenant on a more accurate basis. For example, a restaurant might have a pro rata share of 10 percent of the entire shopping center, yet the other tenants only offer service and office uses. A 10 percent allocation for water or garbage service would not be an accurate representation of the true impact of the restaurant tenant's use. Therefore, it's common and a generally acceptable accounting principle (GAAP) to allocate such expenses based on use or number of fixtures (i.e., toilets or sinks), to require tenants to contract directly for garbage service, or to provide a submeter to get an accurate reading of water use. In this way, the fact that the restaurant uses the majority of the service does not put a greater financial burden on the office tenant who might not generate the same amount of garbage per week. In addition, vacancies obviously will not generate water expenses. Therefore, the GLA would be altered to remove the vacancy from the water calculation and the rest of the tenants who actually use water. These various accounting tactics ensure the highest possible recapture of expenses to an owner, increasing NOI and the property's value, which is a more reasonable way to allocate expenses—especially for tenants who have a higher pro rata share but do not generate an equally higher impact on a certain expense.

Escalations. Because retail leases have long terms, escalations have to be written into the lease in order for them to take effect automatically. For an anchor tenant, a 20- or 30-year lease is common, and for ancillary tenants, leases usually have three- to 10-year terms. Similar to office space leases, provisions for rent increases may be negotiated as a periodic percentage increase, or they may be based on the *consumer price index (CPI),* along with base-year and expense-stop provisions.

An escalation provision typically applies only to the base rent, but escalation provisions sometimes apply to expense stops or base-year expenses. The lease for an anchor tenant whose sales generally surpass the agreed-upon breakpoint may mandate an escalation in base rent only once every five years. For an ancillary tenant, the lease usually calls for an annual increase; the specifics depend on market conditions at the time of the lease negotiation.

Retail leases can include the simple option to renew or vacate the premises. The option will usually state that notice has to be given to the owner at some point, but no less than a certain number of days before the lease expires, and it usually specifies the length and the rental rate of the extension. For leases that have long initial lease periods, it's important to keep in mind that the market at the end of the lease is unknown. If the initial lease term is 10 years, there is no way of knowing what a market rent will be at year 11. Therefore, the option period could state that the rent will be at market rates, but no less than three percent more than the rent paid during the last period of the lease. The option period could also include a cap of five percent so the tenant is assured that market rent will not dramatically increase during their option period.

The Retail Lease

The standard lease for a shopping center includes a number of clauses that are specific to this type of property and addresses concerns and contingencies that can arise over the number of years covered by the lease. Additionally, leases for a freestanding store or for space in a small convenience shopping center might not have such specific provisions. Along with the specification of rental rates and how payments are to be made, the following lists the other specific clauses and considerations included in the standard retail lease.

Use. A shopping center is carefully designed and leased to appeal to a specific market in a specific location. If a tenant were to change its merchandise or its image—such as from specialty lines to general merchandise or from upscale to discount—that change could alter the tenant mix of the center. Therefore, a *use clause* prevents tenants from using the premises in a different way than was originally intended.

Exclusive Use. To minimize competition among tenants, prospects might seek a clause covering *exclusive use* to prohibit other tenants in the shopping center from selling a similar product. However, *some* competition within the center is generally beneficial, and an exclusive use clause can be counterproductive. It's important to be aware of certain exclusive-use clauses that might violate antitrust laws enforced by the Federal Trade Commission, which make restraint of trade illegal. Regardless, temporary limits on certain product lines or on competing store sizes might help a retailer meet their rent payment or give a new business a head start. Because it is desirable to have several types of tenants in each retail category in a regional or larger center, and because the merchandise carried by each retailer in a category tends to complement the others' merchandise rather than compete with it, owners rarely grant exclusive use.

In open-air shopping centers, it is common for parcels of land to be owned by different entities or to be built by the developer with that in mind. In such cases, there will usually be documents—or *covenants, conditions,* and *restrictions* (CC&Rs)—that affect the management and maintenance of the center as a whole. These documents dictate everything from pro rata shares of CAM by parcel size, building, and construction limitations, to the parcel owner, or maintenance director, for all common area services that benefit all parcel owners as well as other provisions on the conduct and requirements of each. The following lists the additional uses that CC&Rs can restrict at the shopping center:

- Specific types of uses that are prohibited in the center
- Specific uses on certain parcels or within so many feet of a neighboring parcel
- Building height on potential new pad buildings
- Confirmation of exclusive use clauses that already exist at the time of execution of the document

Simply being aware that these documents exist is the most important step, but understanding how to administer them is another. CC&Rs can be quite cumbersome and sometimes require an attorney to interpret, but on the real estate manager's end of the spectrum, it's important to be diligent in ensuring that these restrictions adhere to all documents that govern the shopping center.

Radius. The *radius clause* prohibits a tenant from opening a similar store or from developing a similar chain of stores within a certain distance from the shopping center—typically three to five miles. Its intent is to prevent the tenant from directing customers to a nearby store in order to reduce percentage rent. The radius provision also requires the tenant to add sales from similar stores it operates—within a certain distance of the shopping center—to the sales of its store in the shopping center when calculating percentage rent.

Store Hours. Among tenants of the same shopping center, variation in store hours should be minimal. This clause authorizes the management of the property to set store hours for the center as a whole. Some anchor tenants such as supermarkets or large drugstores may remain open 24 hours a day. These stores are usually located in open shopping centers where the ancillary tenants maintain their own hours. A store-hours clause may also include provisions for seasonal adjustments and special hours for holiday shopping periods.

Common Area Maintenance. The *common area maintenance* (CAM) *clause* specifies exactly what constitutes the common area of the shopping center and what expenses the tenant will pay. In addition, it spells out the property owner's responsibility to maintain the common areas and repair any damage to them. The CAM clause also gives the owner the right to expand, reduce, or otherwise alter the common area. The common area in an enclosed mall includes the mall corridors, parking lots, escalators, landscaped areas, and other parts of the property that the tenants use in common. In addition to maintenance, CAM charges include expenses for security personnel and alarm systems that protect the shopping center, its tenants, and their customers. These charges can also include some replacement items that some may see as capital improvements (e.g., parking lot or roof replacement) and fees for management of the common area as a direct pass-through of that expense, as a percentage (administrative fee) of the base rent, or as a percentage share of the CAM charges in lieu of management expense.

As previously mentioned, CAM fees are normally prorated based on the percentage of GLA of the center the individual store occupies. On that basis, a store with 3,000 sq. ft. of GLA in a 300,000 sq. ft. shopping center would pay one percent of the center's CAM costs; a separate clause usually specifically states the tenant's pro rata share of CAM and other expenses. CAM clauses also include provisions on when a reconciliation should be completed and delivered to each tenant, and they provide an opportunity for the tenant to audit the owner's books at the tenant's expense—if they should choose. Some leases further dictate that if the landlord does not provide a reconciliation within a certain number of days after the applicable accounting period, the tenant will not have to pay any additional operating expenses. Therefore, it's important to be aware of and adhere to these clauses to ensure that the ownership receives the highest revenue possible and allowable by the lease. Most owners would not be very forgiving if certain deadlines were missed and/or precluded collection of monies due.

Advertising, Signs, and Graphics. The owner retains the right to restrict the size, location, lettering, manner of installation, and language of all signs in the shopping center. Large malls establish uniform graphic images and seek to maintain consistency in the caliber of signage. This is especially important for signs that are permanently mounted on the exterior of the building or are placed in the center's interior. Tenants may be required to spend a certain percentage of their gross income on advertising to promote their stores—and the shopping center. Most large shopping centers have promotional campaigns for the center as a whole, and to support those campaigns, they might require tenants to participate in a *marketing fund* or *merchants' association*—usually through a specific lease clause. Options similar to those described for office leases—to renew, expand, or cancel—may also be part of retail lease negotiations.

Concessions. Comparatively, leasing office space is similar to shopping centers—the owner usually offers concessions to secure a new lease or to retain an established tenancy. Because concessions are a special part of the lease negotiation process, they are usually stipulated in the applicable clauses rather than included as a single specific clause. If there is no applicable clause to amend, they may be listed in separate documents incorporated into the lease by reference (or addenda). Ideally, any concession granted will not lower the quoted rent. It's important to remember that any reduction in rent also reduces the value of the property.

One type of concession, a *tenant improvement* (TI), is money the owner provides for modification of the leased space before the tenant moves in. This may be a dollar amount per square foot, and the tenant may have to repay this as *additional rent* prorated throughout the lease term. Store space is typically leased as a "vanilla shell," consisting of a storefront, demising walls, and HVAC. The TI provisions usually state that the funds can only be used to improve the leased premises, and not for the tenant's signs, fixtures, or personal property. Depending on the area and market conditions, the demised premises may include (or specifically exclude) other items such as utility lines to the interior of the space, a dropped ceiling, and a restroom. Tenants usually finish the interiors of their store spaces and install appropriate display fixtures themselves.

Unlike office buildings, retail TIs rarely have direct impact on structural components or mechanical systems of the shopping center building. However, the tenant will be required to submit a construction or remodeling plan for the owner's approval before work begins. Other concessions include payment of a new tenant's moving expenses, a higher artificial breakpoint for percentage rent, or a period of free rent. Free rent is a good alternative to a TI since it eliminates the out-of-pocket need to move a new tenant into the space—especially if there is no TI reserve in-house or with the lender.

Other Clauses. Other common clauses in retail leases are requirements for *continuous occupancy*, staying in business for the full term of the lease, and *continuous operation*, keeping the business operating smoothly and consistently. Shopping center owners usually include *sales reporting* and *sales auditing clauses* to ensure that tenants report and pay percentage rent accurately and on time. Provisions regarding *alterations* to the store space, *insurance* coverage for the retailer's business, ADA compliance, and related indemnification are also common. For some businesses, a separate clause might also address the tenant's specific rights and limitations on *parking*.

Since *defaults* can be monetary or non-monetary, it's important that the default clause in a retail lease clearly explain what constitutes a default. Failure to pay rent is obviously a monetary default, and failing to open the store for four days is an example of a non-monetary default. Both types should have remedies stated in the lease, along with the rights of the owner, should the tenant fail to cure the default within a stated period of time. If the default remains, the lease should outline the owner's rights for an eviction, obtaining possession, collection of debt, and other expenses for which the tenant is responsible (e.g., re-leasing fees or leasing commissions). The default clause should also include what constitutes a "notice" to the tenant of their default. Failure to properly notify the tenant, as stated in the lease, can severely interfere with the owner's ability to evict the tenant—therefore, it's important to be familiar with the default clauses.

Addenda. The following lists addenda that are usually included in retail leases:

- A site plan of the shopping center outlining the boundaries of the common areas and identifying any individual parcels
- A space plan of the demised premises
- Rules and regulations governing the tenant's conduct and rights to quiet enjoyment
- Outside seating regulations for restaurants that have seating on sidewalks or in common areas
- A copy of the franchisee sublease would be attached if the lease is for a corporate entity that subleases to a franchisee

OTHER COMMERCIAL PROPERTY TYPES

Other professionally managed commercial properties include medical buildings, industrial sites, and warehouses. Each poses distinct challenges to the real estate manager because of the unique requirements of its tenants.

Industrial Properties

Industrial properties include large single-user buildings, incubator space for small business start-ups, multitenant business parks, self-storage facilities, and business continuity services (records maintenance). They often have a mix of uses that combines office, retail, light manufacturing, distribution, and storage at a single site.

Certain technologies have affected space needs in some ways as they have with office and retail uses. For the most part, manufacturers can maintain minimum stocks of materials, parts, and packaging since updated inventory systems—coupled with overnight shipping services—allow *just-in-time delivery* that keeps pace with their production levels.

Most new industrial rental space consists of single-story structures that can be configured to accommodate a single tenant or multiple tenants (*flex space*). Often built in a business park setting, such spaces have no lobbies or fancy fixtures, and they have no load factors or add-on charges—rents are lower and parking is ample. Some tenants such as e-commerce and telecommunications firms that set up data centers, have companies that need large blocks of inexpensive space.

Other firms need their offices in the same building as their manufacturing or warehouse operations. Research facilities and factories are often built to tenants' specifications, which are detailed in a *build-to-suit lease*. Truck access and rail lines may be among their requirements, along with reliable sources of electricity and other utilities such as gas and water.

Existing commercial facilities that are open to the public as well as renovations and new construction are required to meet accessibility requirements of the Americans with Disabilities Act (ADA).

Businesses and individuals may choose to store and secure their goods in *self-storage facilities* containing rows of attached garages. Some facilities include living quarters for an on-site manager; however, other storage facilities that are not climate controlled pose a threat not only as living quarters, but also for the tenant's items in storage. Self-storage units have various requirements and lease clauses that cover issues of abandoned property, lockouts, nonpayment of rent, and even prohibited items that cannot be stored in the units. The lease should clarify how to deal with the disposal of goods left by a tenant, along with the protocol used in locking the storage units.

Warehouses

Warehouses sometimes exist in cities, but most are in suburban areas. Warehouses are leased for storage of inventory, records, or excess raw materials. Real estate management services include shipping and receiving, with charges based on gross weight of materials handled or the number of packages shipped and received. The storage environment (e.g., control of temperature and humidity) is critical for many materials, and federal and other laws mandate labeling to identify specific hazards of materials transported in interstate commerce. Such requirements will affect typical management procedures.

Lease Considerations

Industrial leases include many clauses similar to those in office and retail leases. To maintain the owner's control over the property, the *use clause* should be specific about the tenant's type of business. The tenant often has direct responsibility for maintenance—especially if a single tenant is in a building.

Storage is another important consideration. Industrial tenants often use hazardous materials that require special storage facilities and special waste disposal equipment and procedures. To reduce risk and protect the value of the property, the leases of such tenants should require an annual environmental inspection of their leased spaces—at the tenant's expense. The *insurance clause* will usually be specific as to type and amount of coverage the tenant must maintain.

Tenants in a *research and development park* or similar campus-style property might establish a tenants' association to oversee road maintenance and groundskeeping, budgeting, and collection of fees for common area operations and maintenance, along with any other routine management activities. In a *master-planned development,* tenants in a single-use building are offered some form of net lease, but in *multitenant properties,* the tenant is responsible for maintaining the interior of the leased space, including the HVAC.

Generally, the owner is responsible for the roof, structural elements, and common areas and bills the tenants—both large and small—for their pro rata shares of CAM charges, real estate taxes, and property insurance.

It's common for tenants in a single-tenant building to be responsible for their own interior and exterior maintenance—including that of the common area parking lots and landscaping. These types of leases usually require the tenant to insure not only their interior improvements and personal property, but also the building structure itself and to provide liability coverage for the common areas as well.

MARKETING COMMERCIAL SPACE

Businesses are not inclined to frequently relocate. Even if a business moves, the initial intention was usually to remain at its location for a long time. Because of the infrequency of moves, and because a multiple-year lease translates into many thousands or millions of dollars in rent over its term, commercial tenants are commonly recruited directly—although conventional advertising and promotion cannot be overlooked.

Prospecting for Tenants

To ensure optimum occupancy, a property representative must make direct calls on potential tenants. This is particularly important for proposed developments because lending institutions usually require a certain percentage of a planned property to be *pre-leased*—leased before construction of the building begins or while the construction is taking place—before construction loans will be approved.

A real estate management firm sometimes employs a leasing agent—either temporarily or permanently—whose sole purpose is to seek out potential tenants. The leasing agent accomplishes this through a process known as *cold calling* or *prospecting,* which involves direct calls on the principals of businesses—individuals or corporations—to discuss the possibility of moving their operations to the subject property. In order to achieve success with such a program, the leasing agent is expected to conduct research on various businesses to ensure that their efforts are directed toward the right prospects. This is especially important for retail properties that seek specific types of tenants to provide a certain product or service niche in the tenant mix of a large shopping center. Information regarding businesses that may be considering a move can come from many sources such as the chamber of commerce, company annual reports, and referrals from business acquaintances. The most promising prospects are businesses that anticipate expansion or those whose leases are nearing expiration.

Various online resources list commercial properties for lease by brokerage firms nationwide and even internationally. Such resources help bring prospective tenants to inquire about the site. Other regional websites post vacancies throughout local areas as well. Posting vacancies through these resources is relatively inexpensive; it's simply a matter of collecting the specific data from the property. The following list of information should be provided when posting available spaces:

- Geographic parameters
- Square footage requirements
- Rental rates
- Detailed photographs
- Floor plans
- Leasing contact information

Along with these online resources, it's important to develop a website specifically for the shopping center. Countless resources are available for developing a unique website. As mentioned in Chapter 8, website development can easily be outsourced. When doing so, it's important to remember the seven Cs of website design:

1. **Context.** Above all, the layout and design should always be user friendly.
2. **Content.** Keep it interesting and updated.
3. **Customization.** The user should be able to tailor the site to fit their needs.
4. **Communication.** Contact info such as e-mails, phone numbers, fax lines, and any other appropriate information should be easily available.
5. **Connection.** Possibly add links to similar references.
6. **Commerce.** The site should enable prompt commercial transactions.
7. **Community.** It is always a nice feature when other users can communicate with one another.

Similar to residential marketing, make use of a *prospect report* that records information about prospective tenants for office space, their space needs, current space and lease expiration data, how they were contacted, whether they were qualified for tenancy, and their status as prospects—if they received a brochure or were given a tour of the property. These prospect reports are a cumulative record of the prospects brought to a building by a particular leasing agent. For retail space, information about the type of business, expected lease terms, and TI work is similarly documented along with the source of the contact and the status of individual prospects—if the lease is under negotiation, it's a dead deal. Such records determine the leasing agent's commission—especially when outside brokers are used—as well as the overall progress in leasing available space.

Certain states require licensing for real estate managers who negotiate the terms of a lease and for those that might share in any leasing commissions for new leases or renewal leases. Always stay updated with state laws when performing any leasing activity.

Marketing on Value

Unlike residential property, which is usually marketed on personal appeal, the marketing emphasis for commercial space is usually on the dollar value the prospect will receive for the rent paid. In this case, value directly affects the prospect's profit margin. The four principal ways to market space based on value are to emphasize (1) price advantage, (2) improved efficiency, (3) increased prestige, and (4) economy.

1. **Price advantage.** Well-managed businesses always strive to improve net profits. If a leasing agent can demonstrate a price advantage in a location that fully meets the prospect's expectations or prerequisites, the likelihood of at least stimulating preliminary interest is great.

2. **Improved efficiency.** Convenient access for employees or customers, low utility costs, and excellent tenant services are some attractions that may turn a prospect into a tenant, along with better operating efficiency. Space plans and layouts or other visual aids help illustrate the expectation of more efficient operations. A demonstration of space adaptability is a tangible and especially strong incentive. Such a demonstration, coupled with data on the probable reduction of expenses, might justify the prospect's move. In addition, because of technology upgrades, many businesses relocate to buildings that have superior electrical systems in place so their operations and equipment can easily fit into their new space.

3. **Increased prestige.** In terms of business value, prestige is a marketable commodity. The rent for prestigious space will certainly be higher, but greater visibility may increase the prospect's business so the amount of rent as a percentage of gross income may actually be lower. Prestigious locations also help attract employees.

4. **Economy.** When price advantages are mentioned, a lower cost on a comparable item is implied. In commercial space, however, economy refers to space that is lower in price but not necessarily equivalent to the space currently occupied. Sometimes a business located in a Class A office building could just as well have part or all of its operations in less-expensive space without compromising its strength or reputation. During periods of inflation or slow business activity, a prospect may consider less-luxurious space or outlying locations to control occupancy costs.

Negotiations with commercial prospects are much more common in comparison to residential properties. Through legal counsel, the owner and the tenant may specifically negotiate many lease clauses. Negotiation of leases for commercial space is complex because the financial risks are greater on both sides—for the tenant *and* the owner. Those risks require much more diligence in order to help protect the owner's rights and interests.

INSURING COMMERCIAL PROPERTIES

When an investor makes a "small investment" in commercial property, the purchase price of the store or office building may be several million dollars. "Large investments" do not necessarily have upper limits, but property valued between $100 million and $1 billion is available in most major cities. Whether the investment is small or large by industry standards, the expectation is for the property over its lifetime to generate income in excess of its purchase price. In fact, the purchaser's ability to retain ownership usually depends on the periodic income the property generates.

Owner's Insurance

If the lifespan of the property ended abruptly because of damage, even a so-called small investment could bankrupt the investor. *Comprehensive insurance coverage* provides protection from financial ruin due to the loss of use of the property. However, no single policy can completely protect the investor; even if such a policy were available, the premium cost would be prohibitive.

As with income-producing residential property (Chapter 11), the owner insures commercial property against loss of income, structural damage, and liability. The policy identifies the owner as the named insured party and lists the manager as an additional named insured. However, a major difference for commercial property is that insurance premiums are an operating expense that the owner may prorate and pass through to the tenants.

While almost anything can be insured, the owner must balance the cost of the premium against the risk of leaving all or part of the value uninsured. To illustrate this concept, think of how fragile certain windows can be and the expense involved in replacing them—most basic insurance policies exclude coverage of plate-glass windows or limit the amount paid per year for window breakage. If every policy included this coverage and placed no upper limit on the amount the insured could claim, owners of skyscrapers could easily take advantage of the cost of repair and would benefit more from this coverage compared to owners of buildings with few windows that rarely need replacing. The insurer would have to charge high premiums in order to pay the claims, and the cost to insure a small building would be prohibitive. To avoid such an inequity, insurers exclude plate-glass coverage from basic policies altogether. However, a separate plate-glass policy can be purchased, or an endorsement can be added to the primary policy to pay for plate-glass damage. The owner of a building that has thousands of windows would probably investigate the value of paying for the coverage. For a smaller building, the owner might leave the windows uninsured and pay for the occasional replacement as an operating expense.

On the other hand, retail leases in open-air centers generally require the tenant to be responsible for their own storefronts, which includes front doors, hardware, and plate glass. The nature of the tenants' business determines the amount of use that the store's front doors incur on a daily basis. A fast-food restaurant may have dozens of patrons every hour as opposed to an insurance office that may have just a few customers per day. Obviously, the fast-food restaurant will have a higher degree of repair and maintenance that should not be shared among the rest of the tenants. This is generally another reason that owner insurance policies do not insure plate glass or tenants' store fronts.

After September 11, 2001, owners and managers of commercial buildings in New York City, in particular, discovered that their insurance coverage did not include acts of terrorism, and their claims were denied. In response, Congress passed the *Terrorism Risk Insurance Act* (*TRIA*), which requires insurers to make that coverage available. Insurers sell terrorism insurance coverage separately from other coverages, and the premiums are expensive. However, owners of commercial properties, especially properties located in urban centers, should at least consider purchasing it. Lenders are likely to require such coverage if the building is mortgaged. The owner's insurance agent can advise on how much coverage would be appropriate.

Tenant's Insurance

Because insurance for the property as a whole does not cover the contents of tenants' individually leased spaces, most commercial leases require tenants to carry enough insurance to cover their inventory and whatever furnishings and equipment they have in their leased space. The commercial tenant's insurance coverage should be sufficient, both to preserve the business and to meet the obligations of the lease in case of disaster. Tenants may need other types of insurance as well—such as crime coverage. Commercial tenants are usually required to carry their own liability insurance, and the lease might require them to list the owner of the property and real estate manager as additional named insured parties. Retail leases specifically require tenants to have insurance against plate-glass damage and business interruptions, and state law requires that employers carry workers' compensation insurance to cover on-the-job illness and employee injury.

The relationship of an insurance company with its customers technically gives it the right, or *subrogation,* to sue an entity in the name of the insured party in order to recover a settlement it has paid if evidence shows that the other entity may be liable. Suppose, for example, that an electrical fire damages a building, and the property owner's insurance pays the claim. If later evidence proves that a tenant's employee left a space heater on overnight and it ignited the carpeting, the owner's insurance company might file a suit against the tenant or its insurance company to recover the amount of the claim. The existence of this right can make obtaining insurance difficult for both the tenant and the owner, so both parties are usually obligated to sign a *waiver of subrogation* to prohibit the exercise of this right.

Real estate managers are generally exempt in their management agreements from having to obtain or acquire insurance coverage for their clients. It's important to always be knowledgeable in all insurance-related matters in order to properly advise clients. The insurance agent for the owner can be of great help in reviewing and recommending lease language or for routinely shopping for better coverage at reduced premiums. Groups of properties under a single ownership can save thousands of dollars by insuring those properties under one *blanket policy,* as opposed to each property having an individual policy.

SUMMARY

Most shopping centers are classified by size and by the types of tenants they contain, but the types of shopping centers are constantly evolving. Each shopping center is planned as a single project, usually has a unified image, and provides on-site parking—especially in suburban centers. As with office buildings, shopping center rent is based on the square footage of the leased space, and some operating expenses of the shopping center are passed through to the tenants as a separate charge in addition to base rent; retailers may also pay a percentage of their gross sales as additional rent.

Other types of commercial property include industrial properties, storage facilities, and self-storage facilities. Along with financial and administrative issues, managers of these types of properties must often deal with issues related to storage and disposal of hazardous materials as well as tenants' special needs. In addition to taking care of special items, marketing for shopping centers is more aggressive compared to marketing for residential properties. With the real estate manager's assistance, a leasing agent will attempt to target specific businesses as prospects and will even call them directly to sell the benefits of the property.

As with residential space, the diversity of commercial property types does not permit development of a definitive insurance policy to cover all the damage that may occur at an individual property. When planning a unique combination of policies and endorse-ments, the property owner and the real estate manager must balance the premiums against the cost of self-insuring in order to design an insurance program that is economical and effective.

In today's market, simply defining an anchor tenant is tricky. In the past, anchors were typically supermarkets and department stores, but today's anchors can be anything from full-service department stores, mass merchandising retailers and grocery stores, to movie theaters, restaurants, bookstores, electronic stores, upscale retail-ers, and gourmet food and wine markets. Anchor tenants will not only drive traffic and sales to the center, but they can also influence the remaining in-line tenant mix of the center. Keeping up-to-date with certain trends is important to secure a solid and functional shopping center, which increases revenue and provides a pleasant addition to the areas in which they reside.

Glossary

abatement: The removal of hazardous materials such as asbestos and mold by a licensed contractor. (Compare *containment.*)

absorption rate: The amount of space of a particular property type that becomes leased compared to the amount of that same type of space available for lease within a certain geographic area during a given period.

abstracting: The process of extracting and condensing the most important terms and financial clauses of the lease into a form that is more easily accessible and understandable.

accelerated cost recovery: Type of depreciation in which the government allows a larger deduction during the early years of the depreciation period. (See also *depreciation.*)

Accredited Commercial Manager (ACoM): A designation conferred by the Institute of Real Estate Management on onsite managers of commercial buildings.

Accredited Management Organization® (AMO®): A designation conferred by the Institute of Real Estate Management on real estate management firms that are under the direction of a Certified Property Manager® and meet and comply with stipulated standards as to accounting procedures, performance, and protection of funds entrusted to them.

Accredited Residential Manager® (ARM®): A professional service award conferred by the Institute of Real Estate Management on individuals who meet specific standards of experience, ethics, and education.

accrual-basis accounting: The method of accounting that involves entering amounts of income when they are earned and amounts of expense when they are incurred—even though the cash may not be received or paid. (Compare *cash-basis accounting.*)

active shooter: An individual actively engaged in killing or attempting to kill people in a confined and populated area; most use firearms; there is no pattern or method to their actions or selection of victims.

actual cash value (ACV): Insurance that pays a claim based on the purchase price of the item, usually allowing for depreciation because of age and use. (Compare *replacement cost coverage.*)

adaptive use: The recycling of existing structures through a change of use.

add-on factor: An amount added to the base rent to account for the proration of the common areas among individual commercial tenants. Also called *load factor.* (See also *base rent.*)

adjustable-rate mortgage (ARM): A type of variable-rate mortgage (loan) for which the interest rate can be adjusted (raised or lowered) at specific intervals (e.g., semiannually or annually). The adjustment is based on a predetermined index or formula, such as the prime rate plus two percent. (Compare *variable-rate mortgage.*)

ad valorem tax: A tax levied on the basis of the value of the object taxed. Most often refers to taxes levied by municipalities and counties against real property and personal property.

affidavit of service: A sworn statement completed by a process server that a notice (e.g., eviction) has been properly served.

Affordable Care Act: See *Patient Protection and Affordable Care Act.*

Age Discrimination in Employment Act (ADEA): The federal law that prohibits discrimination against older workers.

agent: A person who enters a legal, fiduciary, and confidential arrangement with a second party and is authorized to act on behalf of that party.

aging in place: The behavior of persons of retirement age who remain in their present residences, whether they own or rent.

air rights: Right to control, occupy, or use the vertical space (air space) above a property, subject to necessary and reasonable use by neighbor(s) and others (such as aircraft). Air rights can be bought, leased, sold, and transferred.

American Society of Heating, Refrigerating, and Air-Conditioning Engineers (ASHRAE): Professional association that provides information on refrigerant chemicals and equipment modifications and costs.

Americans with Disabilities Act (ADA): A federal law passed in 1990 that prohibits discrimination in employment on the basis of physical or mental disability and requires places of public accommodation and commercial facilities to be designed, constructed, and altered in compliance with specified accessibility standards. The accessibility requirements may also apply to common areas of residential properties (e.g., rental offices).

amortization: Gradual reduction of a debt, usually through installment payments.

analysis of alternatives: An investigation of the range of possible changes and evaluation of their anticipated effects on a property that is undertaken in the effort to improve the property's performance.

anchor tenant: A major shopping center tenant that draws the majority of customers.

ancillary tenant: A shopping center tenant that occupies a smaller space and a location that is secondary in relation to the anchor tenant.

annual budget: The most common form of operating budget. Projects the entire year's income and expenses for each account. There are two types: a *historical budget* based on a review of income and expenses from previous years; a *zero-based budget* that consists solely of projections and ignores past operating expenses. (See also *operating budget.*)

appraisal: An opinion or estimate of the value of a property. An estimate of value that is (usually) prepared by a certified or accredited appraiser. Four methods of appraisal are common—the *cost approach,* based on the estimated value of the land plus the estimated cost of replacing the improvements on it less depreciation; the *market approach* (also called *sales approach*), based on a comparison to similar properties in the market that have been sold recently; the *income capitalization approach,* based on the net operating income of the property; and the *discounted cash flow method,* which discounts all future fiscal benefits of an investment property over a predetermined holding period. All four are used to estimate value if sufficient information is gathered in each approach to do so.

appreciation: The increase in the value of an asset over time.

articles of incorporation: A document that states that a condominium association is a corporation under the laws of the state.

artificial breakpoint: See *breakpoint.*

asbestos: A fibrous mineral formerly used in buildings for flooring, insulation, and fireproofing later determined to be a health hazard.

as-built drawing: Representation of a property that indicates the presence and location of certain utilities for future use.

assessment: An amount paid by each owner or tenant of a property to fund its operation; also used in referring to local (municipal) taxes.

asset management: A specialized field of real estate management that involves the supervision of an owner's real estate assets at the investment level. In addition to real estate management responsibilities that include maximizing net operating income and property value, an asset manager may recommend, be responsible for, or participate in property acquisition, development, and divestiture. An asset manager may have only superficial involvement with day-to-day operations at the site (e.g., supervision of personnel, property maintenance, tenant relations).

asset manager: A position in real estate management that focuses on the property—residential or commercial—as a financial asset. (See also *asset management.*)

assignment: The transfer of one person's interest or right in a property (e.g., a lease) to another; the document by which such an interest or right is transferred.

assisted living facilities: Housing intended for seniors who need assistance with most (or all) daily living tasks—because of age or frailty but not because of illness.

at will employment: Employment in which either the employee or the employer may terminate the relationship at any time for any reason (with or without cause). Important exceptions are antidiscrimination (protected classes) statutes, anti-retaliation (whistleblower) statutes, and specific contractual arrangements, including collective bargaining agreements.

balloon mortgage: A loan with a constant monthly rate of repayment and a much larger (balloon) payment at the end of the term to fully amortize the loan.

bankruptcy: A state of financial insolvency (liabilities exceed assets) of an individual or organization; the inability to pay debts.

Bankruptcy Abuse Prevention and Consumer Protection Act: The 2005 federal legislation that changed many provisions of the previous bankruptcy laws; requires all debtors to get credit counseling before they can file a bankruptcy case—and additional counseling on budgeting and debt management before their debts can be wiped out.

base rent: The minimum rent as set forth in a (usually commercial) lease; also called *minimum rent.*

base year: In an office lease, the stated year that is to be used as a standard in determining rent escalations. During the next year, operating costs are compared with the base year, and the difference (higher or lower) determines the tenant's rent adjustment.

Basic Allowance for Housing (BAH): A stipend military personnel receive for housing.

Better Buildings Initiative: An incentives-based federal program to provide more generous tax credits and more incentives for owners who undertake costly retrofits on existing properties.

blanket policy: Insurance coverage that insures several properties under one policy. May offer more favorable premiums than individual policies.

board of directors: The elected governing body of any corporation, including condominium and other homeowners' associations. (See also *corporation.*)

bodily injury insurance: Type of coverage that protects against liability for damages arising out of injury or death occurring on a property.

boiler insurance: Type of coverage that pays for any damage resulting from a boiler malfunction.

BOMA Standard Method: See *Building Owners and Managers Association International.*

breakpoint: In retail leases, the point at which the tenant's percentage rent is equal to the base rent and beyond which the tenant will begin to pay overages; also called *natural breakpoint.* Sometimes a tenant and owner will negotiate an *artificial breakpoint* that requires the tenant to begin paying percentage rent before or after the natural breakpoint is reached.

broker: A licensed individual who provides owners with the knowledge and expertise needed to buy and sell real estate assets as an investment—acquisition and disposition.

budget: An estimation of income and expenses over a specific period for a particular property, project, or institution. (See also *capital budget* and *operating budget.*)

budget variance report: A report produced by most accounting software that compares the operating expenses paid during the month with the amounts budgeted for that month; reflects which expense categories have variances during the month and year (or year-to-date) and can reveal deficiencies in operations.

building engineer: The position in real estate management that manages systems such as HVAC, boilers, elevators, communications, electrical systems, and even green building technologies; must have a wide range of knowledge and expertise in all building systems.

Building Owners and Managers Association International (BOMA): A trade association that serves the commercial real estate building industry and provides operational statistics for office buildings. The *BOMA Standard Method* computes a tenant's rentable area by multiplying the tenant's usable area by an *R/U ratio,* which is the rentable area of a floor divided by the usable area of that same floor. A pro rata share of the building's common areas is then added to the basic rentable area to arrive at the tenant's total rentable square feet.

building standard: A uniform specification that defines the quantity and quality of construction and finish elements a building owner will provide for build-out of space leased to commercial tenants. (See also *tenant improvement allowance.*)

build out: In retail leasing, to construct the tenant's space.

build-to-suit: An arrangement in which a landowner constructs (or pays for constructing) a custom building on the land, and both land and building are leased to the tenant; a frequent arrangement in shopping centers (e.g., for *pad* or *outlot* spaces) and industrial properties.

business cycle: Four successive stages (recession, depression, recovery, and prosperity) that businesses experience during periods of inflation and deflation of an economy.

bylaws: Regulations that provide specific procedures for handling routine matters in an organization—e.g., a homeowners' association.

call center-based management: Management approach in which a regional call center equipped with the latest technology allows the management of projects/properties from anywhere an Internet connection is available.

cap: An upper limit on the amount of change allowed in a year and over the term of the loan in a variable-rate mortgage.

capital budget: An estimate of costs of major improvements or replacements; generally a long-range plan for improvements to a property.

capital improvement: A structural addition or betterment to real property that increases its useful life; the use of capital for a betterment that did not exist before.

capitalization: The process employed to estimate the value of a property by the use of a proper investment rate of return and the annual net operating income produced by the property, the formula being expressed as follows:

Net Operating Income ÷ Rate = Value (I/R = V)

capitalization rate (cap rate): A rate of return used to estimate a property's value based on that property's net operating income. This rate is based on the rates of return prevalent in the marketplace for similar properties and is intended to reflect the investment risk associated with a particular property.

cash-basis accounting: The method of accounting that recognizes income and expenses when money is actually received or paid. (Compare *accrual-basis accounting.*)

cash disbursements report: A chronological record of payments for operating expenses that lists the vendor, the amount, and the check number for all payments and includes items that are not operating expenses (debt service, payment for capital expenditures); also called *check register* or *check voucher*.

cash flow: The amount of cash available after all payments have been made for operating expenses, debt service (mortgage principal and interest), and capital reserve funds; also called *pretax cash flow* to indicate that income taxes have not been deducted.

cash-on-cash return: See *return on investment*.

C corporation: See *corporation*.

central business district (CBD): The concentration of high-rise buildings within a community.

CERTIFIED PROPERTY MANAGER® (CPM®): The professional designation conferred by the Institute of Real Estate Management on individuals who distinguish themselves in the areas of education, experience, and ethics in property management.

chart of accounts: A classification or arrangement of account items.

chlorofluorocarbon (CFC): Refrigerant chemical that contains two types of halogens—chlorine (Cl) and fluorine (F). It is being phased out and replaced with similar compounds that do not include chlorine.

Civil Rights Act (Title VII): Prohibits discrimination in employment—hiring, compensation, promotion, termination; enforced by the U.S. *Equal Employment Opportunity Commission* (*EEOC*).

client trust account: See *operating account*.

closing ratio: The number of prospects who became residents or tenants due to the efforts of a leasing agent. (See also *leasing agent*.)

cogeneration plant: One of the most common forms of energy recycling; uses a heat engine or a power station to simultaneously generate both electricity and useful heat; also called a *combined heat and power (CHP)plant.*

cold calling: Telephoning or personally calling on commercial prospects with whom the leasing agent has had no previous contact in order to interest them in leasing space.

collateral: Property pledged as security for a loan or debt.

combined heat and power (CHP) plant: See *cogeneration plant.*

commercial property: All real estate development that is not exclusively residential.

commingle: To mix or combine; to combine the money of more than one person or entity into a common fund. A prohibited practice in real estate.

common area: Area of a property that is used by all tenants or owners. In a condominium, the areas of the property in which the unit owners have a shared interest (e.g., lobbies, laundry rooms). In an enclosed mall, the mall corridors, parking lots, escalators, landscaped areas, and other parts of the property that the tenants use in common.

common area maintenance (CAM) clause: Lease clause that specifies exactly what constitutes the common area of the shopping center, what expenses the tenant will pay, and what rights and responsibilities the property owner has. (See also *common area.*)

common interest development (CID): See *common interest realty association.*

common interest realty association (CIRA): Real estate that is operated for the mutual benefit of the owners; condominiums, cooperatives, gated communities, and planned unit developments; (PUDs) are examples; also called *common interest development (CID).*

community shopping center: A shopping center usually anchored by a junior or discount department store, supermarket, or large hardware store. The 25 to 40 ancillary tenants may include men's and women's apparel stores, bookstores, card shops, family shoe stores, and fast food operations. Community shopping centers range in size from 150,000 to 400,000 square feet of GLA and usually require a population of 100,000 to 150,000 to sustain them.

comparison grid: A form for price analysis in which the features of a subject property are compared to similar features in comparable properties in the same market. The price (or rent) for each comparable property helps to determine an appropriate market price (or rent) for the subject.

concession: An economic incentive granted by an owner to encourage the leasing of space or the renewal of a lease.

condominium: A multiple-unit structure in which the units and pro rata shares of the common areas are owned individually; a unit in a condominium property.

condominium association: A nonprofit corporation comprised of the unit owners of a condominium that governs its operation. Also called *homeowners' association.*

congregate housing: For those who want to remain independent but require some assistance with daily tasks, these arrangements include meals, transportation, and some housekeeping services.

Consolidated Omnibus Budget Reconciliation Act (COBRA): Federal law that requires employers to offer employees an opportunity to continue their group health care coverage for a time by paying the premiums themselves when they are terminated or leave their jobs.

construction manager: Position in real estate management that provides expertise when an owner or tenant makes improvements to a property.

Consumer Price Index (CPI): A way of measuring consumer purchasing power by comparing the current costs of goods and services to those of a selected base year; sometimes used as a reference point for rent escalations in commercial leases (i.e., as a measure of inflation). (Compare *Producer Price Index*.)

containment: The process by which a licensed contractor works to maintain a hazardous material such as asbestos safely in place. (Compare *abatement*.)

Continuing Care Retirement Community (CCRC): A type of senior community in which residents typically pay a substantial entry fee—usually a six-figure amount—which establishes an ownership interest in a community with available nursing services. In addition to the entry fee, a monthly service fee (in essence, rent) is paid by the resident for services rendered by the community; also called *buy-in communities*.

continuous occupancy clause: Retail lease clause in which the tenant agrees to stay in business for the full term of the lease.

continuous operation clause: Retail lease clause in which the tenant agrees to keep its business operating smoothly and consistently for the full term of the lease.

contract for labor as needed: A work agreement in which money paid is for specific work done and actual hours worked.

convenience shopping center: Shopping center type that usually has a convenience market or a combination gas station and food store anchor and 2 to 10 stores. Most are open all day and all night. Other tenants may be card- or coin-operated laundries, barbershops, dry cleaners, or liquor stores. Usually has 5,000 to 30,000 square feet of GLA. Typical trade area comprises the immediate neighborhood of the site and the traffic on the street. A convenience center can succeed in an area with a population of 1,000 to 2,500. Also called *strip shopping center*.

conversion ratio: The number of prospects who visit a rental property compared to the number who sign a lease.

cooperative: Ownership of a share or shares of stock in a corporation that holds the title to a multiple-unit residential structure. Shareholders do not own their units outright but have the right to occupy them as co-owners of the cooperative association under *proprietary leases.*

corporation: A legal entity that is chartered by a state and is treated by courts as an individual entity separate and distinct from the persons who own it. The federal government classifies most corporations *C corporations.* The entity pays income tax and has no restrictions on the number of shareholders it can have or the types of stock it can issue. An *S corporation* combines the ownership features of a corporation with those of a partnership. It does not pay federal income tax; profits (and losses) pass directly to the shareholders.

corrective maintenance: Ordinary repairs that must be made to a building and its equipment on a day-to-day basis. (Compare *deferred maintenance* and *preventive maintenance.*)

cosmetic maintenance: A type of preventive maintenance that enhances the property's aesthetic value; aids in the future development of the property by maintaining an up-to-date appearance.

cost approach: See *appraisal.*

cost-benefit analysis: A method of measuring the benefits expected from a decision (e.g., a change in operating procedures) by calculating the cost of the change and determining whether the benefits justify the costs.

cost recovery: See *depreciation.*

covenants, conditions, and restrictions (CC&Rs): Documents that affect the management and maintenance of the center as a whole in open-air shopping centers in which parcels of land are owned by different entities.

curb appeal: General cleanliness, neatness, and attractiveness of a building as exemplified by the appearance of the exterior and grounds and the general level of housekeeping.

custodial maintenance: The day-to-day cleaning and other work that is essential to preserving the value of a property; also called *janitorial maintenance* or *housekeeping.*

debt service: Regular payments of the principal and interest on a loan.

declaration: A legal document that creates a condominium. The document describes the property, defines the method of determining each unit owner's share of the common elements, and outlines the responsibilities of the owners and the association.(See also *condominium association.*)

deductible: In insurance, a specified amount the insured party must pay before the insurer pays on a claim.

deed of trust: Instrument some states use in place of a mortgage. The deed pledges the property as collateral—the buyer holds title to the property as a warranty deed, and the financial institution and the buyer execute a note as evidence of the debt. A mortgage requires a court order for foreclosure, but a deed of trust does not. (Compare *mortgage.*)

default: Failure to fulfill an obligation; the nonperformance of a duty.

deferred maintenance: Ordinary maintenance of a building that, because it has not been performed, negatively affects the use, occupancy, and value of the property. (Compare *corrective maintenance* and *preventive maintenance.*)

deflation: An economic condition that occurs when the money supply declines in relation to the amount of goods available, resulting in lower prices. (Compare *inflation.*)

demand: The availability of purchasers for a given amount of goods or services.

demised premises: That portion of a property covered by a lease agreement; usually defined by the walls and other structures that separate one tenant's space from that of another.

demising wall: The partition that separates one tenant's space from another—the interior of the corridor wall, and the interior of the exterior wall.

demographic profile: A compilation of social and economic statistics (including population density, age, education, occupation, and income) for a specific population, usually within a geographic area (as a neighborhood or region). (Compare *psychographic profile.*)

density: The number of apartments in relation to the land area; Number of apartments ÷ Land size = Density.

Department of Housing and Urban Development (HUD): A department of the U.S. government that supervises the Federal Housing Administration (FHA) and other agencies that administer housing programs.

depreciation: Loss of value due to all causes, including physical deterioration (ordinary wear and tear), structural defects, and changing economic and market conditions (see also *obsolescence*). The tax deduction that allocates the cost of an asset over its useful life; also called *cost recovery.*

depression: Part of the business cycle, a period of low economic activity characterized by high unemployment, low levels of investment, falling prices (including rents), reduced purchasing power, decreasing use of resources, and currency deflation.

disability: A physical or mental impairment that substantially limits one or more major life activities, a record of such impairment, or being regarded as having such an impairment.

discounted cash flow method: See *appraisal.*

discretionary income: Money available for spending after physical needs (food, clothing, shelter) have been met and taxes have been paid.

disposable income: The amount that is left over after personal income taxes have been subtracted from personal income. The amount of money that consumers actually have available to spend or save.

Drug-Free Workplace Act: The federal law that requires employers who contract with the U.S. government to certify that they maintain a drug-free workplace and have a published statement notifying employees that drug activity is prohibited in their workplace and specifying the actions that will be taken against those who violate the prohibition. Employees must abide by the terms of the employer's drug-free workplace policy as a condition of their employment.

due diligence service: A legal rule that prevents someone from stating a position inconsistent with one previously stated, especially when the earlier representation has been relied upon by others.

Economic Growth and Tax Relief Act of 2001: The federal law that lowered individual tax rates. (See also *Jobs and Growth Tax Relief Act of 2003.*)

economic obsolescence: See *obsolescence.*

economic shift: Fluctuation in real estate sales prices and rental rates. (Compare *population shift.*)

economic vacancy: The percentage of rental units that are not producing income. Includes unoccupied units, leased space that is not yet producing income, delinquencies, and leasable space that is used for other purposes or is otherwise unleasable.

economics: The science that deals with the production, distribution, exchange, and consumption of goods and services.

effective gross income: The total amount of income actually collected during a reporting period; the gross receipts of a property. Gross potential rental income *less* vacancy and collection losses *plus* miscellaneous or unscheduled income.

effective rent: The cumulative rental amount collected over the term of a lease expressed as an average monthly rental (residential) or an annual rate per rentable square foot (office, retail, industrial).

eminent domain: The right of a governmental body to acquire private property for public use through a court action called condemnation. The court also determines the compensation to be paid to the owner.

employee onboarding: A comprehensive approach to bringing in new hires that goes beyond simple orientation; intended to make new employees familiar with the overall goals of a management company or specific property and support them as they embark on early projects in an effort to achieve success.

Employee Polygraph Protection Act (EPPA): The federal law that prohibits the use of lie detector tests in most business situations; in the event of an economic loss, it allows the use of polygraph tests, subject to notification and other restrictions.

Employee Retirement Income Security Act (ERISA): The federal law that safeguards employees' rights to benefits under a company's pension.

employment at will: See *at will employment.*

Employment Eligibility Verification form (form I-9): Federal form that verifies the employee's identity and right to work in the United States. Employees can present a number of documents to verify their identity and right to work. Employers should retain I-9 forms in the employee's personnel file for at least three years.

employment practices liability insurance (EPL): A type of coverage that protects businesses from the financial consequences associated with a variety of employment-related lawsuits such as charges of racial or age discrimination, sexual harassment, wrongful termination, or noncompliance with the Americans with Disabilities Act; also helps protect businesses against legal dismissals that flare up between employees and third parties, such as vendors or customers.

endorsement: An attachment to an insurance policy that provides or excludes a specific coverage for a specific portion or element of a property; also called a *rider.*

ENERGY STAR: A joint program of the U.S. Environmental Protection Agency (EPA) and the U.S. Dept of Energy (DOE) that can help improve a building's energy performance. (Compare *U.S. Green Building Council.*)

Enterprise Income Verification (EIV) system: A federal database that provides the information needed to verify a resident's income—federal wages, quarterly unemployment compensation, monthly social security, and supplemental security income benefits.

entertainment shopping center: Shopping center type that typically consists of entertainment, dining, and other retail stores. Most have a GLA in the range of 150,000 square feet up to 300,000 square feet, but some are much larger. The trade area varies, depending on the location of any other similar center or competition.

Environmental Protection Agency (EPA): The agency of the U.S. government established to enforce laws that preserve and protect the environment.

Equal Employment Opportunity Commission (EEOC): A U.S. governmental body created under Title VII of the Civil Rights Act of 1964 to end discrimination in the workplace.

equity: The interest or value that an owner has in real estate over and above the mortgage against it.

errors and omissions insurance: See *professional liability insurance.*

escalation clause: In a lease, a provision for increases in rent based on increases in operating costs, sometimes based on a standard index such as the Consumer Price Index (CPI) to account for inflation.

estoppel certificate: A document signed by a tenant stating that certain facts about the tenant's lease are true; the certificate is for the benefit of the property owner and is usually directed to a lender or a new purchaser of the property.

eviction: A legal process to reclaim real estate, usually from a resident's or a commercial tenant's failure to perform under the lease (*for cause*). The two types of causes are monetary (nonpayment of rent) and nonmonetary (breach of a lease covenant).

eviction notice: A written notice to a tenant to cure a breach of the lease immediately or vacate the premises within a specified period.

exclusive use clause: In a retail lease, clause that prohibits other tenants in a shopping center from selling a similar product in order to minimize competition.

Executive Order 13224: See *U.S.A. Patriot Act.*

executive property manager: A real estate management position often held by an officer of a management firm or its owner; responsible for overseeing management, ensuring profitability, and acquiring new business.

executive summary: A section at the beginning of a management plan that highlights the information presented in the report.

exempt status: See *Fair Labor Standards Act.*

expense cap: See *expense stop.*

expense stop: In an office lease, a clause obligating the property owner to pay operating costs up to a certain amount per square foot per year; tenants pay their pro rata share of any costs in excess of that amount. When used in a retail lease, a clause obligating the tenants to pay a pro rata share of operating expenses up to a certain amount (*expense cap, cap*) per year; the owner pays any costs in excess of that amount. An expense stop in an office lease sets a ceiling on how much the property owner pays; a cap in a retail lease defines a limit on how much the tenant pays.

extended coverage (EC): An endorsement to a standard fire insurance policy that adds coverage against financial loss from certain other specified hazards.

facility manager: A type of real estate manager who, when employed directly by a corporation that owns real estate incidental to its primary business, may be responsible for acquisition and disposition in addition to physical upkeep of the property, record keeping, and reporting on its management, although a corporate asset manager is likely to handle acquisition and disposition. More broadly, the responsibilities involve coordinating the physical workplace with the people and purpose of the organization.

Fair Credit Reporting Act (FCRA): A federal law that gives people the right to see and correct their credit records at credit reporting bureaus. It also requires real estate managers to inform rental applicants if a credit bureau is contracted to investigate their credit (and to obtain the applicant's written authorization to do so), advise them in writing if a lease is denied because of a poor credit report, and identify the source of credit information that resulted in their being denied a lease.

Fair Debt Collection Practices Act (FDCPA): A federal law that created a series of guidelines for debt collectors to follow. Designed to prevent collection agencies from harassing debtors, the law was later expanded to include any organization that collects consumer debt (including real estate managers). The law is governed and regulated by the Federal Trade Commission (FTC).

fair housing law: Any law that prohibits discrimination against people seeking housing. There are federal, state, and local fair housing laws. Specifically, Title VIII of the U.S. Civil Rights Act of 1968 prohibits discrimination in the sale or rental of housing based on race, color, religion, or national origin. It was amended in 1974 to include sex as a protected class; the Fair Housing

Amendments Act of 1988 further prohibits discrimination on the basis of familial status (children) or mental or physical disability.

Fair Labor Standards Act (FLSA): The federal law that regulates hourly workers' wage rates and the number of hours worked and requires overtime compensation for time worked in excess of 40 hours per week. Employers must pay workers for all hours worked, including work performed at home and travel as part of the job. Employees (usually salaried) who do not have to be paid for overtime work are considered to have *exempt status*. Under new rules put into effect in July of 2009, the U.S. Department of Labor (DOL) issued specific guidelines for determining exempt status, including salary level. In addition to hourly workers, real estate managers working in the corporate setting whose annual salary is less than $47,476 must be paid overtime when they work more than 40 hours in a workweek—in the past, the hours per day or per week maximum did not affect exempt employees. The new rules also spell out the duties that define the roles of exempt employees. This act is frequently referred to as the federal *Wage and Hour Law.*

familial status: The presence in a household of children under age 18 living with parents or guardians, pregnant women, or people seeking custody of children under age 18.

Family and Medical Leave Act (FMLA): The federal law that requires employers to grant eligible employees up to 12 weeks of unpaid job-protected leave in the event of a serious health condition or to care for a family member. To be required to participate, the firm must have at least 50 employees within 75 miles.

Federal Housing Administration (FHA): An agency that is part of the U.S. Department of Housing and Urban Development (HUD). It administers a variety of housing loan programs.

Federal Insurance Contributions Act (FICA): The federal law that requires employer and employee to contribute funds equally based on the employee's income to the Social Security fund and Medicare.

Federal Unemployment Tax Act (FUTA): The federal law that requires employers to contribute funds to compensate employees who are laid off or terminated. The employer alone makes the contributions, and the amount or rate is based on the number of employees and the number of claims made.

Federal Wage and Hour Law: See *Fair Labor Standards Act.*

fidelity bond: A *surety* issued by a third party (usually an insurance company) that protects one individual against financial loss that might result from dishonest acts of another specific individual.

fiduciary: One charged with a relationship of trust and confidence, as between a principal and an agent, trustee and beneficiary, or attorney and client, when one party is legally empowered to act on behalf of another.

financing: The availability, amount, and terms under which money may be borrowed to assist in the purchase of real property, using the property itself as the security (*collateral*) for such borrowing.

fire insurance: Coverage on property against all direct loss or damage by fire.

fixed-rate mortgage: A loan for real property in which the interest rate is constant over the term of the loan.

flex space: Single-story commercial structure that can be configured to accommodate a single tenant or multiple tenants or to have varying proportions of office and warehouse or manufacturing space according to tenants' needs.

floor plate: Rentable floor size.

for cause: See *eviction.*

foreclosure: A court action initiated by the mortgagor, or a lienor, for the purpose of having the court order the debtor's real estate sold to pay the mortgage or lien.

formaldehyde gas: A foaming agent once used in foam insulation and still present in adhesives used in making pressed-wood products. Its presence in a building can be harmful.

form I-9: *See Employment Eligibility Verification form.*

fractional ownership: A type of property ownership similar to a timeshare, but it divides a property into more affordable segments for individuals and also matches an individual's ownership time to their actual usage time. Unlike timeshares, fractional ownership often allows a longer time on the property and a greater chance of property appreciation, while offering the same rights as any other real estate purchase. Although the cost of a fractional property is quite a bit higher than that of a typical timeshare, it is still less expensive than whole ownership of a luxury home in the same location. Also called *private residence club.* (Compare *timeshare.*)

frequency: The number of times an ad appears in a marketing medium.

friability: The ease with which a material such as asbestos crumbles.

fully amortized loan: A loan characterized by periodic payments that include a portion applied to interest and a portion applied to principal.

functional obsolescence: See *obsolescence.*

garden apartment building: A low-rise building designed for multifamily living, usually located in a suburban area.

general partnership: The business activity of two or more persons who agree to pool capital, talents, and other assets according to some agreed formula, and similarly to divide profits and losses, and to commit the partnership to certain obligations. General partners assume unlimited liability. (Compare *limited liability limited partnership* and *limited partnership.*)

government-assisted housing: Any residential rental property in which the property owner receives part of the rent payment from a governmental body. As a rule, governmental housing subsidies are either resident based or property based. Also called *subsidized housing.* (Compare *public housing.*)

Gramm-Leach-Bliley Act (GLBA): Federal law under which property owners fall within the definition of "financial institutions" because they collect personal and financial information from prospective tenants; requires property owners and managers to safeguard personal and financial information collected from prospective tenants and to dispose of it properly to protect against misuse and identity theft.

graphic rating scale: An employee rating system in which the manager checks the appropriate place on a scale for each task listed; typical scale has a five-point rating: 1 is significantly below standard, 3 is standard, and 5 indicates performance significantly above standard.

Great Recession: A severe global economic problem that began in the United States in December 2007, affecting the entire world economy, and is often characterized by various systemic imbalances and was sparked by a liquidity shortfall in the United States banking system. The Great Recession has resulted in the collapse of large financial institutions, the bailout of banks by national governments, and downturns in stock markets around the world.

great room: A living space that combines the living room, dining room, and kitchen.

green movement: Eco-friendly, consumer-driven movement that has affected property management and development through its efforts to minimize urban sprawl and achieve reductions in the carbon footprint.

gross area: The entire floor area of a building measured to the outside finished surface of its permanent walls. (Compare *office usable area, rentable area.*)

gross domestic product (GDP): Measure of productivity used in the United States since 1991. It indicates the market value of all final goods (tangible objects such as canned food and automobiles) and services (intangible objects such as entertainment activities and transportation) produced *only within the United States* in one year's time. (Nearly all other countries measure productivity as GDP, so use of GDP facilitates comparisons of U.S. economic activity with that of other countries.) (Compare *gross national product.*)

gross floor area: In an enclosed shopping mall, the mall's GLA plus the common areas—courtyards, escalators, sidewalks, parking areas, etc.—that are not used exclusively by individual tenants. (Compare *gross leasable area.*)

gross leasable area (GLA): The total square feet of floor space in all store areas of a shopping center, excluding common area space; the size of a retail tenant's area of exclusive use in a shopping center, usually expressed in square feet. (Compare *gross floor area.*)

gross lease: A lease under the terms of which the property owner pays all operating expenses of the property and the tenant pays a fixed rent. (Compare *net lease, percentage lease.*)

gross national product (GNP): The market value of all final goods (tangible objects such as canned food and automobiles) and services (intangible objects such as entertainment activities and transportation) produced by an economy in one year's time. It measures output attributable to U.S. residents *regardless of their geographic location.* (Compare *gross domestic product.*)

gross potential rental income: The sum of the rental rates of all spaces available to be rented in a property, regardless of occupancy; the maximum amount of rent a property can produce.

habitability: A state of being fit for occupancy (e.g., sanitary, safe, in compliance with applicable codes).

heating, ventilation, and air-conditioning (HVAC) system:
The combination of equipment and ductwork for producing,
regulating, and distributing heat, refrigeration, and fresh air
throughout a building.

highest and best use: The use of real property that will produce
the highest property value and develop a site to its fullest
economic potential.

high-rise apartment building: A multiple-unit dwelling that has
10 or more stories.

historical budget: See *annual budget.*

homeowners' association: See *condominium association.*

home purchase clause: Residential lease clause that allows the
resident to break the lease in the event a purchase transaction is
closed before the lease term ends.

hoteling: A company's practice of setting aside one or more
spaces for staff members who only need to work in the office
periodically rather than maintaining office space for a particular
employee.

housekeeping: See *custodial maintenance.*

Housing and Community Development Act: The 1974 federal
law that authorized the Housing Assistance Payments Program
commonly referred to as the *Section 8 Housing Choice Voucher
Program.* The program provides rental assistance nationwide
to low-income families and elderly and disabled individuals.
Public housing agencies (*PHAs*), which receive funds from the
U.S. Department of Housing and Urban Development, locally
administer housing choice vouchers.

Housing and Economic Recovery Act of 2008: Legislation that
established a tax credit for first-time homebuyers. The *American
Recovery and Reinvestment Act of 2009* expanded the first-time
homebuyer credit by increasing the credit amount for purchases
made in 2009 before December 1, and the *Worker, Homeownership
and Business Assistance Act of 2009* extended that deadline even
further.

illiquid asset: An investment that cannot readily be converted into cash. (Compare *liquid asset.*)

Immigration Reform and Control Act (IRCA): The federal law that requires the employer to verify an *only within the United States* employee's identity and eligibility to work in the United States. Employees must complete Immigration and Nationalization Service (INS) form I-9.

income capitalization approach: See *appraisal* and *capitalization.*

income and expense statement: See *statement of operations.*

individual tax identification number (ITIN): Identification number the Internal Revenue Service issues to a noncitizen who needs to report income for tax purposes but is not eligible for a Social Security number.

indoor air quality (IAQ): An environmental concern specifically related to the work environment. Problems can arise in any type of building, but office buildings are the most susceptible. That is partially because their centralized HVAC systems serve such a large space and partially because they are built new or retrofitted as entirely enclosed systems (the windows cannot be opened), which results in poor air circulation.

inflation: An economic condition occurring when the money supply increases in relation to the amount of goods available, resulting in substantial and continuing increases in prices. (Compare *deflation.*)

initial investment base: The purchase price of a property; some owners include the cost of initial improvements to make the property operational (rehabilitation) or to enhance its ability to generate income—installation of new appliances to upgrade apartments and achieve higher rental rates.

initial investment basis: The difference between the loan amount and the purchase price of a property (i.e., the owner's initial equity).

Institute of Real Estate Management (IREM®): A professional association of men and women who meet established standards of experience, education, and ethics with the objective of continually improving their respective managerial skills by mutual education and exchange of ideas and experience. The Institute is an affiliate of the National Association of Realtors®. (See also Certified Property Manager®.)

institutional owner: A financial institution (bank, trust company, mortgage bank, investment house) or other source of investment capital (insurance companies, pension funds) that invests in real estate.

insurance: An agreement by one party (the insurer, carrier, insurance company) to assume part or all of a financial loss in the event of a specified contingency or peril (e.g., liability, property damage) in consideration of a premium payment by a second party (the insured).

International Council of Shopping Centers (ICSC): The worldwide trade association of the shopping center industry, dedicated to advancing the development of the industry.

inventory control system: A method that provides for each item to be recorded as it is removed from inventory and for the remaining inventory count (item total) to be reduced.

janitorial maintenance: See *custodial maintenance.*

Jobs and Growth Tax Relief Act of 2003: The federal law that lowered individual tax rates, including reducing the long-term capital gains tax rate from 20 percent to 15 percent. (Those capital gains rate cuts were to be effective for the tax years ending on or after May 6, 2003, through December 31, 2008.)

joint and several liability: A situation in which all the participants in a legal agreement are individually responsible for performing the obligations of the agreement and one or more or all of them can be sued for a breach of the agreement. In real estate management, when a lease is signed by unrelated adults who agree that they are all individually, and as a group, responsible for rent payments and other duties of the tenant.

joint tenancy: Ownership by two or more persons specifically designated as joint tenants, with the right of survivorship—upon the death of one joint tenant, ownership is passed to the other joint tenant(s). (Compare *tenancy in common.*)

joint venture: An association of two or more persons or businesses to carry out a single business enterprise for profit.

just-in-time delivery: A system manufacturers use to allow them to maintain minimum stocks of raw materials, parts, and packaging by using computer inventory systems coupled with overnight shipping services to supply the materials they need to keep pace with their production levels.

landlord: One who owns real property that is leased to a tenant; a property owner. (See also *lessor.*)

landlord-tenant law: Laws enacted by various jurisdictions that regulate the relationship between property owner and tenant.

lead-based paint: Type of paint used in housing built prior to 1980 that poses a serious lead-poisoning hazard to resident children. (Its use in the United States was outlawed in 1978.)

Leadership in Energy and Environmental Design (LEED) Certification: An internationally recognized green building certification system; provides building owners and real estate managers the understanding needed to implement practical, environmentally friendly building design, construction, operations, and maintenance solutions.

leaking underground storage tank (LUST): Many older buildings used to maintain their own fuel supply for their boilers, usually in storage tanks on the premises. The threat of contamination of groundwater has led to regulations requiring inspection and replacement of tanks that are still in use. Those no longer in use may have to be removed.

lease: A contract, written or oral, for the possession of part or all of a property for a stipulated period of time in consideration of the payment of rent or other compensation by the tenant. Leases for more than one year generally must be in writing to be enforceable. A residential lease is sometimes called an *occupancy agreement.*

lease abstract: See *abstracting.*

leasing agent: A person who is directly responsible for renting space in assigned properties; also called *leasing broker.*

LEED Certification. (See *Leadership in Energy and Environmental Design Certification.*)

lessee: The tenant in a lease.

lessor: The property owner in a lease.

liability insurance: Insurance protection against claims arising out of injury or death of people or physical or financial damage to property.

lien: The legal right of a creditor to have their debt paid out of the property of the debtor.

lifestyle shopping center: A shopping center type that has anchor tenants such as Ann Taylor, Barnes and Noble, and Pottery Barn. These shopping centers have few small shops because they lack the traditional anchor tenants. The trade area may vary greatly from one center to another, depending on the local competition. They generally have 250,000 to 500,000 square feet of GLA.

limited liability company (LLC): Created by state statute, a business ownership form that functions like a corporation— its members are protected from liability— but for income tax purposes is classified as a partnership. Income and expenses flow through to the individual members. The arrangement offers considerable flexibility in its organization and structure.

limited liability limited partnership (LLLP): A form of limited partnership that limits the liability of the general partners. (Compare *general partnership* and *limited partnership.*)

limited partnership (LP): A partnership arrangement in which the liability of certain partners is limited to the amount of their investment. Limited partnerships are managed and operated by one or more general partners whose liability is not limited; limited partners have no voice in management. *Private limited partnerships* have 35 or fewer investors and usually do not have to register with the Securities and Exchange Commission (SEC), although they may have to file a certificate with state authorities. *Public limited partnerships* have an unlimited number of participants and must register with the SEC when the number of partners and the value of their assets reach certain levels. (Compare *general partnership* and *limited liability limited partnership.*)

liquid asset: An investment that can be quickly and easily converted into cash at or near its market value; examples include savings accounts, money market accounts, certificates of deposit, stocks, bonds, mutual funds, and precious metals. (Compare *illiquid asset.*)

load factor: See *add-on factor.*

locator service: A business in a major city or other large community whose sole objective is matching prospective tenants with rental spaces.

long-range budget: A budget that illustrates the relationship between operating income and expenses over five or more years in the life of a property. (See also *budget.*)

loss to lease: The amount of money lost due to rental rates being less than the maximum market rents (or GPI).

low-rise apartment building: Multiple-unit residential dwelling of three or fewer stories. (See also *garden apartment building.*)

M1: See *money supply.*

M2: See *money supply*.

management agreement: A contractual arrangement between the owner(s) of a property and the designated managing agent, describing the duties and establishing the authority and compensation of the agent and detailing the responsibilities, rights, and obligations of both agent and owner(s).

management by objectives: A process in which employees help set objectives for themselves and define what they intend to accomplish within a given period; employer and employees mutually agree on the goals and objectives.

management fee: The monetary consideration paid monthly or otherwise for the performance of management duties.

management plan: An outline of a property's physical and fiscal management that is directed toward achieving the owner's goals.

manufactured housing: A dwelling that is built in a factory, transported to and anchored on a site, and used as a year-round residential unit. All manufactured homes must be in compliance with the federal Manufactured Home Construction and Safety Standards Act of 1974 (the HUD code) which became effective in 1976. (Usage note: The term *mobile home* is commonly used to identify all manufactured housing even though the legal nomenclature is "manufactured homes" for units built after the enactment of the HUD code.)

market: Broadly, any interaction between buyers and sellers. In real estate management, the geographic area within which a rental property competes for tenants.

market analysis: An evaluation of supply and demand conditions in a particular area for a particular type of goods or services. In real estate management, the process of identifying the specific group of prospective tenants for a particular property and then evaluating the property by that market's standards for rental space.

market approach: See *appraisal*.

marketing: All business activity a producer uses to expose potential consumers to available goods and services, including selling, advertising, and packaging. For rental property, methods used to attempt to lease space.

marketing director: The position in charge of the entire marketing campaign from lease-up of a new property to managing the leasing activities of the property; typically provides services to large, enclosed shopping malls and large apartment communities or office buildings. Also called *marketing manager.*

marketing fund: In a shopping center, an account controlled by the landlord that is specifically for funding shopping center promotions and advertising. Merchants and the owner of the shopping center contribute to this fund based on a predetermined amount stated in their leases. (Compare *merchants' association.*)

material safety data sheet (MSDS): A compilation of information regarding the hazardous properties of chemicals. Usual information includes composition, physical and chemical properties, and known hazards (e.g., toxicity, flammability, explosion potential); recommended cautions for handling (e.g., protective clothing and devices), storage, and disposal; clean-up procedures, and first aid treatment in the event of exposure. An MSDS is provided when chemicals (e.g., solvents, cleaning compounds) are shipped in bulk in pails or drums and when the information does not fit on the labels of small containers. Maintenance and other onsite personnel must retain these documents for reference.

Medical Office Building (MOB): A building whose space is primarily leased to medical and dental professionals.

megamall: A giant shopping center that may contain five million or more square feet of GLA. Such malls are often connected to or contain hotels, amusement parks, or nightclubs in addition to numerous anchor tenants and hundreds of ancillary tenants.

Megan's Law: In 1996, the federal government passed legislation called Megan's Law, which requires disclosure to the public of the presence of convicted sex offenders (names and addresses). This information is available from a variety of sources, including local police departments and the Internet. As interpreted up to 2005, the federal law does not address the responsibility of a property owner to a tenant regarding disclosure.

merchants' association: An organization formed in shopping centers and controlled jointly by the property owner and the tenants to plan promotions and advertisements for the good of the center as a whole. Usually all tenants are required to participate and both tenants and property owner pay dues. (Compare *marketing fund.*)

Method B: See *Office Building: Standard Methods of Measurement.*

micro-market: The neighborhood of an office building.

mid-rise apartment building: A multiple-unit dwelling ranging from four to nine stories tall.

miscellaneous income: Income a property produces from sources other than rent, such as coin-operated laundry equipment, vending machines, and late fees; also called *miscellaneous cash receipts, miscellaneous receipts, or unscheduled income.*

mixed-use development (MXD): A single property, often found in central business districts, that has more than one use, including retail, office, and hotel space, among other possibilities.

mobile home: See *manufactured housing.*

modernization: The process of replacing original or outdated equipment with similar features that are of up-to-date design.

money supply: All of the printed currency and coinage in circulation outside of banks, plus those bank deposits that are immediately convertible to cash (savings and checking deposits owned by individuals but held in banks), plus other negotiable instruments such as traveler's checks, credit union share-draft balances, and negotiable order of withdrawal (NOW) accounts. This amount of money, referred to as *M1*, is the most frequently cited measure of the U.S. money supply. More broadly, the money supply includes less liquid funds such as money market mutual fund shares and small time deposits (e.g., certificates of deposit) on which penalties are imposed for withdrawal before a specified maturity date. Those less liquid funds are added to M1, and the result is called *M2.*

mortgage: A conditional transfer or pledge of real property as security for the payment of a debt. The document used to create a mortgage loan. (Compare *deed of trust.*) (See also *collateral.*)

mullion: A vertical bar that separates the panes of glass in a window. In newer buildings that have expansive windows, the spacing of the mullions usually determines the placement of the walls.

narrative of operations: A report that explains any differences or variances between the actual income and expenses and the amounts projected for them in the budget.

National Apartment Association (NAA): A professional association that compiles statistics on rental apartments.

National Association of Industrial and Office Properties (NAIOP): A professional association that provides operational statistics for industrial properties.

natural breakpoint: See *breakpoint.*

negative balance of trade: The economic condition in which a country imports more goods than it exports.

negligent hiring: An instance of employee hiring in which proper collection and verification of pre-employment information was not done; if a background check would have revealed a prior conviction for a felony (e.g., assault), the employer of an individual who assaults someone on the job could be sued successfully.

negligent retention: Failure on the part of an employer to prevent an employee who exhibits dangerous behavior on the job (e.g., showing a weapon, making or carrying out threats of harm) from repeating the behavior and harming another person.

negligent supervision: An employment situation in which training and oversight of an employee is inadequate and an incident results in injury to another person, employee, tenant, or visitor.

negotiation: The process of bargaining that precedes an agreement; in commercial leasing, the bargaining to reach a mutual agreement on rental rates, term of the lease, and other points.

neighborhood analysis: A study of a neighborhood and comparison with the broader economic and geographic area of which it is a part to determine why individuals and businesses are attracted to the area.

neighborhood shopping center: A shopping center type in which the most common anchor tenant is a supermarket, a super drugstore, or a combination of the two. This type of center usually has 15 to 25 small shops. Ancillary tenants include dry cleaners, bank branches, beauty salons, and card and gift shops. The GLA of a typical neighborhood center is between 30,000 and 150,000 square feet. A neighborhood shopping center usually thrives in an area with a population of 5,000 to 40,000.

net lease: A lease that requires the tenant to pay a share of specific property operating expenses in addition to base rent. Three types of net leases are common: *net* (or *single-net*), *net-net* (or *double-net*), and *net-net-net* (or *triple-net*), depending on the extent of the costs that are passed through to the tenant. Used most often for commercial tenants, the definitions of the terms vary with location and types of property—e.g., office, retail, industrial. (Compare *gross lease, percentage lease.*)

net operating income (NOI): Total collections (gross receipts) less operating expenses.

new urbanism: See *urban village.*

no-cause action: Termination of a tenancy by a property owner without stating a cause if the tenant has a month-to-month lease.

obsolescence: Lessening of value due to being out-of-date (obsolete) because of changes in design and use; an element of *depreciation. Physical obsolescence* is a condition of aging (wear and tear) or deferred maintenance of a property; *functional obsolescence* is a condition of obsolete design or use of a property; and *economic obsolescence* is a loss of value due to external causes (e.g., market conditions) such that the property cannot generate enough income to offset operating expenses.

occupancy agreement: See *lease.*

Occupational Safety and Health Act (OSHA): A law passed in 1970 requiring employers to comply with job safety and health standards issued by the U.S. Department of Labor. It mandates use of protective clothing and devices for certain types of tasks.

Office Building: Standard Methods of Measurement: A publication (ANSI/BOMA Z65.1 2010) that can be obtained from BOMA; includes definitions, illustrations, and calculations. This standard, which is commonly referred to as *Method B,* discusses the *single load factor method,* which is an updated calculation applied to the occupant area of each floor to determine the rentable area and is the same for all floor levels of a building.

office condominium: An office space that a business purchases as an alternative to leasing. The most common purchasers are medical and dental practitioners, real estate firms, financial planners, entrepreneurs, and small companies that need 1,000 to 10,000 square feet of space. (See also *condominium.*)

office park: A discrete business center near an airport, major highway, or other suburban attraction.

office usable area: The rentable area *less* certain common areas that all tenants share, such as the corridors, storage facilities, and restrooms; basically, the actual space occupied by tenants. (Compare *gross area, rentable area.*)

off-price center: See *outlet shopping center.*

onboarding: See *employee onboarding.*

operating account: Bank account set up as an important provision of the management agreement through which the client's (owner's) receipts and expenditures flow; also called a *client trust account.*

operating budget: A listing of all anticipated income from and expenses of operating a property, usually projected on an annual basis. (See also *annual budget.*)

operating expense: Any expenditure made in connection with operating a property with the exception of debt service, capital reserves (and/or capital expenditures), and income taxes.

operating expense escalation clause: A lease clause under which any increases in operating costs are passed on to tenants on a pro rata basis.

operations manual: An authoritative collection of information that describes the organization and its goals, explains policies that guide its operations, outlines specific procedures for implementing those policies, assigns responsibility for performing various functions, and contains the various documents (forms) for performing the work; also called *standard operating procedures manual.* (Compare *property operations manual.*)

option: The right to obtain a specific condition within a specified time. An option is often written into a lease as an addendum.

option to cancel: An option that grants the tenant the right to cancel the lease before its expiration and, if granted, usually requires a financial penalty; also called *termination right.*

option to expand: An option that requires the property owner to offer specific additional space at a stated time in the future, often at the end of the lease term.

option to renew: An option that allows a tenant to renew a lease on the same terms and conditions as the original lease.

outlet shopping center: A shopping center in which at least 50 percent of the stores are factory outlet stores. They may include off-price and discount merchants. At an *off-price center,* retailers offer name-brand merchandise at well-below-normal retail prices. Outlet centers may attract customers from a radius of 20 miles to as far away as several hundred miles in rural areas. They traditionally require a minimum population of 200,000.

outlot: In a shopping center, a separate site that is not attached to the main center. Also called a *pad.* Banks, restaurants, automotive service centers, and movie theaters are common tenants for these spaces.

overage rent: See *breakpoint* and *percentage rent.*

owner, landlord, and tenant (OLT) liability insurance: Type of insurance that covers claims against a property owner, a landlord, or a tenant arising out of injury to a person or persons on the property.

pad: See *outlot.*

parking area ratio: The relationship between the size of the parking area and the size of the building it is intended to serve.

parking index: For a retail property, the number of spaces per 1,000 square feet of GLA.

partnership: See *general partnership* and *limited partnership.*

passive activity income: See *Tax Reform Act of 1986.*

passive loss rules: See *Tax Reform Act of 1986.*

pass-through charges: In commercial leasing, operating expenses of a property that are paid by the tenants, usually on a pro rata basis and in addition to base rent.

pass-through clause: A provision that allows property owners to pass to tenants increases in certain operating expenses and rent escalations.

Patient Protection and Affordable Care Act (PPACA): This 2010 federal legislation makes insurance more affordable by providing small businesses (50 employees or less) with a tax credit to provide healthcare coverage and by providing tax credits to those who need help buying insurance. Also called the *Affordable Care Act.*

payback period: The amount of time required to recover the cost of a capital investment.

percentage lease: A lease contract sometimes used for retail properties; the rent is a percentage of the tenant's gross sales made on the premises. The lease usually states a fixed minimum rent, and the tenant pays a percentage of its gross sales in excess of that amount, depending on the volume of business.

percentage rent: In retail leasing, rent that is based on a percentage of a tenant's gross sales (or sometimes net income or profits), often set against a guaranteed minimum or base rent and referred to as *overage rent.* (See also *breakpoint.*)

physical obsolescence: See *obsolescence.*

physical vacancy: The percentage of units (apartments, office suites, store spaces) that are unoccupied and available for lease.

planned unit development (PUD): A zoning classification that allows flexibility in the design of a subdivision, usually setting an overall density limit that allows clustering of units to provide for common open space. A PUD is a departure from conventional residential zoning; therefore, the term *planned unit development* also refers to a special zoning apparatus that permits the undertaking.

point: One percent of the total loan amount.

polychlorinated biphenyl (PCB): A chemical present in electrical transformers that is relatively harmless if left undisturbed. However, if a PCB-containing transformer leaks or burns, lethal *dioxin* gas may be released. Local or state law may require removal of PCBs during rehabilitation.

population shift: A fluctuation in numbers of individuals in different age and income groups and changes in household sizes. (Compare *economic shift.*)

portfolio manager: The position in real estate management that is responsible for assembling real estate assets to achieve specific investment plans and goals—similar to the management of a mutual fund or other pooled investment.

power shopping center: A type of super community shopping center. Several large, strong, high-volume, heavy-advertising retailers occupy most of the space. Home furnishings, office supplies, sporting goods, home improvements, toys, and consumer electronics (computers, major appliances) stores are common anchor tenants in these centers. Power centers have GLAs ranging from 200,000 to 600,000 square feet and at least four category-specific off-price anchors, each occupying 20,000 or more square feet of GLA. The trade area may extend up to 30 miles, depending on local competition; they need a minimum population of 150,000.

prelease: To lease before construction of a building begins or while the construction is taking place. For proposed developments, lending institutions usually require a certain percentage of a planned property to be leased before construction loans will be approved.

pretax cash flow: See *cash flow.*

preventive maintenance: A program of regular inspection and care that allows potential problems to be prevented or at least detected and solved before major repairs are needed. (Compare *corrective maintenance* and *deferred maintenance.*)

primary trade area: The immediate area around a shopping center; accounts for 60 to 75 percent of the center's sales. (Compare *secondary trade area, trade area, tertiary trade area.*)

prime rate: The lowest interest rate available from banks for short-term loans to their most creditworthy customers.

primogeniture: A rule of inheritance in which estates could be passed to descendants.

principal: In real estate, one who owns property; in real estate management, the property owner who contracts for the services of an agent; in finance, the amount of money that is borrowed in a loan as distinct from the interest on such loan.

private limited partnership: See *limited partnership.*

private residence club: See *fractional ownership.*

Producer Price Index (PPI): A measurement of inflation at the wholesale level. (Compare *Consumer Price Index.*)

professional liability insurance: In real estate management, insurance to protect against liabilities resulting from honest mistakes and oversights (no protection is provided in cases of gross negligence); also called *errors and omissions insurance.*

professional real estate management: The profession of conducting a property's management, operations, marketing, leasing, and financial reporting to meet the objectives of the owner. It also involves planning for the future of the property by proposing physical and fiscal strategies that will enhance the value of the real estate.

progressive discipline: A system of employee reprimand that provides ample opportunity for the employee to change or correct their behavior; such a system usually involves verbal warnings, written warnings, probation, and termination.

Project-Based Rental Assistance HUD: Section 8 program under which HUD makes up the difference between the rent a low- or very low-income household can afford and the approved rent for an adequate housing unit in a multifamily project. Eligible renters pay rent based on their income.

property analysis: A study of a property referring to such items as deferred maintenance, functional and economic obsolescence, land location and zoning, exterior construction and condition, plant and equipment, unit mix, facilities, and expected income and expenses.

property damage insurance: Coverage that protects against liability for damage to the property of others that occurs on the insured property.

property management: See *real estate management.*

property manager: A position in real estate management that may be responsible for operating a single large property or a portfolio of several properties, while also supervising the site managers. Also called *property supervisor.* (Compare *site manager.*)

property operations manual: A manual that a real estate manager or management firm develops for a specific managed property. Some policies and procedures may duplicate or only slightly modify many of the firm's operational policies, others will be property-specific. (Compare *operations manual.*)

proprietary lease: See *cooperative.*

pro rata: Proportionately; in real estate ownership and leasing, based on the size of individually owned or leased spaces in relation to the whole. Condominium owners and commercial tenants commonly pay proportionate shares of operating expenses and other costs.

prospect: A potential tenant or management client.

prospect report: A record of information about prospective tenants for office space, their space needs, current space and lease expiration data, how they were contacted, whether they were qualified for tenancy, and their status as prospects—if they received a brochure or were given a tour of the property.

protected class: See *fair housing laws.*

psychographic profile: An analysis of a retail trade area that goes beyond the numbers to examine the interests and shopping habits of the people who live in the shopping center's trade area. (Compare *demographic profile.*)

public housing: Housing owned by and/or managed for a local or state governmental agency; the principal form of low-income housing available in the United States. (Compare *government-assisted housing.*)

public housing agency (PHA): See *Housing and Community Development Act.*

public limited partnership: See *limited partnership.*

public relations (PR): Any form of promotion that is not paid for, such as press releases and word-of-mouth endorsement.

qualification: The process of judging a prospective tenant's financial status or creditworthiness. In real estate management, the process of determining whether a prospect can afford the rent on the unit applied for and has a good history of bill payments.

quiet enjoyment: A covenant that promises that the grantee or tenant of an estate in real property will be able to possess the premises in peace, without disturbance by hostile claimants. Quiet enjoyment is a right to the undisturbed use and enjoyment of real property by a tenant or property owner.

radius clause: A provision in a retail lease that prevents a retailer from opening and operating a similar—and therefore competitive—business within a certain radius from the shopping center.

radon: A colorless, odorless, tasteless gas that occurs naturally in the radioactive decay of radium and uranium. It became a problem with the advent of energy-efficient buildings that allow only minimal transfer of air between the building's interior and exterior.

reach: The specific audience exposed to a marketing medium; should be the largest possible number of prospects who mirror the target market.

real estate: Land and all improvements in or on it.

real estate cycle: Recurring periods of high and low activity in real estate markets. The cycle has four components: overbuilding, adjustment, stabilization, and development. They generally follow their business cycle counterparts.

real estate executive: A supervisory role that manages multiple real estate managers, numerous personnel within an entire firm, or even several apartment communities that have regional real estate managers that supervise onsite personnel. Also called *senior portfolio manager, director of real estate services, director of client services.*

real estate investment trust (REIT): An entity that sells shares of beneficial interest to investors and uses the funds to invest in real estate or mortgages. Real estate investment trusts must meet certain requirements such as a minimum number of investors and widely dispersed ownership. No corporate taxes need to be paid as long as a series of complex IRS qualifications are met. (See also *shares of beneficial interest.*)

real estate management: A profession in which someone other than the owner (a real estate manager) supervises the operation of a property according to the owner's objectives or consults with the owner on the definition of those objectives and the property's profitability.

receivables ledger: See *statement of receipts report.*

receivership: Court-ordered turnover of a property to an impartial third party (receiver) so that it may be preserved for the benefit of the affected parties.

reconciliation: The process of comparing estimated operating expenses paid by tenants throughout the year to actual operating expenses at year-end when the true costs are known and then billing or crediting the adjusted amounts to the tenants.

recovery: Part of the business cycle, a period or economic upturn following a depression characterized by increasing demand for goods and services and rising prices.

regional analysis: A detailed study of a region, usually the area surrounding and including one or more neighboring cities, to determine the force of various factors affecting the economic welfare of a section of the region, such as population growth and movement, employment, industrial and business activity, transportation facilities, tax structures, topography, improvements, and trends.

regional mall: A large shopping center that has one or more full-line department stores as anchor tenants. The presence of a department store tends to attract such ancillary tenants as men's and women's apparel stores, optical shops, electronic equipment stores, and jewelers. Many include small fast-food outlets arranged in a food court. Some also have cinemas. Regional malls contain 400,000 to one million square feet of GLA. Their trade area has a radius of 7 to 10 miles, and they usually serve a population of 150,000 to 300,000.

regional manager: A position in real estate management that supervises onsite residential or commercial property managers and sometimes the property managers within the management firm. Also called *regional property manager*, *portfolio supervisor,* or *senior property manager.*

rehabilitation: The process of renewing the equipment and materials in the building; entails correcting deferred maintenance.

rent: In real estate, payment made for the use of space; periodic payments made under a lease.

rentable area: The area in an office building on which rent is based and which generally includes the space available for tenants' exclusive use *plus* identified common areas *less* any major vertical penetrations (air shafts, stairways, elevators) in the building. The term is applied to the building as a whole, to individual floors, and to portions of floors. (Compare *gross area, office usable area.*)

rental agreement: See *lease.*

rental ledger: A record of rent received, date of receipt, period covered, and other related information for each individual tenant. (Compare *rent roll.*)

rent control law: A law that regulates rental rates, usually to limit the amount of rent increases and their frequency.

rent loss insurance: Coverage that protects the owner from loss of income resulting from damage that makes all or part of the property unleasable.

rent roll: A listing of all rental units, showing the rental rate, tenant's name, and lease expiration date as well as the status of rent and other payments. (Compare *rental ledger.*)

replacement cost coverage: Insurance to replace or restore a building or its contents to its preexisting condition and appearance. (Compare *actual cash value.*)

request for proposal (RFP): A request for a formal proposal that requires a bidder to provide written specifications for services.

reserve account transactions report: A report that lists deposits to and withdrawals from the reserve fund.

reserve fund: Money set aside to provide funds for anticipated future expenditures.

resident: One who lives (or resides) in a place. Many real estate professionals prefer to refer to residential tenants as "residents." (Compare *tenant.*)

Resident-Based Rental Assistance HUD Section 8 program: The individual or family who receives a housing voucher is responsible for finding a suitable housing unit. The public housing agency pays the subsidy directly to the property owner on behalf of the participating renter. The renter then pays the difference between the amount subsidized by the program and the actual rent charged by the owner (usually limited to 30 percent of the renter's adjusted monthly income).

Residential Lead-Based Paint Hazard Reduction Act: The federal law that requires owners and managers of apartment buildings constructed before 1978 to give renters (1) a disclosure form detailing the presence of lead-based paint; (2) a government pamphlet on lead paint hazards; and (3) a copy of any existing reports that describe lead paint hazards at the property.

residential manager: One who manages a residential property or properties.

resident manager: See *site manager.*

Resolution Trust Corporation (RTC): A governmental agency created to manage and dispose of the assets of thrifts that were in receivership; contracted with real estate management firms to manage and market many of those assets for disposition.

retrofit: To replace fixtures or facilities in a building with new equipment that is more efficient, usually in terms of energy consumption, fire protection codes, or accommodations for new technology.

return on investment (ROI): A measure of profitability expressed as a percentage and calculated by comparing periodic income to the owner's equity in the property. (income ÷ equity = % ROI) It can be calculated either before or after deduction of income tax. Also called *cash-on-cash return.*

rider: See *endorsement.*

right of first offer: As an alternative approach to granting an *option to expand,* a tenant may be granted a first choice to rent a particular space subject to availability of that space.

right of first refusal: An option that gives a tenant the first choice to lease contiguous space or other space in the building when it becomes available. The lease clause specifies the area.

right of reentry: The property owner's right to enter an occupied apartment to make repairs, provide agreed-upon services, and show the apartment to prospective tenants and others, subject to certain limitations.

R/U ratio: See *Building Owners and Managers Association International.*

sales approach: See *appraisal.*

S corporation: See *corporation.*

Sarbanes-Oxley Act (SOX): Legislation that expanded repercussions for destroying, altering, or fabricating records in federal investigations or for attempting to defraud shareholders; required compliance from property management companies.

secondary trade area: The area around a shopping center that usually extends three to seven miles from the site (for a regional shopping center) and accounts for 10 to 20 percent of sales. (Compare *primary trade area, tertiary trade area, trade area.*)

Section 202: Federal housing program that covers supportive housing for the elderly.

Section 8 housing: Privately owned residential rental units that participate in the low-income rental assistance program created by the 1974 amendments to Section 8 of the 1937 Housing Act. Under this program, the U.S. Department of Housing and Urban Development (HUD) pays a rent subsidy to the property owner on behalf of qualified low-income residents so they pay a limited portion of their incomes for rent.

Section 811: Federal housing program that covers supportive housing for the disabled.

security deposit: An amount of money advanced by the tenant and held by an owner or manager to ensure the faithful performance of the lease terms by the tenant. Part or all of the deposit may be retained to pay for rent owed, miscellaneous charges owed, unpaid utility bills, and damage to the leased space that exceeds normal wear and tear. Limitations on withholding may be imposed by local and state ordinances.

self-storage facilities: Storage facilities that resemble rows of attached garages in which individuals and businesses store and secure their goods themselves. Many of these facilities include living quarters for an onsite manager.

semimonthly payroll system: A payroll method that pays employees twice a month—usually on the 15th and the last day of the month.

shares of beneficial interest: Shares sold by real estate investment trusts (REITs); they are traded on the stock markets similar to corporate common stock. (See also *real estate investment trust.*)

shell space: Condition in which new office space and store space is commonly leased—enclosed by outside walls and a roof, with a concrete slab floor and utilities brought in. The plumbing and electrical installations are unfinished, and the space has no partitioning walls, ceiling tiles, wall coverings, or flooring. (Compare *vanilla shell space.*)

shopping center: A generic term applied to a collection of retail stores enclosed in one building or adjacent to each other in separate buildings. Shopping centers are categorized based on their gross leasable area, type of tenancy, and the extent of their geographic trade area (customer base).

single-family home: A residence that has its own entry. Townhouses, which by definition share a common wall but have private entrances, are also classified as single-family homes.

single load factor method: See *Office Building: Standard Methods of Measurement.*

site management: A profession that involves maintaining the physical structure of a property as well as maintaining and updating property-related documents and information.

site manager: An employee who oversees and administers the day-to-day affairs of a property in accordance with directions from the property manager or the owner. For residential properties, the manager may live in the building they manage (*resident manager*) or off site. For commercial properties, the manager may occupy an office on site or off site. (Compare *property manager.*)

sole proprietorship: A business enterprise carried on by one person.

space planning: The process of designing an office configuration for maximum functional efficiency based on a prospective tenant's space utilization needs, aesthetic requirements, and financial limitations.

special assessment: A special tax levied by a local government to fund public improvements (sidewalks, curbs, or other infrastructure) within a small area; only properties directly benefiting from the improvements are assessed the tax. In a condominium, monies collected from owners to fund a capital expenditure (e.g., roof replacement) when reserve funds are insufficient. This is in addition to the regular assessment for maintenance of common areas. (See also *assessment.*)

special form insurance: Coverage that pays for all losses except those that are specifically excluded in the policy. (Formerly *all-risk insurance.*)

special improvement district: A narrowly defined area—a single block or several blocks along a thoroughfare—in dense urban areas in which owners of buildings may band together to form a nonprofit corporation with a specific purpose, such as to clean up the area, to increase security, or simply to give the area a specific identity, such as using signs or banners. The taxing body may levy a special assessment for this purpose. (See also *special assessment.*)

Specially Designated Nationals and Blocked Persons (SDN) list: See *U.S.A. Patriot Act.*

specialty shopping center: A dominant theme or image characterizes this type of shopping center. Those in downtown areas are often the result of adaptive use of a historic building. They do not always have an anchor tenant, and many rely on tourists for most of their sales. Their uniqueness is their main attraction. They usually vary in size from 25,000 to 70,000 square feet, although some of these centers can be as large as 375,000 square feet of GLA. The specific use defines the trade area, and it may extend beyond the radiuses usually associated with centers of this size. Specialty shopping centers require an area population in excess of 150,000 to survive.

standard operating procedures manual: See *operations manual.*

standard tenant improvement allowance: See *tenant improvement allowance.*

statement of operations: An at-a-glance view of the property's gross amounts of income and expenses for a period. It emphasizes the cash flow paid to the owner. Also called an *income and expense statement.*

statement of receipts report: Chronological report of rents and income from sources other than rents that identifies the source and amount of all monies received; also called *receivables ledger.*

steering: An illegal discriminatory practice that encourages a prospective tenant to look at another site for housing or conceals vacancies from a prospect.

store hours clause: A retail lease clause that authorizes the management of the property to set store hours for the center as a whole. It may include provisions for seasonal adjustments and special hours for holiday shopping periods.

strip shopping center: A shopping center designed in a line. The term is sometimes used for convenience shopping centers and can refer to other types of centers as well.

sublet: The leasing of part or all of the premises by a tenant to a third party for part or all of the tenant's remaining term.

sublet clause: A clause in a residential lease that states that, in order for the resident to vacate the premises before the end of the term, he or she must find a suitable resident to sublet the space for the remainder of the lease obligation. The manager must approve that person, and the resident or the subtenant must pay for the credit check.

submarket: A segment of the overall market that is limited by a particular market influence.

subrogation: The substitution of one creditor for another such that the substituted person succeeds to the legal rights and claims of the original claimant; in insurance, the right of an insurer to attempt to recover amounts from an at-fault third party for claims paid to the insured party.

subsidized housing: See *government-assisted housing.*

substitute check: See *Check 21 Act.*

super-regional mall: A large shopping center that includes four or more full-line department stores and 100 to 150 small shops. May include *outlots* or *pads.* It usually has one million to three million square feet of GLA. Its trade area has a radius of 10 to 20 miles, and it serves a population of 300,000 or more.

supply: The availability of goods and services.

surety: A formal guarantee.

syndicate: A type of professionally managed limited partnership formed to invest in different types of real estate.

syndication: A method of selling property in which a sponsor sells ownership interests to investors.

tax: An amount assessed by government for public purposes, usually based on the relative value of property or income.

Tax Reform Act of 1980: Federal legislation that offered numerous incentives for real estate investment and fueled unprecedented development. (See also *Tax Reform Act of 1986.*)

Tax Reform Act of 1986: Legislation that restructured federal income tax and its associated deductions. Of primary importance in real estate are its definitions of *passive activity income* (and loss), which include real property income, and its restrictions against using passive losses to offset active income—i.e., salary. (The Technical and Miscellaneous Revenue Act of 1988 delineated technical corrections to the Tax Reform Act of 1986.)

telecommute: To work at home using a computer linked to an employer's location via a telephone network.

tenancy in common (TIC): Ownership by two or more persons in which each holds an undivided interest in the property. Upon the death of one tenant, that tenant's interest in the property passes to his or her heirs—not to the other tenant(s); the right of survivorship does not apply. A tenancy in common is a fractionalized fee-simple interest in real property used in certain tax-deferred exchanges. While technically a real estate transaction, TICs are in fact sold as securities. (Compare *joint tenancy.*)

tenant: One who pays rent to occupy real estate. Real estate managers often limit the use of the term "tenant" to commercial tenants and refer to residential tenants as "residents." (See also *lessee* and *resident.*)

tenant improvement allowance (TIA): In commercial leasing, an amount a landlord agrees to spend to improve the leased shell space for a tenant before move-in or as a condition of lease renewal. A *standard tenant improvement allowance* is a fixed dollar amount allowed by the owner for items that may be installed in the leased premises at no charge to the tenant. Payment for tenant improvements is part of the lease negotiations. (See also *building standard.*)

tenant mix: The combination of types of businesses and services that lease space in a shopping center, an office building, or (sometimes) an industrial park.

term: The duration of a tenant's lease; the duration of a mortgage (e.g., a 30-year term).

termination right: See *option to cancel.*

terrorism: As defined in the U.S. Code of Federal Regulations, the unlawful use of force and violence against persons or property to intimidate or coerce a government, the civilian population, or any segment thereof, in furtherance of political or social objectives.

Terrorism Risk Insurance Act (TRIA) of 2007: This federal legislation provides for a transparent system of shared public and private compensation for insured losses resulting from acts of terrorism.

tertiary trade area: The area around a major shopping center that extends 15 to 50 miles from the center and accounts for 5 to 15 percent of sales. (Compare *primary trade area, secondary trade area, trade area.*)

timeshare: A specialized form of condominium found mostly in resort areas. As the name implies, the owner has the right to occupy the unit for a specific period. (Compare *fractional ownership.*)

time value of money: The assumption that a dollar today is worth more than a dollar at some future date. The basis of compounding to determine future value or discounting to determine present value.

Title VIII: See *fair housing law.*

trade area: The geographic area from which a shopping center obtains most of its customers, its size depends on the type of center, location of competition, and other factors. (Compare *primary trade area, secondary trade area, tertiary trade area.*)

traffic report: A record of the number of prospects who visit or make inquiries at a property and the factors that attracted them to it.

transfer clause: A residential lease clause that allows the resident to break the lease without penalty in case of a job transfer.

tuckpointing: The periodic replacement of mortar.

umbrella liability insurance: Extra liability coverage that exceeds the limits of a basic liability policy.

unemployment rate: The number of unemployed divided by the number in the labor force (the number of employed plus the number of unemployed).

unit deed: A document that legally transfers title to a condominium unit and a share of the common areas from one owner to another.

unscheduled income: Income that may be unanticipated and/or not planned.

Urban Land Institute (ULI): An independent nonprofit research and educational organization dedicated to improving the quality and standards of land use and development. It publishes comparison data on shopping centers and multifamily housing.

urban renewal: A federal program that opens land in cities to development or redevelopment and new uses.

urban village: A parcel of land that was previously home to an industrial use or an apartment complex that is redeveloped to incorporate a variety of residential and commercial uses into a "pedestrian-friendly" neighborhood. This phenomenon, called *new urbanism*, includes higher-density development with narrow streets complemented by wide sidewalks. This strategy is revitalizing urban areas and creating an identifiable downtown in suburbs that do not have one.

usable area: The area in an office building that is available for the exclusive use of a tenant. (Compare *rentable area.*)

U.S.A. Patriot Act: This federal legislation, along with Executive Order 13224, has increased federal government scrutiny of financial transactions, including real estate transactions. The purpose is to curb and prevent business interactions with terrorist organizations. Commercial property managers in particular should periodically check the *Specially Designated Nationals and Blocked Persons* (*SDN*) list to ensure that current and prospective tenants are not on that list. Residential property managers should also check prospects and existing residents against the list since known terrorists have leased apartments in the United States.

U.S. Civil Rights Act of 1968: See *fair housing law.*

use clause: In a retail lease, a clause that prevents a tenant from using the premises in a different way than originally intended.

useful life: The period of years over which a building will produce income and to recover the cost of the building; the period varies for different types of properties. Also called *depreciation period.*

U.S. Green Building Council (USGBC): A federal program for improving a building's performance that offers a Leadership in Energy and Environmental Design (LEED) Certification. (Compare *ENERGY STAR.*)

valuation: An estimation or calculation of the worth of an object or service; the process of determining an object's or service's worth.

vanilla shell space: A rental space that usually has an American Disabilities Act (ADA) compliant restroom, walls ready for paint, floor ready for floor coverings, and ceiling tiles and lighting in place. (Compare *shell space.*)

variable-rate mortgage: A mortgage in which the lending institution can raise or lower the interest rate of an existing loan depending on prevailing loan rates or a prescribed index. (Compare *adjustable-rate mortgage.*)

wage and hour law: See *Fair Labor Standards Act.*

walk-up: An older four-story apartment building that has stairs only.

weighted checklist: An employee evaluation method in which the appraiser is given a list of statements and checks the items on the list that describe or apply to the employee; some items may be weighted higher than others to arrive at an overall tabulated result.

Worker Adjustment and Retraining Notification (WARN) Act: The federal law that requires employers of large numbers of workers to give affected workers 60 days' advance notice of a layoff if it impacts 33 percent of the employer's workforce, provided that at least 50 employees are to be laid off.

Worker, Homeownership and Business Assistance Act of 2009: See *Housing and Economic Recovery Act of 2008.*

workers' compensation insurance: Coverage obtained by an employer to pay compensation and benefits awarded to an employee in the event of employment-related sickness or injury.

zero-based budget: See *annual budget.*

zoning: Regulation of the character and use of property by areas or "zones," usually by local (municipal) government.

Index

A

abatement, 297, 429
absorption rate, 129, 134–135, 429
abstracting, 125, 429
accelerated cost recovery, 90, 429
accessibility, 3, 366, 399–400
accounting, 161–164
   income categories, 163–164
   methods of, 163
   pass-through costs, 410–411
   payroll and related expenses,
      165–166
   systems for, 161–163
accounting services, 35–36
accounts payable, 173
accounts receivable, 173
Accredited Commercial Managers
   (ACoMs), 2, 429
Accredited Management
   Organization (AMO), 2, 429
Accredited Residential Managers
   (ARMs), 2, 429
accrual-basis accounting, 163,
   429–430
ACoMs. See Accredited Commercial
   Managers (ACoMs)
active income, 10
active shooters, 304, 430
actual cash value (ACV) insurance,
   356, 430
adaptive use, 140, 430
addenda to retail leases, 417
additional rent, 163, 416
add-on factor, 383, 430
adjustable-rate mortgages (ARMs),
   83–84, 430
adjustments, 71–72
administrative costs, 164–165
administrative personnel, 39
ad valorem tax, 68, 430
advertising, 110
   broadcast media and billboards,
      230

print media, 227–229
   shopping center, 415
aesthetic appeal, 399
affidavit of service, 266–267, 430
Age Discrimination in Employment
   Act (ADEA), 430
agents, 31, 430
   owner's, 106
aging in place, 321, 431
air rights, 149, 431
all-cash purchases, 79–80
all-inclusive rent, 256
all-risk insurance. See special form
   insurance
alterations, 416
amenities, 283
   office building, 367, 370–371
American Recovery and
   Reinvestment Act of 2009,
   16
American Society of Heating,
   Refrigerating, and Air-
   Conditioning Engineers
   (ASHRAE), 298, 431
Americans with Disabilities Act
   (ADA), 262–263, 330, 379,
   418, 431
AMO. See Accredited Management
   Organization (AMO)
amortization, 431
amortization schedules, 82
analysis of alternatives, 137–142,
   431
anchor tenants, 392, 431
ancillary tenants, 392, 431
annual budgets, 176, 431–432
annual debt service (ADS), 151
apartments, 314–316
appearance, of office buildings,
   367–368
appraisal, 431
appreciation, 431
   of capital, 86–88
   of currency, 54